VIOLENCE IN AMERICA

Volume 1

VIOLENCE, COOPERATION, PEACE

AN INTERNATIONAL SERIES

Editors: Francis A. Beer and Ted Robert Gurr, *University of Colorado, Boulder*

Violence, Cooperation, Peace: An International Series focuses on violent conflict and the dynamics of peaceful change within and among political communities. Studies in the series may include the perspectives and evidence of any of the social sciences or humanities, as well as applied fields such as conflict management. This international book series emphasizes systematic scholarship, in which theory and evidence are used to advance our general understanding of the processes of political violence and peace.

Volumes in the Series

VIOLENCE IN AMERICA

Volume 1

The History of Crime

edited by
Ted Robert Gurr

VIOLENCE, COOPERATION, PEACE
AN INTERNATIONAL SERIES

SAGE PUBLICATIONS
The Publishers of Professional Social Science
Newbury Park   London   New Delhi

For information address:

SAGE Publications, Inc.
2111 West Hillcrest Drive
Newbury Park, California 91320

SAGE Publications Ltd.
28 Banner Street
London EC1Y 8QE
England

SAGE Publications India Pvt. Ltd.
M-32 Market
Greater Kailash I
New Delhi 110 048 India

Printed in the United States of America

Library of Congress Cataloging-in-Publication Data

Main entry under title:

Violence in America / [edited by] Ted Robert Gurr.
      p.   cm.
   Previously published (1979) in 1 volume.
   Bibliography: p.
   Includes index.
   Contents: v. 1. The history of crime—v. 2. Protest, rebellion. reform.
   ISBN 0-8039-3227-8 (v. 1).—ISBN 0-8039-3228-6 (pbk. : v. 1).—ISBN 0-8039-3229-4 (v. 2).—ISBN 0-8039-3230-8 (pbk. : v. 2)
   1. Violence—United States.   I. Gurr, Ted Robert, 1936–
HN90.V5V54   1989
303.6'2'0973—dc 19   88-37565
                                                              CIP

FIRST PRINTING 1989

Contents

Foreword   7

The History of Violent Crime in America: An Overview   11

1. Historical Trends in Violent Crime: Europe and the United States
   Ted Robert Gurr   21

2. On the Social Meaning of Homicide Trends in America
   Roger Lane   55

3. Diverging Homicide Rates: England and the United States, 1850–1875
   Eric H. Monkkonen   80

4. Violence Arrests in the City: The Philadelphia Story, 1857–1980
   Neil Alan Weiner and Margaret A. Zahn   102

5. Violence and Lawlessness on the Western Frontier
   Roger D. McGrath   122

6. Bootlegging: The Business and Politics of Violence
   Mark H. Haller   146

7. Economic Change and Homicide in Detroit, 1926–1979
   Colin Loftin, David McDowall, and James Boudouris   163

8. Identifying Potential Assassins: Some Situational Correlates of Dangerousness
   James W. Clarke   178

9. Firearms and Violence: Old Premises and Current Evidence
   Don B. Kates, Jr.   197

10. Homicide in the Twentieth Century: Trends, Types, and
    Causes
    Margaret A. Zahn   216

11. Social Change and the Future of Violent Crime
    Wesley G. Skogan   235

12. Crime, Law, and Society: From the Industrial to the
    Information Society
    Richard Maxwell Brown   251

    Index   269

    About the Contributors   277

FOREWORD

TED ROBERT GURR

The first edition of *Violence in America: Historical and Comparative Perspectives* was released by the National Commission on the Causes and Prevention of Violence on June 5, 1969, the first anniversary of Robert Kennedy's assassination. *Violence in America* was a research report to the Commission, prepared by two young scholars, Hugh Davis Graham of the Department of History at Johns Hopkins University, and Ted Robert Gurr of the Department of Politics at Princeton University. The twenty-nine contributors to the two-volume report surveyed what was then known about group violence in the fields of history, law, and the social and behavioral sciences. In the words of Milton S. Eisenhower, who chaired the Commission, the report "offered an uncompromising portrait of a nation whose past was often marred by violence, but it showed by comparison with other nations that the American experience, though more extensive and voluminous, was neither unique nor beyond explanation and remedy."[1]

The National Commission itself was established less than a year earlier by President Lyndon B. Johnson, at a time when Americans were traumatized by the spectacle of violence by ghetto rioters, anti-war protesters, assassins, and terrorists on the right and left. The Commission's purpose was to "go as far as man's knowledge takes it" in searching out the causes of violence and the means of preventing it. Dr. Eisenhower ably chaired a Commission that reflected the contemporary political spectrum. Its research was directed by two accomplished scholars, criminologist Marvin E. Wolfgang and sociologist James F. Short, Jr., and carried out by a dozen task forces, each staffed by experts. Eventually a total of thirteen research reports were published. The Commission's own summary volume, *To Establish Justice, To Ensure Domestic Tranquility*, was issued in December 1969.

Violence in America, the first full report to be released by the Commission, was heralded in a televised national press conference. Laudatory reviews appeared in the national media and academic journals. Only a few radical historians were skeptical. A *New York Times* reviewer called it "a stupendous job" and said the authors "have articulated the challenge and paradox of the American situation: those characteristics of which we are most proud are also responsible for the divisiveness that now paralyzes us."[2] Lewis A. Coser wrote that the report was "a remarkable document. . . . It is a genuine contribution which is likely to be read long after many of the more sensational volumes that our present predicaments have spawned will be forgotten."[3] The Government Printing Office's edition was promptly reprinted by three major trade publishers (Bantam Books, Praeger, and New American Library). More than 300,000 copies eventually were in circulation.

During the 1970s social scientists and historians reevaluated the received wisdom of the 1960s. Some looked more closely at the historical annals of group violence in the United States, finding new social meanings in familiar and forgotten episodes. Social scientists traced the connections from the civil rights movement to ghetto riots, legal reforms, and political backlash. Group violence was no longer regarded as an uncommon disorder. Rather, it came to be understood as a recurring outgrowth of social conflict and change, with predictable kinds of consequences. The second edition of *Violence in America* integrated these new perspectives with the old. When it was issued by Sage Publications in 1979, though, political violence and disruptive social action were too rare to stimulate much public concern. The twenty new and revised chapters that summarized the new scholarship were distinctly better, as a group, than the contents of the first edition. Ironically, scarcely anyone noticed. The first edition had pointed to Americans' "historical amnesia" about previous eras of violent conflict. It was clear, from the reception that greeted the second edition, that by the end of the 1970s few people wanted to be jarred out of forgetfulness. If they had any larger social concerns it was mainly with crime, which was then nearing the highest levels ever recorded in the United States or in any other modern Western society.

This third edition gives equal weight to the two principal dimensions of violence in America: personal crimes and group violence. All twelve chapters in Volume 1, *The History of Crime,* were written for this edition. Their authors survey a wealth of new research on the long-term dynamics of murder and other crimes of violence. They identify and diagnose the circumstances of recurring epidemics of violent crime that have swept the social landscape of the United States during the last 150 years. Waves of immigration, the social dislocations of war, and growing concentrations of urban poverty, affecting both blacks and whites, all are among the indictable causes. Some surprises emerge from historical inquiries into crime in frontier mining towns (property crime was uncommon) and bootlegging during Prohibition (urban politics shaped its violence). Other chapters evaluate the traits of political assassins and assess the pros and cons of gun control for reducing crime. The past and present dynamics of violent crime, projected into the future, suggest grounds for cautious optimism. Resentment against crime has stimulated tougher, more effective criminal justice policies and widespread, grass-roots efforts to remedy the social disintegration that breeds violent crime.

Volume 2 focuses on *Protest, Rebellion, Reform*, the issues that generate group violence. Four of the contributors to the first edition, including its editors, reassess their views about the historical precedents and international parallels of American violence. There are few surprises here, but a wealth of new evidence and theories that deepen our sense of understanding about the sources of recurring conflict and the tenuous nature of consensus in American society. Other chapters deal with new issues: the belated emergence and decline of activism by Native Americans, the steady decline of political terrorism since the early 1970s, and the recurring threat of violence from right-wing extremists like the Klan, the Order, and the Aryan Nations.

The most intractable source of social and political conflict in our history remains the resistance of black Americans to their inferior status, and the efforts of white Americans to keep them there. A set of three chapters analyzes the twentieth-century history of racial activism, reaction, and reform. The Civil Rights movement, like many other social movements, impelled substantial legal and political changes. Urban rioting and rebellion first helped, then hurt the prospects for continued progress. Richard E. Rubenstein suggests, provocatively, that the recurrent failure of limited reforms to resolve fundamental demands for equity and autonomy for all the diverse groups that make up American society may lead to "the fire next time." Hugh Davis Graham, however, concludes that an evolving cultural consensus provides political cohesion to American society. Group conflict and violence are part of our tradition because they have contributed to the incorporation of new groups and expectations into that consensus.

The basic assumption that underlies all the interpretations in *Violence in America: Protest, Rebellion, Reform*, skeptical or upbeat, is that group violence grows out of the dynamics of social change and political contention. The origins, processes, and outcomes of group violence, like the causes and consequences of crime, have to be understood and dealt with in their social context. They arise out of the imperfect but perfectible nature of American society, and they should inform our understanding of what that society does and does not do for its citizens.

Annapolis, Maryland
September 1988

Notes

1. Milton S. Eisenhower, "Preface," in Hugh Davis Graham and Ted Robert Gurr, eds., *Violence in America: Historical and Comparative Perspectives*, rev. ed. (Beverly Hills, CA: Sage, 1979), 10.

2. John Leonard, "Books of the Times: The Children of Cain Never Grow Up," *New York Times,* July 30, 1969.

3. Lewis A. Coser, "The History of Violence in America," *New York Times Book Review*, Apr. 12, 1970.

The History of Violent Crime in America: An Overview

TED ROBERT GURR

Each year in the 1980s about 20,000 Americans were murdered. Most of them were young men, nearly half of them were black. Each year more than 75,000 women reported attacks by rapists to police. Another half a million people reported robberies, more than 650,000 told police they were victims of serious non-sexual assaults.[1] The chapters in this volume provide some historical perspectives on violent crime in America. They represent the most recent efforts of historians, criminologists, sociologists and political scientists to address some of the larger questions. What are the long-term trends in violent crime and what drives them up or down? How was violent crime in America influenced by the frontier experience, by Prohibition, by the Great Depression? Why are political assassinations part of the American tradition, and who are the potential assassins? Is gun control an antidote to violent crime? Given what we have learned in the last decade of research on crime trends, what are the prospects for an abatement of deadly violence in the next decade? Some answers suggested by the contributions to this volume are sketched below. No chapters deal specifically with the police, courts, or prisons because our foremost concern is with the dynamics of violent crime rather than the institutions that respond to it. But their effects, or lack of effects, on violent crime are noted at a number of points.

In the very long run, homicidal violence has declined sharply throughout Western society. Chapter 1 summarizes the historical evidence. Our medieval European ancestors had few inhibitions against clubbing and knifing their neighbors during angry brawls. In thirteenth- and fourteenth-century England, when murders were well documented, people killed one another at rates at least ten times greater than those of contemporary Britain, and at twice the rate in the United States today. Oxford in the 1340s had the highest rate estimated for any medieval English jurisdiction, 110 murders per year per 100,000 population. Detroit was the murder capital of the United States and Europe in 1986, with a rate of 59 per 100,000. During the six intervening centuries, short-term increases in violent crime occurred during times of social unrest, war, and in the early stages of industrialization and urbanization, but the long-run trend was down. In most European countries it reached its lowest recorded levels in the second quarter of the twentieth century. Beginning no later than the 1970s, though, violence and robbery surged upward in virtually every Western country. The pattern, traced over time, is a distorted U-shaped curve.

Roger Lane's historical research on violent death in American cities, in chapter 2, provides an interpretation of North American and European trends in violent crime during the last 150 years. The well-documented decline in serious crime during the nineteenth century coincided with the inculcation of habits of discipline among urban industrial workers by schools, churches, and factories . . . a discipline that was enforced by increasingly professional police forces. The bottom of the U-shaped crime curve, from the 1920s to the 1950s, coincided with the maturation of industrial society. The rising rate of violent crimes that began in Britain and the United States in 1960s is a consequence of the transition to post-industrial society, which provides ever fewer job opportunities for poorly trained people at the bottom of the social ladder. The black underclass in our urban ghettos has its counterpart among the growing numbers of alienated, unemployable youths in Europe's old industrial cities.[2]

A closer look at the historical records of American urban crime is provided by Eric H. Monkkonen in chapter 3 and by Neil Alan Weiner and Margaret A. Zahn in chapter 4. Murder and assault probably declined in North America until the middle of the 1800s, though the evidence is scanty. In Northeastern cities it appears that this trend continued downward for white Anglo-Americans through the last part of the nineteenth century and into this century. But the most striking features of violent crime in America during the last 150 years are periodic upwellings associated with immigration, war, and economic deprivation. From the 1840s to the end of large-scale European immigration after World War I, each new wave of migrants—Irish, Germans, Italians—added disproportionately to the official tallies of mayhem. These immigrants did not necessarily come from violent cultures. Rather, many were rootless young men abroad in a new environment, with a disposition and opportunities for drinking and brawling.

Eric H. Monkkonen's comparative study of homicide in New York, London, and Liverpool in the last half of the nineteenth century suggests three reasons why the American pattern of violent crime began to diverge so sharply from the British pattern of steady decline. In addition to the role of immigrants, he finds a significant increase in the use of guns in the aftermath of the Civil War. He also cites the general laxity of the authorities (in New York, the city he has studied most closely) when prosecuting cases of homicide, especially if both the killer and victim were young immigrants. Wiener and Zahn's statistical portrait of violent crime in Philadelphia from 1856 to 1980 shows in more detail how violent crime, and official attention to crime, changed in an American city. The arrest rates for most violent offenses in Philadelphia tended to move upward over the long run: Rape and aggravated assaults have increased more or less steadily since the Civil War, while arrests for homicide and robbery began to increase after 1900.

In the aftermath of the Civil War many demobilized veterans went West, some to the mining boom towns of the Rockies and the Sierra Nevada. Roger D. McGrath's study of crime in several of these towns, in chapter 5, confirms some stereotypes and challenges others. The miners did kill one another with great frequency, at 20 to 30 times the prevailing homicide rates in Northeastern cities. In Bodie, California, around 1880 the homicide rate was 116 per 100,000 while in Boston and Philadelphia the rate was below 4. Sexual assault was virtually unknown in the boom towns, for two reinforcing reasons: the Victorian code that protected "respectable" women and the ready availability of women of easy virtue. Property crime also was rare: robberies were no more common in Bodie, California, than in Boston in 1880, occurring at only one-third the national robbery rate in 1980, a century later. Burglaries almost never happened in Bodie or Aurora. Property was secure in the mining towns for reasons made perfectly clear in contemporary accounts: Theft was risky business in places where virtually every man carried a gun and was willing and able to use it.

Armed and violent men also were responsible for some of the high rates of violent crime during the 1920s. Bootlegging during Prohibition, from 1920 to 1933, was a very lucrative business in which young entrepreneurs, mostly immigrants or sons of immigrants, fought hijackers and rivals for control of booze and markets. Historian Mark H. Haller shows in chapter 6 that the political setting had much to do with the incidence of violence. In Chicago, warfare among competing distributors escalated after 1923 because a reform-minded mayor established centralized police control and tried to enforce Prohibition laws. In doing so he undermined the ability of ward politicians and police captains to enforce (and profit from) territorial agreements among dealers. In German-American Milwaukee, by contrast, authorities shared the widespread aversion to Prohibition. The police followed a simple policy: they tolerated the distribution and sale of liquor but vigorously prosecuted acts of violence by bootleggers. As a result bootlegging in Milwaukee was a thriving and largely non-violent enterprise.

Much of what we know about trends in violent crime is hedged with uncertainty because of the limitations of official crime statistics. Contributors to this volume reaffirm the common view that homicide is the offense recorded most consistently over time and among jurisdictions, but also point out significant qualifications. During the latter part of the nineteenth century and the early decades of the twentieth, coroners' offices became better able to identify homicides and police had increasing resources to devote to violent crime of all kinds. These factors, combined with increasing public sensitivity to lesser offenses, tended to push up violence arrest rates, as is evident from the Philadelphia data examined in chapter 4, even though the "true" rate of offenses may not have changed. A specific example: many cities' records show substantial increases in official rates of homicides and homicide arrests between 1900 and 1920, not because of a "crime wave" but because most local authorities regarded the rising tide of deaths in auto accidents as culpable homicide and arrested the drivers responsible for them.

Since 1933, however, we are on solid ground when tracking long-term trends in homicides. Both the FBI's Uniform Crime Reports (UCR) data on homicide and national Vital Statistics (VS), compiled from coroners' death certificates, move precisely in unison for the last half-century. Homicide rates declined from the Depression years of the 1930s to their lowest recorded levels in American history in the 1950s. They began to move sharply upward in the early 1960s, as Margaret A. Zahn demonstrates in chapter 10. Between 1963 and 1980 the VS homicide rate more than doubled to a high of 10.7. Since then it has begun a gradual decline to about 8.0, mainly because of a decline in homicide deaths among black Americans.

Rates of violent crime vary irregularly across the social landscape. In the handful of Northeastern cities that have been studied, we know that nineteenth-century homicide rates, calculated from coroner's reports, news accounts, and arrests, generally ranged from 3 to 5 per 100,000. There is reason to think that homicide was considerably more common in the South and West during this period, especially after the Civil War. Historians have argued that a subculture of violence emerged in the South during this era because of the social dislocation and grievances that followed from military defeat. The greater lethality of firearms and a greater willingness to use them probably also played a role, as they did in the West, which was the destination of both northern and southern veterans of the Civil War.[3] When Vital Statistics first began to be reported nationally, during the early twentieth century, it became clear that homicide was far more common in the predominantly rural South and West than in the more urbanized New England and the Midwest. During the recent decades of rising crime rates, however, violent crime has become more and more concentrated in cities. In 1976 the thirty-two largest cities in the United States had 15 percent of the population but 38 percent of the murders, 56 percent of the robberies, and 33 percent of the rapes reported to police.[4]

The low rate of most kinds of violent crime during the Depression, noted above, may be puzzling in view of the common belief that economic hardship is associated with crime. In chapter 7 Colin Loftin, David McDowall, and James Boudouris explore this relationship in Detroit from 1926, before the Depression began, to 1979. Their evidence, like many other studies, shows little convincing evidence of a twentieth-century connection between unemployment and crime. What is clear, from this and many other studies, is that in the United States and Western Europe *persistent* poverty leads to increased homicide. Moreover the Detroit study shows that both common types of murder are increased by persistent poverty: killings by family members, lovers and acquaintances; and killings by strangers in the course of robbery and other crimes.

One of the most disturbing and perplexing features of violent crime in America is the fact that both offenders and victims are disproportionately black. Every study of race and crime from the mid-nineteenth century to the present finds that blacks have been more likely than whites to be arrested for homicide, and more likely to be killed. Five chapters in this book comment on some of the evidence: chapters 1, 2, 3, 10, and 11. We know, for example, that arrest and victimization rates are equally good indicators of the race of killers, since homicide in the United States has always been 90 percent or more intraracial, that is, white on white or black on black. In northern cities in the second half of the nineteenth century, blacks were two to three times more likely to be murdered, and arrested for murder, than whites. In the twentieth century the gap widened considerably: Vital Statistics for the mid-1920s show that blacks were eight times more likely to be murdered than whites. The gap between white and black homicides reached its greatest extent in some northern cities during the 1970s and 1980s, with blacks as much as fifteen times more likely to be murdered than whites.

Roger Lane's explanation, in chapter 2, for the widening interracial gap in homicides is that, except for a brief period during and after World War II, Afro-Americans were never absorbed in significant numbers into the industrial labor force. Thus, many were immune to the social controls that led to declining rates of interpersonal violence among Anglo-Americans and successive waves of immigrants. But while this helps explain the persistence of relatively high homicide rates among blacks, it does not account for the run-away twentieth-century increase. Concentrated and persistent poverty among inner-city minorities in an increasingly affluent white society provides the second part of the explanation. Detroit has become increasingly black and poor during the last half-century, which underlies Loftin, McDowall, and Boudouris's finding of a substantial connection between increasing poverty and murder rates. Wesley G. Skogan cites national evidence, in chapter 11, that the greater the gap between black and white incomes in American cities, the higher the arrest rates of blacks for crimes of violence. This evidence gives added plausibility to the argument that black crime arises out of relative deprivation and resentment. Resentment against poverty stimulates anger, interpersonal aggression, and predation, especially among young black men.

One test of this kind of argument is whether other minorities followed the same pattern. A number of immigrant groups had high rates of violent crime, as Roger Lane and Eric H. Monkkonen have shown. Poor, young immigrant Irishmen were sharply overrepresented among the perpetrators and victims of urban homicide in New York and Philadelphia in the 1850s, 1860s, and 1870s, as were immigrant Italians in early twentieth-century Philadelphia. Once the immigrants were absorbed into the New World's industrial economy, their involvement in crime declined. Most of the bootleggers of Prohibition were children of impoverished, recently arrived immigrants from Eastern and Southern Europe. They were responding to the opportunities they found in Americans' thirst for illegal booze, Mark H. Haller suggests, just as young black men respond now to the opportunities inherent in Americans' craving for illicit drugs. Immigrant Hispanics occupy a similar position in contemporary America, relatively poor—as a group—but assimilating into the mainstream economy more rapidly than the black underclass. Evidence is cited in chapter 1 that murder rates among Hispanics are intermediate between those of black Americans and of whites.

If this thesis is correct, though, black victimization rates should have begun to decline as a result of the political and legal assault on racial discrimination during the 1960s. As I report in chapter 1, this has in fact occurred. The rate of homicide deaths among blacks fell by about 30 percent between 1970 and 1983, from more than 40 to less than 30 per 100,000. Among whites, by comparison, homicide deaths increased by about 30 percent during the same period, from 4.3 to 5.6 per 100,000. Several factors may underlie the increase in white homicides. There is evidence, cited by Wesley G. Skogan in chapter 11, of a significant increase in social disorganization and poverty among white families. The decline of decent job opportunities for unskilled young men, which has had powerful criminogenic effects in Europe, has similar effects on young Americans of all races. And there may be a cultural shift, as I suggest in chapter 1, which has loosened the inhibitions against interpersonal violence that have evolved in Western cultures during the last several centuries. This factor, like the others cited above, is a hypothesis in search of more definitive evidence.

Political assassinations and attempts are the rarest yet best known crimes of violence in America. Even so, they are often misunderstood. James W. Clarke suggests in chapter 8 that of the fifteen men and two women who have tried to kill presidents or other national political figures since 1835, only three were insane, seven were emotionally disturbed, and the motives of the remaining seven were unrelated to psychological disorders. Political motives were central for most assassins, yet only two were unequivocally part of conspiracies: John Wilkes Booth, who killed Abraham Lincoln, and James Earl Ray, the assassin of Martin Luther King. Clarke argues that the actuarial and clinical models used to diagnose dangerousness among other potentially violent offenders do not apply to this select group of seventeen. The question is whether there are any commonalities among them that might be used to assess the danger posed by any of the 200 to 400 individuals who at any point in time are on the Secret Service's "watch list" for surveillance. He identifies seventeen "situational indicators" of dangerousness, that is, traits that characterized a number of past assassins. A majority of them had five traits in common: weapons possession, strong ideological commitments, intense interest in the victim, and three kinds of personal disengagement: occupational instability, estrangement from their family, and transience. Most recent assassins also were known to authorities beforehand because of suspicious activities centered on their eventual victim, and had engaged in attention-seeking behavior. Clarke concludes by proposing a situational approach for assessing dangerousness that is based on these traits.

Americans looking for simple solutions to high crime rates and to political assassinations have repeatedly proposed and sometimes imposed restrictions on gun ownership. Since about two-thirds of murders and all recent assassinations have been committed with guns, the argument goes, dry up guns and violence will decline. Don B. Kates, Jr. reviews the detailed evidence in chapter 9 and demonstrates the implausibility of the argument. In a country with an estimated stock of 60 million handguns and more than 100 million long guns in private ownership, not even the most Draconian policies could remove guns from the hands of people who were determined to get and keep them. Those determined gun owners include far more citizens concerned about defending themselves and their homes than predatory criminals. The irony of most gun control proposals is that they would criminalize much of the citizenry but have only marginal effects on professional criminals. Moreover, an overemphasis on such proposals diverts attention from the kinds of conditions that are responsible for much of our crime, such as persisting poverty for the black underclass and some whites and Hispanics; the impact of the post-industrial transition on economic opportunity for working-class youths; and the shortage of prison facilities that makes it difficult to keep high-risk, repeat offenders off the streets.

There is little doubt that if universal civilian disarmament could be achieved in the United States, deadly crime would decline. Wife murderers, tavern toughs, and robbers would resort to knives and clubs, as our remote European ancestors did, and modern medicine would save more of the victims. But we also must balance the criminogenic effects of the widespread availability of guns against their deterrent effect. Half of American households have weapons for the same reason that police have them: guns can be an effective defense. McGrath's historical evidence from the mining towns, cited above, shows that widespread gun ownership deterred property crime while simultaneously making brawls more deadly. Contemporary studies, summarized by Kates, also show that widespread gun ownership deters crime. Surveys sponsored by both pro- and anti-gun groups show that roughly three-quarters of a million private gun-owning citizens report using weapons in self-defense, while convicted robbers and burglars report that they are deterred when they think their potential targets are armed. The final irony in the gun control-crime equation is that prosecutors, judges, and juries are reluctant to enforce existing laws, not even laws that prescribe greater penalties for gun felonies. Court dockets are too full, prisons are too crowded with repeat offenders to make it possible to implement consistently laws that stipulate "use a gun, get ten." These are the political reasons that comprehensive gun control will never be imposed in the United States, not the work of the gun lobby.

Crime and citizens' presumed right of self-defense are intricately interwoven in American history, as Richard Maxwell Brown points out in chapter 12. Vigilantism, locally controlled police forces, and private gun ownership are all facets of the American tradition that communities and individuals have the right to defend themselves against threats to life and property. The community crime-prevention movement today is a well-respected and effective manifestation of that tradition. And for the last 150 years the evidence of this book is that Americans have had more crime to defend against than have Western Europeans. Waves of immigration, a Civil War that desensitized an entire generation to violence, persisting structural inequalities along racial lines, and the tradition of local rather than more efficient, centralized law enforcement—all have shaped the American experience of crime.

While it is true that Americans are a relatively violent people in crime, as well as in political action, crime rates are not constant across time and social space. We know a great deal about the circumstances in which they rise and fall, and about which groups are most likely to be the perpetrators and victims. All of this provides opportunities for social and policy interventions that can reduce crime. We know, for example, what factors increase or decrease the likelihood that spouses will kill one another, and that robbers will murder their victims. In chapter 10 Margaret A. Zahn summarizes a wealth of research on these questions. Both kinds of murder will be diminished by reducing poverty, income inequality, and racial segregation. Cultural factors that contribute to spouse killings include traditional beliefs in male dominance, the "hands-off" policy of many authorities toward domestic disputes, and the relative lack of safe houses for battered women. Another set of cultural factors leads young men, black and white, into violent crime: family disorganization, materialism, the search for thrills, a perception that they can get away with it, and the presence on television and in urban neighborhoods of positive images of violence and crime.

Alcohol and drug abuse are closely linked to all kinds of violent crime in all social groups.

Some, not all, of these criminogenic factors can be reduced by consistent and persistent application of national policy and local action. The criminal justice system is no longer in the disarray that it seemed to be in the 1970s. In chapter 12 Brown reviews the more stringent policies adopted in the 1980s, including expansion of prisons, sentencing reform, and a shift by the courts away from due process considerations toward more repressive policies. Two features of our emerging Information Society particularly affect the control of crime. Data management technologies make it much easier for authorities to track offenders, while the new surveillance technology vastly extends the capacity of the police and private citizens to monitor crimes in the making. These factors, he suggests, have contributed to the downward drift in crime rates during the 1980s.

The more skeptical view is that public policy is not likely to change enough to overcome the underlying structural and cultural causes of violent crime. Given current conditions and trends, Wesley G. Skogan asks in chapter 11 how crime is likely to change in the next twenty years. Because birthrates declined in the 1970s before rebounding slightly in the 1980s, violent crime is likely to fall significantly, but only temporarily, in the 1990s. More important are the joint effects of hardship, inequality, and social disorganization, or "social poverty," on crime. Minority neighborhoods in the inner cities have the greatest concentration of these criminogenic conditions. There also is evidence of a significant increase in social disorganization and poverty among white families. Although crime and its victims remain most heavily concentrated in inner-city ghettos, the economic and personal security of white Americans is threatened by many of the same conditions that breed crime in the ghettos. Richard Maxwell Brown contends that grass-roots social movements are beginning to respond effectively to these conditions. Community self-help and crime prevention movements are active in high-crime areas as well as in the suburbs. There are promising efforts by leaders and citizens in black communities to motivate youths, improve schooling, and counteract the corrosive effects of the drug and gang subcultures. He sees a new mood of resolve to tighten social discipline that cuts across all the divisions of American society.

An accounting for violent crime twenty years from now, forty years after the National Commission on the Causes and Prevention of Violence issued its first reports, will depend first and foremost on how well the citizens and governments of the United States deal with fundamental problems produced by cultural and economic change: social disarray, lack of economic opportunity, and racial inequality. In the long run I place my bet not on the intractable nature of social reality, but on the ability of Americans, in times of crisis, to take control of their lives and change what they do not like about their society.

Notes

1. According to data from the Uniform Crime Reports, about 42 percent of murder victims in the 1980s have been black. In the period 1980–86 rapes known to police averaged 84,000 annually, robberies 535,000, and aggravated assaults 700,000. The incidence of assaults increased sharply in 1985–1986 to over 800,000 per year.

2. A new long-term study of theft in Sweden shows that two factors together have combined to push up theft rates in the period 1950 to 1984: a declining number of job vacancies (therefore fewer job opportunities, especially for unskilled young people) and the rising availability of durable consumer goods (therefore more opportunities for theft). See Thor Norstroem, "Theft Criminality and Economic Growth," *Social Science Research* 17 (March 1988): 48–65.

3. The classic studies of the southern subculture of violence are cited in note 74 to chap. 1. A recent study that reviews the historical argument but casts doubt on the relevance of gun ownership to understanding regional subcultures of violence is Jo Dixon and Alan J. Lizotte, "Gun Ownership and the 'Southern Subculture of Violence,' " *American Journal of Sociology* 93 (no. 2, 1987): 383–405.

4. From Wesley G. Skogan, "Crime in Contemporary America," in the 1979 ed. of *Violence in America,* 381.

Chapter 1

Historical Trends in Violent Crime: Europe and the United States[1]

TED ROBERT GURR

Most criminologists and other social scientists agree that the real incidence of serious crimes against persons increased very substantially in the United States and most European societies during the 1960s and 1970s, though experts debate about the accuracy of official data on the magnitude of increases. Margaret A. Zahn's chapter 10 in this volume surveys information about trends in American homicide during the last half-century, including evidence that the murder rate began to slacken in the 1980s. Wesley G. Skogan, in chapter 11, summarizes what we know about the social causes of homicide in the United States and concludes that, despite a short-run decline, rates of violent crime are likely to remain high well into the next century. In chapter 13 of the 1979 edition of *Violence in America* I showed that serious crimes had skyrocketed in virtually all Western European countries between 1950 and the 1970s.[2] The most recent comparative evidence, for 1980–84, is that property crime continues to increase in most of Europe whereas homicide rates have held steady. U.S. homicide rates have begun to decline but violent crime in the United States is still far more common than in Europe. In 1984 the U.S. homicide rate was five times greater than in Western Europe: 7.9 homicides per 100,000 people contrasted with an average rate of 1.5 in European countries. Reported rapes were more than six times as common in the United States (35.7 vs. 5.4 per 100,000 in Europe), robberies four times as common (205 vs. 49 per 100,000).[3]

What is less widely recognized is the growing body of historical evidence that the recent increase of serious crime against persons and property in European countries, and perhaps also in the United States, has followed a much longer downward trend. When the historical and contemporary evidence are joined together, they depict a distended U-shaped curve. Figure 1.1

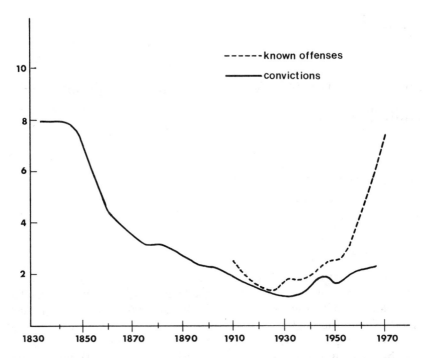

Figure 1.1: The Common Trend in Crimes of Theft and Violence in Western Societies, 1830–1970

shows the composite trends for three Western cities—London, Stockholm, and Sydney—whose crime records extend back 150 years. A century-long period of decline, marked by the convictions data on the left-hand side of the curve, has given way to a shorter period of rapid increase in offenses known and a lesser increase in convictions. Note that the numbers on the horizontal axis represent ratios: a decline from 8 to 4 means that the rates fell by half.[4]

The thesis that rates of serious crimes in Western societies have traced a reversing U-shaped curve is a simplification of a much more complex reality. It characterizes some but not all offenses. The evidence for it is substantial in some societies, especially the English-speaking and Scandinavian countries, but is either lacking or contradictory in others. There are severe problems in the interpretation of official data on crime compiled in different eras. Even where a reversing trend is clearly present, as in England and Wales during the last 150 years, there are substantial short-term deviations around it. For these and other reasons, the U-shaped curve is used here as a hypothesis, not a proven social law, against which we can evaluate evidence on the trends in violent crime.

This chapter is limited mainly to evidence about trends in homicide, with occasional references to assault and robbery. In terms of social importance these offenses are less common than burglary and larceny, but are of greater concern to most people: offenses that inflict bodily harm are and probably have always caused greater fear than has theft. From the perspective of the social and cultural historian, the variation in violent offenses across time, space, and social groups is of great interest because of what it tells us about social stresses, interpersonal aggression, and the complex of social attitudes toward violence. And from a methodological viewpoint, when dealing with data on homicide in particular we can be more confident that long-run trends reflect real changes in social behavior rather than changes in the practices of officials who record and respond to crime.

The first part of this chapter comments briefly on what can and cannot be inferred from data on violent crime. The next three parts report statistical evidence on trends in violent crime for England, the United States, and some other advanced industrial societies. The conclusion offers evidence and ideas about the social dynamics that underlie the long-term trends in violent crime, and the variations around it.

Official Data on Interpersonal Violence

There is a great deal of slippage between the occurrence of an offense and the chain of events by which it does or does not enter the official records from which rates and trends are estimated.[5] The reporting and prosecution of offenses depends in part on public concern, police resources, and many other factors. The alternative sources of information about violence offenses in crime statistics include police tabulations of known offenses and arrests, and court records of indictments or committals to trial, convictions, and sentences. Survey studies of people's victimization by crime show that the more serious the offense, the more closely citizen reports correspond with police data,[6] which supports the commonly held view that murder is the most accurately recorded violent crime. But offenses known to police have been recorded for only a relatively brief period in most Western societies, which is why the "offenses known" data in Figure 1.1 begin in 1930. Arrest data go back somewhat further in time. In many American cities they began to be recorded soon after uniformed police forces were established in the third quarter of the nineteenth century. However, as Neil A. Weiner and Margaret A. Zahn show in their historical study of arrests in Philadelphia (see chap. 4 in this book), there are many inconsistencies in the way arrests have been categorized and reported.

Most studies of crime in the nineteenth century, and virtually all research on earlier periods, use court records on indictments or committals to trail, or on convictions. The slippage between the commission of a felony and the success of private citizens or officials in getting the accused to trial is considerable, and probably was greater before modern police forces were established than since. On the other hand, since homicide is usually committed by people known to the victim (as evinced by many microstudies), and because homicide in Western societies usually has attracted close official attention, the slippage between act and court record is probably less for this crime than for assault, robbery or rape.

Coroners' records of homicides and death registration data are alternatives to police and court records.[7] In principle, data from these sources should be closer to the "true" incidence of homicide than any other, but in fact, as Roger Lane found in his study of nineteenth century Philadelphia (see chap. 2), there may be serious systematic sources of error in recording the cause of death. And of course death records are of no help in assessing the incidence of other kinds of interpersonal violence. Such problems have led a few historians, among them Eric H. Monkkonen (see chap. 3) to supplement official records on homicide deaths with newspaper accounts, a very time-consuming procedure that has an important payoff: it provides more information on offenders, victims, and circumstances than do most police or court records.

Official records thus are not perfect for assessing the true incidence of violent offenses, but closer to the mark for homicide than for others. This is not always a problem for determining trends because sometimes it is plausible to assume that the slippage within a jurisdiction is more or less constant over time. But not always, and there is the rub. Official categories of violent crime may change, for example by shifts in the inclusion or exclusion of involuntary manslaughter, infanticide, or attempted murder. Underlying legal definitions also may change, for example, the distinction between murder per se and manslaughter. No distinction was drawn between these two forms of violent death in English criminal procedure until the sixteenth century.[8] Most difficult of all to detect are changes in police and prosecutorial procedures. Coroners and police in England and the United States became better able to identify death from unnatural causes during the nineteenth century and, as a consequence, homicides were increasingly likely to come to police attention as the century progressed.[9] In the first two decades of the twentieth century many American police forces treated the fatalities of the auto age as homicides. The sharp increase in "homicide" rates that followed has led to some dubious conclusions. Careful study of the sources and their historical and institutional context is necessary to identify and screen out the potentially misleading effects of these factors on long-term trends.

Changing social values also play a role in the recording of violent crime. Western societies have experienced a centuries-long process that Soman calls the "sensitization to violence," a process that was manifest in the gradual "exclusion of most violence from ordinary daily life, and a heightened sensitivity to some of the residual violence."[10] How this process affected trends in violent crime is evaluated in the conclusion. Here we must be concerned with the fact that this shift in values disposed more private citizens to seek redress for lesser acts of violence, with a parallel increase in officials' disposition to prosecute such cases. The implication is that official data on such offenses as assault and attempted murder can be expected to increase over time (especially before the twentieth century) even if the true incidence of offenses stayed constant. Something similar has happened with respect to the incidence of rape, whose victims have become ever more willing to bring complaints.

Because of increased sensitization to interpersonal violence, any long-term upward trend in assault, especially prior to the twentieth century, is prima facie suspect as an indicator of change in social behavior. This is especially so if the trend in assault runs counter to the trend in homicide. Homicides usually are the result of particularly successful (or unlucky) assaults and it is implausible that the real incidence of serious assaults could increase without a parallel increase in homicide. On the other hand, evidence of a long-term statistical decline in the assault rate has prima facie plausibility because it runs counter to increased public sensitization and official attention. These comments apply to trends in assault observed over a number of decades, not to sharp upward and downward waves of a few years' duration. Such waves are too brief to be a product of slow change in social values. Short-term peaks in serious assault and homicide rates probably are reflections of real events.

The two other main categories of violent crime are sexual assault and robbery. We can do little more than guess about long-term trends in sexual assault, first because time-series data are sparse and second because it is an offense more often concealed than reported by the victim: The "dark figure" of unreported offenses was unknowably large until victimization surveys began to be used in the 1970s. Robbery trends, though, may be more reliably estimated and used as a supplemental indicator of changes in interpersonal violence. They are second in reliability only to homicide rates per se, though subject to many of the same questions about validity. Robbery—defined as theft with the threat or use of force against the victim—has always been regarded as a particularly serious crime in Western societies and usually leaves victims who are more than willing to complain to authorities. The legal definition of robbery has not changed appreciably over time in England or the United States, and thus records of cases brought to official attention should be relatively consistent over time. The most substantial slippage to affect our knowledge of trends in robbery arises from the fact that the offender is usually unknown to the victim. Thus court cases (and arrest and clearance rates) are usually much less numerous than offenses, but are likely to have increased—relative to the number of offenses—after the development of modern police systems during the past century. Therefore there may be some artifactual increase in the number of robbery cases brought to trial during the nineteenth century, relative to their true or "known to police" incidence. We know, for example, that in London the gap between robberies known to police and convictions narrowed appreciably between the 1880s and 1930.[11] Gatrell says that the same principle applies to nineteenth-century English data on serious offenses in general: "The rate of recorded crime crept ever closer to the rate of actual crime."[12]

In summary, three general guidelines are suggested here for interpreting the long-term trends in violent crime, with special reference to the period of decline that ended in the early twentieth century. (1) The declining historical trend in homicide probably is understated somewhat, because of closer official attention and a stretching of definitions to include more cases of voluntary manslaughter. Since the establishment of modern, centralized systems for recording crime and death data, official homicide data are the most accurate of all data on interpersonal violence. A cautionary note: Since homicide is a relatively rare offense, it is highly variable over the short run and in smaller localities. Thus homicide rates are best used as an indicator of middle and long-run trends in interpersonal violence.[13] (2) Data on robberies are a rather distant second to homicide data in reliability. Long-term trends in trial and conviction data for robbery are probably unreliable across those periods in which police systems were being established, but should be internally comparable before and after that transition. (3) Long-run trends that show increases in assault are suspect because of increasing concern about these offenses. Long-run declining trends in assault are more likely to reflect real change in social behavior.

Finally, we can be more confident about the underlying trends in interpersonal violence if different studies and different indicators point in the same direction. Conclusions about the directions and magnitude of change in interpersonal violence are convincing to the extent that they are supported by any of the following kinds of parallel evidence: (1) similarity in trends of indicators of an offense obtained from several different sources, for example, police and coroner's records of homicides; (2) similarity in trends of indicators of an offense registered at different stages in the criminal justice process, for example, offenses known vs. committals to trial and convictions; (3) similarity in trends of indicators of an offense from different cities or regions within countries; and (4) similarity in trends of linked pairs of offenses, for example, homicide and assault, or assault and robbery. Divergence among indicators, especially of types (3) and (4), is not necessarily a threat to the validity of conclusions about trends because the social dynamics of interpersonal violence may vary among regions, or from one type of offense to another. If they do vary, plausible and testable explanations for the differences are needed. If there are no such explanations, then the data are seriously suspect.

Violent Crime in Medieval and Contemporary England

Were the rates of murder and assault in London, and all of England, as high in the eighteenth century as they were after 1805, when officials first began to compile country-wide statistics? This question is not entirely a matter of antiquarian curiosity because an unambiguous answer would help us interpret the nineteenth century's decline and, possibly, the late twentieth-century's rise in violent crimes. There are two general possibilities. The developmental possibility is that the nineteenth-century decline continued an earlier trend. This implies that the decline was due to some fundamental, very long-term social dynamics in the evolution of Western society: perhaps the transition from rural to town and city life, or the emergence of some civilized values that inhibited aggressive interpersonal behavior. The cyclical alternative is that the high level of interpersonal violence of the 1820s was an aberration, the result of a cresting wave caused by the Napoleonic wars, or by economic or demographic dislocations. The two interpretations are not mutually exclusive. It is possible that violent crime has tended to decline over the longer run but with short-term reversals, in other words a cyclical pattern of variation around a declining trend.

There are two major obstacles to testing these alternatives. One is the lack of official tabulations of any kind of crime statistics before the nineteenth century. The second is the lack of accurate population data, without which no precise estimates can be made of crime rates. Regular population censuses, like crime statistics, were largely a nineteenth-century innovation. The first national census in the United States was taken in 1790, in Britain in 1801. Nonetheless, there are a handful of historical studies of homicides (and other felonies) in medieval and early modern England that suggest some answers.

Homicide in Medieval and Early Modern England

None of the quantitative historical studies of English crime are national.[14] Instead, all are based on painstaking analyses of surviving coroners' rolls and court records for specific years in specific counties or cities. Second, they are concerned mainly with describing the characteristics of violent crimes: how many occurred, their circumstances, the traits of offenders and victims, the outcomes of trials, and how they varied among jurisdictions. Third, if rates of offenses, or indictments, are calculated, they are subject to substantial error because population data for pre-census English towns and counties were considerably less accurate than records of violent deaths. One author chooses "to avoid all discussion of rates of crime until, if ever, there is more reliable demographic information for the fourteenth century."[15] Fourth, all the studies combine data on murder and manslaughter. Finally, few of these studies estimate trends because most are necessarily limited to scattered years by the availability of records. It is only when we juxtapose the results of a number of different studies in different eras that evidence about long-term trends in homicide begins to emerge.

The first systematic records of English homicide appear in the thirteenth-century records of the eyre courts, panels of royal justices that visited each county every few years. They had the exclusive prerogative of judging all cases of homicide. Coroners and juries were required to report independently to the court on all violent deaths that had occurred since the previous visit of the court and were fined if there were inconsistencies or omissions in their reports. The transcribed records, where they have survived, "portray violent conflict in medieval England with a completeness that is unmatched by the records of any other country in northern Europe in the Middle Ages." Given's study of a wide sample of the eyre rolls shows convincingly that murderous brawls and violent deaths at the hands of robbers were everyday occurrences in medieval England. The average annual homicide rates for five rural counties, studied at scattered intervals between 1202 and 1276, ranged from 9 per 100,000 population in Norfolk to 23 in Kent, compared with a contemporary rate of about 2 per 100,000 in all of England and Wales.[16] Most of these violent deaths resulted from fights among neighbors, while between 10 and 20 percent were attributed to robbers or bandits. Knives, axes, cudgels, and other implements found in every agricultural community were the typical instruments of death. Usually several assailants were charged in each homicide, another item of evidence that most deaths resulted from brawling among small groups rather than one-on-one attacks.

The medieval English population was more than 90 percent rural. Fourteenth-century London had only 35,000–50,000 people, Oxford about 7,000. Estimates of urban homicide rates for this period vary enormously. In the thirteenth century, according to Given, the London rate was about 12 per 100,000 and in Bristol 4 per 100,000.[17] On the other hand Hanawalt estimates that London in the first half of the next century had homicide rates of 36 to 52 per 100,000, depending on which population figures and which year's homicides are used.[18] And in Oxford, Hammer's very thorough study for the 1340s shows an extraordinarily high rate of about 110 homicides per 100,000, a rate to which scholars contributed no more (as victims or assailants) than might be expected from their proportions in the population. Analysis of the details shows that virtually all victims and assailants in Oxford were males and, except for scholars, were almost always of low status. Scarcely any homicides occurred within families and at least one-third involved "strangers," such as people having no fixed residence in Oxford. Unlike the rural pattern, very few homicides in Oxford resulted from robbery or burglary.[19]

These early estimates of homicide rates and their contemporary description sketch a portrait of a society in which men (but rarely women) were easily provoked to violent anger and were unrestrained in the brutality with which they attacked their opponents. Interpersonal violence was a recurring fact of rural and urban life. Had medieval Englishmen been equipped with firearms rather than knives and rustic tools, one can only assume that they would have killed one another with even greater frequency. There are only two circumstances that might inflate somewhat the homicide rates estimated from this period by comparison with the present. First, the medieval English population included a somewhat larger proportion of young men, who are universally more likely to be involved in murderous violence than older men.[20] Second, more victims may have died because of lack of medical knowledge and services—a factor that probably is more than offset by the fact that modern firearms are more likely to kill victims than are knives and clubs (see Don B. Kates' chap. 9 in this volume). Two critical historians who have reviewed the evidence of this chapter concur that medieval homicides occurred at about ten times their modern rate.[21]

The eyre courts largely ceased to function during the fourteenth century and it was not until the late sixteenth century, during the reign of Elizabeth I, that county assize courts left records of indictments in sufficient detail to permit statistical study. These records refer to persons charged with crimes rather than offenses per se. Cockburn calculates these estimates of homicide indictment rates for 1559–1603 for three counties, the first two close to London and the other more distant: Essex, 6.7 per 100,000; Hertfordshire, 16, and Sussex, 14.[22] In a more detailed study of Essex during an overlapping period, Samaha relies on records from coroners' inquests and lower courts as well as the assize records. He also uses different population estimates. Nonetheless, the homicide rate calculated from Samaha's data is virtually the same as Cockburn reports for Essex: 6.8 per 100,000.[23]

Homicide rates in Elizabethan England were noticeably lower than those for the medieval centuries, but still far higher than contemporary figures. Spontaneous violence was still common among rural people. According to Cockburn, few of the killings investigated at assizes during this time resulted from calculated violence; "rather, they occurred during acts of sudden, unpremeditated aggression and resulted from attacks with a variety of knives and blunt instruments. Fatal quarrels could originate in almost any context—at work, in drink or at play." Handguns, known as "pocket dags," were in limited use by this time and about 7 percent of the violent deaths involved firearms.[2]

In contemporary Western societies assaults are far more common than homicides. Not so in the sixteenth century records. Indictments for homicide in Cockburn's study outnumbered assaults 280 to 133, not because assault was less common, one suspects, but because most people did not think it was serious enough to bring to the assize courts.[25] Samaha excludes assaults entirely from his parallel Essex study because the assault indictments he examined usually state that the defendant put the plaintiff out of possession of his land. He concludes that they were not assaults in the ordinary meaning of the term but rather that plaintiffs were using the criminal law to try civil property disputes.[26]

Moving ahead to seventeenth- and eighteenth-century England, we find Beattie's statistical analysis of indictments brought in the higher courts of Surrey and Sussex for a sample of years between 1662 and 1802. Surrey included London south of the Thames and Sussex was predominantly rural. The rates of murder and manslaughter indictments per 100,000 in Surrey begin at about the level of Elizabethan England and decline thereafter:

1663–1665	6.1
1690–1694	5.3
1722–1724	2.3
1780–1784 and 1795–1802	less than 1

The decline was registered in both urban and rural parishes of Surrey, and was "confirmed in Sussex, where there were on average between two and three indictments for murder every year in the seventeenth century and rarely more than one in the eighteenth." Beattie concludes, not surprisingly, that these absolute numbers almost surely reflect a real decline in killing, not changes in public attitudes or judicial efficiency.

Trends in the rate of indictments for assault are much different than those for homicide. In Surrey assault rates followed a wavelike pattern, rising to a very high peak in the 1720s and 1730s, with lesser peaks in the 1760s, 1780s, and at the beginning of the nineteenth century. In rural Sussex, though, the assault rates were lower, the peaks of lesser amplitude, and the long-run trend was generally downward. Two kinds of factors apparently underlie the shifting patterns of indictments for assault. Evidently there was a long-term decline in assault in rural Sussex, and real but short-term increases in assault in Surrey (and much greater ones in property offenses) by disbanded soldiers and seamen who periodically flooded London and its environs at the conclusion of the six wars in which England was involved between 1690 and 1802. Second, Beattie thinks that some of the short-term peaks were due to an increased inclination of injured parties to bring cases to court, and greater apprehensiveness of authorities about threats to public order, especially in the 1720s. In other words, public and private responses to the fear of assault during what we would now call "crime waves" may have inflated the number of indictments.[27]

Violent Crime in the Nineteenth and Twentieth Centuries

Beginning in 1805, English officials compiled national data on commitals to trial for indictable (serious) offenses, and after 1834 began to report them by county. The rate of all offenses against persons tried in upper courts was 12.3 per 100,000 in 1836–1840, falling to 9.0 in 1896–1900 and 7.7 in 1906–1910. Beginning in the 1850s there are series on homicides known to the police, which trace a similar decline from 1.4 per 100,000 in 1856–1860 to 0.8 in 1906–1910. Gatrell, whose study is the source of these estimates, argues trenchantly that the trends cannot be explained away by changes in public attitudes or official practices: they reflect a real decline in interpersonal violence. Nor is deterrence a likely explanation, because impulsively violent offenders are not likely to be deterred by the threat of arrest or punishment. The explanation must be sought in "heavy generalizations about the 'civilizing' effects of religion, education, and environmental reform."[28]

The national trends are paralleled by the evidence from my study of London from the 1820s to the 1970s. In Middlesex County, which included London north of the Thames, committals to trial for homicide during the 1830s ranged from 15 to 35 per year in a county with about 1.4 million inhabitants. The committals rate in this period averaged about 2 per 100,000 (about twice the rate in adjoining Surrey at the beginning of the century) but by the 1850s had declined to less than 1 per 100,000, with temporary upswings in the late 1840s and the 1860s. Conviction rates were consistently about half the committal rates. Committals to trial for assault declined more sharply. When first recorded in the 1830s and 1840s they ranged from 15 to 25 per 100,000 annually but had fallen by 1870 to an average rate of 6 per 100,000.[29]

From 1869 to 1931 data for all of London's Metropolitan Police District show that homicide rates continued to decline. For this period the trend study focuses on convictions. The annual conviction rate for murder and manslaughter gradually fell from about 0.5 per 100,000 in the 1870s to half of that in 1930. Convictions for assault and attempted murder declined from ca. 5 to ca. 1.5 over the same span. After the 1940s, however, both London and all of England and Wales experienced increasing rates of violent crime. In London the incidence of homicides known to police tripled from about 0.7 per 100,000 in the 1950s to more than 2.0 in the 1970s. In absolute numbers, the London police reported 18 murders and 22 cases of manslaughter in 1950 compared with 127 murders and 15 cases of manslaughter in 1974. During the same period indictable assaults increased still more sharply, from 10 per 100,000 in 1950 to 120 in 1974.[30]

In the United States, violent crime is disproportionately concentrated in large cities. Not so in London until recently. National trends in England and Wales started inching upward in the 1940s, a decade earlier than in London. By the beginning of the 1980s London's rate was nearly double the national rate of 1.2.[31]

Summary: The Long-Term Trend in English Homicide

When the above evidence is juxtaposed, the general trend that emerges is unmistakable: rates of violent crime were far higher in medieval England than in the twentieth century—probably ten and possibly twenty or more times higher. The estimates discussed above are displayed graphically in Figure 1.2. Each estimate for a county and city before 1800 is represented by a dot, even though the estimate may cover a period of several decades.[32] A speculative trend curve is fitted to the data points. Elizabethan Essex and London from 1820 to 1975 are represented by five-year moving averages. The 750-year trend is so pronounced that no amount of quibbling about imprecise population data or incomparability of sources can make it disappear.

There are still two problematic features of the long-term trend. One is the extraordinarily high incidence of homicide in two fourteenth-century cities by comparison with the preceding century. If the handful of estimates is not grossly in error, there evidently was a tremendous upsurge in violent crime in England (or at least in its cities) during the early fourteenth century. Hanawalt suggests as much. In general the fourteenth century was more disorderly than the thirteenth. The Hundred Years War, which began in 1337, and the Black Death, which killed perhaps one-third of the population, precipitated social and economic crises of major proportions.[33]

The other question is whether homicidal violence remained more or less steadily high until the decline which set in during the late seventeenth century. The evidence ca. 1600 consists of estimates for three different counties for which population data are dubious. This question, like that of the previous paragraph, cannot be answered definitively until substantially more research is done by historians working on different periods and places.

The evidence clearly favors the possibility, raised at the outset of this section, that the century-long decline of violent crime in England that ended by 1950 was the latest phase of a much longer trend. The seemingly high rates of homicide in early nineteenth- and late twentieth-century London were actually very low when contrasted with the more distant historical experience. The possibility of cyclical or wavelike movements away from the underlying trend is not ruled out, however. There probably was a surge in violent crime in fourteenth-century England. Violent crime also evi-

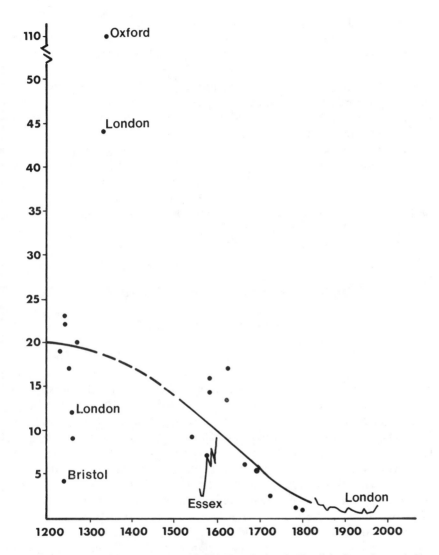

Figure 1.2: Homicide Rates per 100,000 Population in English Counties and Cities, 1200–1970

dently increased in Elizabethan times. More certainly, Beattie offers evidence of several such waves between 1660 and 1802, and it is also likely that London's violent crime rates were unusually high in the 1820s and 1830s. The relatively high rates of contemporary London may prove to be the peak of another such wave.

Did assaults also decline over the longer run? For the medieval and early modern period we simply cannot say because the court data on assaults are either nonexistent or unreliable. In Elizabethan times they appear in court records less often than homicide, but a century later assaults were much more numerous. Since most homicides of this period resulted from violent altercations, the real incidence of assault was presumably much higher. The paucity of assaults in early court records almost surely reflects a significant social fact: physical assault ordinarily was not thought serious enough to warrant indictments unless someone died. Sporadic increases in assault rates during the period studied by Beattie, between 1660 and 1802, are evidence of increased concern by victims and courts but not of a real long-term increase. During the last 150 years we are on more solid ground. Trends and peaks in official data on assault in London and all of England and Wales have closely paralleled those for murder and manslaughter. We can be reasonably confident that assaults, like murder, became less common during most of this period but increased after about 1950.

Trends in Violent Crime in the United States

North America was settled mainly by the English and we might expect some parallels in violent crime between the two countries during the colonial era and the early years of the new American Republic. We know that crime trends in England and Australia were similar from the 1830s to the 1970s. But North America was or became different in social composition from England in ways that fundamentally affected the American way of crime. England had no counterpart of Afro-Americans, first slave and then free, whose experience of crime as victims and perpetrators has been radically different from that of Anglo-Americans. And from the 1840s until 1919 American cities absorbed tens of millions of immigrants from Ireland, Germany, Scandinavia, Italy, and Eastern Europe. These groups had their own lifeways that only gradually were reduced in the American melting pot: turn-of-the century Italy, as Roger Lane remarks elsewhere in this volume, had the highest homicide rate in Europe. Moreover many of the immigrants were rootless young men, a group with a very high propensity for getting into trouble.

The problems with records and statistics that make it difficult to discern long-term trends in English crime are worse in North America. Court records are fragmentary, municipal police forces in the nineteenth and early twentieth centuries were too busy dealing with offenses to count them reliably, and no national agency was directed to collect comprehensive crime statistics until 1933, when the Federal Bureau of Investigation was given the task. Moreover it took years after 1933 for the FBI to establish standard guidelines for classifying and counting offenses and to secure the cooperation of thousands of local police forces (see Margaret A. Zahn's chap. 10 in this volume). England and Wales, by contrast, have centralized government and courts and, since the 1830s, a nationally-administered police system.

One clue to the long-term trends in North American violence is provided in Figure 1.3, which shows the rate of judicial executions per 100,000 population from the early colonial period. A total of 14,570 executions have been recorded in the 13 colonies and the 50 states between 1608 and mid-1987. The great majority of those executed, 79 percent, were people convicted of murder. Another 11 percent were executed for rape and other offenses involving the use of violence.[34] Of course the data do not reveal anything directly about the incidence of violent crime. Most evident from Figure 1.3 is a long-term decline in the disposition of officials to use the harshest penalty at their disposal. Opposition to capital punishment did not become widespread until after 1945. We also know, from evidence cited below, that the incidence of homicide in American cities drifted downward from the 1870s to about 1950, with some increases in the first and third decades of the twentieth century. For this period the homicide and execution rates parallel one another. Thus we can infer that the longer-run downward trend in executions probably tracks, in an imperfect way, a long historical decline in murder.

VIOLENT CRIME IN NINETEENTH CENTURY AMERICA

How much did murder decline in nineteenth century America? The evidence begins around 1840, when annual indictments for homicide in Philadelphia averaged about 3.3 per 100,000 (Lane) and in Suffolk County (Boston) 2.1 per 100,000 (Hindus), slightly greater than the London rates at that time.[35] In the 1850s, however, these and other eastern cities show evidence of a significant upturn in homicide victims, arrests, and indictments. A variety of evidence, some of it discussed in chapters by Lane and Monkkonen elsewhere in this volume, strongly implicates working-class Irish immigrants, who appear with far greater than chance frequency in police records and accounts of public disorder from the 1840s onward.[36]

Homicide rates declined temporarily during the Civil War because most young men were in uniform. After 1865 rates turned sharply upward for a decade or more. In Suffolk County, for example, murder committals immediately before the Civil War (1859–61) averaged 3.1 per year, then jumped in 1869–70 to 7.0 per year (Hindus). In Philadelphia the homicide indictment rate increased to 3.1 in 1867–73 before falling to an average of 2.1 from 1881 to 1901 (Lane).

Homicide arrests in the same city averaged 3.9 per 100,000 in 1868–72, then declined to 2.2 in the last decade of the century (Weiner and Zahn, this volume). Three reasons have been proposed for the post-war surge: the return of demobilized veterans, some of them habituated to violence;

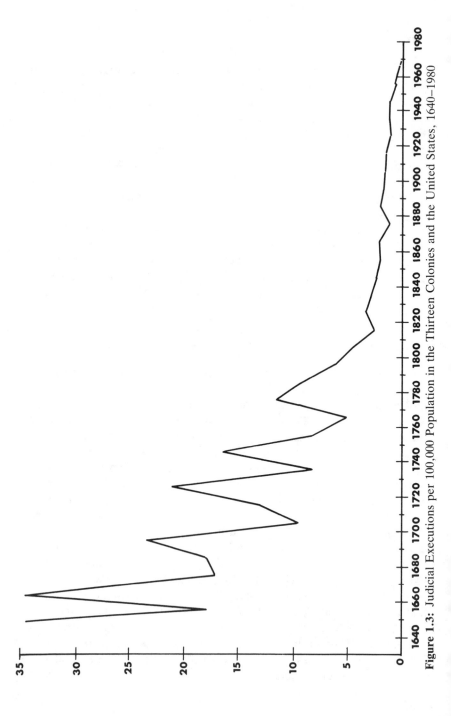

Figure 1.3: Judicial Executions per 100,000 Population in the Thirteen Colonies and the United States, 1640–1980

the widespread availability of guns; and continued emigration from Europe. In New York City, where about 40 percent of the population in 1850–70 consisted of emigrants, both killers and victims during this period were disproportionately likely to be young Irish and German men between 20 and 30 years of age (see Monkkonen, this volume).

The effects of Irish emigration and post-war disruption on homicide seem to have dissipated by the last two decades of the century. In Philadelphia homicide indictments declined by one-third between the post-Civil War high and 1900 (Lane, *Violent Death in the City*), the arrest rate by almost half (Wiener and Zahn, this volume). Similar declines of 40 to 50 percent are registered between the 1870s and 1890s in white homicide rates in New York City (Monkkonen, this volume), arrest rates for homicide in Boston (Ferdinand), and aggregate homicide arrest rates in twenty-three large cities (Monkonnen). Moreover these declines took place against a backdrop of increased sensitivity to marginal cases. Lane's examination of individual homicide indictments in Philadelphia "reveal a further stretching of definitions" of murder over time.[37]

The late-century decline in murder also occurred despite fresh waves of emigration from elsewhere in Europe, a fact that suggests the presence of some other social dynamic. Lane proposes that it was the shift toward industrial society and its imperatives: Children were socialized by public schools to cooperative, regulated behavior and their adult lives were subject to the discipline of factory shift work. The implication is that the immigrant factory worker in the 1880s had less time and inclination for drinking and brawling than the Irish-born casual laborer of the preindustrial 1840s.[38]

Did other offenses against the person follow the same general pattern of an increase from the 1850s to the 1870s, superimposed on a gradual long-term decline to the turn of the century? The evidence is mixed. In Boston the arrest rates for assault and robbery follow this pattern (Ferdinand). So do commitals to trial for rape, robbery, and arson in all of Massachusetts (Lane, "Crime and Criminal Statistics"); arrest rates for all offenses against persons in Buffalo, New York (Powell); and arrests for all crimes with victims in twenty-three cities (Monkonnen). In Philadelphia, by contrast, sustained increases in arrests for aggravated assault and rape more than offset a slight downward drift in robbery arrest rates (see Wiener and Zahn, this volume). The rise in assault rates, since it goes against the common trend, may reflect a growth of public and private antipathy toward familiar behavior rather than a real growth in assault.

VIOLENT CRIME IN THE TWENTIETH CENTURY

If American social behavior followed the Northern European pattern, the decades from 1900 to World War II should have marked the ebb tide of interpersonal violence. At first glance the statistical evidence suggests otherwise. A study of the death registration records of twenty-eight large cities for 1900 to 1924 showed that their aggregate homicide rate increased steadily from 5.1 to 10.3 per 100,000.[39] The aggregate homicide arrest rate in twenty-three cities increased by the same proportion, from 6 at the beginning of the century to 13 in 1920 (Monkonnen). At the root of this epidemic of "homicides" was the onset of the auto age and a commensurate rise in traffic fatalities, which the outraged authorities repeatedly recorded and prosecuted as murder. As late as 1926, twenty-three trolley, truck and auto operators in Philadelphia were tried for "murder" in cases that would now be categorized as vehicular manslaughter.[40]

Other circumstances combined to keep the real rate of murder (excluding manslaughter) higher in American cities than in Europe. The Prohibition era of the 1920s was the source of a great deal of violence as bootleggers fought over hijackings and distribution rights.[41] Not all immigrants were quickly and easily absorbed into the work-a-day routines of the industrial world. In Philadelphia during the first two decades of the century, people of Italian origin were 20 times more likely to be imprisoned for murder than other white social groups. Their participation in violence gradually abated; not so the almost equally great overrepresentation of black Philadelphians, most of whom were barred from industrial jobs until World War II.[42]

A detailed survey of later twentieth-century trends and patterns in homicide is provided in Margaret A. Zahn's chapter 10. The national rate of known homicides in the United States, documented in the FBI's new *Uniform Crime Reports*, declined from about 6.5 per 100,000 in the mid-1930s to a low of 4.8 in the 1950s, interrupted by a temporary increase after World War II. In the early 1960s began a well-documented upsurge, reaching a high point of 10.5 in 1980 before declining slightly to about 8 in the late 1980s. The American and European trends thus parallel one another between the 1930s and the present, but the American rates have been far higher throughout—five times higher in the mid-1980s, for example.[43]

The most disquieting feature of violent crime in the United States is not its absolute level but the fact that its perpetrators and victims are so heavily concentrated among black Americans. A major and long-neglected question about crime trends is whether the trends and dynamics of homicides among blacks are similar to those among whites. Some evidence on this question is summarized in Figure 1.4 and discussed below. The evidence comes mainly from studies of homicide mortality rates by race. These rates correlate closely with homicide arrest and imprisonment rates by race because murder in the United States has always been almost entirely intra-racial.[44]

We begin, once again, in nineteenth-century Philadelphia. Homicide deaths among blacks averaged 7.5 per 100,000 over the period studied by Lane, almost three times higher than the white rate of 2.8. By the 1950s the

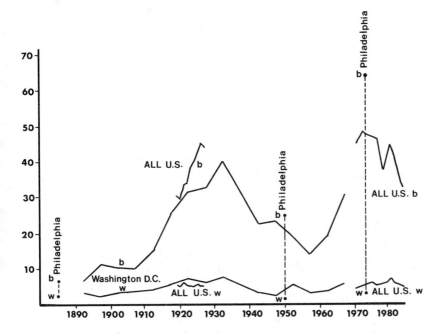

Figure 1.4: Homicides per 100,000 by Race in the United States, 1800s–1984
NOTE: Types of Data: Philadelphia, race of victims in homicide indictments in
1838–1901 (mean) Washington, D.C., arrests for homicide by race, decennial averages 1890–1970 All U.S., homicide mortality rates by race,
1918–1927, 1970–1984

white victimization rate had declined to 1.8 per 100,000 while the black rate
was an incredible 64.2.[45] Data from New York, summarized below for
selected decades, show that black victimization rates began to escalate
after 1900 and by the 1930s were 12 times as great as the white rate.[46]

	Murder Victimization Rates	
	White	*Black*
1852–1860	6.5	19.3
1866–1875	5.4	10.7
1881–1890	4.2	10.2
1901–1910	4.2	12.7
1921–1930	4.8	22.2
1931–1940	4.2	31.3
1945–1953	1.9	24.3

A study of homicide arrests in Washington, D.C., from 1890 to 1970,
provides further evidence of the same diverging trends. These are the
homicide arrest rates for whites and nonwhites in selected decades:[47]

| | Homicide Arrest Rates | |
	Whites	Nonwhites
1890–99	2.9	9.1
1910–19	5.1	20.0
1930–39	6.3	36.1
1960–70	5.0	25.4

Studies of deaths registration data show that the divergence between black and white homicide victimization is a national phenomena, not one confined to Northeastern cities. An early study by Brearley of the 1919–1927 period found that white homicide rates remained virtually constant over the decade at 5.3 per 100,000. The rate for blacks, however, increased from 30.5 to 43.8. Moreover, separate figures by states show that every state in the registration area experienced an increase during this decade in black homicide rates.[48]

One prevalent explanation for high homicide rates among blacks is their poverty relative to whites, and the barriers of racial discrimination that historically have kept them poor.[49] Resentment against poverty stimulates anger, interpersonal aggression, and predation. Consistent with this explanation is the fact that black homicide victimization increased to unprecedented levels during the Depression years of the 1930s (in Washington and New York). World War II provided upward economic mobility for many blacks, and it appears that black homicides declined somewhat in the aftermath of that war.

If the relative deprivation argument is correct, black victimization rates also should have begun to decline as a result of the political and legal assault on racial discrimination during the 1960s. A recent study by the federal Centers for Disease Control shows precisely this trend. The rate of black homicides declined from more than 40 at the beginning of the 1970s to less than 30 per 100,000 by 1983. The white homicide rate, in contrast, edged upward from 4.3 in 1970 to 5.6 in 1983.[50] The black victimization rate remains much higher than the national average in large cities like Chicago and Philadelphia, in other words in cities with the greatest concentrations of the black poor. In the five southwestern states, where Hispanics occupy an intermediate social and economic position between whites and blacks, their homicide rate in 1977–82 was three times higher than Anglos but less than half that of blacks.[51]

SUMMARY: THE LONG-TERM TRENDS IN AMERICAN HOMICIDE

The composite picture of violent crime in nineteenth-century America is a stable or declining trend with a pronounced upward swing that began shortly before the Civil War and persisted into the 1870s. The evidence is limited mainly to cities on the eastern seaboard and the Midwest, which may not be representative of what was happening in towns or on the frontier. Roger McGrath's study of crime in two California mining towns in chapter 5 shows, paradoxically, that property was safer there and life more dangerous than in the eastern cities.

Homicide and most other violent crimes declined in the 1880s and 1890s, then increased somewhat (how much remains uncertain) during the first thirty years of the twentieth century. A sharp rise in black homicides contributed substantially to the overall trend. Bootlegging robberies and killings added to the violence of the 1920s. Violent crime subsided during the 1930s and remained low until the 1960s. Current national homicide and robbery rates surpass any previously recorded in this century, and far exceed those of any other advanced industrial society. The difference is due only in part to black homicides. The homicide rate among U.S. whites in 1984 was twice that of Canada and Finland, the Western countries with the second and third highest rates.[52]

The dominant feature of the American experience is not a reversing U-shaped curve but rather the occurrence of three pronounced upsurges of interpersonal violence that began roughly fifty years apart: around 1850, 1900, and 1960. There were lesser increases in violence in the aftermath of the Civil War and the two World Wars of the twentieth century. These waves are of such amplitude that we cannot say conclusively whether they are superimposed on a longer-run decline. It is likely that homicide rates among white Anglo-Americans drifted downward and remained relatively low for most of the period. The more important social fact is that violent crime in the United States has been much more affected during the last 150 years by the changing socioeconomic status of immigrants and Afro-Americans, and by war, than by underlying cultural dispositions. In societies that are sharply stratified along economic and ethnic lines, as the United States has been, social historians should give more attention to the social characteristics of offenders and victims than to aggregate trends and waves.

Violent Crime Trends in Europe and Australia

It was suggested earlier in this chapter that there might have been a long-term decline in serious crime common to all Western societies on the basis of a comparative study of London, New South Wales (including Sydney), and Stockholm. All of them experienced declines in homicide and other offenses against persons beginning in the 1820s and 1830s, when data first were recorded, to very low levels a century later. The rates did not turn sharply upward until the 1960s, as in the United States. Since New South Wales imported most of its population and crime problems from England, as well as its institutions of criminal justice, one might expect its trends in violent crime to parallel those of the mother country. The most substantial difference was that murder and assault were far higher at the beginning of the century of decline than they were in England, not surprising in view of the fact that, until 1840, the majority of Sydneysiders were convicts and emancipists. The decline, once it began, was precipitous: the rate of high court convictions for murder and assault in the 1890s were one tenth their 1830s level. It is more remarkable to find Scandinavian evidence of similar long-term trends. In Stockholm convictions for murder and attempts were ca. 3.5 per 100,000 population in the 1830s, ca. 1.5 in the 1850s, and less than 1.0 by the turn of the century. Data on offenses known to police from 1841 trace a similar decline.[53]

The trends on the European continent were somewhat different. France has the best and most thoroughly studied nineteenth-century crime statistics. The most detailed English-language analysis, by Zehr, reports that homicide trials declined from about 3.5 per 100,000 adults in the 1830s to about 2 in the 1860s, then increased and varied between 2.5 and 3 during the rest of the century. Serious assaults tried before the higher courts declined, probably because they were shifted to the lower courts, while cases of assault and battery doubled between the 1830s and the first decade of the twentieth century. When assault trends are examined in a sample of eight Departments, it becomes clear that they responded to the social and economic changes of urbanization. Zehr's most general conclusion is that "most major upswings in violence appear to be relatable to urban-industrial growth or more precisely, to the initial and/or most disruptive stages of the process."[54]

Similar conclusions follow from the study of crime trends in Germany between 1882, when the first national data were compiled, to the outbreak of World War I in 1914. The overall trend in offenses against persons (using court data on trials and convictions) shows a 50 percent rise from the early 1880s to the late 1890s followed by a more gradual decline.[55] But, as in France, the upward trend was due to changes in the incidence of assault, and as I suggested earlier, positive trends in assaults during the nineteenth century are more likely a reflection of growing sensitization and closer official attention to assaults than evidence for real increases in interpersonal violence. Indeed, the trend in homicide trials in Germany was downward, declining from an initial rate of about 1.0 trials per 100,000 to 0.76 after 1900.[56]

What of the correlates of trends in crimes against persons in Germany? In general, McHale and Johnson found that the incidence of all categories of crime in Germany was highest in regions where social stress was greatest, due either to depopulation (in rural areas) or to very rapid population growth (in the swelling urban-industrial centers). As stress increased and then lessened in a particular district, so did crime rise and ebb.[57] There is converging evidence from Zehr's time-series analysis of assault trends in thirteen German towns and cities during the same period. Though the results are mixed, they suggest that rising assault coincided with the initial, not the later stages of urbanization. Once industrial and urban growth were well under way, social adjustment set in and interpersonal violence tended to decline.[58]

The two World Wars had a profound impact on crime in Central Europe, and lesser effects on crime in all the combatant nations. In Germany and Austria most kinds of property and personal offenses declined during World War I, a pattern widely observed during wartime in other Western societies and readily explained by the fact that most young men were in military service. Immediately after the war most kinds of crimes against persons rose sharply.[59] Homicide rates usually increase after wars, as Archer and Gartner have demonstrated in a wide-ranging comparative study. Their procedure is to compare average homicide rates during the first five years before the outbreak of war with rates during the first five postwar years. They found substantial increases, averaging 40 percent, in eight of fourteen combatant nations in World War I, little or no change in three, declines in three others. Among fifteen combatant nations in World War II, homicide rates increased substantially in eleven, by an average of 89 percent. They use the evidence to test alternative explanations about why war leads so often to increases in homicide and conclude "that wars . . . tend to legitimate the general use of violence in domestic society."[60]

The European evidence tells us more about the causes of "crime waves" than about very long-term trends. The rates of homicide in Continental Europe during the late nineteenth and early twentieth centuries were about as low as those of contemporary England and Wales and lower than those of cities in the United States. It also is evident that the social dislocations of urban growth, industrialization, and war tended to push rates of personal crime up. But, oddly, the stresses of the Great Depression, which began in late in the 1920s, seems to have had no such general impact. In England and the United States, Stockholm and Sydney, the rates of offenses against persons remained at or near their all-time historic lows through the 1930s. Property offenses evidently increased, especially in England, homicide rates did not. More fine-grained studies, such as Loftin, McDowall, and Boudouris's study of unemployment and murder in Detroit (see chap. 7 in this volume) suggest that the impact of depression on personal crime is more complex than might be supposed from the national data.

The "crime waves" in the European countries most affected by World War II had largely subsided by 1950. The most remarkable subsequent phenomenon is the near universality of rising crime during the period of unprecedented prosperity of the 1960s and early 1970s. Criminologists cite "opportunity theory" as an explanation for the fact that property crime tends to rise during periods of prosperity: the more abundant and less well protected property is, the easier it is to steal.[61] There is no such easy explanation for the rise in crimes of violence documented above for England and the United States. The English and American experience was by no means unique. In Stockholm after 1950 virtually every category of offense against persons skyrocketed. Some twenty-year increases in rates of offenses known to police are: murder and attempts, 600 percent; assault and battery, more than 300 percent; rape and attempted rape, 300 percent; robberies 1000 percent. Stockholm experienced in more serious form a malaise that affected all the Scandinavian countries beginning no later than the 1960s. In Germany, Austria, and France the rates for these offenses stayed relatively low until the 1970s, then also surged upward. Switzerland was the only Western European country where crimes against persons remained relatively low throughout this period.[62]

One factor that helps account for the differential timing of increases in personal crimes among Western countries is the shape and timing of the "baby boom" that followed World War II. In Britain and the United States the proportion of the population aged 15 to 29 increased by about 50 percent between the mid-1950s and the mid-1970s, and crime rates surged upward as the postwar generation of youths came of age.[63] The American birthrate was lower in the 1960s and early 1970s than in the first postwar decade, with the result that crime rates have subsided somewhat in the 1980s.[64] Germany and Austria, by contrast, had baby "boomlets" that began after economic recovery set in during the 1950s, and their crime increases began later and continue high.

There is nothing automatic about the youth/crime connection. In most Eastern European countries the youthful population increased substantially between 1964 and 1977 with little impact on the incidence of violent crime.[65] If the incidence of criminal violence among young men was constant, a 50 percent increase in their proportion would cause a 50 percent rise in rates of violent crime, not 500 percent. Cultural values and social practices are crucial intervening variables. In Switzerland, Clinard suggests that crime has remained relatively uncommon because of the persistence of traditional "small town" values, including an active interest in monitoring the activities of one's neighbors.[66] There is also the countervailing evidence of Japan, a very prosperous country with a large and youthful population where serious offenses against persons and property declined steadily from the mid-1950s through the 1970s. In 1984 Japan had the lowest recorded rates of homicide, robbery, and rape among all the industrialized countries of the world.[67] Cultural values and lifeways are different in Japan than in the advanced industrial countries of the West; so are policing practices.[68] Both presumably help explain what might be called the other Japanese miracle: rapid economic transformation without social disorder.

Conclusions: The Dynamics of the Long-Term Trends

How well does the U-shaped curve of declining, then rising violent crime fit the evidence reviewed here? The English evidence on homicide covers the longest run and is the most convincing. It also makes the post-1960 upturn appear to be a minor perturbation, proportionally no greater than temporary upsurges in homicide rates in Elizabethan times and during the Napoleonic wars. In the United States the occurrence of three generation-long waves of violent crime, beginning ca. 1850, 1900, and 1960, makes it difficult to say whether these increases are superimposed on a long-term decline. The evidence suggests that homicide rates among whites moved gradually downward from the mid-1800s until the 1960s, whereas homicide rates among blacks not only have been higher but surged upward from the beginning of the twentieth century until the early 1970s. Declines in homicidal violence also are established for nineteenth-century Stockholm, New South Wales, France, and—beginning late in the century—Germany. We have no evidence from any country or jurisdiction that there was a sustained *increase* in homicides during the later nineteenth century. An increase in homicide rates from the 1960s to the early 1980s is also a common though not quite universal phenomenon in Western societies.

The evidence on assault and robbery, including data not reviewed in this chapter, in general parallels the trends in homicide, especially during the last thirty years. In this era of rising crime, robbery and assault rates usually have increased much more than homicide. In the nineteenth century, however, assault rates moved contrary to homicides in France, Germany, and some American cities. There is reason to attribute this mainly to increased official attention to minor offenses, not to real and sustained increases in assault. Serious assault and robbery usually trended downward.

The discussion of the long-term decline in violent crimes has touched on a number of explanations for trends and variations around them. There are two separate questions: What social dynamics underlie the long-term decline? And what explains the big deviations of crime above this trend, especially those sustained upwellings of violence that persist for ten or twenty years before subsiding again? I think there is a simple and singular answer to the first question, but multiple and complex answers to the second. I also think that no special, *sui generis* explanation is needed for the late increase in violent crime. Its explanation should follow from an understanding of the dynamics of the long-term decline and of the deviations from it. In other words I suggest that the upturn of the U-shaped curve is simply the latest, and best-documented, deviation from the underlying trend.

A plausible explanation for the long-term decline in interpersonal violence is what Norbert Elias calls "the civilizing process" and all that it implies about the restraint of aggressive impulses and the acceptance of humanistic values.[69] By their own accounts, medieval Europeans were easily angered to the point of violence and were enmeshed in a culture that accepted, even glorified, many forms of brutality and aggressive behavior.[70] The progress of Western civilization has been marked by increasing internal and external controls on the show of violence. People are socialized to restrain and displace anger. Norms of conduct in almost all organized activity stress non-violent means of accomplishing goals. Interpersonal violence within the community and country is prohibited and subject to sanction in almost all circumstances. The process has a darker side. States claim an ever-more-effective monopoly on violence and use it, in the guise of "legitimate force," to maintain internal order and to promote "national interests" against other states. In many modern societies there also has been a long-term increase in structural violence—the social and political arrangements that compel individuals, minorities, and lower economic strata to accept restraints and subordination against their will. But the risk of unpredictable danger in daily life from violent attack has declined.

The "civilizing process" has been both a cultural and political one, and like most such changes had its origins in the changing values of Western elites. They have sought both political order and social peace. The process, so far as it pertains to violence, contributed not only to the decline in homicide and assault but also to the humanization and rationalization of social policy. It led, for example, to the decline and ultimate abandonment of executions in most Western nations, the end of slavery and the brutalization of wage labor, the passing of corporal punishment in schools and prisons, and many other humane features of contemporary life that are often taken for granted.[71]

The cultural process of sensitization to violence, to use Soman's phrase, has not been uniform. It took root first among the urban upper and middle classes and only gradually and selectively was promulgated among rural people and the lower classes. It has been suggested, for example, that a major social function of the new nineteenth-century police forces was to serve as missionaries of upper and middle class values to the theretofore dangerous lower classes.[72] The same message was spread by the expanding public school system and by churches like the Methodists, who were especially active in British working-class neighborhoods.

The thesis that sensitization to violence spread from the social center to the periphery and from upper to lower classes is intrinsically plausible as an explanation of some basic features of violent crime, past and present. Interpersonal violence historically may have been higher in rural than urban areas—the evidence is mixed—because of the persistence there of traditional patterns of interpersonal behavior. It tended to increase in cities during the early phases of urbanization and industrialization because new immigrants from the countryside, or from overseas, only gradually accepted the lifeways and values of the industrial city. Interpersonal violence declined overall during the nineteenth century and the first half of the twentieth because Western societies became increasingly urban and formal education became universal. The further down the class and status ladder, then and now, the more common is interpersonal violence, because the lower classes did not assimilate and still have not wholly assimilated the aggression-inhibiting values of the middle and upper classes. And the black minority in the United States has had far higher rates of violence than the white majority not merely because of poverty-induced frustration but because the barriers of discrimination and segregation have fostered a subculture that encourages aggressive behavior. What is true of Afro-Americans is likely to be true of other stratified minorities in Western societies.

One other group may become desensitized to violence: youth. The historical process of sensitization to violence must be replicated in the socialization of each new generation of children in each society. To the extent that socialization fails, or is incomplete because it is not reinforced by other social institutions, youth are susceptible to other kinds of values, including those that celebrate violence. This factor is independent of, but reinforced by, the social fact that young males are more disposed to interpersonal violence than any other demographic category.

The long-run downslope of interpersonal violence is irregular and some of the irregularities take the form of sharp and sustained increases. We have seen evidence from France, Germany, and Eastern American cities that violent crime tends to rise during the early stages of industrialization and urban expansion. Rapid modernization may have been one of the sources of high rates of violent crime in early nineteenth-century England and in the United States in the 1860s and 1870s, especially because it pulled in many young migrants. But urbanization and industrialization usually are gradual processes, not likely in and of themselves to create a national tidal wave of disorder.

The connection between warfare and waves of violent crime is more precise. In fact, war is the single most obvious correlate of the great historical waves of violent crime in England and the United States. Civil and foreign wars contributed to the crime peak of the 1340s.[73] A mid-eighteenth century wave of crime coincided with Britain's involvement in a succession of wars from 1739 (war with Spain) to 1763 (the end of the Seven Year's War). The upsurge of crime at the onset of the nineteenth century began while Britain was fighting the Napoleonic wars, from 1793 to 1815, and continued through the severe economic depression that followed their end. In the United States, Irish immigration evidently contributed to the urban crime wave that began in the 1850s, but its peak in the 1860s and 1870s coincided with the social and political upheavals of the Civil War. The disproportionate fondness for dueling and less genteel forms of violence among white southerners may not have originated with the Civil War,[74] but certainly was reinforced by it. The second high wave of violent American crime crested during the decade after World War I. The third began near the onset of the Vietnam War. Lesser increases in violent crime followed both world wars in England and Wales, the United States, and most continental democracies.

War may lead to increased violent crime for a number of reasons. I opt for Archer and Gartner's interpretation that it does so mainly because war legitimizes violence. It does so directly for young men who become habituated to violence in military service. It does so indirectly for others who find in the patriotic gore of wartime a license to act out their own feelings of anger. The interpretation is difficult to prove. But it is consistent both with the evidence on crime trends and with the social dynamics I have proposed for the long-run decline in interpersonal violence. If the civilizing process has been accompanied by sensitization to violence, then war, including internal war, temporarily *de*sensitizes people to violence.

Another basic factor that influences the extent of personal crime is the size of the youthful population. If their relative numbers are high in a particular city or era, its crime rates are likely to be higher than in times and places where the population is older. Substantial short-term increases in the numbers of young males have happened periodically in Western societies, often as a result of socioeconomic change or war. A population boom was underway in England during the first half of the nineteenth century, thanks to better nutrition and higher birth rates. One result was a remarkably high proportion of young males in London. Over the long run, 1801 to 1971, the changing proportions of males aged 15 to 29 in London's population trace a time-path very similar to, though of much lower amplitude than, the time-path of felonies.[75]

This evidence and speculation suggests a composite explanation for the upsurge of common crime in Western societies during the last several decades. Begin with the demographic explosion of young people. Add the consequences of the transition to post-industrial society, which almost everywhere has meant a decline in the factory jobs that once provided economic opportunity to working-class youths. The result is a high level of structural (persisting) unemployment among the least well-educated young people in virtually every European and North American city. Many are intensely resentful of their status at the lower margins of affluent societies. Because of their class background and social experiences they also are the people who are least likely to feel inhibited against interpersonal violence. And their lack of regular employment means they have ample reasons and time for exciting and illegal behavior: to steal, to deal drugs, to riot at soccer matches, to assault and kill one another. In this larger context, unemployed ghetto youths in the United States are locked in the same kind of criminogenic social prison that can be found in most large European cities.

The strands of this speculative discussion can be brought together by concluding that each great upsurge of violent crime in the histories of the societies under study has been caused by a distinctive combination of altered social forces. Some crime waves have followed from fundamental social dislocation, as a result of which significant segments of a population have been separated from the regulating institutions that instill and reinforce the basic Western injunctions against interpersonal violence. They may be migrants, demobilized veterans, a growing population of resentful young people for whom there is no social or economic niche, or badly educated young black men trapped in the decaying ghettos of an affluent society. The most devastating episodes of public disorder, however, seem to occur when social dislocation coincides with shifts in values, because of war or changes in popular culture, that legitimate violence which was once thought to be illegitimate.

Notes

1. This is a substantial revision of an essay first published in Michael Tonry and Norval Morris, eds., *Crime and Justice: An Annual Review of Research* (Chicago: University of Chicago Press, 1981), 3:295–333. An extensive summary and commentary on parts of the original essay appear in Lawrence Stone, "Interpersonal Violence in English Society, 1300–1980," *Past & Present* 101 (Nov. 1983): 22–33.

2. "On the History of Violent Crime in Europe and America," in Hugh Davis Graham and Ted Robert Gurr, eds., *Violence in America: Historical and Comparative Perspectives* (Beverly Hills, CA: Sage, 1979), 353–74. See also Gurr, "Crime Trends in Modern Democracies since 1945," *International Annals of Criminology* 16 (1977): 41–85.

3. Bureau of Justice Statistics, *Special Report: International Crime Rates* (Washington, DC: May 1988). This report, prepared by Carol B. Kalish, reports rates from multiple sources. The rates from Interpol data are used in this chapter.

4. Fig. 1.1 is adapted from two figures in Ted Robert Gurr, Peter N. Grabosky, and Richard C. Hula, *The Politics of Crime and Conflict: A Comparative History of Four Cities* (Beverly Hills, CA: Sage, 1977), 644–5. It summarizes information on time-series data for six different rates: for homicide and assault combined, and robbery and burglary combined, for each of the three cities. Sydney is represented by data on all of New South Wales, London by data from the Metropolitan Police District. Each time-series was standardized by setting its lowest recorded rate at 1.0 and calculating other years' rates as ratios. The figure traces the mean of the ratio scores on all six time-series. Of course there is substantial variation around the mean, but all six time-series examined separately trace the same general U-shaped trends.

5. The limitations of contemporary American crime data have been widely discussed, for example, by Herbert A. Bloch and Gilbert Geis, *Man, Crime, and Society: The Forms of Criminal Behavior* (New York: Random House, 1962); Donald Mulvihill and Melvin Tumin, *Crimes of Violence, Report to the National Commission on the Causes and Prevention of Violence* 11 (Washington, DC: U.S. Government Printing Office, 1969); and Wesley G. Skogan, "Measurement Problems in Official and Survey Crime Rates," *Journal of Criminal Justice* 3 (1975): 17–32. Detailed discussions of the interpretation of American historical statistics on crime are to be found in Eric H. Monkkonen's work, including *The Dangerous Class: Crime and Poverty in Columbus, Ohio, 1860–1885* (Cambridge, MA: Harvard University Press, 1975); "The Quantitative Historical Study of Crime and Criminal Justice," in James A. Inciardi and Charles E. Faupel, eds., *History and Crime: Implications for Criminal Justice Policy* (Beverly Hills, CA: Sage, 1980); and *Police in Urban American, 1860–1920* (New York: Cambridge University Press, 1981). On the reliability of British historical statistics see V. A. C. Gatrell and T. B. Hadden, "Criminal Statistics and Their Interpretation," in E. A. Wrigley, ed., *Nineteenth Century Society: Essays in the Use of Quantitative Methods for the Study of Social Data* (Cambridge, UK: Cambridge University Press, 1972); and V. A. C.

Gatrell, "The Decline of Theft and Violence in Victorian and Edwardian England," in V. A. C. Gatrell, Bruce P. Lenman, and Geoffrey Parker, eds., *Crime and the Law: A Social History of Crime in Western Europe since 1500* (London: Europa Publications, 1980). My views about what can be inferred from official crime data are spelled out in Gurr, Grabosky, and Hula, *Politics of Crime*, 16–26.

6. Wesley G. Skogan, "Citizen Reporting of Crime: Some National Panel Data," *Criminology* 13 (1976): 535–49.

7. They have been used by, among others, H. C. Brearly, *Homicide in the United States* (Chapel Hill: University of North Carolina Press, 1932); James Buchanan Given, *Society and Homicide in Thirteenth Century England* (Stanford: Stanford University Press, 1977); and Roger Lane, *Violent Death in the City: Suicide, Accident, and Murder in Nineteenth-Century Philadelphia* (Cambridge, MA: Harvard University Press, 1979).

8. J. M. Kaye, "The Early History of Murder and Manslaughter," *Law Quarterly Review* 83 (1967): 365–95.

9. On England see Gatrell, "The Decline of Theft and Violence," 247–8; on Philadelphia see Lane, *Violent Death in the City*, 76.

10. Alfred Soman, "Deviance and Criminal Justice in Western Europe, 1300–1800: An Essay in Structure," *Criminal Justice History: An International Annual* 1 (1980): 1–28. Changing attitudes toward interpersonal violence are a recurring theme in Norbert Elias's work: *The Civilizing Process: The History of Manners* (New York: Urizen, 1978, originally published 1939) and *State Formation and Civilization* (Oxford: Oxford University Press, 1982).

11. Gurr, Grabosky and Hula, *Politics of Crime*, 120.

12. Gatrell, "Decline of Theft and Violence," 250–1.

13. See Howard Zehr, *Crime and the Development of Modern Society: Patterns of Criminality in Nineteenth Century Germany and France* (Totowa, NJ: Rowan and Littlefield, 1976), 85–6.

14. This section makes use of these in-depth historical studies: J. M. Beattie, "The Pattern of Crime in England, 1660–1800," *Past & Present* 62 (February 1974): 47–95; J. S. Cockburn, "The Nature and Incidence of Crime in England, 1559–1625: A Preliminary Survey," in J. S. Cockburn, ed., *Crime in England, 1550–1800* (Princeton: Princeton University Press, 1977); Given, *Society and Homicide*; Carl I. Hammer, Jr., "Patterns of Homicide in a Medieval University Town: Fourteenth-Century Oxford," *Past & Present* 78 (February 1978): 3–23; Barbara A. Hanawalt, "Violent Death in Fourteenth- and Early Fifteenth-Century England," *Comparative Studies in Society and History* 18 (1976): 297–320; Hanawalt, *Crime and Conflict in English Communities, 1300–1348* (Cambridge, MA: Harvard University Press, 1979); and Joel Samaha, *Law and Order in Historical Perspective: The Case of Elizabethan Essex* (New York and London: Academic Press, 1974). A more general statistical study is P. E. H. Hair, "Deaths from Violence in Britain; A Tentative Secular Survey," *Population Studies* 25 (1971):5–24. For good contextual studies of crime in the post-medieval era see Gatrell, Lenman, and Parker, *Crime and the Law: A Social History of Crime in Western Europe since 1500*, and Douglas Hay, Peter Linebaugh, John G. Rule, E. P. Thompson, and Cal Winslow, *Albion's Fatal Tree: Crime and Society in Eighteenth-Century England* (New York: Pantheon Books, 1975).

All the above studies are concerned with cities and counties in England proper. The "national" data referred to below are usually for England and Wales. Scotland, the third component of Great Britain, has its own criminal justice system and its own official statistics, none of which are examined in this survey.

15. Hanawalt, *Crime and Conflict in English Communities*, 287.

16. Given, *Society and Homicide*, estimates 36, quotation 13.

17. *Ibid.*, 36.

18. Hanawalt, *Crime and Conflict in English Communities*, 301–2.

19. Hammer, "Patterns of Homicide," 9–19.

20. Hanawalt suggests this point in *Crime and Conflict in English Communities*, 127.

21. Stone, "Interpersonal Violence in English Society 1300–1980"; J. A. Sharpe, "Debate: The History of Violence in England: Some Observations," *Past & Present*, 108 (August 1985), 206–15; Lawrence Stone, "A Rejoinder," same issue, 216–24.

22. Cockburn, *Crime in England*, 55–6.

23. Samaha, *Law and Order*, 19–22, 115–16.

24. Cockburn, *Crime in England*, 58–9, quotation 57.

25. *Ibid.*, 55.

26. Samaha, *Law and Order*, 17.

27. Nothing in Beattie's description of typical assault cases ("Pattern of Crime in England," 62–3) suggests that any of them were really civil property cases as they were in Elizabethan Essex.

28. Gatrell, "The Decline of Theft and Violence," 282–93, quotation 300. Official data were reported with increasing reliability and detail as the century progressed.

29. David Peirce, Peter N. Grabosky, and T. R. Gurr, "London: The Politics of Crime and Conflict, 1800 to the 1970s," in Gurr, Grabosky, and Hula, *Politics of Crime*, 166–7.

30. *Ibid.*, 116–7, 162–4.

31. See F. H. McClintock, *Crimes of Violence: An Enquiry by the Cambridge Institute of Criminology into Crimes of Violence against the Person in London* (London: Macmillan, 1963); and McClintock and N. Howard Avison with G. N. G. Rose, *Crime in England and Wales* (London: Heinemann, 1968). The national rate is from Bureau of Justice Statistics, *Special Report: International Crime Rates*, 2.

32. The sources of the data in figure 1.2 are referred to in the text, with two exceptions. The estimate of 20 for ca. 1270 is the mean of high and low figures for Bedfordshire, as calculated by Hair, "Deaths from Violence," 18, using minimum and maximum estimates of population. The estimate for ca. 1550 is the mean of high and low figures for Nottinghamshire for 1530–58, *ibid.*, 17. Hair's estimates of London homicide rates for the seventeenth through nineteenth centuries, based on the London bills of mortality, are not shown because the source is highly suspect.

33. Hanawalt, *Crime and Conflict in English Communities*, 260. The high urban homicide rates she reports cannot be attributed to the social disorder that followed the onset of the Black Death because her London and Oxford estimates are for the first half of the fourteenth century whereas the plague arrived in England late in 1348.

34. The data were compiled by M. Watt Espy from an extraordinary variety of historical, journalistic, and official sources. The analysis in figure 1.3 makes use of a machine-readable datafile that is documented in M. Watt Espy and John Ortiz Smylka, *Executions in the United States, 1608–1987: The Espy File* (Ann Arbor, MI: Inter-university Consortium for Political and Social Research, 1987). Will Moore and I aggregated the executions by decade and calculated decennial rates using population estimates for the colonies (through 1770) and the United States from *Historical Statistics of the U.S., Colonial Times to 1970* (Washington, DC: Government Printing Office, 1976), 1:8 and 2:1168.

35. Studies of nineteenth century American crime trends cited in this and the following two paragraphs are in Theodore N. Ferdinand, "The Criminal Patterns of Boston since 1869," *American Journal of Sociology* 73 (1967): 688–98; Michael Stephen Hindus, *Prison and Plantation: Crime, Justice, and Authority in Massachusetts and South Carolina, 1767–1878* (Chapel Hill: University of North Carolina Press, 1980); Roger Lane, "Crime and Criminal Statistics in Nineteenth Century Massachusetts," *Journal of Social History* 2 (1968:156–63; Lane, *Violent Death in the City*; Monkkonen, *Police in Urban America, 1860–1920*; and Elwin H. Powell, "Crime as a Function of Anomie," *Journal of Criminal Law, Criminology, and Police Science* 57 (1966):161–71. Chapters in this volume by Lane, Monkkonen, and Neil Alan Weiner and Margaret A. Zahn are the sources of other estimates.

36. There was significant Irish immigration from the 1780s onward but it did not reach its

peak until the 1840s. Paul A. Gilje documents the prominent role of Irishmen in New York City's riots and clashes, the first of which occurred in 1799. He says that the Irish "injected a more virulent strain of violence into the popular disorder" of the city and cites two reasons: "the violent tradition of resistance that Irishmen brought with them" and the antagonism of Anglo-Americans toward Catholics. In *The Road to Mobocracy: Popular Disorder in New York City, 1763–1834* (Chapel Hill: University of North Carolina Press, 1987), quotes from 129. The crime data, and some of Gilje's own accounts, suggest that the Irishmen had a general disposition to aggressive behavior, whoever challenged them—including other Irishmen.

37. Lane, *Violent Death in the City*, 70–1.

38. *Ibid.*; see also chap. 2 in this volume.

39. From F. L. Hoffman, *The Homicide Problem* (Newark: Prudential Press, 1925). Other studies utilizing the death registration data during this period are H. C. Brearley, *Homicide in the United States* (Chapel Hill: University of North Carolina Press, 1932) and E. H. Sutherland, "Murder and the Death Penalty," *Journal of the American Institute of Criminal Law and Criminology* 15 (1925):522–9.

40. For documentation see chap. 2 by Roger Lane and chap. 4 by Neil Alan Weiner and Margaret A. Zahn in this volume.

41. See chap. 6 by Mark H. Haller in this volume.

42. See Roger Lane's chapter in this volume and his more detailed study of *The Roots of Violence in Black Philadelphia* (Cambridge, MA: Harvard University Press, 1986).

43. See note 3 above.

44. The race of both victim and assailant is known to the FBI in about three-fourths of all homicide cases from 1976 to 1983. Among these, 94 percent of black victims were killed by blacks, 87 percent of whites were killed by whites. Centers for Disease Control, *Homicide Surveillance: High-Risk Racial and Ethnic Groups—Blacks and Hispanics, 1970 to 1983* (Atlanta: Centers for Disease Control, 1986), 5.

45. Lane, *Violent Death in the City*, 112–3.

46. My calculations from annual data in Eric H. Monkkonen's chap. 3 in this volume, table 3.1.

47. My calculations from Gloria Count-van Manen, *Crime and Suicide in the Nation's Capital: Toward Macro-Historical Perspectives* (New York: Praeger, 1977), 200–1.

48. Brearley, *Homicide in the United States*, 19–20.

49. For evidence on the poverty-crime connection see the chapters in this volume by Wesley G. Skogan and Colin Loftin. For further evidence about and interpretations of crime among and against Afro-Americans see Samuel L. Myers, Jr., and Margaret C. Simms, eds., *The Economics of Race and Crime* (New Brunswick, NJ: Transaction Books, 1988) and the books reviewed by Andrew Hacker, "Black Crime, White Racism," *The New York Review of Books*, March 3, 1988, 36–41.

50. Centers for Disease Control, *Homicide Surveillance*, table 4B.

51. *Ibid.*, 5. The rates are Anglos 7.9, Hispanics 21.6, blacks 46.0.

52. Bureau of Justice Statistics, *Special Report: International Crime Rates*, 3.

53. Gurr, Grabosky, and Hula, *Politics of Crime*.

54. Howard Zehr, "The Modernization of Crime in Germany and France, 1830–1913," *Journal of Social History* 89 (1975): 117–41, quotation 128. A more detailed report is Zehr, *Crime and the Development of Modern Society*, note 13 above. Other English-language studies of French crime correlates and trends are Abdul Qaiyum Lodhi and Charles Tilly, "Urbanization, Crime, and Collective Violence in 19th-Century France," *American Journal of Sociology* 79 (1973): 296–318; and A.R. Gillis, "Crime and State Surveillance in Nineteenth Century France," *American Journal of Sociology*, forthcoming.

55. Vincent E. McHale and Eric A. Johnson. "Urbanization, Industrialization, and Crime in Imperial Germany," Part I in *Social Science History* 1 (1976–77): 45–78, Part II in *Social Science History* 1 (1976–77):210–47; also Zehr, "Modernization of Crime," 91–4.

56. Zehr, "Modernization of Crime," 115–6.

57. McHale and Johnson, "Urbanization," Part II, 243–4.

58. Zehr, "Modernization of Crime," 94, 107–14.

59. See Moritz Liepmann, *Krieg und Kriminalitaet in Deutschland* (Stuttgart, Berlin, and Leipzig: Deutsche Verlags-Anstalt; New Haven: Yale University Press, 1930); and Franz Exner, *Krieg und Kriminalitaet in Oesterreich* (Vienna: Hoelder-Pichler-Tempsky; New Haven: Yale University Press, 1927).

60. Dane Archer and Rosemary Gartner, "Violent Acts and Violent Times; A Comparative Approach to Postwar Homicide Rates," *American Sociological Review* 41 (1976): 937–63, quotation 958. See also, by the same authors, *Violence and Crime in Cross-National Perspective* (New Haven: Yale University Press, 1984).

61. A time-series study that provides strong support for opportunity theory is Lawrence E. Cohen, Marcus Felson, and Kenneth C. Land, "Property Crime in the United States: A Macrodynamic Analysis, 1947–1977; with Ex Ante Forecasts for the Mid-1980s," *American Journal of Sociology* 86 (1980):90–118.

62. See the sources in note 2, above. On Switzerland see Marshall B. Clinard, *Cities with Little Crime* (New York: Cambridge University Press, 1978).

63. See Theodore N. Ferdinand, "Demographic Shifts and Criminality: An Inquiry," *British Journal of Criminology* 10 (1970): 688–98, and Gurr, "On the History of Violent Crime in Europe and America," 368–69.

64. See Wesley G. Skogan's chap. 11 in this volume.

65. From a comparative study by a Polish scholar, Slawomir Redo, "Crime Trends and Crime Prevention Strategies in Eastern Europe," paper read to the Sixth United Nations Congress on the Prevention of Crime and the Treatment of Offenders, Caracas, 1980. Redo implicitly accepts the accuracy of the official data. There is no prima facie reason why the homicide and assault data should be misreported in the internal documents on which he relies.

66. Clinard, *Cities with Little Crime*.

67. See Gurr, "On History of Violent Crime in Europe and America," 69–70, and Walter A. Lunden, "Violent Crimes in Japan in War and Peace, 1933–74," *International Journal of Criminology and Penology* 4 (1976): 349–63. The 1980s data are from the Bureau of Justice Statistics, *Special Report: International Crime Rates*. The Japanese homicide rate is 0.8 per 100,000, half the European average. Rape is reported at about one-third the European average, robberies are one-twentieth as common as in Europe and less than 1 percent of the robbery rate in the United States.

68. For an interpretation of low crime rates in Japan see David Bayley, *Forces of Order: Police Behavior in Japan and the United States* (Berkeley: University of California Press, 1976).

69. See note 10; also see Mary Fulbrook, "The Emergence of Modernity: Patterns and People in Sociocultural History. A Review Article," *Comparative Studies in Society and History* (1985): 130–4.

70. See Given, *Society and Homicide*, chap. 1; also Elias, *Civilizing Process*, 191–205.

71. The effects of humanitarian thought on criminal justice policies are discussed in Gurr, Grabosky, and Hula, *Politics of Crime*, chap. 5.

72. See Alan Silver, "The Demand for Order in Civil Society: A Review of Some Themes in the History of Urban Crime, Police, and Riot," in David J. Bordua, ed., *The Police: Six Sociological Essays* (New York: John Wiley, 1967); and Monkkonen, *Dangerous Class*.

73. Hanawalt, *Crime and Conflict in English Communities*, 228–39.

74. Scholars have debated the existence of a southern subculture of violence and its relation to criminality historically and at present. Its effects evidently have weakened over time. See Sheldon Hackney, "Southern Violence," *American Historical Review* 76 (1969): 906–25; Raymond D. Gastil, "Homicide and a Regional Culture of Violence," *American*

Sociological Review 36 (1971):412–26; Colin Loftin and Robert H. Hill, "Regional Subculture and Homicide: An Examination of the Gastil-Hackney Thesis," *American Sociological Review* 39 (1974): 714–24; and Jo Dixon and Alan J. Lizotte, "Gun Ownership and the 'Southern Subculture of Violence,'" *American Journal of Sociology* 93 (1987): 383–405.

75. Gurr, Grabosky, and Hula, *Politics of Crime*, 43.

Chapter 2

On the Social Meaning of Homicide Trends in America

ROGER LANE

The serious historical study of crime, still less than a generation old, has already fractured a number of popular myths—and created an equal number of new puzzles and problems of interpretation. Among the long-standing myths is the notion of a peaceable past best exemplified by the medieval English village—now shown to have been wracked by frequently murderous violence. Careful examination of the frontier towns of our own Wild West, during the late nineteenth century, has shown that duelling gunslingers were virtually unknown, and while drunken homicide was common most other offenses were quite rare. In the puzzle category, no one has been able to show conclusively why changes in the rates of both violent and property crimes, during the late twentieth century, have tended in the short run to go up and down in tandem, in contrast to the nineteenth century pattern in which violence went up in times of prosperity and down in depressions, while theft responded to the business cycle in precisely opposite fashion. It is not clear either why armed robbery, now the quintessential urban street crime, was so rare in the 1890s that a holdup in the North Bronx rated front page stories in Philadelphia, with the New York cops eventually concluding that the gunman must have worked for Buffalo Bill.[1]

But perhaps this last item is just a part of the most intriguing puzzle of all: that is the long term direction of crime over the past 150 years. All of us in the late twentieth century have lived through a period of rapidly rising rates, especially frightening in the urban United States, and the inspiration for much scholarly historical interest. Yet historians have found a sharply different pattern in the cities of the late nineteenth century, when criminality was not rising but rather falling beneath all the movement, noise, and smoke of urban growth.[2]

Recent rises, then, are best conceived not in isolation but rather as part of a larger pattern, as one end, the far right side, of what amounts to a distended "U-curve" in crime rates whose left side extends well back into the previous century. And what this essay intends, as part of the effort to comprehend the curve as a whole, is to compare the dominant explanations for it, to use new data from Philadelphia to help illumine what is in this country its murkiest segment, that is the early twentieth century, and of course to suggest the direction of future research.

Three Interpretations: An Evaluation and Critique

There are in fact very few attempts to explain the whole of the long U-curve. Most studies of crime rates are naturally concerned with contemporary data, or with the short-term impact of past events such as war and depression. These studies, dealing with relatively neat sets of data over finite periods of time, often result in precise and testable relationships among the variables considered. Studies of long-term trends, in contrast, are typically based on untidy data, from scattered times and places, in forms which defy direct comparison. It is not surprising that the short-term studies are not very helpful in interpreting this material, or even that they are often written in ignorance of it. But despite its shortcomings, the long-term evidence is on some points overwhelming and on others suggestive.

An historical perspective at the least helps to dismiss much of what passes for explanation of what has been happening over the past generation. Many of the alleged causes of crime which currently worry popular and academic observers were also common to the late nineteenth century, often more sharply then than now—whether the disruption of traditional society, rapid urbanization, massive population shifts, expressions of class consciousness, ethnic tensions, or (in the United States) the spread of cheap handguns. Equally important, the fact that the U-curve is an international phenomenon undercuts many of the parochial explanations common to political discourse in this country: whatever the significance of the changing racial composition of our cities, the impact of Supreme Court decisions, or the politics of a given administration, it is impossible to extrapolate their impact to account for long-term changes in London, Stockholm, or Sydney.

But while it is useful simply to note that recent rises in criminal activity form only one side of a larger U-curve, it is not so easy to explain why. And in fact only three scholars have attempted, in any detail, to explain developments stretching across 150 years and three continents: Ted Robert Gurr, James Q. Wilson, and myself. All three of these efforts suffer from one or more obvious weaknesses, partly as a result of problems in the data. But they do have several points in common, and offer at least a place to start.[3]

No one has studied arrest records in more jurisdictions, over more time, than Ted Robert Gurr, who has also written the best recent surveys of the international literature. For him the U-curve is set within a much larger historical framework, one which reaches back to those medieval studies that suggest homicide rates far higher than those across the modern west. From this truly lofty perspective the whole curve seems less a "U" than a kind of gigantic reverse "J," with the long decline resulting from an increasing "sensitization to violence," part of the broad advance of humanitarian values over the past several centuries.[4]

Still, for Gurr, the U-curve of the past 150 years, based on more nearly continuous data from more nearly comparable societies, remains a distinct unit for analysis. And his explanation, as of 1979, is characteristically broad. The key to the downturn of the late nineteenth century is "modernization": the transformation from a rural agricultural way of life into an urban industrial. This may happen in two stages. In the first (which does not always occur), rural society is simply disrupted as people migrate into cities not yet able to absorb them. This stage may at least temporarily result in increased criminal disorder. But thereafter—and this is sometimes the only relevant stage—"modern cities which offer immigrants real economic opportunities within the framework of social control exercised by schools, associations, police, and courts, are not likely to have high rates of crime among immigrants." Indeed once the process of urbanization is in "full swing," rates are likely to decline.[5]

At the other end of the U-curve, the "explosion" of crime in the 1960s and 1970s may have been partly due to a youthful "age bulge," somewhat differently timed in different western societies. But "it is not entirely convincing to attribute crime increases of 300 to 500 percent to a 50 percent increase in the size of the youthful population." More important were two somewhat contradictory developments, although both had a special impact on the young. One was the glorification of violence beginning in the 1960s, fostered both by real war and by fantasies in the media, which encouraged "a significant reversal in the long secular tendency toward restraining and condemning violence." The second was paradoxically related to the antiwar movement, or to a perversion of its message. "Peace, tolerance, and social progress," Gurr speculated, were transmuted to fit into a larger "post-industrial" pattern of values which "might be called aggressive hedonism." This new ethic, with its deemphasis of work, and its insistence more on sexual and social than directly material satisfactions, encouraged a resentment against external authority of all kinds. And in a situation in which "no self-confident consensus on standards of behavior is to be found in most of western society," the old institutions of social control—law, schools, police, prisons—have lost their effectiveness, despite frequent infusions of manpower and money.[6]

This emphasis on moral standards links Gurr's explanation with James Q. Wilson's. Wilson's 1985 study of *Crime and Human Nature*, coauthored with the psychologist Richard J. Herrnstein, is an ambitious attempt to explain differences in the propensity toward criminal behavior in terms of differences in the ability to control impulsively violent or predatory behavior. And while his own work has been largely concerned with contemporary criminality, the whole of chapter 16 and parts of others attempt to make this case historically, to explain the U-curve in terms of developments which in the nineteenth century tended to inhibit and in the late twentieth to encourage reckless impulsiveness.

Wilson's argument is complicated and involves some purely hypothetical suggestions as well as others based on harder evidence. At one end of the spectrum, in keeping with a larger stress on the importance of intelligence in controlling impulse, he offers a kind of speculative Darwinism: some modern criminals may simply be people who would not, in the past, have lived long enough to cause trouble, as modern medicine saves many malnourished and thus learning-disabled infants to survive into adulthood. A more nearly conventional argument is that growing alcohol and drug abuse may weaken self-control by "shortening the time horizons of users." But the most important reason for the recent rises in criminal behavior is not biological but social, and it depends explicitly upon an interpretation of history: that is, "the rise and then the decay of social arrangements designed to foster self-control."[7]

The social arrangements accounting for the left side decline in the "U-curve" Wilson identifies as a series of associated reform movements dating, in the United States, from the second quarter of the nineteenth century. They include the creation of police and prisons, the establishment of public schools, and perhaps most characteristically the temperance movement. All "rested firmly on a religious foundation," and he gives special credit to increases in church membership and the spread of Sunday schools, both of which contributed to the most nearly measurable result of all of this, that is, a long decline in per capita consumption of alcohol.[8]

Since then, of course, "the broadly based effort at moral uplift, and the religious convictions of those elites who led and sustained it, have been weakened or abandoned." The 1920s marked the turning point, with what was considered—despite a real drop in the use of alcohol—the failure of national Prohibition. At the same time a vulgarization of Sigmund Freud's thought, together with a more accurate popular understanding of the work of Margaret Mead and other comparative anthropologists, encouraged the values of self-expression over those of self-control. The stage was then set for the great crime explosion of the 1960s, created by much the same forces as those cited by Gurr, with one characteristic addition: as part of his argument for the deterrent value of swift and sure sanctions, Wilson points out that arrested felons, between 1962 and 1979, were progressively and dramatically less likely to suffer punishment of any sort.[9]

My own work for reasons of precision has largely, although not entirely, dealt with single jurisdictions—Massachusetts and then Philadelphia—and for reasons of statistical trustworthiness has largely, although not entirely, dealt with the single crime of homicide. In its matured form my explanation for the U-curve in murder rates begins with Martin Gold's concept of a "Suicide-Murder Ratio." Gold's argument, published in 1958, is that homicidal and suicidal behavior are differing, even opposing, reactions to frustration, and that individuals and even groups are inclined to either one or the other, statistically, as a result of differing kinds of socialization. Using clinical data together with statistics from the 1940 census, he argued that people socialized into cooperative, careful, or—to put it negatively— regimented behavior were more likely to resort to suicide in times of stress. On the other hand people without such socializing experiences were more likely to erupt into recklessly homicidal violence. And while Gold confined his conclusions to differences in class, and to some degree in gender, it seemed that the concept itself might be applied to ethnic variables as well, and most importantly might be put in motion to explain changes in similar populations over time—such as rising or falling homicide rates.[10]

The research for my 1979 study of *Violent Death in the City* tended to confirm these hypotheses. A variety of indices, local and national, showed that ethnic groups with high murder rates in the late nineteenth century tended to have low suicide rates, and vice versa, all in neat rank order. Over time, too, the curves describing the two phenomena moved in opposite directions. And with the additions of another curve, that for fatal accident—the psychological profile of the accident-prone suggests the same kind of aggressiveness shown by most murderers—the timing of the movement could be established with some precision. Homicide and (nonindustrial) accident rates began to move sharply down, and suicide up, within a few years of 1870. The reason, I hypothesized, was the contemporary movement away from pre-industrial forms of work and education toward three related and highly organized social forms: factory, bureaucracy, and public school, all of which grew dramatically in the post-Civil War era.[11]

The left side and bottom of the U-curve, then, coincided with the growth and maturation of personal habits demanded by the urban-industrial revolution. The logic of this argument suggested simply that the murderous upsurge of the 1960s and after reflects the decay of industrial society in its older form, an idea bolstered by the fact that the patterns of homicide in the post-industrial city of the 1970s—that is, who and how many did what to whom, when, and where—strongly resembled those of the pre-industrial 1840s and 1850s.[12]

Further work on *The Roots of Violence in Black Philadelphia*, published in 1986, added a refinement to all this. The experience of American blacks has long been the kind of exception that proves the rule, in that they were almost totally excluded from the office and factory jobs of the urban-industrial revolution until World War II. The group as a result never fully experienced the downturn in homicide shown for example by Irish and then Italian immigrants who participated fully in the new economic order, and many turned instead toward illegal activities that fostered violent behavior and attitudes. There was a brief break in the pattern when factory and office work opened in the 1940s and 1950s. As national black unemployment reached record lows there was at the same time, and for the first time, a drop in black murder rates. But the 1950s also witnessed the beginnings of urban decay and the shrinkage in the total number of traditional blue-collar factory jobs. Since the 1960s, double digit unemployment and soaring crime rates have been especially marked among young male Afro-Americans in the cities. And their experience suggests that not simple conditioning alone but also less tangible matters involving opportunity/exclusion, or security/insecurity, can have a profound effect on crime rates, as a history of denial can help create, in effect, a criminal subculture with a life of its own.[13]

All of these interpretations have much in common. Gurr, Wilson, and I have all used many of the same original studies, including in several cases each other's; perhaps more important, we have several times arrived independently at parallel or at least compatible conclusions. But at the same time all three theories have demonstrable weak points. Of the original studies, only my own was designed specifically to test for an explanation of the U-curve itself, and that is much more explicit about the falling rates of the late nineteenth century than the rises in the late twentieth. Some of our differences may be testable with new data. But it is necessary first to establish the similarities and differences themselves.

All of us, first, share a definition of "crime" as common law offenses involving theft and violence. While I am not sure that such offenses as assault and homicide respond to the same kinds of social changes as burglary and larceny, there are clearly some connections, and in very broad terms both violence and theft have tended to move in tandem over time. These are all actions that are less subject than "white collar" crimes to changing legislative or administrative definition, which, unlike vice, have individual victims, and, unlike either of these other categories, are almost universally condemned by people of all classes and cultures. Again in contrast to some vice and most white collar crimes, thefts and assaults tend to be impulsive, irrational actions, not, with some exceptions, the result of coolly calculated decisions.

To restrict the definition of "crime" in this fashion has the disadvantage of leaving out the most lucrative and numerous forms of illegal activity. "White collar" criminals steal much more than burglars, and moral violations such as gambling, drug use, drunkenness, and the whole array of sexual offenses are far more common than simple theft and illegal violence. But restriction to the common law crimes, by minimizing problems of definition, social tolerance, and reportage, contributes to a shared faith that we can indeed measure at least broad changes in the incidence of some forms of criminal behavior.

If we ordinarily begin in the nineteenth century, and largely rely on figures from urban jurisdictions, this is simply because trustworthy evidence from earlier periods or rural areas is so rare. Wilson implies the existence of a peaceable rural society before the onset of trouble in the city; Gurr and I, mindful of those bloody medieval villages, are not so sure, but we do limit our observations to changes within largely urban or urbanizing places.[14]

All note an initial period of disorder at some point before the downturn. In accounting for the downturn all three accounts agree further on the importance of education—although for somewhat different reasons—and on the healthy effect of decreasing drunkenness. All note, too, the role played by the justice system, police, courts, and prisons.[15]

What distinguishes Wilson's interpretation is simply the strength of its reliance on government sanctions, together with moral suasion and schooling. Historians have in fact linked these and parallel movements, and the fact that in this country they date from the second quarter of the nineteenth century, some decades before any measurable drop in major crime rates, is not an insuperable barrier to linking them further to wider improvements in self-control. It may be argued that the ongoing effort to reform behavior took some time to work, and certainly that it was buried for some time under waves of immigration, especially Irish, during mid-century. The unique aspect of Wilson's argument, rather, is that he describes the reform movement as essentially self-generated and self-sustaining, operating virtually within a socio-economic vacuum, without links to the wider Urban-Industrial Revolution.

While both Gurr and I agree that the justice system, schooling, and the temperance movement helped push down nineteenth century crime rates, both of us explicitly argue that these were secondary to prevailing economic needs and forces. For Gurr the primary force is "modernization," defined in terms of economic opportunity; for me it is "the urban industrial revolution." This is not to argue that the efforts to reform behavior was mere "superstructure." But it is to argue that the effectiveness of reforms in actually changing mass behavior was dependent upon their "fit" with other needs. The important thing about drunkenness, for example, was not so much that it was labelled criminal but that it was clearly dysfunctional in an increasingly interdependent economy, just as the important thing about schooling was not the moral intent of the lessons so much as the fact that the process of learning to sit still, take turns, hold your water, mind the teacher, and listen for the bell was perfect training for later work in factory or office.[16]

The differences between Gurr and me—his broader and looser definition tending to subsume mine—reflect in part a difference in method. The very strength of Gurr's approach, involving the collation of aggregate arrest statistics or offenses known to the police, is at the same time its weakness. The fact that declining crime rates were noted in so many independent nineteenth century jurisdictions makes that decline undeniable. But at the same time the angle and the timing of change varies considerably not only across differing social and economic systems but as a result of differing definitions and practices within the criminal justice systems which generated the statistics. More detailed measurement, in depth, enables in contrast more careful correlation between criminal statistics and other evidence, more precise specification about different occupational and ethnic groups, more exact location in time. This makes it possible to explain as well as to note what Gurr describes as (sometimes) a two-stage process. Whatever the specific impact, in this country, of Irish immigration and cheap hand-guns, the more fundamental downward change did not occur until about 1870 because it was only then that bureaucratic and industrial employment, and public schooling, began really to involve large numbers of people in cities. Until then, immigration into the older, pre-industrial or commercial city could bring no more than the miseries associated with overcrowding and underemployment.[17]

But if my explanation for the nineteenth century side of the U-curve is more precise than those of either Wilson or Gurr, the same cannot be said for my explanation of the more recent upsurge or right side. That subject has twice been left to the final chapters, in effect the epilogues, of two books mostly concerned with the previous century. It makes sense *a priori* to link the two sides of the curve, to suggest as Wilson does that the increasing violence in the twentieth century essentially results from the weakening of the forces that curbed it earlier. But things may not be so neat, and while I have outlined the pre-industrial-to-industrial transition in some detail, I have simply not done the same for the industrial-to-post-industrial. The precise ways in which the jobs and job-related experiences and attitudes of the late nineteenth century socialized people in different ways from the jobs and job-related attitudes of the late twentieth are hard for an historian to document. Some things may be shown; the curve of black homicide does reflect the impact of the promising period 1940–1960, followed by insecure employment from 1960 on. But while blacks account disproportionately for criminal statistics in this country, roughly half of all homicides and two-thirds of all armed robberies, they do not account for all of the observable rise, and certainly not for parallel developments abroad. There remains much which I frankly cannot explain.[18]

Neither Gurr nor Wilson is so reticent, however, and both make a number of sensible or provocative observations. Much property crime can doubtless be blamed on the emphasis on instant satisfactions in a modern consumer economy: Wilson notes that goods are "out there," for the taking, as never before, and Gurr's "aggressive hedonist" may simply be the ideal consumer gone a little off the tracks. Wilson's concern about the effect of drugs on impulsiveness also parallels Gurr's concern about "sexual and social" gratification. At the same time both point out that abundance in itself is not sufficient to produce high crime rates of any sort, and that culture, as illustrated by the Japanese case, is an important variable in itself. Japanese rates are lower than American by an order of magnitude— the nation has proportionately less than 1 percent of our armed robberies— and these rates were falling in the post-World War II period when ours were rising.[19]

The two political scientists do differ on some important points. One, as noted, concerns the deterrent effect of formal sanctions. Another involves the timing of the modern process of moral breakdown. Gurr's 1979 description, from a man who has done more international comparison than any of us, seems heavily weighted toward the specifically American experience of young people in the 1960s, the simultaneously hot-and-cold breath effect of the Vietnam war and the peace movement. Wilson describes a much more fundamental process, a massive failure of nerve among the reigning elite which dates from the intellectual ferment of the 1920s. Uncertain standards, ever since, have weakened the ability to inculcate morality in children, the most important function of the family. And while most dramatically evident over the past generation, the malaise is older and deeper than is shown simply by the statistics of criminality.[20]

Gurr on the other hand has his own and even longer perspective, which makes his work qualitatively different from Wilson's Jeremiad. Given the truly massive fall in homicide rates since the Middle Ages, even the sharply disturbing rise of the past generation can be seen as only a temporary blip, an interruption in the progressive decline.

Despite these differences, however, there is an overriding similarity between the two interpretations. Since Gurr's account of more recent developments abandons the insistence on underlying economic forces that informed his explanation of earlier change, both he and Wilson attribute growing crime rates essentially to a general climate of moral weakness and uncertainty. This climate, in Wilson's case apparently affecting all kinds of crimes, virtually all western societies, and all groups and classes within them, is described without reference to any structural social or economic changes that might have produced it.[21]

While Gurr is more sensitive to group differences in the modern world, much the same problem afflicts his longer perspective. The sensitization to violence he describes, persuasively, as having occurred over some centuries is attributed to the changing values of the social and intellectual elite—but this development is cited in isolation from any social or economic conditions that may have inspired or encouraged it.[22]

All of this is, by nature, hard to test. But some help may be provided by a body of data that none of us has fully used or accounted for. There is some evidence that in the United States, uniquely, the long ragged "U-curve" that we have all been describing may at best look more like a "W," with a sharp rise in homicides and perhaps other crimes occurring neatly in the middle, that is during the period from roughly 1900 into the early 1930s. At worst the statistics from the period even threaten the notion that the long curve has any meaningful shape at all. Close examination is clearly needed; and in fact analysis of some new data, primarily from Philadelphia, helps not only to resolve this issue but at least contributes toward a solution to some of the others suggested above.

On "Homicide," "Murder," and "Manslaughter": Philadelphia Figures Illumine the "Dark Period," 1899–1933

Existing studies, Ted Robert Gurr has noted, suggest that the urban United States has experienced three pronounced upsurges of interpersonal violence, which began roughly 50 years apart: around 1850, 1900, and 1960. The first of these is the one associated with Irish immigration into the still pre-industrial city, a movement which happened to coincide with the first widespread use of pocket revolvers. Its magnitude is a little unclear simply because it also coincided with the beginnings of urban police, so there are few baseline statistics from any earlier period. The last upsurge, which has witnessed an increase in homicides of several hundred percent, has yet to recede; together with the first it marks the twin arms of the putative U-curve in this country. But the one in the middle, for Gurr, puts the very concept of a U.S. U-curve in jeopardy: "we cannot say conclusively whether the cycles are superimposed on a longer-run decline."[23]

In fact the early twentieth century presents a kind of gap in trustworthy statistical information about homicide in the United States. A number of studies have convincingly shown a drop in the murder rate from the middle to the late nineteenth century, while the FBI's Uniform Crime Reports, beginning in 1933, show a ragged fall from that time into the late 1950s. But if these findings may be accepted as given, the period in between remains relatively uncharted. For theoretical purposes, it is obviously important to determine just who did what during these years, how often, and above all why. But the answer to this last and most important question depends upon the answer to the first two. And the search for (relatively) reliable aggregate figures on the actual incidence of murder, and then for information about who was doing it, provides a textbook case in the practical difficulties of doing longitudinal research in the field.

The idea that the first third of the twentieth century witnessed a steep upturn in homicides is most forcefully suggested in Eric Monkkonen's aggregation of the available arrest records of the 23 largest American cities between 1860 and 1920, supported in varying degrees by other studies which also depend in general upon police reports. Monkkonen, and a few others, show a truly manifold increase in "homicide" arrests. But the idea that these represent "homicide" as usually defined by historians of crime— that is, murder and voluntary manslaughter—will not stand examination.[24]

Monkkonen speaks for us all in suggesting that the state of early criminal records is enough to drive an historian into hysteria. His own painstaking compilation of arrests suffers from a narrowing effect toward the end, as the nineteenth century Golden Age of official statistical reportage fades into the early twentieth, and much police data turns thin or disappears. More distorting is the effect of seriously misleading reportage from the biggest city of all, which particularly in the early years tends to dominate the rest. New York's police typically listed 1392 "homicide arrests" during 1899–1901, a number that nearly matches the 1404 totalled by all other cities. No other place had rates like that; big bad Chicago, by then about half the size of the First City, reported just 103 arrests for the same years; most telling, New York's own coroner counted just 389 homicides. Clearly either the words "homicide" or "arrest" had a special meaning for the New York department that do not translate outside its own walls, and any search for accurate national trends must simply slice the Big Apple out of the totals. The effect, since the New York data are proportionately far bigger around 1900 than around 1920, is to lower the national rates but steepen their apparent climb.[25]

The most relevant sets of data, then, are given in Table 2.1, expressed in rates per 100,000 of population. Monkkonen's big city "homicide arrest" figures, minus New York, are given in column A, and as another kind of benchmark the homicides reported annually by the New York Coroner, in column B. The others, all from Philadelphia, are that city's "homicide arrests," that is "murder" plus "manslaughter," in Column C, its strictly "murder" arrests alone in Column D, and its imprisonments for murder and voluntary manslaughter in Column E.[26]

These are not, on careful examination, purely random numbers; whatever indices are used there is clearly an upward trend. But there is a great discrepancy in the apparent magnitude of that trend. The dramatic upward surge in "homicide arrests" in the largest cities (column A), is (roughly) paralleled by the same increase in Philadelphia (column C), which suggests something like a tripling of rates. Meanwhile New York's coroner, Philadelphia's murder arrests, and Philadelphia's imprisonments for murder and voluntary manslaughter all show much more modest rises, flattening after an initial jump, while even the highest column, D, averages only half that for the "big cities"—minus New York. Which set of figures, then, best represents the "real" tendency of urban homicidal violence?

This problem, at least, has a relatively simple solution. The years in question coincide very neatly with the most important change affecting

Table 2.1. "Homicide" Statistics per 100,000, 1899–1934: A Sampler

Column A "Homicide" Arrests, Largest Cities (minus New York)
Column B "Homicides" found by NYC coroner
Column C "Homicide" Arrests (Murder plus Manslaughter)—Philadelphia
Column D "Murder" Arrests, Philadelphia
Column E Convictions, Murder plus Voluntary Manslaughter, Philadelphia

Year	A	B	C	D	E	Year	A	B	C	D	E
1899	5.1	4.1	5.0	3.2	1.2	1917	13.7	4.5	14.4	4.7	3.7
1900	6.0	4.1	2.1	1.7	1.7	1918	15.4	4.5	22.4	6.5	3.2
1901	6.3	3.1	4.1	4.1	1.5	1919	11.9	5.0	20.4	3.6	1.7
1902	6.2	3.4	4.3	3.2	1.8	1920	12.1	5.7	19.5	5.0	1.0
1903	6.1	3.4	5.0	4.0	2.9	1921	n.a.	5.2	16.4	4.6	1.6
1904	5.7	4.4	5.3	4.8	2.9	1922	n.a.	5.7	21.8	5.2	2.7
1905	8.1	4.0	4.6	3.3	2.7	1923	n.a.	5.1	25.6	7.3	2.5
1906	7.6	5.9	7.1	5.1	2.0	1924	n.a.	6.3	n.a.	n.a.	1.7
1907	8.5	6.5	8.3	6.2	3.3	1925	n.a.	5.3	n.a.	6.3	2.5
1908	8.4	5.1	8.2	6.0	1.3	1926	n.a.	5.3	n.a.	6.0	2.7
1909	6.6	3.9	8.0	4.0	1.4	1927	n.a.	5.6	n.a.	6.7	1.9
1910	8.3	6.0	14.6	7.0	1.9	1928	n.a.	6.0	n.a.	6.6	3.3
1911	7.3	5.8	7.8	3.8	1.5	1929	n.a.	6.2	n.a.	5.3	n.a.
1912	9.3	6.0	10.7	3.8	1.0	1930	n.a.	7.1	n.a.	6.9	n.a.
1913	9.7	6.5	9.6	4.4	2.2	1931	n.a.	8.3	n.a.	n.a.	n.a.
1914	10.2	5.8	10.0	4.1	3.5	1932	n.a.	8.2	n.a.	5.8	n.a.
1915	10.4	5.0	9.6	6.8	2.9	1933	n.a.	7.6	n.a.	5.1	n.a.
1916	13.5	4.8	12.5	4.6	3.4	1934	n.a.	6.1	n.a.	4.1	n.a.

police work since the Civil War—that is, the impact of the internal combustion engine. In Philadelphia, the first deaths from automobiles were recorded at the very beginning of the period; by the 1920s the annual toll reached into the 300s, far higher than today, as the treatment of trauma was still primitive and citizen-pedestrians were still more used to gauging the oncoming velocity of milk wagons than of Studebakers.[27]

The effect of all this on "homicide arrests" was dramatic. Gurr is quite right to cite the long-term effect of a growing sensitivity to violence on the administration of criminal justice. But decades before this was expressed as empathy for killers, curbing capital punishment, it was expressed as abhorrence for them, refusal to accept the deaths of victims. In Philadelphia this sentiment accounted for a tendency, increasingly evident in the late nineteenth century, for district attorneys to prosecute as "homicide" deaths which would earlier have been dismissed as mere accident, or perhaps Acts of God. This was part of a larger pattern of "overcharging" by at least one and sometimes two "degrees" of homicide. The practice was formally to indict killers for "murder" even when, as in incidents resulting from street brawls and the like, the more accurate legal charge would have been "voluntary manslaughter." The latter was reserved then for deaths resulting from accidental gas leaks, boiler explosions—or traffic accidents. These accidents, growing even before the automobile as the result of the electrification of trolleys, resulted in an ever larger number of indictments for manslaughter and even murder. As late as 1926, fully 23 trolley, truck, and auto operators were tried for "murder."[28]

As with prosecutors, so with police, who arrested careless or merely unlucky drivers for "manslaughter," and sometimes even "murder." While some studies make an effort to subtract these, the nature of police records, used alone, make this virtually impossible; only in 1930, typically, do the published Philadelphia data make a distinction between the routine vehicular manslaughter cases and "non-negligent manslaughter," the latter a small fraction of the total. But if the clearly involuntary cases are eliminated—as in the New York coroners' homicide count, the strictly "murder" arrests in Philadelphia (remembering that this apparently covered most voluntary manslaughters as well), and the same city's imprisonments for all voluntary homicides, a clearer picture emerges. Through most of the period the trends among these three sets of data from the two cities are remarkably similar, as shown in Figure 2.1. All remain at far lower levels than those in Monkkonen's original "homicide arrest" table. And after an initial rise early in the period it is only toward the end, with a relatively modest "spike" in the late 1920s and early 1930s, that Philadelphia's "murder" arrests, uniquely, break upwards to levels higher than usual for the late nineteenth century.[29]

Do the New York and Philadelphia figures represent urban trends in the whole country? Their own congruence, and the fact that Philadelphia's "homicide arrests" so closely parallel those for all available big cities outside New York (see Table 2.1), strongly suggest this. It is accidental deaths, most but by no means all of them in traffic, that account for the apparently high and rising levels of early twentieth century homicides. Beyond that broad conclusion the use of aggregate or published data leaves a number of puzzles and mysteries.

Different places had of course different levels of murderous violence. In the early years, before one might expect much "contamination" with auto accidents, southern cities such as New Orleans and St. Louis tended (in general) to report higher rates than northern, suggesting that such factors as history, regional culture, and racial composition had a significant effect. But later on the actual extent of murder and manslaughter was less important in determining reported numbers than police policies in classifying accidents; it seems significant that Henry Ford's Detroit was by the late 1910s the city with the highest reported rates, reaching a peak of 28.5 in 1918. (Philadelphia was second at 22.4, more than twice the reported arrest rates for New York, whose relative numbers had fallen far below those reported earlier.)[30]

The one clear thing is that the homicidal "crime wave" of the early

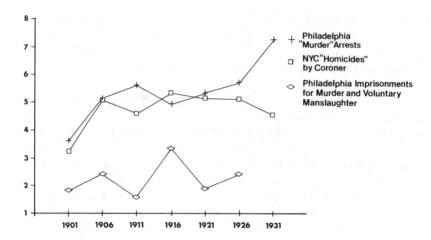

Figure 2.1: Comparative Trends in Urban Murder Statistics per 100,000 Population, 1899–1934 (5-year moving averages)

twentieth century tends to dry up under a hard look. Moreover, there is some reason to question even the modest rises shown in Figure 2.1. Homicides, in comparison with other crimes, are less likely to go wholly undetected, most resulting from street fights, barroom quarrels, or domestic arguments which may leave doubt as to "why" but little as to "what" was involved, and less as to "who." But even in the case of homicide the gap between the "real" and the officially counted may change over time. And there is ground to believe that the gap was closing during the early twentieth century, resulting in more bodies counted, more arrests and imprisonments, even in the absence of any "real" increase in the rate of killings.

By modern standards it seems clear that many nineteenth century killings went unreported by, or to, the police department, which was only slowly evolving from the multi-purpose agency of its early years to its modern focus on traffic control and crime. As late as 1898, the City of Philadelphia—while it reached roughly three-quarters of its present population—had only fifteen men on its detective force, none of them specialists in homicide. The newspapers indicate, too, that the coroner, in listing causes of death, often delivered dubious "suicide" or "accident" verdicts, evidently to avoid burdening this little force with difficult cases, especially involving people about whom no one much cared. The citizens of the nineteenth century, meanwhile, when faced with criminal problems, even homicide, were far less dependent on police than we are. While some murders skewed the official figures by sparking mass roundups of "the usual suspects," there were other times when killers were collared and brought in directly by private citizens, or taken into custody by the coroner, and so never appeared on the department's own books.[31]

The early twentieth century, however, was a time of growth. Philadelphia, fairly typical, adopted a telephone system, fingerprinting, and motorized patrol all in the single year 1906, and finally installed radio communication in 1922. The police force meanwhile grew much faster than the population, especially toward the beginning of the period. The 15 detectives of 1898 had grown to 33 just five years later, while the whole roster steadily increased from 2779 men in 1900 to 3612 by 1910. Perhaps most indicative was the addition, during a series of Progressive Era reforms in 1913, of an annual table listing the number of all known "murders," together with every step in their disposition—arrest if any, indictment, trial and verdict. Adoption of this sort of box score—previously reserved for liquor and gambling violations—was significant recognition that criminal violence was moving toward the top of the department's priorities.[32]

But while better police work may account for some of the rise in official figures just after the turn of the century (see Figure 2.1), it probably had less effect thereafter. It must, instead, be thrown with many other things into that maddening mare's nest of variables, impossible to quantify, which complicate all calculations. During the years for which they are available, between 1913 and 1932, the numbers of "murders known to police" were growing faster than Philadelphia's "murder arrests." Among possible reasons may be the fact that the will and ability to discover homicide—perhaps related to a still growing "sensitization to violence"—was improving faster than the ability to "clear" it through arrest. Another may be that the movement toward "professionalism" cut down on the nineteenth century practice of rounding up large numbers of suspects in notorious cases, making the number of arrests often exceed the number of murders.[33]

Two other factors are more easily established, through examination of some 686 Philadelphia cases, from court dockets, newspaper accounts, scattered trial transcripts, and arrest files for the years 1902, 1908, 1914, 1920, 1926, and 1932. When compared with a similar study of all homicides between 1839 and 1901, these show two differences that would tend to lower the annual ratio of arrests made to murders found. One is a decline in the number of "multiple" cases, in which several men were accused of a single killing. This situation, usually the result of a ruckus involving much dust and many participants, was quite characteristic of the pre-modern era, and still common in nineteenth century Philadelphia, but it was less often found in the increasingly modern city. And while it was rarely possible to convict men who had been in the thick of these things—they tended to blame unseen and absent opponents—it was easy to arrest them in number. The other offsetting factor was an evident increase, especially in the 1920s, in "gangland" killings and armed robbery-murders. It may be that the "getaway" automobile was at least partly responsible for a sudden rise in armed robberies, so rare just a generation earlier. In any case, those which ended in death were harder to "solve" than the fatal fights which comprise most homicides.[34]

The growing number of these unsolved and gangland cases is one of several bits of evidence which suggest that the official rise in "murder" arrests during the 1920s reflects a genuine increase, modest but real, in aggregate urban violence. While Wilson is quite right in pointing out that the "noble experiment" of alcohol Prohibition did succeed in limiting drunkenness—which by itself should have cut down on the murder rate—this little-noted success was more than balanced by the kind of lawlessness that popular legend, just as rightly, associates with "the Roaring 'Twenties." In fact even before then the entire period seems to have witnessed an ever wider use of handguns, a trend which would naturally increase the proportion of routine and often senseless arguments which suddenly turned fatal. Police reports from 1910 to 1923 list an increasing number of fatal gunshot accidents. And while only 25 percent of killings tried between 1839 and 1901 were caused by gunfire, the figure for (known) cases in the years selected is 42 percent, peaking at well over half in the 1920s.[35] The best estimate, then, is that "true" aggregate rates of murder and manslaughter during this "dark period" zig-zagged, at far lower levels than had been thought, along a relatively flat line, with (probably) some rise toward the beginning and (perhaps) another toward the end.

WHO DID IT AND WHY: THE SIGNIFICANCE OF RACE, ETHNICITY, AND OPPORTUNITY

Whatever the aggregate figures for the dark period, they turn out in practice to be less significant than those which indicate just who was responsible for urban violence. And in contrast to the often problematic figures used to establish the comparative incidence of homicide, those used to establish the ethnic and racial identity of killers are refreshingly unambiguous. Despite other deficiencies, the dockets used in jails and prisons to "log in" new convicts may be trusted to distinguish black from white, and to a lesser degree native from foreign-born. And of the 1107 men and women consigned from Philadelphia to the Eastern State Penitentiary, Moyamensing and Holmesburg Prisons for murder and voluntary manslaughter between 1899 and 1928 (the last year for which the prison records are available), some 463 were black, and 213 had been born in Italy. Over the whole span of years the city's blacks and Italians together amounted to little over 10 percent of Philadelphia's population; how and why did they account for fully 61 percent of its convicted killers?[36]

These figures cannot be laid to discrimination in the justice system. While Philadelphia was in some respects the northernmost of southern cities, and racist in many crucial respects, this period, like the nineteenth century earlier, seems to have been largely free of systematic prejudice in determining guilt or innocence. Elderly black men and women, survivors of "The Great Migration" north in the era of World War I and after, recall the justice system as essentially fair. While black killers were more likely to be executed than white ones, this was at least partly because they were more likely than others to have used guns. But in most identifiable measures of discrimination, such as degree of charge and conviction rate, neither blacks nor those with Italian names seem to have differed significantly from others brought to the dock.[37]

The numbers involved here are shown below in Table 2.2, which gives yearly figures for population and incarceration for blacks, Italians, and "all other whites." The trends are indicated in Figure 2.2 which charts the rate per 100,000 among the same groups.[38]

Philadelphia's racial and ethnic mix around 1900 was reasonably similar to that of most American cities; perched just above the Mason-Dixon line, it had proportionately more blacks and fewer immigrants than those to the North, fewer blacks and more immigrants than those to the South. But despite the growth shown in Table 2.2, over the next three decades it changed less than its two biggest rivals in particular. The "Great Migration," from World War I and through the 1920s, had a sharper effect on New York and Chicago, whose black populations for the first time passed Philadelphia's both absolutely and relatively. While Italian immigration meanwhile peaked between 1900 and 1915, even an almost fourfold growth in the local Italian community left the city as the major American metropolis with the highest proportion of native-born residents.[39]

In any case, the presence and in-migration of both Italians and blacks had a truly dramatic impact on murder rates, here and presumably elsewhere. The stark contrasts shown in Figure 2.2 help to underline the evident simplicity of the explanation for it.

What the "Italian" graph measures is, in the earlier years, the arrival of disproportionately male and single immigrants from a region with the highest murder rates in Europe, their dispositions unimproved by the ocean voyage and their arsenals upgraded by American weapons. Within a short time, however, as these people found jobs in the still thriving urban industrial economy of Philadelphia, the graphic decline reflects the way in which they went to school, got married, and settled into the orderly pattern of home ownership, neighborhood stability, and focus on family and future that have marked South Philadelphia ever since.[40]

The black line, in contrast, measures the very different impact of continuing economic exclusion. Factory jobs, and certainly white collar ones, were still not open to black migrants, except for a brief time during World War I. And so for better and worse they were also denied the experience of regimentation, the need to adjust to the psychological and emotional demands exacted by urban-industrial discipline. The overwhelming majority

Table 2.2. Imprisonments from Philadelphia, 1899–1934

Column A: Black population, in 100s
Column B: Blacks Imprisoned for Murder and Voluntary Manslaughter
Column C: Italian-Born Population in 100s
Column D: Italians Imprisoned for Murder and Voluntary Manslaughter
Column E: Rest of Philadelphia Population, in 1000s
Column F: All Others Imprisoned for Murder and Voluntary Manslaughter

Year	A	B	C	D	E	F
1899	598	5	155	4	11944	6
1900	626	6	176	4	12138	9
1901	646	7	196	3	12333	10
1902	666	6	215	2	12503	16
1903	686	8	236	3	12733	29
1904	708	15	259	3	12936	18
1905	730	9	284	9	13142	20
1906	752	10	312	7	13354	12
1907	775	15	343	12	13556	21
1908	799	2	376	8	13766	10
1909	824	7	413	9	13975	5
1910	849	17	453	7	14188	6
1911	888	9	469	7	14384	7
1912	930	5	485	8	14582	1
1913	974	18	502	6	14782	11
1914	1019	21	519	10	14986	27
1915	1067	9	537	15	15191	24
1916	1117	22	556	17	15399	18
1917	1169	25	575	15	15610	25
1918	1224	20	595	16	15823	20
1919	1282	16	616	6	16039	9
1920	1342	6	637	1	16259	13
1921	1410	11	642	6	16675	13
1922	1481	20	646	7	16709	22
1923	1556	29	650	3	16748	15
1924	1635	16	655	2	16784	14
1925	1717	30	658	4	16819	14
1926	1804	33	663	5	16861	13
1927	1895	25	668	2	16899	9
1928	1991	41	672	8	16937	14

of those who participated in the straight economy at all were confined to two job categories: domestic or personal service, and purely unskilled labor, work more characteristic of the Middle Ages than of the urban industrial era. Virtually all lived lives marked by insecurity, dependence, and unpredictability, most in neighborhoods in effect "zoned" by the authorities as centers of vice. Many were pushed, a few jumped, into established patterns of criminal activity, potentially violent occupations that reinforced a long felt need to carry weapons routinely.[41]

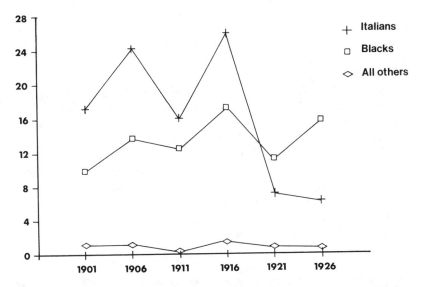

Figure 2.2: Racial and Ethnic Trends in Imprisonment for Murder and Voluntary Manslaughter per 100,000 Population, Philadelphia, 1899–1928 (5-year moving averages)

The city's principal white immigrants, outnumbering the Italians, were Jews from Eastern Europe, people with peaceable traditions who fit easily into a variety of jobs that offered more than they had known before. Even so, the foreign-born were generally over-represented among convicted killers in the "non-Italian white" category. The native white descendants of earlier waves of migration, as late as 1930 over 80 percent of the whole, were clearly no small elite, and fairly represented at every level of the urban-industrial economy. Nothing better illustrates the psychological power of that economy than its ability to transform the habits and traditions of those who—unlike the blacks—were allowed to work in it. Just as the maturing industrial city of the mid-to-late 19th Century had pacified the Wild Irish, so the fully matured industrial city was able to pacify the even more violent Italians. Of the 1107 people convicted of murder and voluntary manslaughter in Philadelphia between 1899 and 1928, only 18 were *descendants* of immigrants with Italian names, and just one of them was born and presumably raised in the city itself.[42]

In sum, just as controlling for anomalies and traffic accidents cuts the level of early twentieth century homicides by more than half, so controlling for the in-migration of blacks and Italians halves it again, and turns the relatively modest rises or peaks shown in Figure 2.1 to the flat or even downward curve shown in the "All Other White" column in Figure 2.2.

The exaggerated contribution of these two marginalized groups, one excluded throughout, the other only beginning to force its way in, serves to underline the fact that the urban-industrial revolution was continuing to pacify its participants.

The period from 1899–1933 can then be fitted neatly back into the U-curve as a whole. At one end it largely extended the downward trend of the later nineteenth century for most native citizens. At the other end, the FBI's index, beginning in 1933, shows a decline from a point, during the Great Depression, when black urban migration had greatly slowed, and Italian immigration had not only halted but reversed. National rates then fell through the 1940s and 1950s as a reflection of minimal immigration from abroad coupled, more importantly, with black inclusion into the full employment of the urban-industrial economy. The upsurge of the 1960s and after then represents the death of that economy, and the movement into our present post-industrial phase.

Conclusion: On Analyzing the Past—and Projecting the Future

The evidence, then, from Philadelphia and elsewhere, essentially reinforces the concept of the long U-curve in homicide rates. And in addition to reinforcing the author's thesis about the relation between urban industrialism and murder rates, the figures have the virtue of showing the importance of two other approaches that social historians have been advancing over the past generation. First is the diminished emphasis on major historical "events," as distinct from long-term trends, and second is the need to avoid generalizations about large population groups, cities or nations, composed in practice of many different peoples and classes. In this case, both help to illustrate the importance of the link between methods and explanations, suggesting the need to establish and analyze a variety of data before drawing conclusions.

The simple fact of using several indices at once has one important advantage, in that it tends to minimize the problem, raised by Eric Monkkonen, of how to deal with or interpret annual variations. It is best, it seems, to ignore them as insignificant. A single set may jump up or down in a given year, prompting historians to look vainly for the immediate impact of some broad event characteristic of that year, such as war, depression, or the onset of Prohibition. But a look back at Table 2.1 shows that the annual highs and lows in the two sets most chronologically comparable—that is, Philadelphia's arrests and New York's homicides found by the coroner—show little correspondence. The explanations behind "murder rates" are, it seems, at least relatively a matter of "La longue durée" rather than the short. The events which spark most homicides are painfully banal, involving arguments over stew or dumplings, the numbers on bits of paper or bones, the differences between Jeanne and Joanne. By extension it seems relatively unimportant just when the event occurred; what made Smith a killer was less the aggravation of the moment than the long personal history, shaped in part by prevailing social conditions, that led him to deal with that aggravation in murderous fashion.[43]

The other issue involves the use of aggregate versus more specific sets of figures. A number of statistical series may be used to establish "murder rates" of some sort, but all have characteristic advantages and disadvantages. While they are all we hope related, linked in differing ways to a single series of incidents, none is directly comparable with the others, and none may be traced uncritically over any long period of time—witness the problems with "homicide arrests" in the discussion above. Gurr's excellent summary of the problems involved suggests, as a subset of Murphy's Law, that the longest series, and those most easily compiled, such as aggregate arrests, generally contain the least trustworthy information about the true incidence of criminal behavior. And they may tempt analysts into over-simple generalizations.[44]

An entire argument may then be miscast, as with Wilson's point about punishment as deterrent. Whatever its merits with respect to other crimes, it is hard to make this fit homicide, historically. It may in general be said that during the long fall in aggregate murder rates, following the Civil War, justice did move far more swiftly than it does now, and capital punishment was more frequent—but at the same time fewer killings were "solved,"juries were less likely to convict, prison sentences were shorter, and pardons much more common. If this is not murky enough, the situation turns truly opaque when the experience of a particular group, such as blacks, is isolated from the whole. Between 1865 and 1899 black killers in Philadelphia were less likely than white to suffer execution; between 1900 and 1928 they were more likely; in both periods their murder rates went up. And to pursue disaggregation to the ultimate—what should be made of, say, William Lane? Lane, a butler, went berserk on the 1st of April, 1902, fatally shooting the widow he worked for and then her two daughters. He was tried the next day, hanged the next month: justice uniquely swift, even then, and clearly intended as a message. But was the message directed at potential killers, or prospective servants? It was clearly read, if little needed, by white employers over breakfast—was it also heard, and with what effect, by southern migrants shooting craps, or jealous husbands in Little Italy?[45]

In dealing with murder, even more than with most phenomena, it can be misleading to draw conclusions about the whole of the society or, worse, what has historically passed for the whole, that is, the socially elite and articulate. In the real world, homicide in modern societies is overwhelmingly done by and to marginal people, often members of minority groups. This is obvious in the United States—with its richly diverse heritage, and increasingly true of England, with its Commonwealth immigrants—and West Europe in general, with its southern "guest workers." Aggregate graphs for any complex society may look deceptively simple, while concealing sharply different movements among its component parts, as in the United States between 1899 and 1933. Perhaps the principal problem with "moral" explanations of crime rates is that too often moral characteristics are attributed to whole societies; socio-economic analysis, in contrast, demands dissection, requiring analysis of differing subgroups, structural inequality, the ways in which even the most widely shared traits are unevenly distributed.

It is this reluctance to explore differing subcultural experiences and values that most handicaps Wilson's analysis of differing crime rates. Rightly insisting, but without the needed qualifications, that all groups deplore theft and unwonted violence, he is left largely with alleged differences in intelligence to "explain" the unique experience of American blacks, for example. And to explain all behavior in terms of the behavior of dominant groups—or worse of the attitudes of a small elite—leads beyond error to silliness; Wilson, read literally, seems to blame black crime rates in the 1920s on the unfortunate impact of Viennese psychiatry.[46]

While Ted Robert Gurr's "increasing sensitization to violence" remains detached from specific social and economic conditions, Gurr does recognize explicitly that values promoted by an elite may be ignored or even resisted by others who differ in terms of class, culture, or merely age. The best modern work, as he surveys it, is careful to make such distinctions; while the historical records are harder to analyze, the need remains.[47]

Much useful work has already been done on the reasons for long-term changes in rates of violence. But this and other chapters in the present volume make it clear that much remains, that even simple information is hard to establish, and that careful answers to questions about who, what, and how often must precede any definitive answers as to why.

The most important question dividing us will be answered simply by the passage of time. It is Gurr, the political scientist, ironically, who offers the long historical perspective which suggests that modern problems may represent no more than an epicycle within a larger movement toward humaneness and civility. If in fact an increasing elite distaste for interpersonal violence remains the dominant influence that it has been, the current "crime wave" in the Western world should soon recede. I hope so, but rather suspect that the contemporary situation has no real precedent, and see no way out.

While not sure just what has created the post-industrial surge in violence, I am sure that whatever created the earlier, urban-industrial, decline is no longer working. The new economy makes unprecedented educational demands on its successful participants, as large numbers trade down those good old industrial jobs for others, at best, in the fast food sector. Until the post-industrial economy offers some equivalent of the kind of socialization that their parents and grandparents experienced, many descendants of the old white working class will face a future that looks—black. Here and indeed across the post-industrial world the history of the American "underclass" may represent the future for millions more. That is a recipe for trouble of many kinds, and suggests that the right-hand side of the U-curve will continue to rise raggedly.

Notes

1. See chap. 1 in this volume by Ted Robert Gurr and chap. 5 by Roger McGrath. My own partial explanation for the relation between economic cycle and 19th century violence is that most people still lived close to subsistence, alcohol consumption went up in "good times" and down in bad; Ted Robert Gurr, in "Development and Decay: Their Impact on Public Order," in James A. Inciardi and Charles E. Faupel, eds., *History and Crime: Implications for Public Policy* (Beverly Hills, CA: Sage, 1980), 34, suggests that nineteenth century property crime went up in response to want, while modern rates go up in response to opportunity, often affluence; on urban robbery, see Roger Lane, *Roots of Violence in Black Philadelphia, 1860–1900* (Cambridge, MA: Harvard University Press, 1986), 103–4.

2. The most detailed surveys of the relevant literature are Ted Robert Gurr, "On the History of Violent Crime in Europe and American," in Hugh Davis Graham and Ted Robert Gurr, *Violence in America: Historical and Comparative Perspectives*, rev. ed. (Beverly Hills, CA: Sage, 1979), 353–74; Roger Lane, "Urban Police and Violence in Nineteenth Century America," in Norval Morris and Michael Tonry, eds., *Crime and Justice: An Annual Review of Research* (Chicago: University of Chicago Press, 1980), 2:1–43; the appendix to Eric Monkkonen, *Police in Urban America, 1860–1920* (Cambridge: Cambridge University Press, 1981); Ted Robert Gurr, "Historical Trends in Violent Crime: A Critical Review of the Evidence," in Morris and Tonry, eds., *Crime and Justice* (Chicago: University of Chicago Press, 1981), 3:295–353.

3. In addition to those cited above, the most relevant works by Gurr and Lane are Ted Robert Gurr, Peter N. Grabosky, and Richard C. Hula, *The Politics of Crime and Conflict: A Comparative History of Four Cities* (Beverly Hills, CA: Sage, 1977); Roger Lane, "Crime and Criminal Statistics in Nineteenth-Century Massachusetts," *Journal of Social History II* (1968), 156–63, and Lane, *Violent Death in the City: Suicide, Accident, and Murder in Nineteenth Century Philadelphia* (Cambridge, MA: Harvard University Press, 1979); for Wilson, see James Q. Wilson and Richard Herrnstein, *Crime and Human Nature* (New York: Simon and Shuster, 1985).

4. Gurr, "Historical Trends," 360.

5. Gurr, "History of Violent Crime," 365.

6. *Ibid.*, 367, 369–70.

7. Wilson, *Crime and Human Nature*, 418–9, 421, 430.

8. *Ibid.*, 430–4.

9. *Ibid.*, 434–7, 424–5.

10. Martin Gold, "Suicide, Homicide, and the Socialization of Aggression," *American Journal of Sociology* 62 (May 1958): 651–61.

11. Lane, *Violent Death in the City*.

12. *Ibid.*, 137–8.

13. Lane, *Roots of Violence*.

14. Wilson, *Crime and Human Nature*, 430.

15. Gurr, "History of Violent Crime," 365; Wilson, *Crime and Human Nature*, 431; Lane, *Roots of Violence*, 110–1.

16. Gurr, "History of Violent Crime," 366, 370; Lane, *Violent Death*, 122–3, 138.

17. Lane, *Violent Death*, 116 and chap. 6.

18. Lane, *Roots of Violence*, 166–8.

19. Wilson, *Crime and Human Nature*, 411–3, 421; Gurr, "History of Violent Crime," 364, 379; Wilson, *Crime and Human Nature*, 453.

20. Gurr, "Development and Decay," 43–4, 49; Gurr, "History of Violent Crime," 369–70; Wilson, *Crime and Human Nature*, 434–7.

21. Gurr, *The Politics of Crime and Conflict*, chap. 5; Wilson, *Crime and Human Nature*, 436–7.

22. Gurr, "Historical Trends," 342.

23. *Ibid.*, 324.

24. Monkkonen, *Police in Urban America*, 76–77; for other studies, see ibid., app., and Gurr, "Historical Trends," 320–4.

25. Eric Monkkonen, chap. 3, this volume. Prof. Monkkonen has kindly provided me with two sets of data critical to the discussion below, and to Table 2.1: a printout of the raw data on which he based his aggregate "homicide arrest" figures, and an annual list of "homicides," number and rate, as reported by New York's coroner and compiled in Haven Emerson, *Population, Births, Notifiable Diseases, and Deaths, Assembled for New York City, New York, 1866–1938* (New York: DeLamar Institute of Public Health).

26. For cols. A and B see note above. Philadelphia's "homicide" arrests compiled by adding figures for "manslaughter" to those for "murder" in the *Annual Police Reports*; imprisonments for murder and manslaughter counted from docket books for Eastern State Penitentiary, Moyamensing and Holmesburg jails. The penitentiary dockets are available only through 1928, and police reports are missing for some years. See Lane, *Roots of Violence*, 179–81.

27. *Annual Police Report* (1930) lists 318 vehicular deaths, up from the 40 in 1912. The Pennsylvania Department of Health, State Health Data Center, provides (by phone) 156 resident motor vehicle deaths in Philadelphia for 1986.

28. Lane, *Violent Death*, 65 ff; for 1926 figures see note 34.

29. *Annual Police Report* (1930).

30. Criminal justice data for fig. 2.1 are derived from those in table 2.1; population figures are given below, in table 2.2.

31. Lane, *Violent Death*, 84–90.

32. *Annual Police Report* for the years 1900, 1903, 1906, 1910, 1913, and 1922.

33. "Murders" in *Annual Police Report* for the years 1913 (70), 1914 (65), 1915 (67), 1916 (90), 1917 (82), 1918 (109), 1919 (98), 1920 (105), 1921 (101), 1922 (126), 1923 (163), 1924 (NA), 1925 (159), 1926 (151), 1927 (161), 1928 (175), 1929 (153), 1930 (150), 1931 (NA), 1932 (144), 1933 (131), 1934 (101). Compare arrest figures in table 2.1.

34. The computerized study mentioned here was based on a study of all death-related indictments for the period 1839–1901, based in turn on Marvin Wolfgang's questionnaire for his classic *Patterns in Criminal Homicide* (New York: John Wiley, 1966). See Lane, *Violent Death*, app. B. Dockets from the Court of Quarter Sessions are largely complete. Information about each case was sought in the *Philadelphia Public Ledger*, after 1926 the *Inquirer*. The archives also contain many trial transcripts, although not a complete set, a fairly full "arrest record" from 1914 and after, and for 1922 and after some police case files. The end product is some 686 worksheets with much standardized information for the Statistical Package for the Social Sciences. I would like to thank research assistants Amanda Crane, Lydia Martin, Peter Shulman, and especially Eric Pollack, for compiling this, cited as "Docket Study, SSPS." Only 2 robbery-murders were tried in 1902, none in 1908 or 1914, but these and "gangland"

murders totalled 2 in 1920 (2 more unresolved in arrest-files), 2 in 1926 (plus 9 unresolved), and 8 in 1932 (plus 4 unresolved).

35. Docket Study SSPS gunshot figures for all six years sampled are: 228 of 542, 42% with 144 or 27% unknown. 1920 figures are 78 of 137, 57% with 16 or 12% unknown; 1926, 105 of 187, 56% 22 or 12% unknown. "Unknowns" are by definition not newsworthy, and doubtless weighted toward accidents.

36. For imprisonments, see note 26. Figures in Lane, *Roots of Violence*, 163, were from penitentiary only, from 1902 to 1928. The 1107 figure here includes the three earlier years and the two county jails.

37. Lane, *Roots of Violence*, 87–94; Charles Hardy III, "Southern Migrants and the 'Negro Problem' in the City of Philadelphia During the Era of the Great Migration," paper presented at the annual meeting of the Organization of American Historians on Apr. 5, 1987, 13; Philadelphia executions in Negley K. Teeters, *Scaffold and Chair: A Compilation of Their Use in Pennsylvania, 1682–1962* (Philadelphia: Pennsylvania Prison Society, 1963), 177–84; accounts identify 59 of 60 men executed 1899–1928 as 24 white, 33 black, 2 Chinese; Docket Study SPSS shows 60% of blacks accused of murder or manslaughter used guns, compared to 42% in whole sample—although this is partly because blacks were less likely to drive motor vehicles.

38. See notes 26 and 36 for imprisonment, and Lane, *Roots of Violence*, 204, note 1, for population.

39. Lloyd M. Abernathy, "Progressivism, 1905–1919," in Russell Weigley, ed., *Philadelphia: A 300-Year History* (New York: W.W.Norton, 1982), 524–65.

40. Arthur Dudden, "The City Embraces 'Normalcy': 1919–1929." in Weigley, *Philadelphia: 300-Year History*, 566, 589–90.

41. Lane, *Roots of Violence*, 164–6.

42. Abernathy, "Progressivism," 529; Lane, *Roots of Violence*, 140–1, 163.

43. Eric Monkkonen, chap. 3, this volume, note 4.

44. Lane, *Violent Death*, 66–7, 81–2, 88–90; Lane *Roots of Violence*, 92–4; note 37, above; *Philadelphia Public Ledger*, May 29, 1902.

45. Wilson, *Crime and Human Nature*, chap. 18 and 434–7.

46. Gurr, "Historical Trends."

Chapter 3

Diverging Homicide Rates: England and the United States, 1850–1875

ERIC H. MONKKONEN

The contemporary differences in homicide rates between Britain and the United States are of such magnitude that no one bothers to contrast them. However, no one has actually begun to explain why these differences exist. Given that the origins of much of what is fundamentally American in the arena of crime and justice is British in origin, an historical comparative account seems an appropriate way to begin to understand today's national differences. The best evidence we now have suggests that the divergence of the United States from Britain, as well as the rest of the Western world, began in the period 1850–1875. For instance, in this period the native born white New York homicide rate was only about 50 percent higher than Liverpool's, a difference which is relatively small compared to later divergences. But after the 1870's, Britain's homicide rate declined dramatically, while, in comparison, that of the United States declined only modestly. Today's differences, in other words, have come out of a long-term historical change.

Explaining National Differences

Two empirical generalizations established by criminal justice historians force us to reopen apparently closed questions relating to national homicide differences. These two generalizations have been reasonably well founded through a series of research endeavors over the past twenty years and they have unintentionally made most ahistorical accounts for the national differences in rates highly fragile. The generalizations: First, crimes of violence were very high during the Middle Ages; and second, they have been declining in the industrial world since then.[1] The United States has shared in this decline, but its decline has been much less steep and far more uneven. The United States' rates are anomalous, therefore, but in a way subtly different from that commonly understood: Violent crime rates have followed similar patterns, but with different timing and magnitude.

In 1974, the murder rate of the United States was about 40 times that of Britain, and the usual magnitude of difference is always over a factor of 10. A contrast of big city differences between the two nations would be similarly dramatic. The higher rates seem "natural" to most observers and therefore in need of no explanation. Although there is no generally accepted or rigorously investigated hypothesis accounting for these well known differences, there are many pet hypotheses, each partially bridging the chasm. These pet hypotheses are all plausible; are all reasonable. They range from the widespread availability of handguns in the United States, to its diverse racial and ethnic mix, to "relative deprivation"—the poor in the United States feel more deprived—to explanations which invoke for the United States a unique "culture of violence," to the idea that its nineteenth century frontier and the cultural values it engendered made the United States more prone to violence.[2]

In and of themselves, these hypotheses are insufficient. Some are so vague as to be untestable, others circular, others easily rejected, and all are partial. Consider, for instance, the three most plausible explanations for the high homicide rate in the United States: guns, race, and culture. Homicides with guns account for about 63 percent of all United States' homicides today. Presumably some unknown fraction of these homicides would have occurred were there no guns. And because the homicide rate of the United States is over ten times as high as that of Britain and also because the removal of guns from the United States could not lower the rate by over half, the United States rate would still surpass that of Britain. Or consider the racial hypothesis: The United States is about 12 percent black, and half of all homicide victims are black. We could claim that the rate would fall by something less than a half were the black rate to fall to that of whites, but again, this in itself does not begin to account for the more than tenfold difference between the two nations. In other words, today, discounting the United States' homicide rate for the presence of guns and racial differences still leaves it nearly three times as high as it "should" be by comparison with Britain. This leaves the vague notion of a "culture of violence" to account for the very large residual difference. By the last quarter of the nineteenth century, the United States had a much higher homicide rate than that of Britain or European nations. How is it that less than a century after political independence the United States had created a culture wholly different from those in the British Isles and Europe in this singular respect?

Virtually every analysis put forward to explain the very high United States' homicide rate has been ahistorical, with the exception, perhaps, of the frontier hypotheses. Had they been proposed as historical, they would have foundered quickly, for the explanatory inadequacy of these "pet" theories becomes immediately apparent in a historical context. For instance, prior to 1910, when blacks composed less than 1.5 percent of New York City's population, it still had a homicide rate many times that of London or Liverpool. Thus the historical as well as the current differences by definition require an integrated explanation, one which accounts for both.

Neither comparative historical analyses nor the study of crime are straightforward, even when they seem natural or obvious. "Rustic," writing to the *New York Times* in 1857, pointed out that crime poses observational problems. "The nearer one comes to it, the less he knows of it. Looking at it blinds the analytic faculty. . . . You [New Yorkers], being in the thickest of the conflict, see not the havoc made; and even when stabbed, it is in hot blood, so that you scarce feel the wound" (April 24, p. 2). Even though they are highly unreasonable criminal offenses, homicides are in fact the most reasonable crimes of violence to study.

Conventional wisdom among criminal justice historians asserts three virtues to the nature of homicides as a crime susceptible to historical analysis. First, of all criminal offenses, homicide is the least definitionally ambiguous. Second, it is the most likely to be reported and "cleared" by arrest; today the arrest of the accused killer follows about three fourths of all homicides. And, third, in some sense it constitutes an offense which indexes other forms of personal violence. Historians James Sharpe and Lawrence Stone recently reiterated this wisdom in a fascinating and acerbic exchange in *Past* and *Present* (1985) concerning trends in the history of violence in England. In spite of some thirty pages of fiery contention, they both affirm the tripart value of homicide to the historian.[3]

Yet even though the experts agree that homicide is the most accessible crime in the past, an historical explanation of diverging homicide rates poses source and measurement problems not presented to analysts of recent data. Although British homicides known to the police are reported in the parliamentary papers, only those for London are clearly urban; other cities reported their homicides with those of the whole county. The question of source reliability is of great importance. Do the often very high variations from year to year indicate unreliable data? In 1867, for instance, there were 6 reported homicides in Liverpool; one year later, in 1868, the number leaped to 27; and a decade later it had fallen to only 1. In 1865 there were 68 homicides in New York City; one year later, in 1866, 36. Could these wild fluctuations indicate unreliability in reporting?

It is probable that source or reporting inconsistencies had little to do with annual variation in Britain for the period of interest here. The offenses known to the police and reported annually in the parliamentary papers correspond with those reported in the newspapers. A closer look at Liverpool makes them seem believable, for a non-systematic newspaper scan indicates a high level of homicide cases in 1868, none related in any obvious

way to each other, contrasted with very few in 1867. Thus the wild recorded variation in these adjacent years is reflected in an independent
source. For London, the number of reported homicides in the parliamentary papers corresponds exactly with those indexed in the *Times* in the
middle years of the century, again suggesting that the official reports were
at least consistent with public reporting and probably accurate. One can
gain confidence because in London there were so few homicides that each
can be identified. Half a century later, the impression of thorough homicide reporting, was held by the leading U.S. statistician of mortality, Frederick L. Hoffman, who admired England's death registration system as a
model.[4]

The United States had no integrated national crime reporting system
until the 1930s, one reason why newspapers constitute the best guide to
nineteenth century homicides. For the data used in the project reported
here, I employed the official New York City coroners' tallies only after
1870, when they correspond closely with the homicide incidents reported as
news items in the *New York Times*. The Appendix details some of the more
difficult decisions made in constructing the data series. Finally, I should
note that in the mid-nineteenth century, two forms of murder do not seem
to me to fit our contemporary notions of murder: infanticide and a
woman's death during an abortion. Both the former, while surely intentional, and the latter, more surely unintentional, had a motivation so very
different from that of ordinary killings, and a rate of reporting so very
uneven, that when possible I have excluded them from the cases analyzed
here.

The complexity of measuring a crime so simple as homicide is in itself
reason enough to begin a comparative historical study by focusing on New
York and London. The biggest cities in each nation, both had relatively
large numbers of homicides, consistent newspaper coverage (although the
New York Times did not begin publication until September, 1851), and the
most articulated criminal justice systems. Neither was the most violent spot
in its nation: London was in fact so tame that I have also included Liverpool for comparative purposes, while in the United States, white rural
Southerners were more dangerous than New Yorkers. There are several
other reasons to construct a systematic comparison based on cities, these
three cities in particular. Cities represent the most comprehensive reporting units; their record keeping is better; they have excellent written institutional histories; and by the mid-twentieth century, they have the most
homicide per capita.[5] And cities, by the mid-twentieth century, had the
bulk of the total number of homicides.

At the middle of the nineteenth century, the three cities of Liverpool,
London, and New York had distinctive demographic and economic pro-
files. London, over three million people, had long been the center of the
British empire. It was a huge metropolis with a strong metropolitan police,

a complex local government, and a prosperous mercantile economic base. No one would have had the temerity to compare it to Liverpool or New York. Liverpool, with under a half-million people, a relatively new port city serving the industrial midland, had the most immigrants—Irish—of any British city and was in some sense a city of economic and industrial opportunity. New York, a city of nearly a million growing far more rapidly than any city in Britain, was a port, a commercial and manufacturing center at the economic hub of the United States. A city of immigrants, its electoral politics directly reflected the Irish and German immigrants who constituted the bulk of voters. It was a brash and booming city where money, whatever its origins, counted.

Although London dominated urban Britain, it was neither the immigrant entrepot nor the manufacturing center that New York was. Therefore, Liverpool, with a relatively high proportion of Irish immigrants, forms a better comparison to New York, even though New York was nearly two times as large and had over twice the proportion of immigrants, 17 percent and 41 percent respectively. And Liverpool had, in fact, a much higher homicide rate than did London. This study therefore includes both. New York is the "natural" starting place for a United States study, simply because it was and is the largest United States city. By virtue of its preeminence the city was and still is atypical, and until a great deal more is known about the actual rates of crime throughout the United States, the claim that any particular place may stand for many places simply must be avoided. The graphed annual homicides per 100,000 persons for New York and Liverpool are presented in Figure 3.1; London's graph is not presented as it is virtually flat when plotted on the same scale. The New York data are decomposed into white and black rates, while Table 3.1 gives the numerical values for all the plotted data points plus London and the proportion of all New York homicides with black murderers.

Liverpool in the two decades at mid-century had a homicide rate about half that of New York City with the exception of one year, 1868. This therefore is the last period for which one can make a sensible comparison between British and American cities. Within a decade, by the mid-1870s the differences had drifted towards an enormous gap. And by 1880, both Liverpool and London had stabilized at very low levels—less than 0.5 homicides per 100,000—which continue to represent some of the lowest urban homicide rates in the modern world.

New York City had a parallel decrease in homicide beginning in the midnineteenth century. Figure 3.1 gives the visual impression of a long, very gradual decline in New York City's white homicide rate, interrupted by two abrupt increases in 1906 and 1930. Neither reversed the direction of long drift downward. While not nearly as steep as the decline in London and Liverpool, New York's is unmistakably steady. In sharp contrast, the city's black homicide rate has almost the opposite appearance. Visually less

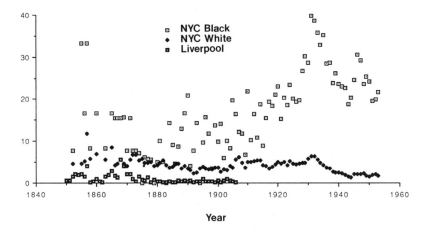

Figure 3.1: Homicides in New York City and Liverpool per 100,000 Population, 1850–1953

clear, in part because of the small black population of New York was such that one or two homicides more in one year doubled the rate and made the graphed image unfocused, there is still visible a gradual drift upward in black homicide rates to a peak in the early 1930s. The magnitude of the differences between white and black rates was slight or nonexistent in the middle part of the nineteenth century, but by about 1910 the two rates had begun to diverge dramatically and apparently irreversibly.

In spite of its slope opposite to the white homicide trend, the trend in black homicides did not really affect the larger picture of homicide in New York until 1917, simply because the white population numerically predominated and its homicide rate determined the overall rate's composition. But during the decades of heavy black immigration into the city, the increasing black rates began to affect the overall rate. Black homicides never accounted for more than ten percent of all homicides until World War I, and after World War I, black homicides began to form a larger and larger part of the picture, until the end of World War II when black homicides accounted for more than half of all homicides in the city. By the 1950s, black homicide rates were ten times as high as white rates, mirroring but not causing the disparity between New York and London's white homicide rates, for New York's exceeded those of London in turn by three to five times.[6]

Five major points may be drawn from these contrasts. First, white New Yorkers did participate in the larger trends downward in homicide throughout the Western world. Second, not all racial groups experienced this basic trend. Third, all racial and nationality groups' homicide rates could

Table 3.1. Homicides per 100,000, London, Liverpool, New York White and Black, and Percent of All New York Homicides Black, 1850–1953.

			NEW YORK CITY		
YEAR	LONDON	LIVERPOOL	WHITE VICTIMS	BLACK VICTIMS	PERCENT OF ALL HOMICIDE VICTIMS BLACK
1850	.13	.54	—	—	—
1851	.25	.53	—	—	—
1852	.12	1.56	4.6	7.7	4
1853	.12	2.04	—	—	—
1854	.12	2.00	—	—	—
1855	.23	2.21	4.7	33.3	12
1856	.45	1.45	5.2	16.7.	6
1857	.15	4.04	11.8	33.3	5
1858	.33	.23	5.8	8.3	2
1859	.43	.46	—	—	—
1860	.14	.91	6.9	16.7	4
1861	.34	.45	—	—	—
1862	.37	.22	—	—	—
1863	.37	1.55	5.6	8.3	2
1864	.46	1.97	—	—	—
1865	.26	2.81	8.5	16.7	3
1866	.29	1.71	4.2	15.4	6
1867	.35	1.27	4.6	15.4	5
1868	.41	5.65	5.5	15.4	4
1869	.22	4.14	4.7	15.4	4
1870	.30	2.05	4.0	7.7	3
1871	.30	2.03	5.6	15.4	4
1872	.27	1.00	6.8	7.7	1
1873	.26	.40	6.8	7.7	1
1874	.29	1.57	5.5	7.1	2
1875	.51	.77	5.7	.0	0
1876	.14	.57	4.9	6.2	2
1877	.47	1.32	4.8	5.9	2
1878	.11	.19	5.0	5.6	2
1879	.24	.74	4.0	.0	0
1880	.38	.37	4.3	5.0	2
1881	.29	.36	4.8	10.0	3
1882	.24	.18	5.5	5.0	1
1883	.31	.18	4.4	.0	0
1884	.51	.35	3.6	14.3	6
1885	.28	.17	3.8	9.1	4
1886	.25	.17	4.4	4.6	2
1887	.27	.50	4.6	8.7	3
1888	.76	.33	3.5	13.0	6
1889	.46	.65	4.1	16.7	6
1890	.39	.32	3.4	20.8	9
1891	.31	.63	3.1	4.0	2
1892	.45	.16	2.3	7.7	5

(continued)

Table 3.1. Continued

1893	.47	.31	2.5	14.3	9
1894	.32	.46	3.4	.0	0
1895	.44	.91	3.8	9.7	4
1896	.48	.45	3.4	15.6	8
1897	.45	.45	3.2	11.7	6
1898	.40	.44	3.3	3.6	2
1899	.47	.15	3.7	13.8	6
1900	.37	.57	3.7	9.8	5
1901	.53	.14	2.6	14.0	9
1902	.46	.56	3.2	6.0	3
1903	.37	.98	3.1	10.0	6
1904	.44	.56	4.1	8.2	4
1905	.48	.41	3.6	19.7	9
1906	.37	.27	5.5	16.5	5
1907	.26	—	6.1	12.2	4
1908	.43	—	4.8	11.8	4
1909	.43	—	3.8	6.8	3
1910	.59	—	5.1	21.7	7
1911	.55	—	5.1	10.2	4
1912	.55	—	5.1	16.3	6
1913	.44	—	5.4	10.9	4
1914	—	—	5.3	18.8	7
1915	—	—	4.3	8.9	5
1916	—	—	4.1	15.5	8
1917	—	—	3.5	19.3	12
1918	—	—	3.8	18.4	11
1919	.47	—	4.4	21.1	11
1920	—	—	5.0	23.0	11
1921	—	—	4.6	15.3	9
1922	1.01	—	4.9	20.3	12
1923	.96	—	4.3	18.5	13
1924	.63	—	5.3	23.4	14
1925	.81	—	4.6	20.0	14
1926	.63	—	4.5	19.4	15
1927	.90	—	4.6	19.6	16
1928	.61	—	4.8	26.6	20
1929	.32	—	4.8	30.2	23
1930	.68	—	5.8	28.7	20
1931	.64	—	6.4	39.9	24
1932	—	—	6.3	38.7	25
1933	—	—	5.7	35.7	26
1934	—	—	4.8	32.9	28
1935	—	—	4.3	35.1	32
1936	—	—	3.6	28.3	32
1937	—	—	3.4	28.6	34
1938	—	—	2.7	23.8	36
1939	—	—	2.6	26.1	39
1940	—	—	2.4	23.6	39
1941	—	—	2.3	23.0	41

(continued)

Table 3.1. Continued

1942	—	—	1.9	22.7	47
1943	—	—	1.5	18.7	49
1944	—	—	1.4	20.4	54
1945	—	—	2.2	24.5	49
1946	—	—	2.2	30.5	55
1947	—	—	2.2	29.2	55
1948	—	—	2.3	23.6	50
1949	—	—	1.8	25.3	59
1950	—	—	1.7	24.2	62
1951	—	—	1.8	19.4	54
1952	—	—	2.2	20.0	51
1953	—	—	1.8	21.6	59

Source: All data from the Parliamentary Papers, from the *New York Times* as discussed in the text, or from Haven Emerson, *Population, Births, Notifiable Diseases, and Deaths, Assembled for New York City, New York: 1866–1938* (New York: DeLamar Institute of Public Health, 1941).

change. Fourth, by observation we can conclude that homicide is an historically variable phenomenon, and as such it has no natural causes in race or ethnicity. And fifth, the period 1850–1870 stands out as the moment when the modern divergence in homicide rates between England and the United States took form. The next section of this article explores the middle decades of New York City's homicides in greater detail in order to determine how much more specifically these differences can be described.

Homicide in New York During the 1850s and 1860s

Thousands of elegant novels cannot hide the fact that murder is not glamorous. The typical murder in nineteenth century New York concluded a screaming, bloody fight between drunken acquaintances, one of whom successfully beat or slashed the other to death with whatever weapon lay at hand. Usually the killer and victim were immigrant males between 20 and 30 years old, and usually the killer faced arrest but no further formal punishment. Those killers who were arrested, indicted, tried, found guilty, and sentenced received prison terms of a year or two. Probably 10 percent of these stays were shortened by a pardon. In mid-nineteenth century New York City, about one homicide in four resulted in trial; about one homicide in five saw a sentence (usually around two years in prison); about one homicide in 80 resulted in an execution. Charge or plea bargaining appears to have been common, in part because pleading to a lesser charge could reduce murder's death penalty to manslaughter's various shorter terms of imprisonment. Juries seldom convicted on first degree murder, preferring a manslaughter conviction's less terminal consequences.

The homicides which occurred during brawls and drinking bouts and which actually went to trial inevitably carried the most minimal manslaughter charges. For example, in October 1857 a jury found Owen Kiernan (or McKearnam) guilty of beating to death with a cart rung his pal James McDermott, an Irishman with a wife and two children. The two "had been drinking freely together when an altercation ensued, during which Kiernan, in a fit of sudden passion, seized a cart-rung and struck McDermott on the head, felling him to the pavement" (*New York Times* [10/12/57] p. 5). For this the court convicted Kiernan of fourth degree manslaughter, sentencing him to one year in prison. On the same day, the same court put Holmes, a forger, away for fifteen years, six months (*New York Times* [11/23/1857] p. 2). How long, or even if, either actually served time is unclear.

The reason for this astonishing discrepancy in punishment can be inferred from the news reports. The jury learned that Holmes, the forger, was "a man of notoriously bad character," of whom, the judge claimed, "few men in the community would speak well." The killer Kiernan, on the other hand, had many friends, one of whom he had just killed. "Councilman Reilly presented a petition in his favor, and others testified to his general peaceful and good character." Kiernan posed no danger to judges or lawyers; Holmes did. Kiernan came from a world where the state let bullies be bullies. One could interpret this as a cultural feature of his world; one can also read it as a cultural feature of the world of judges and lawyers. That is, one can claim that the manly fighting abilities of American working class culture sanctioned Kiernan's behavior; however, one can equally well claim that in a world where the intervention of the state is almost nonexistent, the weak or unsuccessful fighters will have little to say about what is valued. Historians of American working class culture have not seriously confronted this problem in interpretation and have tended to celebrate manly virtues without asking about the costs and damages they incurred in a culture where physical brutality went unchecked by the state.[7]

In order to draw more precisely the transatlantic comparison during the two decade period of the 1850s and 1860s when New York began its violently different course from London and Liverpool, I have pooled the years 1852 to 1871 (excluding 1850–51, prior to the publication of the *New York Times*). For New York, I interpolate for 1853–1854, 1859, and 1862. In this period, there were at least 912 homicides in New York City; 181 in Liverpool; 170 in London. During these two decades, New York's population rose 80 percent, from 515,457 to 942,292; Liverpool grew the least, 30 percent, from 376,000 to 493,000. And London grew 40 percent, from 2,362,000 to 3,336,000. Using 1870 populations as denominators, the annual homicides rates per 100,000 for the two decade period, were 4.44, 1.83, and 0.25 for New York City, Liverpool, and London respectively.

These rates may be adjusted even more for population at risk differences. Race and ethnicity loom as the first "explanations" of the differ-

Table 3.2. Race or Nativity of Killers and Victims, New York City, 1852–1869

	VICTIMS				
KILLERS	Unknown	Foreign	Native	Black	Total
Unknown	367	102	13	7	489
Foreign	58	126	9	3	196
Native	11	8	3	2	24
Black	5	6	3	8	22
Total	441	242	28	20	731

CHI-SQUARE = 244.236,   D.F. = 9,   PROB. = −.00000043

Source: see text.

ences, although it is notable that the newspaper accounts of the period did not draw such inferences. For this two decade mid-century period, in New York, the race or ethnicity of 242 killers, 290 victims, or both in 168 situations, have been identified (Table 3.2). In some cases I used names and the ethnicity of the second person in a killer-victim dyad to identify the Irish, but otherwise did not use names as ethnic identifiers. The population at risk figures discussed here are interpolated from the 1865 state and 1870 federal censuses. My guess is that when unnoted in the records, the killer or victim was somewhat more likely to have been native born: that is the missing information was not random, nor was it totally biased in favor of the native born. Probably all blacks were noted, just because there were so few black homicides. Two extreme assumptions, the first that missing information indicated that a person was born in the United States, and the second, that missing information was random, may be used to frame upper and lower ethnicity and racial estimates. No information at all on ethnicity was obtained for the 107 cases in 1864, so by definition the values for this year were randomly distributed, reducing the denominator in the lower bounds estimate.

At the lower bounds then, 39 percent of the victims and 31 percent of the killers were foreign born; somewhat over 3 percent were black. At the upper bounds, just over 80 percent were foreign born, 7 percent of the victims and 9 percent of the killers black. The population of New York was about 41 percent foreign born over this period and about 1.4 percent black. Had foreign born or black died or killed at rates comparable to the native born populations, New York City's overall homicide rate would have been reduced substantially, by at least a fifth, more likely 25–40 percent. This would have left the native born white homicide rate of New York City 50 percent higher than Liverpool's for the whole period, the closest the two have been since then. This conclusion, though necessarily imprecise, is worth reiterating: net of the ethnic/racial differences, New York's homicide rate was still somewhat higher than Liverpool's, but the two were closer than they would ever be again.

For the year about which we know the most due to the publication of the coroner's list, 1865, we can be more precise. I have identified 68 homicides for the year. (There were 135 in *all* of England and Wales.) Twenty five of the 28 positively identified killers and 37 of the 55 identified victims were black, Irish, British or German. These are very conservative numbers, for a glance at the list of names shows where one could guess at ethnicity by name: for example, Andrew Mulligan, William Ahearn, or Michael Gorman were probably Irish while Christian Schlemmer was probably German. Eighteen cases had victims and killers in the same racial/ethnic category. Eleven of the total cases had no positive identification of either victim or murderer. Only two cases had both victim and killer identified who were neither Irish, German, British, nor black.

We can use these numbers to compare with the earlier upper and lower bounds estimates. At the minimum, 36 percent of the killers were of these ethnic/racial groups; at the maximum, 90 percent. At the minimum, 54 percent of the victims were in these groups; at the maximum, 67 percent. At the minimum, 64 percent (n = 44) of all cases had at least one participant who was in these groups; at the maximum, only 3 percent had no one. At this juncture, it is reasonable to claim that young Irish and German males were slaughtering each other in New York City, that at mid-century homicide was an ethnic problem.[8]

The larger point then is fairly straightforward. New York City's homicide rates would have been from at least one third lower, possibly even two thirds lower, were it not for the presence of immigrants. While this puts its native born rate near to that of Liverpool, it still would have soared three to five times over that of London.

The mean age of killers was greater than of their victims: about 29 to 25. No doubt they were stronger too. For the 56 cases where the ages of both killer and victim are known, a regression confirms the tendency for the killers to be a little older than their victims. The age group between 16 and 36 accounted for over 70 percent of the victims, 80 percent of the killers.[9] Any ethnic/racial group with large proportions of men concentrated in this age range would have a larger percentage of murders: This no doubt accounted for some of the higher rates of immigrants and blacks, as able-bodied young men moved to the city. One might note that an even more distinctive age/sex group moved to the frontiers and gold fields, where they distinguished themselves with high homicide rates (see Roger McGrath's chapter, this volume). Does the ethnic/race differentiation have anything to do with age/sex structures? Unfortunately, there are no existing population data which allow us to percapitize rates by age/sex/ethnicity.

Family relationships played a large part in determining who killed whom, in the nineteenth century as today. Nearly a third of the identified relationships linking killer and victim were within the family for nineteenth century New York City. Here missing data are a problem, for in virtually all male-female killings, the newspaper identified the nature of the relation-

Table 3.3. Killer and Victim Sex and Relationship, New York City, 1852–69

	KILLER		
	Male	*Female*	*Total*
Family and friends	238	32	270
Working partners, incl. superiors	25	1	26
Schoolmates	2	0	2
Govt. officials	15	1	16
Attack, robbery, burglary	20	2	22
Old antagonists	17	1	18
Business relation (i. e. barkeeper)	42	1	43
Political argument	18	0	18
Cellmates	6	2	8
(275 missing cases)			
TOTAL	384	40	423
	VICTIM		
	Male	*Female*	*Total*
Family and friends	145	125	270
Work partner	24	1	25
Schoolmate	3	0	3
Officials	15	1	16
Old antagonists	17	2	19
Business relations	37	7	44
Political disputants	18	0	18
Cellmates	7	2	9
(266 missing cases)			
TOTAL	292	140	432

Source: see text.

ship; thus we may assume that most if not all spousal killings have been identified, as have a large proportion of identified killings in immediate families. More distant relationships were in all probability not so consistently identified or even known. In order words, when the homicide was of a spouse, it was more likely to be noted than when the homicide was of an acquaintance or cousin. This measurement bias reduces the proportion of family killings to about 20 percent of the total. Clearly violence was not limited to single males and the barroom fighting world. In the 1980s, about 14 percent of all homicides are of immediate family members, about 9 percent spouses. Readers might wish to take cheer in the suggestion here that family violence has declined a bit both per capita and as a proportion of all violence.[10]

Men killed more than did women (91.4 percent of the killers); a large proportion of their victims (28 percent) were women. In contrast, when women killed, they more often killed women than did men: 44 percent of their victims were other women. Table 3.3 clarifies these gender differences further. For women, the home and family formed the usual context of homicide, for victims and perpetrators. Political arguments and "business" quarrels (most often over the price of a drink) were almost an exclusively male domain. Table 3.3 displays the differing locales of terminal discord for men and women. Men killed and were killed at home and in public, while women mainly were limited to family and friends.[11]

The murders in mid-nineteenth century New York make evident that guns are not required for homicides. For the period 1852–1869, 25 percent of the homicides were with gun, 31 percent with knife, and the remainder a combination of feet, stones, poisons (less than 4 percent), sticks and hands. The Civil War ushered in the era of gun murders with a bang: before 1863, 20 percent of the murders involved guns, after over one third. To confirm this percentage evidence, a regression predicting gun homicides per year by the total number of homicides and a dummy variable for 1863 shows the 1863 division to be of more impact than the total number of killings.[12] Accounts of gun murders in the post war era convey the distinct impression that they would have been even higher had the gun owners been more sober.

Conclusion

In the mid-nineteenth century the United States' homicide rate exceeded that of Britain, but the two were far closer to each other than they have been ever since. In the decades surrounding the Civil War the United States began its bloody divergence from the rest of the Western world. The homicide rate in the city of New York declined, but that of Britain in the post Civil War years fell far more precipitously. Only some of the differences can be clearly accounted for.

A portion came from guns. The evidence from the 1852–1869 data suggests that in the United States the Civil War ushered in an increased use of guns in homicides. Had the usage of guns continued at the lower pre-war rate, there might have been 10 to 20 percent fewer homicides per capita. One wonders also if the notoriously high rates of Southern rural homicides resulted from a similar post-Civil War gun culture. Did the nature of the war, a mass effort with loosely organized soldiery often casually armed, introduce the personal weapon on a wider scale than before?

In addition to the seemingly more plentiful means to kill, it also appears that the punishment mechanism in New York was feeble. It is impossible to know if vigorous and harsh punishment would have made a difference, though impressionistic evidence suggests that the even more violent South meted out even less punishment for murder.[13] Why were nineteenth century homicides so carelessly, or perhaps laxly, punished? Here, nothing seems to have changed, for Henry Lundsgaarde's study of homicide in Houston finds equally lax modern justice standards in one kind of case, where the killing was "reasonable."[14] And evidently, most killings in New York or in the rural South were reasonable, in the sense that the victim had not done everything possible to escape from the killer, that the killing resulted from a personal dispute, or because the killer and victim were the kinds of people who kill each other.

If two Irish toughs fought and one died, the killer could expect to escape with one year in prison at most, as in the case of Kiernan, above. If the tough killed a peaceable middle class man, then the killer might well hang. James Rogers did. A nineteen year-old fire house tough, he killed a man walking with his wife in an unprovoked attack in 1857. He was arrested, prosecuted, and hung within a year. On the other hand, if an Irish couple drank and fought for years until one was killed, the state did little. But if a respectable woman killed her husband, or even worse, her paramour, then she could meet severe punishment. In 1857, Mrs. Cunningham apparently killed her dentist friend, Dr. Burdell. She was never convicted or punished, but it was not through lack of trying. The vigorous, if incompetent and bizarre, prosecution of the case lasted two years. The message comes through the pages of nineteenth-century newspapers with great clarity and force: Murder was okay for some people, as long as they kept it within the bounds of social propriety.

When these two specific conditions, modest punishment and an increase in gun usage, are considered in conjunction with the city's enormous immigration and population growth, the decline (Fig. 3.1) of New York's homicide rate over the final decades of the nineteenth century seems all the more remarkable. Of course, the rates at any moment in time after 1870 were much lower in Britain, but we should not allow these contrasts to obscure the remarkably similar trends. And one can only speculate about the influence of the *laissez-faire* American state and homicide. Is it possible that if New York, and by extension other cities and counties, had punished homicides consistently and vigorously the United States could have kept in step with other nations including other former British colonies like Australia? Instead, in the opportune decades after the Civil War, the United States benefited from a declined in homicide but did not make the difficult and costly local effort to push the rate down even further. Thus the twentieth century began in the United States with an unacknowledged problem of grave and worsening dimensions, what one of the few early twentieth century experts on the subject called "America's darkest page in an otherwise inspiring history."[15]

Appendix: Some Observations on Theory and Measurement

I share James Sharpe's uneasiness about the notion that homicide is a systematically, socially produced index, and think the idea should remain a question ("Debate. The History of Violence in England: Some Observations," *Past and Present*, 108 [August 1985]: 206–15). For the notion that homicide indexes something else as well as murder is based on yet another assumption, one which I have begun to find difficult to accept. This is the notion laid out by Quetelet (Adolphe Quetelet, *Physique Sociale* [St. Petersburg, 1869]) and Durkheim, and accepted by most of us as a truth, that crime and violence are socially produced. Roger Lane (*Violent Death in the City: Suicide, Accident, & Murder in 19th Century Philadelphia* (Cambridge, MA: Harvard University Press, 1979), for example, uses as a headnote to chapter 2, "relations of suicide to . . . social environment are . . . direct and constant. . . . " (Durkheim, *Suicide*). Quetelet supported the notion by reference to the regular production of seemingly discrete and unrelated events like suicides and homicides. He wrote,

Experience . . . proves that not only is the annual number of homicides nearly constant, but that even the weapons employed are used in the same proportions. . . . Society contains within itself the germs of all the crimes that are about to be committed. It is society, in a way, which prepares them, and the criminal is only the instrument that executes them. Every social state supposes, then, a certain number and certain order of crimes as a necessary consequence of its organization." (Quetelet, 1869, I, 95–7; cited by William A. Bonger, *Criminality and Economic Conditions* [Boston: Little Brown, 1916], 32)

Because a social body produced what seemed to be unrelated events with regularity, Quetelet concluded that the events were in fact related.

Given Quetelet's thesis as an assumption, one may then turn to the rates at which a society produces events, like suicides or homicides, and use these rates as indexing something else about the society. When the homicide rates change dramatically, we automatically turn to larger things in the society for explanation. Thus we accept Quetelet.

And having accepted him, even the wildest variations in homicide rates prove less than problematic. There are several ways of handling such variation. The first is aggregation. This is why we may plot homicide rates monthly, annually, or decennially. We spread out the time frame so as to cast a wider social net and make each data point relatively similar to the previous and following ones. Historians who would be horrified by the idea of discovering a social "law," on the one hand, are quick to "smooth" to make their data demonstrate (or conform to) our vision of reality. Quetelet exemplified smoothing by showing how a design up close may seem to be only points, but that "if the observer continues to recede, he loses sight of the individual points. . . . [and] grasps the law that has presided over their general arrangement" (Quetelet, 1869, I, 42, cited by Bonger, 1916, 31). Even for very homicidal places, we do not plot rates daily, for the graph would bounce from zero to a very high number most erratically if we did so. It is hard to avoid the irony here: Quetelet observed stability in rates, and therefore concluded that regular social process produced the rates; they were not idiosyncratic events. When we observe wild variation in rates, we look for social change, rather than questioning the soundness of the empirical observations which prompted Quetelet's generalizations in the first place.

Ask any researcher familiar with the sources about data quality for nineteenth century homicides and the likely answer is laughter, or tears, or both. And on inspecting the data more and more closely, even the hard-bitten quantifier like me can be tempted to opt for texture, nuance, and narrative detail as the feasibility of exact counts shimmers and disappears like the hound of the Baskervilles. But of course it is the very lack of precise selection which makes the individual stories all the more difficult to use. Just as sampling error introduces unknown bias into the data-analytic approach, it introduces unknown bias to the narrative detail. Nuance is interesting but meaningless without some sense of its representativeness. For this reason then, any historical study of homicide must be concerned with data, testing different sources against each other, comparing them to discover possible biases, weighing and measuring the probabilities of error.

For New York City I have combined sources whenever possible and have been cautious in using what seems like the most reliable source: the coroner's reports. Roger Lane has pointed out to me that coroner's juries tended to acquit, as did courts, on the basis of Victorian sentiment. That is, a good story of emotional stress brought them around to empathizing with the killer. There are suggestions that lenient juries were not new to America. See Kathryn Preyer, "Coping with Crime," *Reviews in American History*, 15 (June 1987), 243, who agrees with Dwight F. Henderson, *Congress, Courts, and Criminals: The Development of Federal Criminal Law, 1801–1829* (Westport, CT: Greenwood Press, 1985), about the refusal of early nineteenth century juries to convict. Thus coroner's reports undercounted homicides. This is why there were more arrests for murders than official numbers of murders recorded and is the first major filtering of cases out of the criminal justice system. Another consequence of such an exclusion of homicides from the possibility of prosecution is that appeals courts won't show much about attitudes towards homicides, because only convictions get appealed. When the jury/courts are lenient, then the appeal process cannot demonstrate one edge of the legal boundary system. The relative accuracy and completeness of United States sources changed over the nineteenth century. By the second decade of the twentieth century, Hoffman argued vigorously for coroners or vital records over other forms of homicide reporting, claiming that the only decision medical examiners made was the means of death, not the circumstances. "What is murder in fact may not be murder in law . . . The death certificate tells the true story" (Frederick Ludwig Hoffman, *The Homicide Problem* [Newark: Prudential Press, 1925], 1.)

One thing is clear: in mid-nineteenth century New York, sources mattered greatly. For the 1850s and 1860s, at least, one must construct the rates on a case by case basis. For instance, sometimes even the same source will produce different numbers. That of the coroner for 1867 (2/1/68, *New York Times*, p. 8 c. 4) listed number only, at 42, while the authoritative compilation into a serial source by Dr. Haven Emerson (1941) gives 34. Based on my name matching of newspaper reports and coroners reports for the one year, 1865, it is possible, I conclude, that for the city of New York, unless it can be shown otherwise, accurate estimates of homicide rates must use actual names of victims. Taking what seem to be differing upper and lower measures from different sources is very deceptive. The lesser number may not simply represent a subset of the larger number, as one would like to imagine. Newspapers/indexes/coroners reports/court reports cannot be averaged or even construed as boundary estimates. Using for instance the *New York Times* "Record of the Coroners' Office" (Jan 5, 1866, p. 8, cols. 3–4) to compare with data from the *New York Times Index* is most instructive. For 1865, the Index listed 47 homicides in New York City, one a death following an abortion. The Coroners' Record, on the other hand, indicated 56 homicides during the year. There was substantial overlap, of course, but not complete agreement. Such name by name comparisons can only be made when coroner's name lists can be found. The score for 1865, then, is as follows:

SOURCE	TIMES INDEX	CORONER'S REPORT	OVERLAP	TOTAL
NUMBER	47	56	35	35 + 12 + 21 = 68

In other words, the amount of undercounting is considerably larger via the newspaper index than via the coroner, but both are large enough to reject either as a solitary data source. And this exploration of two sources does not consider that the newspaper itself, if its pages were searched without the index (as I did for this project), would yield other deaths. There is also some possibility that errors come from misassignment of year, though most cases moved from crime to court conclusion in a matter of days. In the early 1870s, the official reports and the newspaper tabulating came much closer to one another, so for the post 1870 data I have relied on the former, taking the similar annual number of homicides as evidence of corroboration.

For the purposes of more detailed, individual case analysis, data on about 734 homicides in New York for 14 of the 19 years between 1851 and 1869 were gathered from the *New York Times* through a reading of the daily papers. Only years which were in between two very ordinary years were skipped. Consequently, only early 1851, 1853, 1854, 1859, and 1861 escaped detailed scrutiny. The *New York Times Index* proved uneven but was also used as a supplement. A daily search is the least unsatisfactory way to obtain data for years prior to accurate or thorough death registration. The hazards include non-reporting in the newspaper (as may have been the case for 1863, when the Civil War news drove out the customary and extensive local reporting), unknown biases (a probable higher reporting of murders among "respectable" people, sensationally violent cases, or those involving the politically prominent), missing information, and lack of follow up stories.

The latter poses two problems. The language of the mid-nineteenth century allowed the use of the word fatal as in "fatal stabbing affray" for both actual killings as well as when the victim was expected to die, but prior to any death. In a related mode, the newspaper reported that victims of violence would, "surely die," but provided no subsequent notice if they did not. A reader of these items is left dangling, as were the witnesses and perpetrator who sat in prison awaiting the outcome of the injuries. Presumably the witnesses were released when the victim lived. A second and related problem is in discovering whether or not the murderers were tried, convicted, and actually punished. Most original notices included arrest information. The series of decisive steps following the arrest cannot be reliably established. The decisions of the coroner's jury, indictments, actual trials in either the General Sessions or Oyer and Terminer courts, the results of the trial, the sentencing of the guilty, the granting of pardons or commutations, cannot be determined through the newspaper with a comfortable sense of completion. The data collection on capital punishment at the Criminal Justice Archives and Information Network reports all known executions in the United States, so both actual punishments and annual rates may be constructed for those handful of cases so concluding. The New York Secretary of State's annual reports can be used to supplement the annual aggregates: They do not tell who was tried but they do tell how many, and the outcome of the trial. These I have used to supplement the data gathered from the *Times*, as I have used for a few years the reported number of arrests for murder and manslaughter. The arrest figures usually are equal to or greater than the number of homicides because the police tended to arrest everyone in sight after a fatal barroom brawl.

Notes

Note: The research reported here represents a portion of a continuing project investigating differential homicide rates. It has been supported by grants from the University of California, Los Angeles Academic Senate, the University of California, Los Angeles College Foundation, the International Studies Overseas Program at University of California, Los Angeles, and by a National Endowment for the Humanities Fellowship. Chenquan Jia, Jose Galvez, Rob Michelson, Naoki Kamimura, Sheila O'Hare, Carole Winter, and Matthew Lee have acted as research assistants for the project, and I am indebted to them for their assistance.

1. Ted Robert Gurr, "Historical Trends in Violent Crime: A Critical Review of the Evidence," in Michael Tonry and Norval Morris, eds., *Crime and Justice: An Annual Review of Research* (Chicago: University of Chicago Press, 1981), 3:295–353.

2. For a reinterpretation of the frontier hypothesis, see David T. Courtwright, "The Frontier as a Concept in Deviant Behavior" (unpublished ms., Trinity College, Hartford, CT). See also Robert B. Toplin, *Unchallenged Violence: An American Ordeal* (Westport, CT: Greenwood, 1975).

3. Lawrence Stone, "Interpersonal Violence in English Society, 1300–1980," *Past and Present*, 101 (November 1983): 22–33; James Sharpe (who refuses to assent completely to the indexing question), "Debate. The History of Violence in England: Some Observations," *Past and Present*, 108 (August 1985): 206–15; Stone, "Rejoinder," *Past and Present*, 108 (August 1985): 216–24.

4. Frederick Ludwig Hoffman [b. 1865], *The Homicide Problem* (Newark: Prudential Press, 1925), often wrote of the quality of British and European statistics, despairing over the miserable quality of U.S. vital records.

5. Horace V. Redfield's *Homicide, North and South: Being a Comparative View of Crime against the Person in Several Parts of the United States* (Philadelphia: Lippincott, 1880) is a remarkable study of homicide in the 1870s that establishes rather convincingly that southern rural homicide rates were close to (he thought higher than) northern urban ones.

6. Although they do not break their data down by race and ethnicity, Dane Archer and Rosemary Gartner, *Violence and Crime in Cross-National Perspective* (New Haven: Yale University Press, 1984), provide the most extensive compilation of recent international homicide data.

7. Elliot J. Gorn, "Good-Bye Boys, I Die a True American: Homicide, Nativism, and Working-Class Culture in Antebellum New York City," *Journal of American History* 74 (1987): 388–410; Sean Wilentz, *Chants Democratic: New York City and the Rise of the American Working Class, 1788–1850* (New York: Oxford University Press, 1984) takes careful note of street violence, and argues that working class violence delineated a separate cultural strand from the articulate unionist strand.

8. Roger Lane, for his Philadelphia study, *Violent Death in the City*, used names to assess ethnicity, and he estimated that the Irish over the latter half of the nineteenth century made up 20 percent of the population while accounting for 30 percent of the homicides. For the Germans, in contrast, he found a strong underrepresentation, due to the presence of the so-called Pennsylvania Dutch, native born Americans of German heritage. For the Irish, he found, using a slightly more conservative name based criterion, a declining proportional rate of homicide, 24 percent (1839–59), 27 percent (1860–1880), and 17 percent (1881–1901), and he makes the highly plausible argument that a "process of pacification" drove down Irish rates of violence. My data do not permit me to generate more precise comparisons, but the proportions of immigrants must have been far higher in New York.

9. The tables below show the age of killers and victims: though limited to 95 and 164 person samples, there is no reason to suspect bias in reporting.

Killers's Age, New York City, 1852–1869.

KILLER'S AGE	FREQUENCY	PERCENT	...CUMULATIVE... FREQUENCY	PERCENT
1– 6	0			
6–11	3	3.2	3	3.2
11–16	3	3.2	6	6.3
16–21	16	16.8	22	23.2
21–26	14	14.7	36	37.9
26–31	19	20.0	55	57.9
31–36	14	14.7	69	72.6
36–41	12	12.6	81	85.3
41–46	3	3.2	84	88.4
46–51	3	3.2	87	91.6
51–56	4	4.2	91	95.8
56–61	1	1.0	92	96.8
61–66	1	1.0	93	97.9
66–71	1	1.0	94	98.9
71–76	1	1.0	95	100
			TOTAL 95	

Victim's Age, New York City, 1852–1869.

VICTIM'S AGE	FREQUENCY	PERCENT	...CUMULATIVE... FREQUENCY	PERCENT
1– 6	5	3.0	5	3.0
6–11	6	3.7	11	6.7
11–16	5	3.0	16	9.8
16–21	19	11.6	35	21.3
21–26	24	14.6	59	36.0
26–31	31	18.9	90	54.9
31–36	28	17.1	118	72.0
36–41	15	9.2	133	81.1
41–46	10	6.1	143	87.2
46–51	7	4.3	150	91.5
51–56	3	1.8	153	93.3
56–61	5	3.0	158	96.3
61–66	0	–	158	96.3
66–71	4	2.4	162	98.8
71–76	0	–	162	98.8
76–81	1	.6	163	99.4
81–86	1	.6	164	100
			TOTAL 164	

Dependent Variable: Age of Victim

VARIABLE	COEFFICIENT	(SEE)	T	SIG.
Killer's age	.5608	.1360	4.124	.00018
Constant	10.6838			
SEE = 10.6928				

R^2 = .2932

F Ratio   17.010   Prob. .00018 N = 41

10. Relationship of Killer and Victim, New York City, 1852–1869.

	FREQUENCY	PERCENT
Spouse	*95*	*20.0*
Lovers	*24*	*5.0*
Family	*22*	*4.6*
Acquaintance	*145*	*30.4*
Personal enemies	*19*	*4.0*
Working partners	*26*	*5.5*
(inc. boss-worker)		
School mates	*3*	*.6*
Officials/citizens	*16*	*3.4*
Attackers/burglars	*25*	*5.3*
Business (e.g.,	*44*	*9.3*
barkeep/customer)		
Political fights	*19*	*4.0*
Cell mates (inc.	*9*	*1.9*
poorhouse, lunatic		
asylum, or jail)		
Strangers	*28*	*5.9*
TOTAL	*475*	*100*

(256 missing cases)

11. For an historical overview of family violence see Elizabeth Pleck, *Domestic Tyranny: The Making of American Social Policy against Family Violence from Colonial Times to the Present* (New York: Oxford University Press, 1987).

12.

Dependent Variable: Number of Gun Homicides per Year, 1852–1869

VARIABLE	COEFFICIENT	(SEE)	T	SIG.
Total Homicides	.1726	(.0745)	2.315	.04314
Dummy 1863 and after	6.7443	(2.0451)	3.298	.00804
Constant	-.7507			
Std. Error of Est. = 3.6528				

Adjusted R^2 = .5144 R^2 = .5953

F Ratio 7.355 Prob. .0109 N = 11

13. Edward L. Ayers, *Vengeance and Justice: Crime and Punishment in the 19th-Century American South* (New York: Oxford University Press, 1984); Redfield, *Homicide, North and South*.

14. Henry P. Lundsgaarde, *Murder in Space City: A Cultural Analysis of Houston Homicide Patterns* (New York: Oxford University Press, 1977).

15. Hoffman, *Homicide Problem*, 10.

Chapter *4*

Violence Arrests in the City: The Philadelphia Story, 1857–1980

NEIL ALAN WEINER and MARGARET A. ZAHN

Background and Issues

For much of our history violence has been banished to our lost American heritage. This "historical amnesia," as Hofstadter and Wallace have aptly referred to it, resulted in part from the fact that the United States "has a history but not a tradition" of violence.[1] Without an ideological foundation and a geographical center to rivet social and intellectual attention, the national consciousness of and conscience about violent people and their acts has tended to be diffuse and of limited duration and vitality. When the national memory has been jarred to recall and reflect on violence, the tendency has been to rediscover and interpret our violent past as part of legitimate national heritage (such as the Revolutionary and Civil Wars) or romantic folklore (for example, the James Gang, Bonnie and Clyde, John Dillinger).

The coincidence in the 1960s of the civil rights movement, urban riots, and protests against the Vietnam War galvanized national concern about domestic disorder and its violent collective forms, and about kindred forms of interpersonal violence and crime. Three national presidential commissions were inaugurated during the decade to reflect and report on the more immediate and enduring roots of these phenomena. The first, the President's Commission on Law Enforcement and Administration of Justice (the Katzenbach Commission), empaneled in 1966, focused on the dimensions and effects of crime and the criminal justice system.[2] The second, the National Advisory Commission on Civil Disorders (the Kerner Commission), created in 1967, investigated the origins of collective action and disorder and, importantly, their increasingly violent turns.[3] The third, the National Commission on the Causes and Prevention of Violence (the Violence Commission), initiated in 1968, explored the interior and exterior topographies and dynamics of personal, interpersonal, and collective violence.[4] Under these different but interwoven mandates—but especially under that of the Violence Commission—violence in America was systematically, politically and intellectually rediscovered. This heightened awareness has fueled a continuing vigorous interest in the investigation of violence using the full repertoire of scientific perspectives and technologies.

One strand of this growth in violence research is the historical analysis of violent interpersonal crime. Much of this work has concentrated on violent crime in the city. We too have been motivated to pursue this line of inquiry by the starkly high incidence of violence in our urban centers.

Analyses reported here focus on long-term patterns in violent crime in Philadelphia. Our observations are inferred from separate statistical time-series of arrests for murder, rape, robbery, aggravated assault, and firearms violations over a 123 year span, from 1857 to 1980. Lane has forged the most detailed historical treatments of the varieties of personal and interpersonal violence in Philadelphia.[5] In many ways, Lane's analyses and conclusions have informed our own: Both his writings and advice have proven to be invaluable in organizing our thoughts on the historical and theoretical problems posed by the vicissitudes in the patterns in violent behavior that have scarred Philadelphia's human landscape. A kindred dissertation by Naylor on crime, criminals, and punishment in Philadelphia has also informed our efforts to make some sense of the violent Philadelphia scene over the last century and a quarter.[6] We hope to amplify these two earlier research efforts by expanding the types of criminally violent acts that are examined, introducing violence-arrest statistics for more recent years, and comparing selected violence arrest series internally to one another and externally to criminal violence series for other urban jurisdictions and time periods.

Historical Studies

Gurr[7] and Lane[8] have developed the main explanations of the historical patterns in violent crimes in Western urban centers. Gurr cuts the wider historical swatch, piecing together evidence from the thirteenth to the twentieth century. Lane wrestles with a much shorter time period—the late 1830s to the mid-1930s. Within this more delimited time range, Lane develops more specific interpretations.

Gurr maintains that the irregular but persistent declines in rates of violent crimes in Western society over the past eight centuries have been governed primarily by modernization, comprising the quartet of urban growth, industrialization, expansions in state power, and the embracement and consolidation of humanistic values. The last of these influences holds a prominent position in Gurr's explanatory framework. Humanistic values—most centrally, the growing sensitization to violence—increasingly began to identify violence as morally repugnant and to banish it to the social and behavioral fringes, first in the social elites and then at the social margins, resulting in the progressive pacification of interpersonal belligerence in Western society.

The thesis of the ameliorative influence of modernity is echoed by the statistical portrait that Gurr constructs from more narrowly focused historical studies. Together the bits and pieces of statistical evidence lead Gurr to propose as an explanatory model the thesis of the "U-curve." Beginning in late medieval England, murder rates and, perhaps, rates of other seriously violent behaviors were at high points in comparison to those of the nineteenth and twentieth centuries. From the thirteenth to the nineteenth centuries, murder and other violent crime rates irregularly declined in response to the pacifications of modernity, tracing the initial (leftmost) vertically declining portion of the U-curve. From the late nineteenth century until the mid-twentieth century, violence rates in England and in other European societies remained at their low points, forming the lower portion of the U-curve. Increases since the mid-twentieth century in serious violent crimes in almost all Western societies, resulting from societal dislocations and readjustments (for example, post-war influences, the bulge in the age structure by the post-war baby-boomers, post-industrial destabilization) trace the (rightmost) upward sweep of the U-curve. Over the long historical run, the recent upsurges of violent crime appear to be modest perturbations of the more dominant pattern of historical recession.

Lane adds a modern anchor to this broader historical account. He argues that social and psychological demands of the industrial revolution are at the root of the contemporary trends in criminal violence. Early industrialization resulted in migratory influxes into cities that led to short-term increases in murderous violence. However, with time and social assimilation, lethal confrontations began to recede. The regulated lives of industrial workers lessened the motivations and opportunities to become violently involved. Industrial social relations required behavioral routines—self-control, orderliness, punctuality, rationality, cognitive concentration, and emotional modulation, to name a few—that are inherently antithetical to violent outbursts. These habits—reinforced by the behavioral routines imposed by, and the substantive content of, ever-widening public education—drove down the violence rates. The historically modest levels of deadly violence observed by Lane in Philadelphia during the heyday of the industrial revolution, followed by the increasing rates of violence in post-industrial modern America, support his thesis.

Studies of violent crime by Monkkonen, Ferdinand, and Powell focused on time periods that overlap with ours. Monkkonen, using arrest data for twenty-three U.S. cities for the period 1860 to 1920, compared the patterns in overall arrests, which declined almost steadily over this period, with homicide, which first declined through the late nineteenth century but then rose dramatically in the early twentieth century.[9] Ferdinand examined trends in seven major violent and property crimes in Boston from 1849 to 1951. He found that the aggregate crime rate declined almost without interruption from 1875 to 1951. However, patterns in several of the violent crimes differed from the aggregate pattern: Murder and assaults declined over the entire time period, although with some fluctuation, which is consistent with the aggregate trend. However, manslaughter increased steeply in the first quarter of the twentieth century, mainly due to vehicular accidents, fluctuated until the late 1930s, and finally sharply decreased. Robbery moved erratically. Rape was the only violent crime to exhibit generally sustained increases over the entire period.[10]

Powell, who compiled arrest statistics for Buffalo for nearly the same time period studied in Boston, found that violent crimes peaked in 1870, declined steadily until the turn of the century, rose again until 1918, and then declined through the mid-1940s. Data for specific violent crimes were not presented, so analyses of crime-specific patterns are not possible.[11] Together these three studies suggest an overall decline in violent crime from the mid-nineteenth century to the mid-twentieth century, although particular types of violent crimes do not always follow this path.

Historical studies of violent crime generally focus on a limited number of these behaviors. For example, neither Gurr nor Lane introduces much evidence about violent crimes other than homicide. In the following sections we enlarge the focus, tracing long-term patterns in violence arrests in Philadelphia for the most serious, or potentially serious, crimes of murder, rape, robbery, aggravated assault, and firearms violations. These arrest series are compared to one another and to related official statistical series that have been compiled for both Philadelphia and other locations. Additionally, Lane's analysis of lethal assaults in Philadelphia ends in 1930. The present study extends the time period another half-century through 1980. Our investigations are exploratory and suggestive, and attempt to shed further light on historical themes of violent crime in urban settings.

The Violent Crime Data and Some Methodological Considerations

Statistics on arrests for violent crimes in Philadelphia were obtained from the *Annual Message and Reports of the Departments* (the *Annual Mayors Reports*), drafted by the city's mayor's office, for the nearly continuous sequence of years 1857–1923, after which time, through 1959, reporting became much sparser with respect to the kinds of crimes that were listed.[12]

For the years 1960 and 1963–1980 arrest statistics were obtained from the Federal Bureau of Investigation, which compiled them expressly for this study.[13] Decennial population data for the city were obtained from the U.S. Bureau of the Census.[14]

Any researcher who has conducted an historical study using criminal justice statistics—especially statistics extending over a long time period—is mindful of the pitfalls of relying on this kind of information. Criminal statutes are modified periodically, official responses to crime vary (through both formal and informal decisionmaking dynamics), and civilian reporting practices and official recording procedures change. Despite these important caveats, quantitative historical analyses of violent crime are not, thereby, fatally flawed and useless. For example, some researchers have argued that problems of data validity due to changes over time in public reporting and official recording practices are least problematic for the most serious crimes such as murder and robbery.[15] Gurr points out that over the nineteenth century, when police detection and coroner designation of deaths as homicides began to improve as a function of greater professional organization and more advanced medical procedures, homicide records provided an increasingly accurate reflection of the actual incidence of non-accidental interpersonal fatalities. The longstanding vigorous condemnation of robbery probably makes the statistical documentation of this crime the next most valid indicator, after criminal homicide, of criminal prevalence and incidence. Statistics on aggravated assault and forcible rape, although probably less valid than those on criminal homicide and robbery, are still productive research tools when used for purposes of comparison with the more accurate statistical evidence. Convergent trends may strengthen conclusions about the historical shape of interpersonal criminal violence. Divergent patterns may make conclusions more tentative but do not, thereby, neuter them, particularly if plausible hypotheses can account for the divergence. Overall, then, the variability over time in reporting and recording criminal homicides and robberies is probably less than that of other violent crimes, making inferences drawn from these time series the firmest.

In addition to using multiple types of violent crimes, we can enhance the validity of interpretations by comparing findings with those reported for other locations and times. Researchers must be, then, cautious and creative in the use and comparisons of official statistical registries rather than immobilized by their deficiencies.

Contemporary debates about the relative merits of rival sources of information about violent crimes and criminals are generally moot in the context of long-term historical analyses. There are only five sources of information about the types and extent of violent crimes: (1) direct observation, (2) informant investigations (which involve questioning, for example, family, friends, and associates), (3) self-reports by offenders who are interviewed,

(4) surveys of persons who have been victimized, and (5) official records maintained by the criminal justice system. Although antiquarian self-report and victimization documents can be identified and make for delightful reading, these fragmentary anecdotes and journalistic accounts typically articulate the perspectives and concerns of social elites. The socially skewed sources of these violence accounts impair their objectivity and general validity. Official records are the only sources of long-term information that have any claim to generality.

One of our analytical concerns has centered on the use of arrest statistics rather than some alternative source of official data such as court indictments. To explore this issue, we have examined the arguments made by Lane, who studied interpersonal fatalities in nineteenth-century Philadelphia by using documents detailing incidents that resulted in homicide (murder or nonaccidental manslaughter) indictments.[16] Table 4.1 adapts, from Lane, seven-year moving average rates of fatal incidents resulting in homicide indictments, beginning in 1860 and ending just after the turn of the century. These rates are compared to corresponding five-year average homicide (murder or nonnegligent manslaughter) arrest rates from our data.[17] The indictment-incident and arrest statistics are presented in tandem in columns 1 and 2. The two data arrays indicate the unremarkable fact that the arrest rates are uniformly higher than their corresponding indictment-incident rates, although not always by very much. However, more remarkable—but not unexpected—is the finding, discussed in detail below, that arrest statistics appear to reflect the same trajectories as the indictment-incident rates, thereby supporting their use in our exploration of long-term trends in violent crimes.

Patterns in interpersonal criminal violence would be identical in the two time series if one series was an exact multiple of the other—if, for example, for any year or averaged set of years, the homicide arrest rate was invariably two times higher than the corresponding rate of incidents that resulted in homicide indictments. This is not so with respect to homicide for those seven-year and five-year average intervals presented in the table, as column 3 indicates. However, departures from this perfect correspondence are not extreme. Figures listed in column 3 represent the ratios of the five-year homicide-arrest averages to their corresponding seven-year homicide-indictment averages. The ratios cluster narrowly between 1.1 and 1.4, with one exception in the late 1870s.

Despite moderate variability in the ratios between the two rates, the trends are generally the same across the two time series. Columns 4 and 5 lay out, for the homicide indictment rates and the homicide arrest rates, respectively, a running index of whether the rates increased or decreased over successive adjacent time intervals. Each ratio represents the later time interval in comparison to the immediately preceding time interval. (Thus, the first ratio in column 4 equals 1.4, which is the ratio of 3.1 to 2.3.)[18]

Table 4.1 Average Annual Rate (per 100,000 Population) of Incidents Resulting in Homicide Indictments and of Arrests for Murder and Nonnegligent Manslaughter

(1) Seven-Year Averages for Nonaccidental Incidents Resulting in Homicide Indictments[a]		(2) Five-Year Averages of Murder and Nonnegligent Murder Arrests[b]		(3) Ratio of Column 2 to Column 1	(4) Ratio of Later to Immediately Preceding Seven-Year Average	(5) Ratio of Later to Immediately Preceding Five-Year Average
Years	Average	Years	Average			
(1860–1866)	2.3	(1861–1865)	2.9	1.3		
					1.4	1.3
(1867–1873)	3.1	(1868–1872)	3.9	1.3		
					.9	1.7
(1874–1880)	2.9	(1875–1879)	6.8	2.3		
					.7	.4
(1881–1887)	2.1	(1882–1886)	2.9	1.4		
					1.0	.8
(1888–1894)	2.1	(1889–1893)	2.2	1.1		
					1.1	1.1
(1895–1901)	2.2	(1896–1900)	2.3	1.1		

[a]Adapted from Roger Lane, *Violent Death in the City* (Cambridge, MA: Harvard University Press, 1979), 71. The rates pertain to those nonaccidental incidents (not persons) resulting in an indictment for murder or manslaughter.
[b]Pertains to persons arrested for murder or nonnegligent manslaughter.

Comparison of the ratios in columns 4 and 5 shows that when the rate of fatal incidents resulting in homicide indictments surged, receded, or remained stable, so did the corresponding homicide arrest rate in three of the five comparisons—the first, third, and fifth. The fourth comparison (1.0 vs. .8), although not perfectly congruent, is certainly not wildly discrepant, especially when one considers that all of the ratios are based on small numbers for which modest differences in absolute values can profoundly influence the resulting computation. Indeed, in view of the very small numbers involved in forming these ratios, it is remarkable that this much consistency is observed.

One might plausibly argue that seven-year and five-year averages comprise periods that are too brief to provide a confident indication of variability in, and comparability between, potentially rival statistical series like the indictment-incidents and arrests under discussion here. Unusual activities in just a few of the years embedded within an averaged set of years can have a major impact on that average. To shed some light on this issue, we compared the 21-year average rates of fatal incidents resulting in homicide indictments computed by Lane for the years 1860–1880 and 1881–1901 (2.8 and 2.1 per 100,000 population, respectively) to the corresponding arrest rate averages based on our data for murder and nonnegligent manslaughter (4.5 and 2.5).[19] The ratios of the two are in the same "greater-than-one" direction (1.6 = 4.5:2.8; 1.2 = 2.5:2.1), indicating the familiar, consistent finding of a surplus of arrests in comparison to indictment-incidents. Also, the ratios are not very different from one another. Moreover, the time trend ratios within each statistical series are congruent, indicating a decline in each series. The ratio of the later 21-year average to the earlier average with respect to indictment incidents is .75 (2.1:2.8); the corresponding arrest rate ratio is .60 (2.5:4.5). Over longer periods, then, these two sources of violent crime statistics also appear to correspond to each other without misleading distortion.

We know of no readily available Philadelphia data with which this issue can be explored for later time periods or for the four other violent crimes comprising the core of our analyses. Nevertheless, we press ahead cautiously, drawing and qualifying inferences based on the joint patterns revealed by the time series on violent crime (murder, rape, robbery, and aggravated assault) and firearms violations, and by comparison of these patterns to those reported in related studies. These methodological considerations, together with the delimited time-series comparisons discussed above, mitigate the proper concern with Murphy's Law that Lane voices in this volume: " . . . the [time series] sets that are the longest, and the most easily compiled and compared, such as aggregate arrests, generally contain the least information."[20] At least for the nearly half-century time span that we have just examined, collateral data on fatal incidents resulting in homicide indictments and homicide arrest statistics yielded quite similar information. The choice of an incident-based or an arrest-based index does not appear, then, to pose a "tiger-behind-the-door" dilemma to researchers tracing broad patterns in secular homicide trends. For Lane, the detailed information contained in indictment documents was essential to his analytical goal of rendering the rich chiaroscuro of fatal urban violence. However, in light of this finding of aggregate statistical congruence, researchers interested in pursuing long-term statistical analyses of criminal homicide in urban areas in America over the last century and a half can now do so more confidently using the more readily available arrest data.

Violence Arrests in Philadelphia

Overall the Philadelphia data show that the progression of arrests for serious violent crimes in the city began at a low ebb in the mid-nineteenth century, continued at this comparatively modest level, with some minor, generally upward movements until about the turn of the century, began to rise again through 1920, and then spiraled upward after the middle of the twentieth century, especially through the 1960s and 1970s. Figure 4.1A represents this pattern in terms of the proportion of the total arrest rate that is accounted for by the total violence arrest rate.[21] For the ninety-year decennial sequence beginning in 1860 and ending in 1950, violence arrests in Philadelphia accounted at most for barely more than 2 percent (regis-

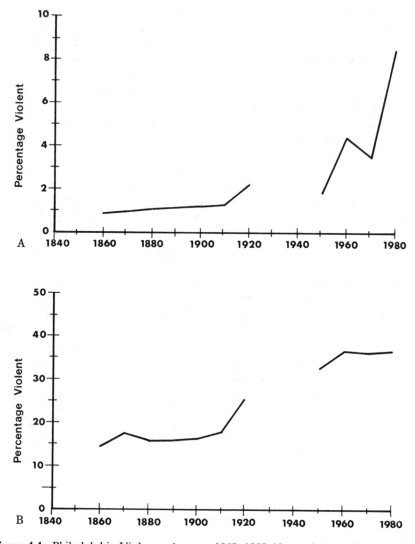

Figure 4.1: Philadelphia Violence Arrests, 1860–1980 (decennial years)
NOTE: A. Violence arrest rate as percentage of total arrest rate
          B. Violence arrest rate as percentage of index arrest rate

tered in 1920) of the total recorded arrests. After just one more decade, by
1960, the figure was up to 4.3 percent; and, as striking, two decades later,
the percentage had almost doubled again, to 8.5 percent.
    We were sensitive to the potential objection that using the total arrest
rate might introduce significant incomparabilities into these calculations,

because crime categories sometimes move in and out of the arrest listings in the *Annual Mayors Reports*, resulting in dissimilar bases for making annual tabulations. For this reason, we also calculated for each decennial year the arrest rate for the crime group that included murder, rape, robbery, aggravated assault, larceny, and burglary. This more restrictive definition, which roughly approximates the contemporary definition (through 1981) of the FBI's *Uniform Crime Reports* (*UCR*) "index crimes," yields an offense-type grouping that is somewhat more resistant to incomparabilities resulting from shifting listings of crime categories.[22,23] For each decennial year under consideration, arrests for each of these crimes were reported.

Figure 4.1B presents a picture that mirrors in its main aspects the one painted in Figure 4.1A. The percentage of the arrest rate for index crimes accounted for by the violence arrest rate rose from its lowest point in 1860 of 14 percent to its highest point in the most recent decennial year of 37 percent—an almost threefold increase. The proportionate rise in violence arrests does not appear, then, to be mainly an artifact of official foibles in reporting in the *Annual Mayors Reports*.

This increase in the violence percentage of both total arrests and index arrests reflects any number of changes, behavioral and administrative. Serious violent behavior may have increased at a faster pace than property offenses; or, criminal justice officials may have issued directives, either formal or informal, to concentrate limited resources on violent offenses, resulting in more violence arrests, fewer nonviolence arrests, and, in turn, the appearance but not the fact of more violence. Changes in public reporting and official recording of violent crimes may also have influenced these patterns.

Strong evidence in favor of one or the other of these competing explanations is not forthcoming. However, the following analysis of violent crime trends shows increases for both those rates that are probably least sensitive to official decisionmaking (such as murder and robbery) and those which are most sensitive (such as firearms violations). Furthermore, these upwardly spiraling patterns are confirmed nationally for urban centers for the most recent two decades, weakening the potential argument that the increase is mainly a matter of administrative decisionmaking only in Philadelphia. We suspect that the long-term historical records of other urban areas, when they are compiled, will reflect the Philadelphia experience. Changes in underlying rates of criminally violent behavior have very likely influenced these patterns, though not exclusively so.

The swelling contemporary rates of arrest for violent crimes—murder, rape, robbery, and aggravated assault—in Philadelphia are vividly depicted in Figure 4.2. Between 1860 and 1920 the total violence arrest rate more than doubled, from 42 (per 100,000 population) to more than 100, respectively. By 1960 the rate more than doubled again to 217. From 1960 to 1980, the rate again catapulted upward, two and one-half times to 523.

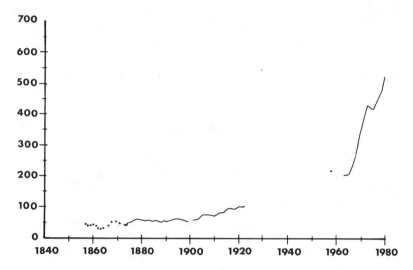

Figure 4.2: Philadelphia: Total Violence Arrest Rate per 100,000 Population, 1857–1980 (5-year moving averages)

Over the 123-year period, serious violence arrests registered, therefore, a twelvefold ascent.

The data indicate that those broad social forces that pushed upward the overall violence arrest rate in the city appear to have operated similarly over the whole period on each of the component forms of violence— murder, rape, robbery, and aggravated assault, and also on firearms violations—albeit at different paces (Figures 4.3–4.7). The murder arrest rate rose almost fourfold, from nearly 5 (per 100,000 population; 5-year average) in 1857 to 18 in 1980; forcible rape thirteenfold, from 3 to 39; robbery twentytwofold, from 13 to 264; and aggravated assault almost ninefold, from 24 to 201. The rate of firearm use, which has become increasingly associated with murderous and serious assaults, as well as with robbery, has similarly recorded a large upswing: nearly eightfold, from 14 to 108. In each arrest-rate sequence, the watershed year occurred in or shortly after 1960. The steep increase in robbery arrests captures most dramatically the profound transformations undergone by the municipality over the century and a quarter, making robbery in Philadelphia, as it is in other cities, the chief criminal stigmata of its urbanity.

Although the violence arrest patterns in the 1960s and 1970s were similar, in earlier years, from 1857 to 1923, the separate arrest rates behaved somewhat differently. Murder tended initially to fluctuate until the turn of the century, hovering between 2.5 and 5 (per 100,000 population), spiking up in the 1870s to its high point of about 6.5, and then subsiding to about

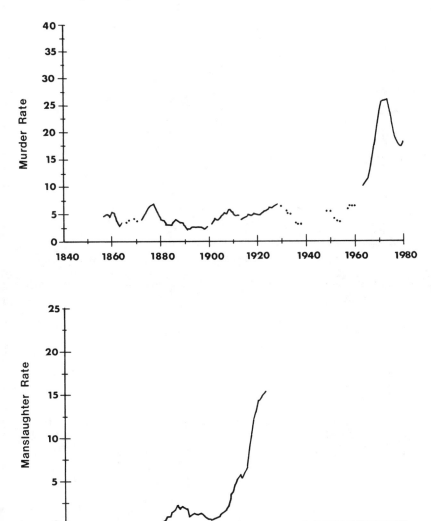

Figure 4.3: Philadelphia: Murder and Manslaughter Arrest Rates, 1857–1980
NOTE: Top figure shows murder arrest rates per 100,000 population (5-year
       moving averages); bottom figure shows manslaughter arrest rates per
       100,000 population (5-year moving averages)

2.5 by 1900; and turning up again over the first quarter of this century,
remaining in the vicinity of 5 (Figure 4.3, top panel). The robbery arrest
rate, on the other hand, fluctuated through 1890, then rose from about 10
in the 1890s to about 30 in the early 1920s (figure 4.5). Both rape and

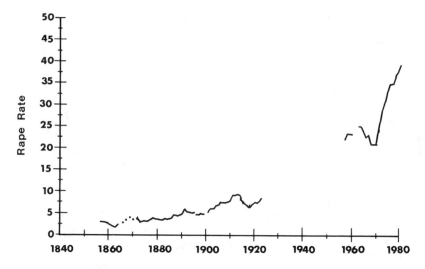

Figure 4.4: Philadelphia: Rape Arrest Rates per 100,000 Population, 1857–1980 (5-year moving averages)

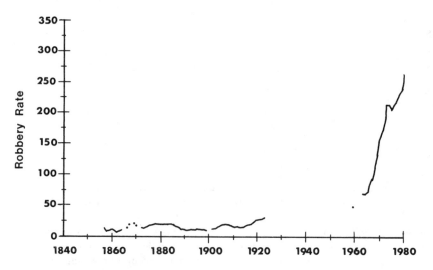

Figure 4.5: Philadelphia: Robbery Arrest Rates per 100,000 Population, 1857–1980 (5-year moving averages)

aggravated assault rose between 1857 and 1923, rape fourfold from about 2 to 8, and aggravated assault more than threefold from 17 to 62 (Figures 4.4, 4.6). The slight acceleration in the rape rate between 1900 and 1915 may reflect the political stirrings of the women's suffrage movement, encourag-

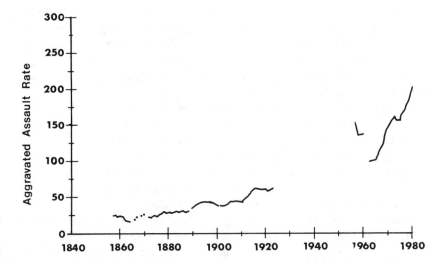

Figure 4.6: Philadelphia: Aggravated Assault Rates per 100,000 Population, 1857–1980 (5-year moving averages)

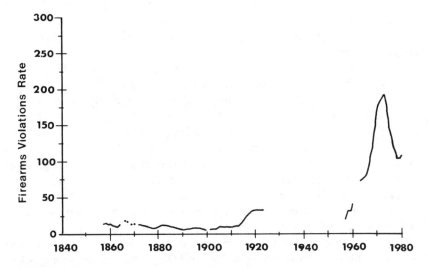

Figure 4.7: Philadelphia: Firearms Violations Arrest Rates per 100,000 Population, 1857–1980 (5-year moving averages)

ing less tolerance for and silence about sexual attacks. Aggravated assault displays a clear, persistent, almost fourfold rise from a low of about 17 in 1864 to a high of nearly 63 in 1916.

One of the more striking findings in these arrest series is the way murder and firearms violations have tracked each other since just after the turn of the century (Figures 4.3, 4.7). With few exceptions, when the firearms-violation rate went up, so too did the murder rate; when the firearms-violation rate went down, the murder rate also did so. Especially intriguing are the dramatic increases in these rates in the 1960s followed by just as dramatic drops in the early 1970s.

The parallel movements between the rates of murder and firearms violations observed after 1900 are not reflected prior to this year. We are uncertain why this discontinuity exists but speculate that since the turn of the century, firearms possession and use have increasingly expanded, which, in turn, has increasingly placed these weapons in settings that are emotionally volatile (such as familial disputes) and instrumentally explosive (such as robberies). Rising firearms violations may indicate more widespread firearms use and, unfortunately, widening occasions for their lethal misuse.

Just as striking as the parallel recent trends in the rates of murder and firearms violations is the overall discordance between the rates of murder and aggravated assault (compare Figures 4.3 and 4.6). If one views some murders as aggravated assaults that got fatally out of hand, then one would expect the two arrest series to exhibit some consistency. That they do not, except during the 1960s and early 1970s, when both rates rose rapidly, suggests either that this hypothesis is unsound or that the assault data are invalid because of biased reporting and recording of nonlethal assaults. If the latter, then there is a pressing need for more valid measures of grievous assaultive behavior.

The arrest-rate series for robbery and firearms violations (Figures 4.5 and 4.7) exhibit long-term concordance from 1857 through the early 1970s, over which time both rates rose irregularly. Subsequently, robbery rates continued to rise steeply, whereas firearms rates declined just as steeply. These findings are troubling. The concordance between the two time series occurred over a period when firearms were probably less often used to commit robberies; the discordance occurred over a period when firearms were probably more often used. Therefore, a weak substantive linkage obtains at precisely the same time as we observe a strong statistical association. Conversely, a strong substantive linkage obtains during a period when we observe a weak statistical association.

If it is so that robbery rates more accurately reflect, because of the gravity of this crime, underlying behavioral trends than most other types of unlawful activities, then the long-term parallel movements in the initial segments of the two time series should indicate a valid relationship, reinforced by the consistency observed in the putatively less valid firearms-violations series. If the early consistency is valid, then the later inconsistency should also be so. The divergence in more recent years may reflect changes that occurred in the city's firearms ordinances, a possibility requiring further investigation.

During the 1970s, the rates of rape, robbery, and aggravated assault all increased in the same steep fashion (Figures 4.4–4.6), which departs from the declines in murder and firearms violations noted above. Over the initial time span of 1857 to 1923, rape and aggravated assault increased in close parallel, indicating either that the same social groups were responsible for increasing sexual and nonsexual assault or that the public or officials viewed rape as primarily assaultive rather than sexual at that time. It is also possible that officials became increasingly likely to make arrests for both kinds of assaults that previously might have gone without complaint or official notice. Again, we are unable to explain definitively these complex consistencies and inconsistencies.

The Philadelphia violence arrest statistics also reflect some social and technological changes. For example, Lane, among others, has noted the effect in the first quarter of the twentieth century of the exponential growth in automobile use on the rate of criminal homicide.[24] Deaths resulting from careless driving and unwary pedestrians became increasingly objectionable, as had become accidental deaths from other causes before the turn of the century.[25] Not generally viewed as accidents but rather as crimes, vehicular fatalities began to populate increasingly the manslaughter tallies as automobile use skyrocketed. Figure 4.3 (bottom panel) exhibits the steeply climbing rate of manslaughter arrests over this period, which continued the clear earlier trend, beginning in 1880, of responding to certain accidental deaths as criminally liable incidents.

Including manslaughter with other homicides, which is done in some studies and tabulations, greatly inflates this rate from 1910 to 1920 (compare Figure 4.3A with 4.3B). The unsuspecting investigator might conclude that an epidemic of criminal violence had spread through Philadelphia from 1900 to 1920, resulting perhaps from the combined contagions of local organized gang warfare, the normative dislocations of contemporaneous Italian migration to the city, and the economic and social obstacles faced by black residents who were increasingly trying to enter the industrial workplace. In fact, the proliferation of poorly regulated and hazardous vehicles—along with other perilous new technologies—combined with modestly rising murderous attacks to swell the overall homicide rate.[26]

Note also that the murder rate (Figure 4.3, top panel) rose over two and one-half times during this period, from about 2.5 at the turn of the century to nearly 6.5 in 1930. The upward slope is likely a product of the combined influences identified above of local gang warfare, Italian and black migration to the city, and frustrated social and economic opportunities experienced by blacks. Evidence supports, then, the hypothesis of increasing murder rates in the decades following the turn of the century.

Changes in drug use and trafficking patterns in the 1960s and 1970s were related to the rising murder rate in Philadelphia.[27] Increased youth gang activity in Philadelphia during the 1960s may also have contributed to the

rising murder rate, motivating gang members to arm themselves for purposes of self-protection and, in the process, heightening the risks of lethal
confrontations. The decline in the murder rate after 1973 might have resulted to some extent from reductions in youth gang activities in response
to vigorous interventions and dispute mediations by gang-crisis units that
had been created by the city. Whether reductions in the levels of violent
gang activities were also responsible for reductions in firearms arrests, also
observed after 1973, is unclear. (The reduction in the rate of firearms
violations might also have followed on the heels of reduced police monitoring of gang members. Less supervision results in fewer occasions to stop
and search youngsters, which results, in turn, in fewer arrests.) We are
unable to determine whether reductions in the carrying and use of firearms
are directly related to the downward trend in the Philadelphia murder rate.

The Philadelphia Story: Summary and Conclusions

The Philadelphia data represent one of the longest time series on violent
urban crime in existence. The data show that, in the aggregate, violent
crime in the city first underwent a gentle rise from the early 1860s to the
early 1920s and then a very sharp and nearly continuous upswing from 1960
to 1980. However, patterns differed among the specific types of criminal
violence: Murder fluctuated from 1857 through 1940, rose steeply from
1960 to the early 1970s, and then rapidly declined. Rape and aggravated
assault rose during the second half of the nineteenth and the first quarter of
the twentieth centuries but behaved quite differently over the most recent
two decades—rape decreasing during the 1960s and then increasing sharply
during the 1970s, and aggravated assault rising almost invariably over this
same period. Robbery also rose through the early twentieth century, although more irregularly and gradually than rape and aggravated assault,
and then increased almost continuously from 1960 onward. These divergent patterns clearly suggest that violent crimes are not all of one cloth.
Understanding violent criminal behavior will require, therefore, some specific but integrated explanations.

Comparing the Philadelphia findings to those in other studies is not
straightforward. For example, the Philadelphia data are probably most
comparable to those of Boston reported by Ferdinand.[28] Both studies examine disaggregated violence arrest statistics for long overlapping periods.
Despite these similarities, comparative analysis is problematical. The arrest rate scales used in the two studies are not always the same; the numbers of years used to smooth the two time series are different; and, although the two studies overlap for substantial time periods, the Boston
data do not cover the most recent years. Despite these impediments, several comparisons nevertheless suggest themselves. First, in Boston, murder

and assault moved downward over the more than 100-year span of 1849 to 1951, whereas in Philadelphia, murder moved more irregularly and aggravated assault rose. Second, in both cities, rape rates rose, making this violent crime the only one that changed similarly in both locations. Third, between 1857 and 1923, robbery rates increased in the two cities, gradually in Philadelphia but later and more abruptly in Boston. Although the robbery rates rose during this early period, nonetheless they were lower than in later years.

These comparisons raise some intriguing research questions. Perhaps the foremost question, due to the gravity of the crime, pertains to murder: What forces operated to bend the Boston rates downward while those in Philadelphia were pushed irregularly upwards? Sorting out the causal dynamics will be central to the development of broad remedial strategies. Other striking consistencies and inconsistencies in violence arrest rates pose similar challenges for explanation and for public policy.

These data shed some additional light on the broader historical question of the U-shaped pattern in serious interpersonal violence in western societies. Using data from several western societies, beginning in thirteenth-century England, Gurr inferred a U-shaped curve for most serious violent crimes. We are unable to examine this issue fully in the American setting because we do not have city data for most of the centuries represented by the initial, declining portion of the U-curve. The data that we do have, which pertain to the central and rightmost portion of the U-curve (its J-curve segment), suggest that this configuration best depicts the Philadelphia robbery rate, which exhibited a stationary rate through 1900, a gentle rise in the early twentieth century, and then a sharp, almost continuous rise beginning in the 1960s. The other violent crimes either rose in the initial period extending from 1857 to 1923 (for example, rape and aggravated assault), which is inconsistent with the flat central portion of the U-curve trajectory, or, if they remained relatively stable in the initial period, rapidly rose and then just as rapidly dropped in the two most recent decades (for example, murder and firearms violations), which again is inconsistent with the continuously rising final portion of the U-curve. The U-curve formulation does not appear, then, to be entirely consistent with the Philadelphia experience. However, the inconsistencies are not strong enough to compel rejection of the U-curve thesis. Modification is called for rather than rejection.

Future studies will need to investigate the reasons for the inconsistencies among the various types of violent crimes and their respective departures from the U-shaped curve. A productive way to begin these analyses will be to examine the differential impacts of modernity—industrialization, urbanization, ethnic migration, and the embracement of humanistic ethics—on each type of violent behavior. These analyses will surely help to provide greater closure to the Philadelphia story and to those of other American cities.

120   VIOLENCE IN AMERICA

Notes

1. Richard Hofstadter and Michael Wallace, eds., *American Violence: A Documentary History* (New York: Vintage Books, 1971), 3.

2. President's Commission on Law Enforcement and Administration of Justice (Katzenbach Commission), *The Challenge of Crime in a Free Society; Final Report* (Washington, DC: U.S. Government Printing Office, 1967).

3. National Advisory Commission on Civil Disorders (Kerner Commission) (Washington, DC: U.S. Government Printing Office, 1968).

4. National Commission on the Causes and Prevention of Violence, *To Establish Justice, To Ensure Domestic Tranquility; Final Report* (Washington, DC: U.S. Government Printing Office, 1969).

5. Roger Lane, "Crime and Criminal Statistics in Nineteenth-Century Massachusetts," *Journal of Social History* 2 (1968): 156–63; *Violent Death in the City: Suicide, Accident, and Murder in 19th Century Philadelphia* (Cambridge, MA: Harvard University Press, 1979); "Urban Police and Violence in Nineteenth Century America," in Norval Morris and Michael Tonry, eds., *Crime and Justice: An Annual Review of Research,* Vol. 2 (Chicago: University of Chicago Press, 1980); *Roots of Violence in Black Philadelphia* (Cambridge, MA: Harvard University Press, 1986).

6. Timothy J. Naylor, "Crime, Criminals and Punishment in Philadelphia, 1860–1916," Ph.D. diss., University of Chicago, 1979.

7. Ted Robert Gurr, "Crime Trends in Modern Democracies Since 1945," *International Annals of Criminology* 16 (1977): 41–85; "On the History of Violent Crime in Europe and America," in Hugh Davis Graham and Ted Robert Gurr, eds., *Violence in America: Historical and Comparative Perspectives*, rev. ed. (Beverly Hills, CA: Sage, 1979); "Development and Decay: Their Impact on Public Order," in James A. Inciardi and Charles E. Faupel, eds., *History and Crime: Implications for Public Policy* (Beverly Hills, CA: Sage, 1980); "Historical Trends in Violent Crime: A Critical Review of the Evidence," in Norval Morris and Michael Tonry, eds., *Crime and Justice: An Annual Review of Research,* Vol. 3 (Chicago: University of Chicago Press, 1985).

8. Lane, *Violent Death in the City* and *Roots of Violence.*

9. Eric H. Monkkonen, *Police in Urban America 1860–1920* (Cambridge: Cambridge University Press, 1981), 65–86.

10. Theodore N. Ferdinand, "The Criminal Patterns of Boston Since 1849," *American Journal of Sociology* 73 (1967): 677–98.

11. Elwin H. Powell, "Crime as a Function of Anomie," *The Journal of Criminal Law, Criminology, and Police Science* 57 (1966): 161–71.

12. Arrest data were obtained from the *Annual Philadelphia Mayor's Reports* published in the years 1858–65, 1867–68, 1870–71, 1873–1900, 1902–24, 1927–29, 1931, 1933–35, 1937–39, 1949, 1951, 1953–55, and 1958–60. Especially thin are the arrest statistics other than for murder. Because reporting of these other violent crime statistics is so erratic between 1924 and 1959, we eliminated these years from our analyses of manslaughter, rape, robbery, aggravated assault, and firearms violations.

13. U. S. Department of Justice, Federal Bureau of Investigation, Philadelphia City Arrest Tabulation for 1960, 1963–80 (untitled). (Washington, DC: U.S. Department of Justice, FBI, prepared for this study).

14. U.S. Bureau of the Census, "Census of Population, 1, Characteristics of the Population, part a, Number of Inhabitants" (Washington DC: U.S. Government Printing Office, 1961); "Census of Population, 1970: Detailed Characteristics; Final Report PC(1)-D-40, Pennsylvania" (Washington, DC: U.S. Government Printing Office, 1972); "General Population Characteristics: Pennsylvania, PC80-1-B40" (Washington, DC: U.S. Government Printing Office, 1981). Annual population figures were estimated through linear interpolation for inter-decennial years in order to calculate the annual arrest rates.

15. Gurr, "Historical Trends in Violent Crime," and Lane, *Violent Death in the City.*
16. Lane, *Violent Death in the City.*
17. We used 5-year arrest averages rather than 7-year averages in order to be consistent with the 5-year curve smoothing procedure adopted for the graphs that are used in the text.
18. A ratio that is equal to 1 indicates perfect stability in the rates across the two time periods. A ratio of less than 1 indicates a drop in the rate. Conversely, a ratio of greater than 1 indicates a rise in the rate.
19. Lane, *Violent Death in the City,* 71.
20. See Roger Lane, chap. 2 in this volume.
21. Total arrests comprise the sum of all arrest types listed for the year in the *Annual Mayor's Reports.* Violence arrests include murder, rape, robbery, and aggravated assault.
22. Motor vehicle theft was excluded because this crime did not occur prior to the invention and marketing of these vehicles.
23. Although this aggregate group approximates the *UCR* "Index Crimes," which is commonly considered to consist of serious crimes, clearly some are not very serious, especially petty larcenies. Despite the fact that less serious crimes like petty larceny are often not reported and, thus, do not result in an arrest, thereby impairing the validity of arrest statistics based on these crimes, we decided to include larcenies in the aggregate group for two reasons: (1) in order to provide a definition that coincides with contemporary criminological usage and, (2) because few crimes other than the most serious violent ones are immune to the impairments and validity resulting from under-reporting. The index crimes provide, then, a base against which to judge the changing proportion over time of the violent subset.
24. Lane in this volume, and Ferdinand, "Criminal Patterns."
25. Lane, *Violent Death in the City.*
26. Lane, ibid. and *Roots of Violence.*
27. Margaret A. Zahn and Mark Bencivengo, "Violent Death: A Comparison Between Drug Users and Non-Drug Users," *Addictive Diseases: An International Journal* 1 (1974): 283–96; Margaret A. Zahn and Glenn Snodgrass, "The Structure of Homicide in Two American Cities," in Edith Flynn and John Conrad, eds., *The New and The Old Criminology* (New York: Praeger, 1978), 134–50.
28. Ferdinand, "Criminal Patterns."

Chapter 5

Violence and Lawlessness on the Western Frontier

ROGER D. McGRATH

Dave Bannon was a good boy who had gone bad.[1] He had once been described as a quiet, industrious young man, but periods of unemployment left him spending ever more time in saloons where he passed the hours gambling, drinking, and fighting. On the Friday afternoon of January 21, 1881, he reeled drunkenly into the Dividend Saloon, one of nearly fifty that the mining town of Bodie boasted, and found several of his friends at the bar. One of them was Ed Ryan, a Civil War veteran who had made his living as a professional gambler since the war's end. In what was termed a playful gesture, Ryan grabbed Bannon by the lapel of his coat. The lapel tore. Bannon, already in a black mood, exploded with anger and punched Ryan in the face. Ryan stumbled backwards but regained his balance and told Bannon that there was no reason to take offense.

"You damn son of a bitch," Bannon replied. "You've fooled with me long enough. You tore my coat once before." Without waiting for a response Bannon punched Ryan again and pulled out a British Bulldog revolver. Holding the gun in his right hand, Bannon threw several more blows at Ryan with his left.

Officer James Monahan spotted the commotion from the sidewalk in front of the Dividend and rushed inside. He grabbed hold of Bannon and tried to pull him away from Ryan. Monahan's sudden involvement gave Ryan the opportunity to pull a sawed-off Colt revolver out of his back pocket. A split-second later Bannon broke loose from Monahan's grip and lunged at Ryan. The two men fell together, grappling, punching, and shooting.

The vicious struggle continued for nearly a minute before Bannon and Ryan separated and staggered off in opposite directions. Ryan fell against the swinging doors of the Dividend's entrance and tumbled onto the sidewalk. Blood dripped from a wound in his left hand and oozed from a hole in his side. Bannon stumbled through the swinging doors that led to the saloon's cardroom and dropped unconscious to the floor. A bullet hole in his lung and a round lodged in his neck caused blood to gush from his mouth and nose. His breath came in labored gasps. Fifteen minutes later he was dead. Ryan, meanwhile, drifted in and out of consciousness and hovered near death. He continued in such a state for days before he slowly began to recover.

It is popularly assumed that the frontier was full of Bannons and Ryans—brave, strong, reckless, and violent men—and that they helped make the frontier a violent and lawless place. The first assumption is correct; the second is mostly wrong.

Aurora and Bodie

A look at two frontier mining towns—Aurora, Nevada, and Bodie, California—illustrates these points.[2] The towns were home to Bannons and Ryans aplenty and saw a considerable number of homicides but they were remarkably free from most crime: robbery, theft, and burglary occurred infrequently and bank robbery, rape, racial violence, and serious juvenile crime seem not to have occurred at all. While the homicide rate was high, the killings were almost always the result of fights between willing combatants. Thus, in Aurora and Bodie, the old, the young, the unwilling, the weak, and the female were, for the most part, safe from harm. If, as many popularly assume, much of America's crime problem is a consequence of a heritage of frontier violence and lawlessness, then it is ironic that the crimes most common today—robbery, burglary, theft, and rape—were of no great significance and, in the case of rape, seemingly nonexistent in Aurora and Bodie.

Located high in the mountains of the trans-Sierra country—a region of rugged mountains and high deserts immediately east of the Sierra Nevada—Aurora and Bodie were two of the most spectacular mining towns of the Old West. They had widespread reputations for violence, boasted populations of more than five thousand, and produced gold and silver bullion worth a billion dollars in today's money. Aurora boomed during the early 1860s and reflected the divisions created by the Civil War. Bodie had its heyday in the late 1870s and early 1880s and was, as one prospector later called it, the last of the old-time mining camps. The trans-Sierra itself was one of America's last frontiers, not thoroughly explored, mapped, settled, and politically organized until the 1880s.

Aurora and Bodie were typical frontier mining towns. They each experienced a spectacular boom period of a few years, followed by a year or so of decline, then bust. The towns were alive twenty-four hours a day, contained dozens of saloons and brothels, and had disproportionately high numbers of young, single males. Women were outnumbered ten to one by men. Much of the population was transient, with men arriving or departing daily.

The population was anything but homogeneous, and half of it was foreign born. In Bodie in 1880 there were some 5,400 people: approximately 850 of them had been born in Ireland, 750 in Canada, 550 in England and Wales, 350 in China, 250 in Germany, 120 in Scotland, 100 in Mexico, 80 in France, 60 in Sweden or Norway, and so on.[3] The towns were distinctly cosmopolitan. Different languages, nationalities, races and religions all met in Aurora and Bodie. The men were adventurous, enterprising, brave, young, single, intemperate, and armed. A few had struck it rich; most had not. Gold and silver worth millions was gouged out of the hillsides. It all should have added up to a reign of terror, but it didn't. A look at robbery, burglary, theft, rape, and homicide in Aurora and Bodie is revealing.

Robbery occurred only infrequently.[4] When it did occur the stagecoach was as likely to be robbed as was the individual citizen. There were eleven robberies and three attempted robberies of stages during Bodie's boom years and a nearly equal number during Aurora's heyday. During the same periods there were ten robberies and three attempted robberies of individual citizens in Bodie and a somewhat smaller number in Aurora. When highwaymen stopped a stagecoach, they normally took only the express box and left the passengers with their possessions intact. Passengers frequently remarked that they had been treated courteously by the highwaymen. Only twice were passengers robbed. In the first instance the highwaymen later apologized for their conduct, and in the second the road agents were drunk. Highwaymen seemed to understand that they could take the express box without arousing the general populace, but if they began robbing passengers they would possibly precipitate a vigilante reaction.

Occasionally the stagecoaches carried bullion shipments to the outside world. These shipments were often of great value: some of them would be worth $5 or $10 million in today's dollars. Yet, not one of the bullion stages was ever attacked by highwaymen. The reason is obvious. The bullion stages, unlike the regular stages, were always guarded by two or three or more rifle and shotgun toting guards. Highwaymen preferred to prey on unguarded coaches, take whatever was in the express box, and escape with their health intact. Only once did highwaymen and guards exchange gunfire—a highwayman was killed and a guard wounded—and in that case the highwaymen had not expected to encounter any guards.

Fear of arrest could not have served as much of a deterrent to stage robbery. Only three road agents were ever apprehended, and just two of them were convicted of robbery.

Although bank holdups are probably the form of robbery, after stagecoach holdups, most popularly associated with the frontier West, none of the several banks that operated in Aurora and Bodie ever experienced a robbery attempt. Bankers went about armed, as did their employees, and robbers, like the highwaymen who avoided the guarded bullion stages, evidently were not willing to tangle with armed men.

Individual private citizens in Bodie and Aurora very rarely suffered from robbery. There were only ten robberies and three attempted robberies of individuals—other than those robbed as part of a stage holdup—in Bodie during its boom years, and there seem to have been even fewer in Aurora during its heyday. In nearly every one of these robberies the circumstances were so similar as to be interchangeable: The robbery victim had spent the evening in a gambling den, saloon, or brothel; he had revealed in some way that he had on his person a tidy sum of money; and he was drunk, staggering toward home late at night when the attack occurred.

More robberies might have occurred if Aurorans and Bodieites had not gone about armed and ready to fight. They were, unless staggering drunk, simply too dangerous to rob. Robbers occasionally made mistakes though. Late one night when a robber told miner C.F. Reid to throw up his hands, Reid said "all right" and began raising them.[5] As he did so he suddenly drew a foot-long bowie knife from an inside coat pocket and drove the steel blade into the robber's shoulder. The robber screamed with pain and took off running "like a deer." Reid gave chase but soon lost sight of the man. Nonetheless, Reid was satisfied, feeling certain he had "cut the man to the bone." Sober, armed men were not to be trifled with.

The few robberies and attempted robberies of individuals, unlike the stage holdups, outraged the citizens and provoked talk of vigilantism.[6] "This business of garroting," as the *Bodie Standard* termed mugging and robbery, "is getting a little too common. The parties engaged in it may wake up one of these fine mornings and find themselves hanging to the top of a liberty pole." Another Bodie newspaper, the *Daily Free Press*, later called for the formation of a vigilance committee, arguing that one or two examples of vigilante justice was usually "sufficient to purify" a mining camp.

Rates of Larcenous Crime

Yet Bodie actually suffered little from robbery. Altogether Bodie experienced only 21 robberies—11 of stages and 10 of individuals—during its boom years. Conversion of this data to the Federal Bureau of Investigation crime index gives Bodie a rate of 84 robberies per 100,000 inhabitants per year.[7] By contrast Detroit led major U.S. cities in 1986 with a robbery rate of 1,497, closely followed by Miami's 1,456.[8] Highland Park, Michigan, easily surpassed all of the major cities with a startling 2,212.[9] On the other hand, Appleton, Wisconsin, a town with crime rates consistently at or near the bottom of the scale, had a robbery rate of 6.4.[10] The rate for the United States as a whole, including small towns and rural areas, was 225.[11] Thus

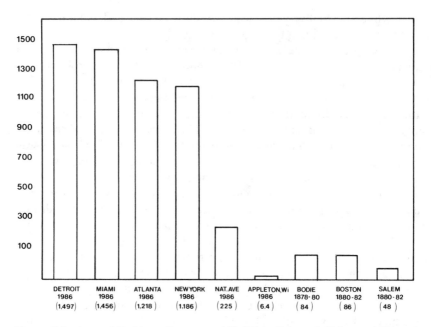

Figure 5.1: Annual Robbery Rates per 100,000 in Selected Cities, c. 1880 and 1986

Bodie, even with its stagecoach robberies included, had a robbery rate just slightly more than one-third of the national rate in 1986 and only a tiny fraction of the rates of the major cities.

Comparison of robbery (or most other crimes) in Bodie directly with robbery in Eastern towns during the nineteenth century demands some extrapolation. All crime studies of eastern towns during that period are based on numbers of arrests and not on number of offenses.[12] Since numbers of offenses, except in the categories of murder and manslaughter, are many times greater than numbers of arrests, conversion factors must be used. For example, according to FBI data in 1986 nearly four robberies (3.72 to be precise) were committed for every one arrest.[13] This ratio (and those for other crimes) has varied only slightly over the last couple of decades and probably was not greatly different during the late nineteenth century.

Theodore N. Ferdinand has found that during the years 1880 through 1882 Boston had a robbery arrest rate of 23, and Salem a 13.[14] Using the conversion factor for robbery of 3.72 gives Boston a robbery rate of 86 and Salem 48.

It would appear then that Boston and Salem had robbery rates—considering the extrapolation involved—roughly comparable to Bodie's.

However, since stagecoach robberies accounted for about half of Bodie's robberies, it would seem that the individual citizen was more likely to be robbed in long-settled Boston or Salem than in frontier Bodie.

Burglary, like robbery, was an infrequent event in Bodie.[15] Between 1877 and 1883 there were only 32 burglaries, 17 of homes and 15 of businesses. Aurora seems to have had fewer still. Bodie's boom years total of 32 burglaries gives the town an average of 6.4 burglaries a year and a burglary rate of 128. In 1986 the neighboring Texas towns of Fort Worth and Dallas led major U.S. cities with burglary rates of 4,458 and 3,711, but Benton Harbor, Michigan, surpassed them with a rate of 5,285.[16] Even Appleton's rate of 754, while only slightly more than half of the national rate of 1,345, is nearly six times greater than Bodie's 128.[17]

From 1880 through 1882 Boston had a burglary arrest rate of 87 and Salem 54.[18] Using a conversion factor of 7.2—a figure consistent with the ratio of offenses to arrests for burglary—gives Boston a burglary rate of 626 and Salem a 389, rates three to five times greater than that for Bodie.

An obvious factor in discouraging burglary in Bodie was the armed homeowner or armed merchant. No fewer than a half-dozen burglaries in Bodie were thwarted by the presence of armed citizens. When two burglars attempted to enter J.H. Vincent's house, for example, Vincent grabbed a gun and sent them running. Applauding Vincent's response to the would-be burglars the *Bodie Morning News* said: "Our people must be on their guard for this class of gentry, and if possible, when they call, treat them to a good dose of lead." The *Bodie Morning News* was not alone: All of Bodie's newspapers regularly advocated shooting burglars on sight.[19] Moreover, even when not armed, citizens were ready and willing to fight intruders. Harry Bryan, for instance, grappled with a burglar who had broken into his cabin, wrested a knife and a hatchet away from the man, and put him to flight.[20]

Theft was more common than robbery or burglary in Aurora and Bodie but still of infrequent occurrence.[21] Bodie recorded some 45 instances of theft, and Aurora somewhat fewer. Since both towns were nestled in mountain valleys at elevations of 8,400 and 7,500 respectively, it is not surprising to find that firewood and blankets were the items most commonly stolen. Of Bodie's 45 instances of theft only six involved horses. Just two horse thieves were caught, and they were punished far less severely than has been traditionally supposed: one was sentenced to serve six months in the county jail, and the other a year in the state penitentiary. Although thousands of head of cattle grazed to the west of Bodie and Aurora in the Bridgeport Valley and to the south in the Owens Valley, cattle rustling, except for Indian thefts during the Owens Valley warfare of the 1860s, seems not to have occurred.

Forty-five instances of theft during its boom years gives Bodie a theft rate of 180. In 1986 Seattle had a theft rate of 8,308, followed closely by

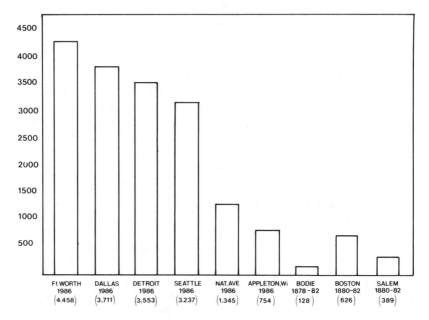

Ft WORTH 1986 (4.458)	DALLAS 1986 (3,711)	DETROIT 1986 (3,553)	SEATTLE 1986 (3.237)	NAT.AVE 1986 (1.345)	APPLETON,Wi 1986 (754)	BODIE 1878-82 (128)	BOSTON 1880-82 (626)	SALEM 1880-82 (389)

Figure 5.2: Annual Burglary Rates per 100,000 in Selected Cities, c. 1880 and 1986

Fort Worth 8,179, and Dallas 7,946.[22] Appleton's theft rate was 2,915, slightly below the national rate of 3,010, and sixteen times greater than Bodie's 180.[23]

Boston's theft arrest rate for 1880 through 1882 was 575; Salem's 525.[24] A conversion factor of 5.2—a factor consistent with the ratio of offenses to arrests for theft—gives Boston a theft rate of 2,990 and Salem 2,730.

Quite clearly, then, Bodie's rates of robbery, burglary, and theft were dramatically lower than those of major U.S. cities in 1986 and were as low as or significantly lower than those for Boston and Salem from 1880 through 1882. The small, midwestern town of Appleton, Wisconsin, could claim only a lower rate of robbery than Bodie. Even if four or five times as much robbery, burglary, and theft occurred in Bodie but went unreported in the newspapers and unrecorded in the jail registers and court records— an unlikely supposition—Bodie would still have rates dramatically lower than those for major U.S. cities in 1986. Using the same hypothetical factor of error when comparing Bodie with Boston and Salem would still leave Bodie with a theft rate several times lower and a burglary rate about equal. Only Bodie's robbery rate would be higher. However, of the three crimes, robbery would be the least likely to go unreported, especially stagecoach holdups which accounted for half of Bodie's robberies. Moreover, if it is true that a portion of Bodie's larcenous crime went unreported, then the same undoubtedly holds true for nineteenth-century Boston and Salem, and for U.S. cities today.

The available evidence suggests that Aurora had even lower rates of robbery, burglary, and theft than Bodie. Such a conclusion, though, must remain speculative because of the intermittent gaps in the newspaper file and incomplete nature of other primary source material for Aurora. (The sources for the town are certainly complete enough to paint a nearly full picture of life there but not for a compilation of statistical data.)

Deterrents to Larcenous Crime

Such low rates of robbery, burglary, and theft cannot be attributed to swift and certain justice meted out by the criminal justice system in Aurora or Bodie. Rarely were any robbers, burglars, or thieves even arrested. Law officers often had a rather casual approach to their job, and some operated on both sides of the law: a gang leader and several of his men served as officers for a time in Aurora, and several Bodie officers may have cooperated with robbers. On the rare occasions when a suspect actually was arrested, chances were good that, if prosecuted, he would not be convicted. Since so few men were convicted, it hardly seems possible that the normal punishment that followed—imprisonment in jail or the penitentiary—could have served as much of a deterrent.

There seems to be little question that the principal deterrent to robbery, burglary, and theft in Bodie and Aurora was the armed citizenry. Not only were the citizens armed but often they had professional training and experience in the use of firearms. Many of the residents of Aurora had fought in the Mexican War and those of Bodie in the Civil War. This was especially true of the Irish-born residents who had arrived in the United States just in time, and in such a condition, to make them likely candidates for service in the wars. Thus the citizens had arms, knew how to use them, and were willing to fight with deadly force to protect their persons or property.

Three other factors may also have worked as deterrents: full or near-full employment, religion, and a collective sense of optimism.

Aurora and Bodie usually could count on full or near-full employment during their boom years, although there were periods, especially in Bodie, when the closing of a mine or the suspension of operations caused some unemployment. The slightly greater amount of larcenous crime reported in Bodie might be explained by the larger number of Bodieites who suffered periodic unemployment.

Religion's role as a deterrent is even more speculative than that of employment. Nonetheless, most Aurorans and Bodieites had been reared with the religion of one Christian denomination or another and the values and morality of the Christian tradition must have exerted at least some influence on them. Regular church services were held by a half-dozen denominations in Aurora and in Bodie. Two churches were actually built in Bodie: a Catholic church, St. John the Baptist, on Wood Street, and a Methodist church on Fuller Street. However, since it was not until the fifth year of Bodie's boom that the churches were erected and then it was the women of Bodie who sponsored the fund-raisers for construction, it would seem that the mostly young, single, and male Bodieites considered the building projects something less than a top priority.

Perhaps the most important deterrent to larcenous crime, but also the most intangible and therefore the most difficult to evaluate, was the optimistic attitude of Aurorans and Bodieites. They had hope. They had hope of a better future, of a big strike, of new adventures. While men have hope, no matter what their present circumstances, they are probably less likely to resort to crime.

It is difficult to find a contemporary example for the comparison of deterrent factors with Aurora or Bodie, although Kennesaw, Georgia, might be similar in one sense: the percentage of its citizens who are armed. In 1982 the town council of Kennesaw unanimously passed an ordinance requiring nearly every "head of household" in the town to maintain a firearm and a supply of ammunition. Since enactment of the ordinance, according to police statistics, robbery, burglary, and theft have declined. Home burglary, for example, has declined from 55 incidents in 1981, the year before the ordinance was adopted, to 26 in 1982, to only 11 in 1985. Kennesaw mayor J.O. Stephenson, who carries a snub-nosed .38 caliber revolver himself, points to those statistics as evidence that more guns in the hands of law-abiding citizens means less crime. "We took a stand for guns," said mayor Stephenson in April of 1987, "and we're proud of it."[25]

Actually, since most residents of Kennesaw were gun owners before the enactment of the ordinance (and this may partly explain Kennesaw's traditionally low rate of robbery and burglary), it would seem that the decline was more the result of publicity over the ordinance rather than an increase in gun ownership. Criminals must have become fully aware that Kennesaw was no soft target: that they ran the frightful risk of being shot and perhaps killed if they plied their trade there. The same conditions prevailed in Aurora and Bodie.

Several national surveys over the last ten years have indicated that armed citizens have used guns to halt an enormous number of would-be robberies, assaults, and burglaries: over 500,000 a year on the average.[26] A few states have adopted laws which protect from prosecution homeowners who use force to defend their home against intruders. Upon passage of such a law in Colorado, a local state legislator said, "We're sending a message that if you [illegally] enter a home, you stand a good chance of getting your head blown off." Another added, "Sometimes blowing dirt balls away is the reasonable thing to do." A third facetiously proposed an annual "bag limit" of ten intruders. Such statements, of course, express an attitude toward burglars identical to that expressed by Aurorans and Bodieites. Since the "Your Home Is Your Castle" or "Make My Day" laws, as they have been called, are all of recent vintage it will be some time before their effects can be evaluated.[27]

Women and Crime on the Frontier

The women residents of Aurora and Bodie, with the exception of those who were prostitutes, rarely suffered from any kind of crime or violence.[28] During Bodie's boom years there were only some 30 violent encounters between men and women, and prostitutes were involved in 25 of the incidents. When women assaulted or fought with other women, prostitutes accounted for 13 of the 17 recorded incidents. Very few of these violent encounters had serious consequences. Only one woman died as the result of an attack—in that case the woman was a former prostitute and her murderer was insane—and only one other was seriously injured.

Prostitutes unquestionably bore the brunt of the little violence against women that did occur. While "decent" women were treated with the greatest deference, prostitutes were socially ostracized and generally shown little respect. Newspapers often treated the punching or slapping of a prostitute humorously, and the attitude of police and judges was only slightly better. Men who assaulted prostitutes were usually arrested for their attacks, but their punishments were far less severe than if they had assaulted "respectable" women. The double standard extended even to the graveyard. Prostitutes who died in Bodie were buried outside the fence of the graveyard. Prostitutes were both figuratively and literally outside the pale.

Nonetheless, even prostitutes do not seem to have been the victims of rape. There were no reported cases of rape in either Aurora or Bodie. Admittedly, rape might have occurred but was not reported. Rape is a crime that has often gone unreported in the past and even today rape victims are often reluctant to report an attack. However, in Bodie there were two reports of attempted rape (in neither case was the allegation substantiated) and this possibly indicates that had rape occurred it would have been reported. Moreover, there is absolutely no evidence of any sort that rape occurred but escaped the attention of the authorities.

On the other hand, there is a considerable body of evidence which indicates that women, other than prostitutes, were rarely the victims of any kind of offense and were treated with the utmost respect. Women enjoyed special status, partly because of the morality of the nineteenth century and partly because they were a rare commodity in western mining towns. Grant Smith, a one-time resident of Bodie, recalled:

132

One of the remarkable things about Bodie, in fact, one of the striking features of all mining camps in the West, was the respect shown even by the worst characters to the decent women. . . . I do not recall ever hearing of a respectable woman or girl in any manner insulted or even accosted by the hundreds of dissolute characters that were everywhere. In part, this was due to the respect that depravity pays to decency; in part, to the knowledge that sudden death would follow any other course.[29]

Smith's warning of "sudden death" may seem like an exaggeration. Nevertheless, there is an example of a Bodieite who was sentenced to 30 days in jail merely for swearing while in the presence of women.[30]

Bodie women did not necessarily depend on men for defense against an attack. There were several instances of prostitutes or brothel madames grabbing guns and putting unruly, drunken customers to flight.[31] Prostitutes were not the only gun-totting women in Bodie. When a dispute arose between a man and a woman over the ownership of a portion of a city lot, the woman, believing herself to be the rightful owner, ordered the man off the property. However, as the *Bodie Standard* put it, since "he was a large man and she was a small lady, he concluded to tarry yet a while." The small lady quickly tired of the standoff, though. She pulled out a six-shooter, took dead aim at the man, and again ordered him to leave. This time he did, and in a hurry.[32]

Women in Bodie (and Aurora too), then, were generally well treated and quite capable, if armed, of defending themselves on the rare occasions when the need arose. Moreover, they do not seem to have suffered rape. Bodie's record of no rape leaves it with a rape rate of zero. In 1986 Atlanta led major U.S. cities with a rape rate of 152.8.[33] Atlanta, though, was topped by Benton Harbor, Michigan, which recorded an astounding rape rate of 295.9, Highland Park, Michigan, with a nearly equally astounding 237.7, and Compton, California 167.7.[34] Appleton had a rate of 8.0, well below the national rate of 37.5[35] From 1880 through 1882 Boston had a rape arrest rate of 3.0 and Salem 4.8.[36] A conversion factor of 2.4—a figure consistent with FBI data in 1986—gives the towns rape rates of 7.2 and 11.5.

Homicide

Aurora and Bodie clearly were not dens of criminal activity, and women residents of the towns were far safer than their counterparts are today in any American city. Nonetheless, when it came to men fighting men, Aurora and Bodie were unquestionably violent.[37] Men fought men with fists, knives, and guns, and they often fought to the death. They occasionally fought over women or mining property, or even politics. But mostly they fought over who was the better man, real or imagined insults, and challenges to pecking order in the saloon. The men involved in the fights were willing—often very willing—participants. Some of them were professionals, hired as gunmen for mining companies. Others were simply miners, teamsters, bartenders, carpenters, woodchoppers, and the like. The men were mostly young and single, and adventurous and brave. The combination, sometimes laced with alcohol, led often to displays of reckless bravado and not infrequently to death.

Thirty-one Bodieites and at least 17 Aurorans were victims of homicide during the towns' boom years. The count for Aurora could be considerably higher—in fact, equal Bodie's—if the grand jury in Aurora can be believed. In March 1864 the jury asserted that "within the last three years some 27 of our citizens have come to their death by the hand of violence."[38] Since four men were homicide victims in Aurora after the jury made its claim, it is possible that Aurora had a total of 31. Nevertheless, only 17 homicides can be verified by the extant historical sources (other than the grand jury's report), and Aurora newspapers at the time thought the jury's figure high.

The large majority of the homicides in Bodie and Aurora would be recorded today in the FBI's crime category of murder and nonnegligent (willful as opposed to accidental) manslaughter.[39] Probably 29 of Bodie's 31 killings, and 16 of Aurora's 17, qualify for such categorization.[40] (It should be noted that most of these killings fall into the nonnegligent manslaughter portion of the category since they were killings in self defense.) Counting 29 homicides for Bodie gives the town a murder and nonnegligent manslaughter rate of 116; counting 16 for Aurora gives it a rate of 64. In 1986 Detroit led major U.S. cities, though not Bodie or Aurora, with a rate of 59.1.[41] Following Detroit were Fort Worth, 46.3, and St. Louis, 44.9.[42] A number of smaller towns scored rates that surpassed Aurora, if not Bodie. Opa Locka, Florida, had a rate of 88.5, Highland Park, Michigan, 84.4, East St. Louis, Illinois, 75.1, and Compton, California, 66.0[43] Near the other end of the scale was Appleton with a rate of 4.8, slightly more than half the national rate of 8.6.[44]

Nineteenth-century Eastern cities had rates similar to Appleton's. From 1880 through 1882 Boston had a murder and manslaughter (Boston police did not consistently distinguish between negligent and nonnegligent manslaughter) arrest rate of only 3.8, while Salem recorded a 0.0.[45] Since numbers of arrests usually almost equal numbers of offenses in cases of murder and manslaughter, there was probably no significant difference between Boston's and Salem's rates of arrests and rates of offenses.[46] Roger Lane has found that from 1874 through 1880 Philadelphia had a homicide rate of 3.7, and its overall rate for the second half of the nineteenth century was 3.0.[47] Since Lane bases his homicide rate on numbers of indictments for homicide and not on numbers of homicides, the actual rates

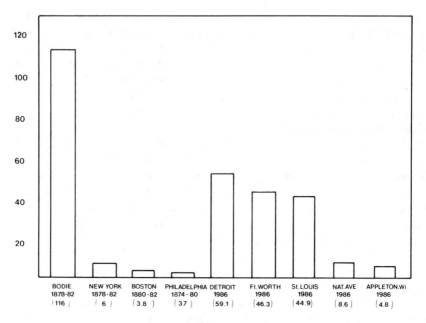

Figure 5.3: Annual Homicide Rates per 100,000 in Selected Cities, c. 1880 and 1986

were probably higher—perhaps double or triple if Bodie is any guide. Still, at worst Philadelphia would only have had a rate of 10 or thereabouts during the 1870s. Eric Monkkonen's investigations of New York City during the 1850s and 1860s reveal a homicide rate ranging from a low of about 4 to a high of approximately 10.[48]

If contemporary Eastern towns did not begin to approach Aurora's and Bodie's high rates of homicide, other Western towns and counties did. Virginia City had 8 homicides during the year and a half following its founding in 1859.[49] In 1876, the year of its birth, Deadwood had 4 homicides.[50] Ellsworth, one of the Kansas cattle towns, had 8 homicides during the twelve months following its establishment in 1867, and Dodge City, the queen of the cattle towns, had 9 in its first year, 1872–1873.[51] Since the populations of all these towns during their first year or two of life were small, not more than two or three thousand, their homicide rates were very high indeed.

Robert R. Dykstra in his study of the Kansas cattle towns, though, compiled data which revealed that an average of just 1.5 homicides occurred per town per cattle-trading season.[52] This would seem to suggest a low homicide rate. However, an average of 1.5 homicides a year is quite high when the sizes of the towns are considered. Dodge City, for example, never had a population of much more than 3,000. Using Dykstra's 1.5 figure gives Dodge City a homicide rate of 50, a rate exceeded by only a handful of cities today. More important, though, is Dykstra's self-imposed limit of not counting homicides for the cattle towns until, as he put it, "the first full shipping season in which each town existed as a municipality." Thus many of the towns' homicides do not figure in Dykstra's data because all of the towns had been established a year or two or more before they had a full cattle-shipping season. Dodge City's nine homicides (some report 12, and one resident claimed 15) in its first year are not counted by Dykstra nor are any other homicides which occurred in Dodge City before 1876. Factoring in these homicides would push Dodge City's homicide rate into Bodie's range.

Thus those who have pointed to Dykstra's study as proof that the numbers of shootings and shootouts in the frontier West have been greatly exaggerated might reconsider their evidence. This is not to criticize Dykstra, who was concerned with the effect of the cattle trade on the towns and therefore found pre-cattle trade homicides irrelevant for his purpose. Moreover, violence was only a very tangential theme, almost an aside, in a study whose principal focus was the entrepreneurial spirit and city-building impulse of the citizens of a small town.

In a study of violence in nineteenth-century Michigan lumber towns, Jeremy W. Kilar has found that there were some 112 homicides in the lumber counties of Bay, Saginaw, and Muskegon during the years 1868–1888.[53] This converts to a murder and nonnegligent homicide rate of about 5 for each of the towns, leading Kilar to conclude that the lumber towns never matched the high homicide rates of many other western frontier communities. However, more than half of the lumber town homicides occurred from 1881 through 1886. During those years their homicide rates would have been about 15 or 16. In 1881 East Saginaw, with a population of some 20,000, had 15 homicides, giving it a rate of 75. Thus the lumber towns certainly had brief periods when their homicide rates were moderately high or very high, although in the long run they do not appear to have had homicide rates to compare with Bodie or Aurora.

Like the Michigan lumber counties, the California counties of San Diego and Nevada had periods when their homicide rates were very high. Clare V. McKanna, Jr., has calculated that San Diego county from 1871–1875 had a rate of 117, and from 1876–1880 a 52.[54] Ben Nickoll has found that during the six-year period 1851–1856 Nevada county had a rate of 83.[55] These figures, of course, closely approximate Bodie's 116 and Aurora's 64. Not all of California was so wild, though. According to Lawrence M. Friedman and Robert V. Percival, Oakland had only two homicides during the entire first half of the 1870s, and its population was more than 11,000 in 1870 and nearly 25,000 in 1875.[56] But then, although Oakland was certainly a Western town, by the 1870s it was no longer a frontier town.

In Bodie and Aurora several factors would appear to have been responsible for their high rates of homicide. First, their populations were composed mostly of brave, young, adventurous, and single males who admired courage above all else. Manly conduct required that a man stand and fight, even if, or perhaps especially if, it could mean death. Ironically, these men had made the dangerous trek to the frontier for a materialistic end—to strike it rich—and yet the values they held most dear—honor, pride, and courage—were anything but materialistic.

Alcohol played a major role in encouraging fighting as well. Aurora boasted some twenty-five or thirty saloons, and Bodie nearly fifty. The boys were kept well watered. It was considered manly to imbibe prodigious quantities of whiskey. Anyone who did not was regarded with suspicion. Because Tom Chapin, the superintendent of an Aurora Sunday school, did not drink, the miners called him Miss Chapin. A visitor to Aurora in 1863 said: "Aurora of a Sunday night—how shall I describe it. It is so unlike anything East that I can compare it with nothing you have ever seen. One sees a hundred men to one woman and child. Saloons—saloons—saloons— liquor—everywhere. And here the men are—where else *can* they be?"[57] Aurorans consumed so much alcohol that they more than doubled the price of eggs when eggnog was in season.

Bodieites were no different. Main Street in Bodie, said the *Bodie Standard* on October 19, 1879, "has more saloons in a given length than any thoroughfare in the world." Drunk and disorderly conduct was the most common entry in Bodie's jail register.[58] A former Bodieite recalled that "nearly everybody drank." They drank the finest imported whiskies but they also drank, according to a report in the *Daily Free Press*, a locally distilled whiskey made "from old boots, scraps of iron, snowslides and climate, and it only takes a couple of 'snorts' to craze a man of ordinary brainpower."

The character of the men of Aurora and Bodie and their value system meant that they would fight. Their consumption of alcohol meant that they would fight often. And their carrying of guns meant that fighting could easily prove fatal.[59] Although the armed state of the citizenry reduced the incidence of robbery, burglary, and theft, it also increased the number of homicides. Men were beaten to death and stabbed to death, but the great majority of homicides resulted from shootings. Without the gun Aurorans and Bodieites would still have fought, but their fights would not have been so deadly.

The carrying of guns was never questioned. Aurorans and Bodieites believed they had a natural and inalienable right to self-defense. The gun was the most effective tool in exercising that right. Nearly every man went about armed. Sam Clemens, who visited Bodie and who spent some time in Aurora working as a miner and writing for the *Esmeralda Star*, said that he had never had occasion to kill anybody with the Colt Navy revolver he carried, but he had "worn the thing in deference to popular sentiment, and in order that I might not, by its absence, be offensively conspicuous, and a subject of remark."[60]

Nor was the high homicide rate a subject of great concern. Aurorans and Bodieites accepted the killings because those killed, with only a few exceptions, had been willing combatants. They had chosen to fight. Commenting on killings in Bodie the *Daily Free Press* said on January 7, 1880: "There has never yet been an instance of the intentional killing of a man whose taking off was not a verification of the proverb that 'He that liveth by the sword shall perish by the sword.' " The old, the weak, the female, and those unwilling to fight were almost never the object of an attack.

Moreover, many of those killed in Aurora and Bodie were "roughs" or "badmen," as they were called. If a badman died in a shootout, he was not to be pitied. Sudden and violent death was an occupational hazard he had assumed upon becoming a gunman.

Extralegal Frontier Justice

On a couple of occasions, however, the citizens of Aurora and Bodie thought it necessary to react to homicides in an extralegal fashion. The homicides in question both involved clearly innocent victims who were given no opportunity to defend themselves. The citizenry was outraged and responded by forming vigilance committees.[61] The committees conformed to Richard Maxwell Brown's model of "socially constructive" committees of vigilance: they were supported by a majority of the townspeople, including the leading citizens; they were well regulated; they dealt quickly and effectively with criminal problems; they left the towns in more stable and orderly conditions; and when opposition developed, they disbanded.[62]

The organization of the Bodie 601 in response to the killing of Thomas Treloar demonstrates these points.[63] Treloar, a Cornish immigrant who had suffered brain damage in a fall down a mine shaft, had suspected his wife Johanna of infidelity for some time when he finally confronted her alleged lover Joseph DeRoche, a French-Canadian who owned a brickyard on the south side of Bodie. DeRoche convinced Treloar that they should talk the matter over. As they walked down Main Street DeRoche fell a step behind Treloar, pulled out a .38 caliber revolver, and shot the Cornishman in the back of the head. Treloar pitched forward into the snow-covered street. Blood gushed from a hole behind his left ear and turned the snow a deep crimson. Within minutes he was dead.

Although it was late at night, two men who happened to be nearby had witnessed the act. DeRoche was arrested and charged with murder, but he later escaped, not from jail but from a hotel room where he had been secretly taken when word spread that a lynch mob was on its way to the jail.

While squads of men searched the town for DeRoche, the coroner's jury assembled. For two days the jury carefully investigated the case and heard the testimony of more than a dozen witnesses, including the two eyewitnesses. Not surprisingly, the jury found that DeRoche had killed Treloar and that the killing was "a willful and premeditated murder." The *Daily Free Press* expressed the mood of the town, saying that the murder was "so cold-blooded and cowardly, and was committed for a purpose seemingly so base and sordid, and under precedent circumstances so revolting to every impulse and sensibility of manhood, that it has stirred the blood of every human being in Bodie to the very springhead of the fountain." DeRoche had obviously stepped far over the line—this was not an act of self defense nor was it the shooting of an infamous badman who had threatened his life—and Bodieites were outraged.

By the time the coroner's jury rendered its verdict, a vigilance committee, the Bodie 601, had been thoroughly organized. The vigilantes operated like the military veterans many of them were. They were organized into companies and squads, had their own elected officers and a command structure, and went about their business in a quiet, orderly, and determined manner.

A patrol of vigilantes eventually discovered DeRoche hiding on a wood ranch outside of town and returned him to the Bodie jail. Within an hour hundreds of men were discussing his fate in a street meeting in front of the Bodie House hotel. Most argued that he should be hanged immediately, while a few urged that the law be allowed to take its course. The more the murder was discussed, though, the greater the indignation, until finally the crowd began to move toward the jail. Into the street jumped Patrick Reddy, Bodie's leading attorney. He brought the crowd to a halt and convinced the men to do nothing rash and allow DeRoche to be examined in justice court.

When the testimony in justice court did not differ materially from that given before the coroner's jury, the Bodie 601, after a "long and deliberate" discussion in a formal meeting, decided that DeRoche should hang. The vigilantes assembled in companies and squads, marched to the jail, and demanded the prisoner. Facing hundreds of organized, determined, and armed vigilantes, the sheriff simply released DeRoche. The vigilantes then marched DeRoche to the very spot where he had killed Treloar and hanged him from a makeshift gallows. While DeRoche was still dangling from the rope a note was pinned to his chest: "All others take warning. Let no one cut him down. Bodie 601."

Two days later the coroner summoned a jury to investigate the death of Joseph DeRoche. The jurors, some of whom could have been members of the Bodie 601, quickly rendered a verdict: "The deceased came to his death at the hands of persons unknown to the jury."

Editorial comment in Bodie newspapers as well as those of nearby towns, such as Virginia City, heartily endorsed the hanging and ignored the obvious failure of the coroner's jury to conduct a proper investigation. The newspapers also predicted that the actions of the vigilantes would have a salutary effect on the town.

The summary execution was not praised by everyone in Bodie, however. Some ninety men organized the Law and Order Association which was dedicated to aiding and protecting the officers of the law in the discharge of their official duties. At about the same time, though, the Bodie 601 disbanded and the Law and Order Association had only one more meeting before it too faded from the scene.

Importantly, the Bodie 601 (and the vigilance committee that operated in Aurora, the Citizens Safety Committee) was formed not because there was no established criminal justice system, but because the system had not been able to convict anyone other than a deranged loner who had beaten a woman to death. Although killers were invariably arrested and charged with murder, most were discharged after justice court had determined that they had acted in self-defense. In Bodie some forty men were arrested for murder (on three occasions more than one man was arrested for the same murder) but only seven of these eventually went to trial in superior court. Of the seven who were tried all but one were found not guilty.

Despite the low ratio of trials to arrests and even lower ratio of convictions to trials, justice prevailed most of the time. The killers had usually been acting in self-defense. However, there were occasions when seemingly guilty men walked free. Since those killed were roughs or badmen, though, the general public was hardly moved. Nonetheless, this meant that when an innocent man was killed Aurorans and Bodieites reasoned that his murderer would probably be able to avoid a guilty verdict also.

Defense attorneys were highly competent and regularly outclassed prosecutors. Not only did the defense have all the advantages that it enjoys today, and properly so, but the defense had the added advantage in the mining towns of a very transient population. A postponement of a trial often meant the loss of prosecution witnesses. The prosecution of Chinese badman Sam Chung for murder was typical.[64] Chung was defended by the redoubtable Patrick Reddy. Chung seemed guilty beyond a reasonable doubt, yet Reddy managed to place doubt in the minds of at least some of the jurors. A mistrial was declared. The jury in a second trial was also unable to reach a verdict. By the time a third trial was held a key prosecution witness had left the state, and Chung was found not guilty.

Crime, Justice, and Minorities

The Sam Chung murder case also demonstrates another point: Chinese were not treated differently from other Aurorans or Bodieites by the legal justice system.[65] Nor were Mexicans. In the only case where white witnesses and Chinese witnesses gave contradictory testimony, the all-white jury accepted the word of the Chinese over that of the whites; and in the one case in which a Mexican was implicated in the murder of a gringo, the Mexican was not even arrested, let alone prosecuted. The finest attorneys made themselves available to Chinese and Mexicans. When convicted of crimes, Chinese and Mexicans suffered penalties similar to those given to other lawbreakers. Moreover, crimes against them were treated just as seriously as if they had been perpetrated against any other Aurorans or Bodieites. Nonetheless, Mexicans and especially Chinese were reluctant to deal with the authorities and often preferred to personally avenge wrongs committed against them. The Chinese let the secret societies handle most of Chinatown's problems. Lawmen found it almost impossible to get Chinese to discuss a crime or testify if the perpetrator of the crime in question was Chinese.

Chinese and Mexican crime was not greatly different from that committed by other Aurorans and Bodieites. The differences were mostly a matter of degree. The Chinese were involved in a disproportionate number of burglaries and thefts, instances of selling liquor to Indians, and assaults on women, while the Mexicans committed a disproportionate number of horse thefts and, like the Chinese, sold more than their share of liquor to the Indians.

No organized violence was ever directed at either the Chinese or Mexicans. They certainly would not have been hapless victims. They too were armed with guns and knives and were not averse to using them. Almost all their fights, though, were with members of their own groups. With the Chinese this occasionally meant clashes between rival tongs. One such battle erupted with gunfire on a warm summer evening in Bodie's Chinatown and continued for more than an hour before police could separate the combatants. Hundreds of rounds were fired during the battle and at least one Chinese was killed and several others seriously wounded. Witnesses said that another three or four Chinese had been killed but their bodies had been carried away before police arrived. Some thirty Chinese were arrested and eight were charged with murder. However, one by one the charges were dropped for lack of evidence. It was simply impossible to get any Chinese to testify. Nor was anything ever learned about the bodies that were supposedly carried away.

Juvenile Crime

Aurora and Bodie, then, do not seem to have suffered from any racially inspired violence. Serious juvenile crime was also absent from the towns.[66] Dozens of teenage boys lived in Aurora and Bodie, and most of them attempted to emulate their elders. This meant smoking (mostly tobacco but occasionally opium), drinking, gambling, fighting, and carrying guns. Yet beyond perpetrating some youthful pranks and committing a few petty thefts and burglaries, the boys stayed out of trouble. In Bodie there was a gang of teenage boys who loitered at the corner of Green and Wood streets, but they were known mostly for their use of foul language and for running their own faro game.

By contrast teenage boys today commit a large percentage of the violent crime that occurs in the United States. In 1986 teenage boys accounted for 14 percent of those arrested for murder, 18 percent of those for rape, and 27 percent of those for robbery.[67] In Los Angeles members of youth gangs commit more than 20 percent of the murders that occur each year. The Los Angeles police department has created a special unit called CRASH (community resources against street hoodlums) solely to combat the gangs. Kevin Rogers, a CRASH detective and fifteen-year veteran of the LAPD, says that the gangs engage in "sport killing" and almost any target, as long as it is in another gang's territory, will suffice. Rogers also notes that nearly all murder victims of the gangs were in a defenseless state when shot. In his entire career he could recall only one instance where an armed combatant died in a shootout.[68]

In recent years the gangs have been ranging farther afield—to the western suburbs of Los Angeles and beyond—searching for easy marks for rape or robbery. Patrick Connolly, the chief of the campus police at UCLA in the suburb of Westwood, says that his force has had to exercise ever greater vigilance to guard against youth gang attacks on or near campus. According to chief Connolly the gangs cruise the area searching for "targets of opportunity" for rape and robbery. He credits good police work with keeping the campus, a small city itself with more than 30,000 students, relatively safe.[69]

There clearly is no comparison between the amount and kind of crime committed by teenage boys in Aurora and Bodie and that perpetrated by youth today. "Sport killing" and searching for rape and robbery prospects were unknown.

Conclusion

Popular wisdom says that generations of living on and conquering frontiers have made Americans a violent and lawless people. Popular wisdom is wrong. So is much scholarly literature that has drawn conclusions about violence and lawlessness from anecdotal evidence and specious assumptions.[70] The kind of crime that pervades American society today has little or no relation to the kind of lawlessness that occurred on the frontier if Aurora and Bodie are at all representative of western communities. Robbery of individuals, burglary, and theft occurred only infrequently and rape seems not to have occurred at all. Racial violence and serious juvenile crime were absent also. The homicides that occurred almost invariably resulted from gunfights between willing combatants. The old, the weak, the innocent, the young, and the female were not the targets of violent men. In fact, all people in those categories would have been far safer in Aurora or Bodie than they are today in any major U.S. city. Even most smaller cities and towns are far more crime ridden and dangerous than were Aurora and Bodie.

There simply is no justification for blaming contemporary American violence and lawlessness on a frontier heritage. The time is long past for Americans to stop excusing the violence in society by trotting out that old whipping boy, the frontier. On the contrary, it would seem that the frontier, instead of representing America at its worst may have, in many respects, represented the nation at its best.

Notes

1. Roger D. McGrath, *Gunfighters, Highwaymen, & Vigilantes: Violence on the Frontier* (Berkeley: University of California Press, 1984), 115, 141, 203–5.

2. For the history of Aurora and Bodie during their boom years see McGrath, *Gunfighters*. Statistical data for Aurora are compiled from the years 1861 through 1865; for Bodie, 1878 through 1882.

3. Dept. of the Interior, Census Office, *Statistics of the Population of the United States at the Tenth Census* (Washington, DC: Government Printing Office, 1883), 108, 382, 428, and 498; *Bodie Standard*, July 27, 1881. Bodie's newspapers during 1879 regularly claimed a population for the town of more than 6,000. See, for example, the *Bodie Morning News*, May 21, 1879, and the *Bodie Standard*, Dec. 22, 1879. Since the U.S. Census traditionally undercounts, Bodie's population might have been close to 6,000 in 1880 also. By 1881, though, the decline had begun. Year by year estimates for Bodie's population are: 1877, 1,200; 1878, 4,000; 1879, 6,000; 1880, 5,500; 1881, 5,000; 1882, 4,000; 1883, 2,000. Thus during the five years that are the focus of this study, 1878 through 1882, the average population was approximately 5,000.

4. McGrath, *Gunfighters*, 70–2, 83, 141, 162, 165–78.

5. Bodie *Daily Free Press* 12 Aug. 1880.

6. For talk of vigilantism and the following quotes see the *Bodie Standard* Feb. 15, 1879, and the Bodie *Daily Free Press*, Jan. 25 and Feb. 19, 1880.

7. Bodie's robbery rate was calculated by dividing the total number of robberies by the span of years over which they occurred (5) and multiplying by the factor (20) necessary to convert Bodie's average population during those years (5,000) to the 100,000 population norm used by the FBI Crime Index.

8. U.S. Department of Justice, Federal Bureau of Investigation, *Crime in the United States: Uniform Crime Reports, 1986* (Washington, DC: U.S. Government Printing Office, 1987), 72, 83. All fractions have been rounded to the nearest whole number. Hereafter cited *UCR, 1986*

9. *UCR, 1986*, 84.

10. Ibid., 109.

11. Ibid., 16.

12. See, for example, Roger Lane, *Violent Death in the City: Suicide, Accident, and Murder in Nineteenth-Century Philadelphia* (Cambridge, MA: Harvard University Press, 1979). Lane briefly discusses the problems of using numbers of arrests rather than numbers of offenses, on 56–57. See also Roger Lane, *Policing the City: Boston 1822–1885* (Cambridge, MA: Harvard University Press, 1967); Eric Monkkonen, *The Dangerous Class* (Cambridge, MA: Harvard University Press, 1975) and *Police in Urban America, 1860–1920* (Cambridge, UK: Cambridge University Press, 1981); Theodore N. Ferdinand, "The Criminal Patterns of Boston Since 1849," *American Journal of Sociology* 73 (July 1967): 84–99; and "Politics, the Police, and Arresting Policies in Salem, Massachusetts, Since the Civil War," *Social Problems* 19 (Spring 1972): 572–88.

13. For the disparity between offenses and arrests in 1986, compare pages 42 and 164 of the *UCR, 1986*. From year to year the ratio between offenses and arrests varies slightly. For 1986 the ratios were robbery 3.7 to 1; burglary 7.2 to 1; theft 5.2 to 1; rape 2.4 to 1; murder and nonnegligent manslaughter 1.07 to 1.

14. Ferdinand, "Criminal Patterns of Boston," 93, and "Politics, the Police, and Arresting Policies in Salem," 579.

15. McGrath, *Gunfighters*, 74, 83, 135, 143, 163, 181–2.

16. *UCR, 1986*, 83, 104.

17. Ibid., 24, 109.

18. Ferdinand, "Criminal Patterns of Boston," 94, and "Politics, the Police, and Arresting Policies in Salem," 579.

19. *Bodie Morning News* July 29, 1879. See, for example, Bodie *Daily Free Press*, March 25 and May 12, 1880.

20. *Bodie Standard*, Nov. 9, 1881.

21. McGrath, *Gunfighters* 74, 83, 86, 135, 143, 163, 178–81.

22. *UCR, 1986*, 104, 109.

23. Ibid., 28, 109.

24. Ferdinand, "Criminal Patterns of Boston," 96, and "Politics, the Police, and Arresting Policies in Salem," 580.

25. *New York Times*, Apr. 11, 1987.

26. Gary Kleck, "Crime Control Through the Private Use of Armed Force," *Social Problems* 35 (Feb. 1988): 1–21.

27. *Los Angeles Times*, Aug. 17, 1986.

28. McGrath, *Gunfighters*, esp. 149–164.

29. Grant H. Smith, "Bodie, Last of the Old-Time Mining Camps," *California Historical Society Quarterly* 4 (March 1925): 64–80.

30. Bodie *Daily Free Press*, Apr. 14,1880.

31. Ibid., Jan. 15, 1881 and July 7, 1882; *Bodie Standard*, July 12, 1882.

32. *Bodie Standard* Sept. 4, 1878.

33. *UCR, 1986*, 73.

34. Ibid., 65, 83, 84.

35. Ibid., 13, 109.

36. Ferdinand, "Criminal Patterns of Boston," 91, and "Politics, the Police, and Arresting Policies in Salem," 579.

37. McGrath, *Gunfighters*, esp. 75–85, 185–224.

38. *Esmeralda Union*, March 31, 1864.

39. Inclusion of homicides by the FBI in the category of murder and nonnegligent manslaughter is based solely on police investigation and not on the findings of a coroner, coroner's jury, or the determination of a court. The FBI does not include deaths caused by negligence, suicide, or accident; or justifiable homicides which the FBI defines as "the killings of felons by

law enforcement officers in the line of duty or by private citizens." The FBI, for purposes of its Uniform Crime Reporting Program, includes self-defense homicides in its nonnegligent manslaughter category whereas the state of California, for example, in its penal code, defines a self-defense killing as a justifiable homicide. See *UCR, 1980* 7, and State of California, Department of Justice, *Homicide in California, 1981* (Sacramento: State Printing Office, 1982), 34.

40. The two homicides in Bodie that I have excepted are a stagecoach guard's killing of a highwayman and the killing of a bystander struck by a stray round during a gunfight; in Aurora it is the killing of a man that may have been an accident, the result of an accidental discharge of a handgun.

41. *UCR, 1986*, 83.

42. Ibid., 87, 104.

43. Ibid., 65, 72, 75, 84.

44. Ibid., 7, 109.

45. Ferdinand, "Criminal Patterns of Boston," 89 and 90, and "Politics, the Police, and Arresting Policies in Salem," 579.

46. The ratio of offenses to arrests for murder and nonnegligent manslaughter was 1.07 to 1 in 1986 and 1.04 to 1 in 1985. See *UCR, 1986* 42 and 164, and *UCR, 1985* 42 and 164. Oftentimes several members of a gang are arrested for one killing, causing numbers of arrests to exceed numbers of offenses in some jurisdictions. This is often the case in Los Angeles where gang-related killings account for nearly one quarter of all homicides.

47. Lane, *Violent Death in the City*, 60 and 79. Lane discusses the problem of determining homicide rates on 56–9.

48. See Eric Monkkonen's chapter "Homicide, America's Darkest Page," in this volume.

49. Myron Angel, ed., *History of Nevada* (Oakland: Thompson and West, 1881), 343–4.

50. Harry H. Anderson, "Deadwood, South Dakota: An Effort at Stability," *Montana: The Magazine of Western History* 20 (Jan. 1970), 40–7.

51. Robert R. Dykstra, *The Cattle Towns* (New York: Alfred A. Knopf, 1968), 113.

52. For Dykstra's discussion of homicide see *The Cattle Towns*, 142–6.

53. Jeremy W. Kilar, "Great Lakes Lumber Towns and Frontier Violence: A Comparative Study," *Journal of Forest History* 31 (Apr. 1987): 71–85.

54. Clare V. McKanna, Jr., of San Diego State University, has recently finished cataloging homicides that occurred in San Diego county during the second half of the nineteenth century. The material, part of a larger project, has not yet been published. Some mention of homicide rates in San Diego county, though, can be found in an article by McKanna and Richard W. Crawford, the archivist of the San Diego Historical Society: "Crime in California: Using State and Local Archives for Crime Research," *Pacific Historical Review* 55 (May 1986): 284–95. Kathleen Jones Bulmash, another researcher working with McKanna, delivered a paper on the subject, "Changing Patterns of Criminal Homicide in the West: San Diego, 1870–1900," before the Western Association of Women Historians at the Huntington Library, Apr. 15, 1984.

55. Ben Nickoll, "Violence on the American Frontier: Nevada County, California, 1851–1856," unpublished senior honors thesis, Dept. of History, UCLA, June 1986.

56. Lawrence M. Friedman and Robert V. Percival, *The Roots of Justice: Crime and Punishment in Alameda County, California, 1870–1910* (Chapel Hill: University of North Carolina Press, 1981), 27 and 29.

57. Francis P. Farquhar, ed., *Up and Down California in 1860–1864: The Journal of William H. Brewer* (Berkeley: University of California Press, 1966), 420.

58. See, for example, Jail Register: Bodie Branch Jail, 10–30.

59. The handgun of choice in Aurora was the Colt Navy, a .36 caliber, octagon-barrel, six-shot revolver, noted for its perfect balance and accuracy. The Colt Dragoon also saw considerable use. In Bodie gunfighters favored the Colt Double Action Model of 1877 known

popularly as the "Lightning," a nickname given the gun by B. Kittredge and Company of Cincinnati, a major Colt dealer. The gun first appeared in .38 caliber but within months was also produced in .41 caliber, which Bodieites used. Although Benjamin Kittredge gave the bigger .41 caliber a new nickname, "Thunderer," Bodieites (and others on the frontier) referred to it as the Lightning. Since the gun was double action it was also commonly called a "self-cocker." For a thorough discussion of the widely-used revolver see Richard C. Marohn, "1877—Colt's First Year of Double Action," *The Gun Report* 28 (October 1982), 14–9. For Colts in general see Charles T. Haven and Frank A. Belden, *The History of the Colt Revolver* (New York: W. Morrow and Co., 1940), James E. Serven, *Colt Firearms from 1836* (Harrisburg: Stackpole Books, 1979), and R.Q. Sutherland and R.L. Wilson, *The Book of Colt Firearms* (Kansas City: R.Q. Sutherland, 1971). For a comprehensive overview of guns used on the frontier see Louis A. Garavaglia and Charles G. Worman's two volume study *Firearms of the American West* (Albuquerque: University of New Mexico Press, 1984 and 1985).

60. Samuel L. Clemens, *Roughing It* (New York: Harper and Row, 1913), 197.

61. See McGrath, *Gunfighters*, 86–101, 225–46, 255–6.

62. Richard Maxwell Brown, *Strain of Violence: Historical Studies of American Violence and Vigilantism* (New York, Oxford University Press, 1975), 118.

63. McGrath, *Gunfighters*, 234–44.

64. Ibid., 135–7.

65. Ibid., 124–148.

66. Ibid., 162–4.

67. *UCR, 1986* 164, 176.

68. Personal interviews with LAPD detective Kevin Rogers during 1986 and 1987. The LAPD keeps careful records of youth gang activities and compiles a large number of statistical tables and charts on gang-related crime for intradepartmental use and analysis. All of these were made available for my use in preparing this study.

69. Personal interviews with Patrick Connolly, Chief of the UCLA campus police, during 1986 and 1987. Before he came to UCLA Chief Connolly Spent nearly twenty years with the Los Angeles County Sheriff's Department.

70. See, for example, James Truslow Adams, "Our Lawless Heritage," *The Atlantic Monthly* 142 (Dec. 1928): 732–40; R. W. Mondy, "Analysis of Frontier Social Instability," *Southwestern Social Science Quarterly* 24 (Sept. 1943): 167–77; Mabel A. Elliot, "Crime and the Frontier Mores," *American Sociological Review* 9 (Apr. 1944): 185–92; Gilbert Geis, "Violence in American Society," *Current History* 52 (June 1967): 354–8, 366; and Joe B. Frantz, "The Frontier Tradition: An Invitation to Violence," in Hugh Davis Graham and Ted Robert Gurr, eds., *Violence in America: Historical and Comparative Perspectives* (Washington, DC: U.S. Government Printing Office, 1969).

Chapter 6

Bootlegging: The Business and Politics of Violence

MARK H. HALLER

On January 17, 1920, the Volstead Act went into effect and began America's thirteen-year experiment with national prohibition. Contrary to popular myth, the best evidence strongly indicates that Prohibition was accompanied by a substantial decline in the use of alcohol by the American public. By the end of Prohibition, in fact, *per capita* consumption may have been only forty percent of the consumption before World War I.[1] But there was another side, as well. The United States had a long tradition of local regulations controlling the use of alcoholic beverages and an equally long tradition that drinkers proudly ignored the regulations. In a continuation of that tradition, millions of Americans defiantly drank through the 1920s. Their drinking was widely reported in the media and has become part of our vision of the "jazz age" of the roaring 'twenties. Some of the best known figures from the 1920s are bootleggers like Al Capone, Frank Nitti, and Jack Guzik in Chicago or Frank Costello, Meyer Lansky, and Dutch Schultz in New York—men who rose from the slums to achieve sudden wealth by the importation, manufacture, wholesale distribution, or retailing of alcoholic beverages.

In their own day and in legend, the bootleggers are perhaps best known for the violence that erupted between bootlegging groups. Indeed, public belief that Prohibition had spawned the violence of bootlegging was a significant factor leading to repeal. Since then, in highly fictionalized television shows and movies, the legend of the violence has been fastened on the American imagination. Oddly enough, however, there have been no scholarly studies of the political or economic factors that underlay the violence of bootlegging.

There were, in fact, powerful political and economic factors that tended to repress violence within bootlegging. Successful bootleggers in many cities established on-going relationships with police and politicians. As early as August 1920, when police Lieutenant Michael Delaney in Chicago announced that he intended to clean up the saloons and cabarets in his district, a saloonkeeper exclaimed incredulously to a reporter: "Clean up? Why, gosh [sic], what does this guy Delaney think everybody's doin'? Saloonkeepers, politicians, gamblers, coppers—they're all cleaning up!" Six years later, during the mayoralty of reformer William E. Dever, newspapers revealed that 400 policemen were on the payroll of the Genna brothers, alcohol manufacturers on the Near West Side. Each month the Gennas received a police roster, along with badge numbers; and, when the police appeared for payment at the Genna headquarters, they displayed their badges and were checked off the list. In Philadelphia in the late 1920s, some local politicians developed a regular payment scheme for neighborhood speakeasies. In the 19th ward, for instance, the ward leader instructed a henchman to collect $55 from each speakeasy every two weeks. The henchman kept $300 per month, the police captain received $1,240, and the rest was deposited in the ward leader's bank account. These are only a few examples of patterns that emerged in America's cities.[2]

The mutually beneficial relationships that developed between bootleggers, on the one hand, and the police or politicians, on the other, provided a framework for the control of violence. Those bootleggers with established relationships to the police or politicians often expected that local authorities would keep out competitors and regulate local bootlegging activities. Because violence attracted newspaper attention and led to unfavorable headlines, violence also had the potential of triggering reform movements designed to put wayward bootleggers, police, and politicians in prison. The police and politicians, as a result, had a strong motivation to take seriously their responsibility to maintain order. Thus the structure of corruption generally constituted a strong force to maintain order and deter violence.

The economics of bootlegging was also a powerful factor underlying cooperation. At each level, bootleggers needed stable relations with other bootleggers. Importers, for instance, maintained business dealings with overseas exporters and shippers, on the one hand, and with wholesalers, on the other. Wholesalers, in turn, needed continuing business relationships with importers, manufacturers, and processors in order to obtain bulk quantities of goods. At the same time, they developed ties to retailers willing to buy the beverages from them on a regular basis. Successful bootleggers, in short, necessarily did business with other bootleggers and therefore joined in local, regional, and even international networks of economic cooperation.[3]

Within the politics and business of bootlegging, then, there were important factors that supported cooperation and minimized violence. Yet in many large cities—and even in rural areas[4]—bootlegging often introduced unparalleled violence into underworld activities. It is important to understand, then, why bootlegging was often violent despite the economic and political forces working to moderate violence.

There is a second, and perhaps related, problem: Why did bootlegging quickly become dominated by men with backgrounds strangely devoid of the business skills and political connections that would seem to be necessary in order to succeed in complex and illegal business ventures?

A person ignorant concerning America in the 1920s might well hypothesize that the successful bootleggers would emerge from among the businessmen previously involved in the legal liquor business. After all, such men already possessed the resources—including breweries, distilleries, and trucks—that were needed to form liquor manufacturing or distribution systems. Because they were bitterly opposed to Prohibition, furthermore, many might not regard violating the laws to be a serious moral problem. Faced with bankruptcy as a result of Prohibition, some could be expected to enter the illegal business and, because of their resources, eventually dominate it. Instead, they largely abandoned the liquor business.

A second hypothesis, inasmuch as legal businessmen abandoned the liquor business, would be that those who were already underworld leaders, especially wealthy gamblers, would become coordinators of bootlegging. As established participants in the urban underworld, they would have no compunctions about engaging in an additional and profitable illegal business. They generally had, in addition, the close relations with local politicians and police necessary to protect a new enterprise like bootlegging, as well as capital to make the initial investments. A few, in fact, did make a start in bootlegging. Arnold Rothstein, a leading New York gambler notorious for fixing the 1919 baseball World Series, backed several early bootlegging gangs in New York. By the time of his death in 1928, though, he had largely withdrawn from bootlegging. "Boo-Boo" Max Hoff, who ran a string of small gambling houses in South Philadelphia before Prohibition, became the leading bootlegger in Philadelphia.[5] Nevertheless, to an overwhelming degree, the leadership of bootlegging in the 1920s was not in the hands of established underworld figures.

Who, then, were the leading bootleggers in American cities? Bootlegging was an area of illegal activity that was seized by newcomers: ambitious, yet relatively unknown men. Of seventy-two important bootleggers identified in thirteen cities in the mid-1920s, most tended to be young men—often in their late teens or early twenties when Prohibition began. They were the children of immigrants, raised in the city slums. Some 50 percent were of Eastern European Jewish background, 25 percent of Italian background, and the rest chiefly Irish and Polish. Most had left school by the age of thirteen or fourteen and then had joined the youthful street life of the city. Although most engaged in crime, they were street hustlers, burglars, and craps shooters, not persons who had achieved success in crime or who had the managerial background for the complicated business activities of bootlegging. Bootlegging, a new and relatively open field of criminal endeavor, allowed ambitious young men from the fringes of crime to catapult to sudden success.[6]

There was, no doubt, a connection between the fact that unknown young men became successful bootleggers and the fact that bootlegging often entailed violence. If legal businessmen abandoned the liquor business because they feared the violence—if even established criminals preferred the safety of their old rackets to the dangers of the new—then the success of the young outsiders can be explained by their willingness to use violence and to risk their lives in the pursuit of wealth. It is crucial to an understanding of bootlegging, therefore, to understand in what ways violence arose from the structure of bootlegging activities.

The Economics of Violence

There were two major factors in the business of bootlegging that tended to result in violence. One factor was the role of hijacking. Alcoholic beverages were relatively bulky and thus not easy to hide. At sea, the booze often had to be carried to port from the large mother ships by small boats. On land, it was trucked from breweries, distilleries, or port cities to warehouses and then from warehouses to the thousands of roadhouses and speakeasies. The easiest way to become a bootlegger was to hijack someone else's booze. Some bootleggers, as a result, got their start as hijackers; and most groups that put together successful bootlegging operations had to be willing to use violence to protect shipments.

A second factor underlying violence was the economics of liquor wholesaling in the city. In the early years, numerous groups in each city competed to become distributors for the speakeasies and other retail outlets in the city. Eventually, for those who survived the early struggles, economic factors impelled them to establish monopolies within their areas of distribution. Already armed to prevent hijacking, distributors sometimes fought to protect or establish territorial monopoly.

HIJACKING

The role of hijacking was perhaps most clearly seen in piracy at sea. In the early 1920s, "Rum Row" developed off the east coast in an arc stretching from Boston to the southern coast of New Jersey. "Mother ships"—large freighters loaded with cases of liquor from Canadian ports, the West Indies, or direct from Europe—anchored five miles or more off the coast. Rum runners in small boats carried money out to the mother ships, purchased the booze, and then sneaked into port to unload. Anyone with access to a small boat and the money to buy liquor could become a liquor importer. From Cape Ann to Cape May, the small ports became centers of bootlegging. The Coast Guard, retrenched after World War I and intended in peace time chiefly to help pleasure vessels in distress, was at first powerless to prevent the smuggling. By 1924, as many as fifty mother ships lay off the coast during the summer months. During the early years, Rum Row was so open that pleasure ships from New York City carried tourists out to watch the rum runners at work. Occasionally, prostitutes put to sea to peddle their charms among the sailors of the mother ships, receiving special hazardous duty pay for their services.[7]

The chief danger faced by the rum runners was not from law enforcement but from hijackers. Pirates sometimes seized their boats on the way out and took the money intended to purchase booze; more commonly, pirates captured the boats on the way back and hijacked the cases of liquor. On occasion, pirates, pretending to be rum runners, boarded a mother ship and overpowered the crew. They could then seize the money aboard ship and also unload the remaining cases of liquor. In March 1924, Thomas Godman, a former U.S. naval officer who went into the business of shipping liquor from the German harbor of Bremen to the Atlantic coast, warned in "Secret Circular No. 15 to our Captains" that the "Captains will understand that the only danger that need be feared on the Atlantic Coast is the danger from rum pirates." He added: "We will endeavor to supply a gunner and also machine guns, grenades, and other suitable weapons."[8] The danger of piracy, then, was a major business problem both for mother ships and for those who smuggled the liquor into ports on contact boats.

Not only did smugglers have to arm themselves but the danger of violence forced a reorganization of importation to make the business safer. Soon the free wheeling and competitive smuggling of the early years gave way to a more systematic smuggling dominated by large-scale exporters and importers. One system was for exporters from Europe or Nova Scotia to meet with importers in advance. The importer paid for the liquor and a secret system of identification was arranged. Then no money would pass at sea, and the mother ship would allow on board only smugglers who were agents of the favored importer. Because the rendezvous was kept secret, the contact ships could hope to sneak ashore without being hijacked. Sometimes American importers became exporters as well and thereby created vertical integration. They would purchase the liquor in Europe, Canada, or one of the Caribbean islands, arrange for its shipment off the coast, and then send contact ships out to unload the liquor. Again, no money passed at sea and the contact boats could operate in greater secrecy.[9]

Frank Costello and "Big Bill" Dwyer, partners in a New York import operation, transformed the small French islands of St. Pierre and Miquelon, located in the Atlantic off the southern coast of Newfoundland, into transfer stations for their operations. Dwyer and Costello ordered liquor in Europe, shipped it to Saint Pierre, and then loaded it onto mother ships that carried it off the coasts of Long Island or New Jersey. The two islands, peopled by poor fishermen, experienced unexpected wealth in the 1920s, and the French government often cooperated in supporting the liquor business there. (According to one Coast Guardsman, the small tax that St. Pierre levied on each case of liquor passing through the island relieved its residents of all local taxes.) The islanders, to protect their new source of wealth, expelled any stranger whom they suspected of being an American official.[10]

At any rate, the need to assure the safety of bootlegging operations at sea triggered the initial attempts to coordinate and bring order to the import business. By spring of 1925, a second major factor intervened. At that time, the Coast Guard acquired destroyers mothballed after World War I, as well as new cutters with advanced technology. The Coast Guard undertook to blockade the booze import business from Boston to Atlantic City. This completed the transformation of importation from a competitive and wide-open affair of small contact ships to a coordinated activity of export and import partnerships working in close cooperation.

On land, too, bootleggers faced the problem of hijacking. Although the problem was especially critical for those who transported liquor between cities, wholesalers within cities also had to protect their warehouses and trucks. One solution was to cultivate ties with politicians or the police in order to secure police protection. In some cities, such protection was an early step in the development of bootleg operations. By September 1921, for instance, the Chicago police chief estimated that over half the force was involved in the liquor traffic. "The trouble has been," he explained, "that a large number of men have been inveigled into guarding whiskey trucks, warehouses, and shipments of booze en route from one point to another and the whole affair has grown to the point where the individual policeman considers it perfectly legal to accept employment of that sort." By the mid-1920s, Roger Touhy, the most important beer brewer and distributor in the northwestern suburbs of Chicago, hired off-duty cops as truck drivers to provide protection against both police arrests and hijacking. In Philadelphia, during the same period, the relationship of wholesalers and police was demonstrated when federal agents raided a liquor warehouse near a police station. As federal agents entered the warehouse, police rushed from the stationhouse to intercept them. But, after identifying the raiders, the police apologized, saying "That's okay; we thought you were hijackers."[11]

Many of the burgeoning bootlegging operations found police protection insufficient, however. This was particularly true for those who trucked booze from port cities to inland markets or from outlying breweries and distilleries to the big cities. Even within cities, bootleggers often had to develop their own protection arrangements as a central part of their operations. The biographers of Benjamin Siegal and Meyer Lansky claim that the pair started in the bootlegging business by hiring out their services to protect booze shipments and used this as a springboard for their later success in bootlegging. In his autobiography, Joseph Bonanno, later the leader of an important New York Italian-American crime family, described his start in the rackets in 1925 when he was barely 21 years old. For Salvatore Maranzano's New York City bootlegging operation, Bonanno coordinated distilleries in western Pennsylvania and upstate New York. A "common occurrence was the hijacking of delivery trucks by rival bootlegging groups," he reminisced; as a result, "I began carrying a pistol."[12]

The dangers of hijacking, then, doubtless drove from bootlegging those businessmen unwilling to face violence as a normal business practice and favored the recruitment of young entrepreneurs who, if they did not have the usual background for business success, had at any rate a willingness to risk their lives in pursuit of the American dream.

WHOLESALERS AND VIOLENCE

Wholesalers, in legal as well as illegal markets, provide a crucial coordinating role. In bootlegging, a major wholesale operation, such as the Capone group in Chicago, cultivated diverse economic ties in order to secure liquor. They purchased liquor from importers in Detroit and New York in the early 1920s and from importers in New Orleans and Florida by the late 1920s. They also obtained alcohol from illegal and clandestine distilleries within Chicago and from distilleries in surrounding suburban towns. Beer was generally purchased from illegal breweries in cities such as Peoria, Illinois, and Racine, Wisconsin. The beer and booze, secured from a variety of sources, usually needed to be warehoused before being distributed to speakeasies, cabarets, and other retail outlets.[13] Wholesalers, then, stood between the numerous suppliers, on the one hand, and the retailers, on the other. In addition to economic coordination, wholesalers were also often responsible for arranging political and police protection to safeguard the shipments and, sometimes, to protect their customers' retail outlets.

At the beginning of Prohibition, numerous small outfits struggled to become distributors and to service the growing number of retail outlets. Over time, some developed into on-going operations characterized by regularized ties both to suppliers and to retailers. As their operations stabilized, wholesalers faced strong economic motives to attain a monopoly of distribution in a particular neighborhood or neighborhoods of a city. To the extent that the retail outlets serviced by a particular wholesaler were spread over the city, costs rose prohibitively: the costs of bribes to numerous ward leaders and police, the costs from increased risk of arrest or hijacking, and the costs of transportation and wasted time involved in deliveries to scattered locations. To the extent that retail outlets were concentrated, all of these costs decline: there would be fewer politicians and police to deal with, and routes, being more compact, could be handled with less cost and less risk. A wholesaler, then, had an economic motive to organize a monopoly of distribution within a city neighborhood by inducing each retailer to become a customer and by eliminating other wholesalers from the neighborhood.

There were a number of strategies for doing this. One strategy, of course, was to provide quality products at a good price and on a reliable schedule. A second was to make arrangements with the police or politicians, so that they would arrest and harass rival wholesalers, while requiring owners of local speakeasies and cabarets to buy only from the favored wholesaler. Indeed, if a local wholesaler developed relations with authorities such that he could provide protection for his own business and for his customers' speakeasies, he had an obvious advantage over rivals. When such arrangements were insufficient, however, wholesalers sometimes turned to violence. Often wholesalers had become successful by hiring gunmen to ward off hijackers. Already accustomed to violent methods, then, wholesalers employed threats and coercion to recruit customers and to eliminate rival wholesalers. The violence directed toward hijackers allowed their businesses to develop; by the mid-1920s violence sometimes helped to rationalize the system of wholesale distribution and thereby paved the way for further growth.

In a number of American cities, then, violence occasionally broke out between rival wholesaling groups. Most newspapers were more interested in the stories of shootings than in the economics of the rivalries. After all, the introduction of the sawed-off shotgun and the Tommy Gun as normal weapons of urban warfare did capture public attention. Originally introduced in 1898 and used by the American Army as a trench weapon during World War I, the sawed-off shotgun had the doubtful advantage of being deadly without careful aim—especially appropriate for assassinations from moving cars, for instance. The Tommy Gun, developed by Colonel John M. Thompson late in World War I, also as a trench weapon, was sold commercially after the War. Its first use in an underworld killing occurred in Chicago in 1925–1926, and the weapon soon spread to other cities. But it was not just that the 1920s saw the introduction of trench warfare weapons as part of the armaments of urban battles between bootleg gangs. The 1920s, the decade when the United States became an automobile society, was also the decade when gangsters shot at each other from moving cars and gave each other "one way rides." Warfare between organized bootleg gangs brought a new dimensions to American urban violence.[14]

Perhaps the most famous bootleg assassination of the 1920s was the St. Valentine's Day massacre in Chicago on February 14, 1929.[15] The massacre was part of an on-going dispute between bootleggers allied with Jack Guzik and Al Capone, on the one hand, and a Northside group of bootleggers centering on George "Bugs" Moran. The Moran group provided alcoholic beverages for the growing nightclub and entertainment district just north of Chicago's Loop. The district was not only a burgeoning market for retail booze but provided bootleggers with opportunities to invest in nightclubs, service slot machines, coordinate gambling, and develop other business ventures. From the early 1920s, the Northside group, with strong political ties in the ward, had generally monopolized liquor wholesaling; by the late 1920s, the Capone partners coveted the area as a way to expand their business opportunities.

On February 13, when Moran received a phone call from a man claiming to be a hijacker and offering a truckload of whiskey at bargain prices, he arranged for delivery to be made the next morning at a warehouse on North Clark Street. Some ten days earlier, three young men rented rooms across from the warehouse, presumably to act as lookouts for the assassins. On St. Valentine's Day, after the delivery of the liquor and while it was being unloaded by seven men inside, a Cadillac drove up and at least four men, two in police uniforms, entered the warehouse. They "arrested" the seven men, lined them against a wall, raked them with Tommy Guns, and then exited as though they were policemen leaving from a police raid. By lucky chance, Moran arrived a few minutes late and escaped the slaughter. Although a long investigation recovered two of the guns (one of which had earlier been used in a New York bootleg assassination) and identified several Capone gunmen as suspects, there were no convictions. The viciousness of the killing and the powerlessness of the police were both part of the abiding image of Prohibition.

The Politics of Violence

City officials, of course, had an interest in moderating or eliminating violence among bootleggers. Their chief resource was the use of the local police to punish bootleggers who engaged in threats or assaults. Cities experienced wide variations in the amount of bootleg violence, reflecting in part those factors that enhanced or hindered the ability of city officials to intervene effectively. Chicago and Milwaukee provide contrasting examples.

Chicago had perhaps the highest level of bootleg violence during the 1920s. This stemmed, in part, from the political structure of the city and the history of city politics during Prohibition. Like most American cities, Chicago had a decentralized pattern of political power within its fifty wards. By long tradition, the ward leader from the dominant party could influence the appointment of the local police captain and generally assure a police policy favorable the activities of the ward leader's allies. With the arrival of the 1920s, then, bootleggers and politicians in many wards seized the new opportunities to coordinate the wholesaling and retailing of alcoholic beverages.[16] These developments took place under the benevolent aegis of Mayor William Hale ("Big Bill") Thompson. Within this environment numerous wholesaling groups organized with roots in different wards of the city.

By 1923 a number of local wholesalers were beginning to expand beyond the neighborhoods in which they had initially developed their bootleg operations. In that same year, William E. Dever, backed by reform elements in the city, was elected Mayor and served until 1927. While he opposed Prohibition (and lobbied nationally to change the law), he also had the quaint notion that he had a responsibility to enforce the law. For the enforcement of vice and prohibition laws, he established centralized control under his police chief and thereby crippled the ability of local politicians and local police to shield bootleggers from arrest. As a result, the territorial agreements that evolved under his predecessor could no longer be enforced, and gang warfare broke out.[16]

Over the next few years, as hundreds of bootleggers died in the streets of the city and its suburbs, Chicago earned a national and international reputation for violence. Because of the unrelenting violence, leading bootleggers called a meeting in a downtown hotel room for October 21, 1926, to negotiate a truce. While reporters were excluded, several respected political fixers were present to provide guidance. Commenting later on the agreement, Capone explained:

> I told them we're making a shooting gallery out of a great business, and nobody's profiting by it. It's hard and dangerous work and when a fellow works hard at any line of business, he wants to go home and forget it. He don't want to be afraid to sit near a window or open a door. Why not put up our guns and treat our business like any other man treats his, as something to work at in the daytime and forget when he goes home at night? There's plenty of beer business for everybody— why kill each other over it?

The nature of the truce—a division of territories and a pledge not to steal each other's retail customers—provides clear evidence that the cause of the conflict was a battle of wholesalers over turf.[18]

Despite the truce, the warfare continued, both because under Dever there was no outside force that could effectively oversee the truce and because bootleggers had by then become accustomed to settling of disputes by force of arms. Even the re-election of Thompson in 1927 did not halt the carnage. The St. Valentine's Day Massacre, occurring in February 1929, was a clear indication that violence had become the accepted way to settle disputes among wholesalers in Chicago.

Milwaukee presented a striking contrast with Chicago.[19] Milwaukee, indeed all of Wisconsin, was described by one observer "as a Gibraltar of the wets—sort of a Utopia where everybody drinks their fill and John Barleycorn still holds forth in splendor."[20] Because of the strong influence from German immigrants and the traditional importance of beer brewing, public opinion bitterly opposed Prohibition; politicians from Milwaukee carefully respected the views of their constituents; and the Milwaukee police had a policy of avoiding enforcement of the Prohibition laws. Yet, although bootlegging was wide open in Milwaukee, there was no violence. This derived chiefly from the structure of politics and police in the city. Milwaukee was perhaps unique among America's large cities in that the enforcement decisions of the police department were generally free from control by local elected leaders. (A sign of the department's independence was that, by the 1920s, the department had had only two police chiefs in its history.) The city was unique, in addition, in that the police did not take bribes or form systematically corrupt relations with the underworld. The police department, then, was in a position to pursue a simple policy: while the police did not arrest bootleggers for bootlegging, they did enforce a policy that violence by bootleggers would be vigorously investigated and prosecuted. By being independent of both the bootleggers and local politicians, the police could regulate bootlegging to control violence.

Bootlegging in Milwaukee, as a result, had a structure unlike that typical of most other cities. Milwaukee wholesalers could not form partnerships with local politicians to carve out neighborhoods in which they held a monopoly of distribution; they also could not use violence to establish territories. There was, then, relatively free entry into bootlegging, and many small distributors peddled booze in the city. Even the largest wholesaling operations tended to be small by the standards of other cities. Equally significant, leading Milwaukee bootleggers, as compared with those of other cities, tended to be older and to have previous careers that were more respectable and less tied to other criminal activities. Because killing or being killed was not an integral part of the business, recruitment to bootlegging in Milwaukee was not primarily from young men on the fringes of the underworld.

The contrasting cases of Chicago and Milwaukee demonstrate that, despite the economic roots of violence within bootlegging, the political environment of a city could shape the level of violence in significant ways. In Chicago, decentralized corruption at first facilitated the rise of a number of wholesaling groups with local monopolies; but the politicians were unable to use the police to control violence when wholesalers expanded into each other's territories after 1923. In Milwaukee, though, the political structure permitted the police to intervene throughout the period and thereby prevented the outbreak of bootleg wars.

Conclusion

Bootleggers in the 1920s confronted the conflicting demands that they be ready to use violence in pursuit of economic gain and that they rapidly put together systems of cooperation. Hijacking of booze, particularly in the early years of Prohibition, forced bootleggers to protect their shipments both on land and at sea. The need to use violence led to the recruitment of young men from the slums willing to risk their lives for a quick profit; this, in turn, drove out the faint-hearted who had no stomach for the dangers and the killings. At the same time, however, systematic bootlegging required that importers work out cooperative arrangements with exporters and with wholesalers. Wholesalers, in turn, needed to mediate between importers and manufacturers, on the one hand, and the hundreds of small retailers, on the other. While many who entered bootlegging had no background in such skills, a few mastered them and developed the network of cooperation that made the servicing of large urban markets possible.

For wholesalers, especially, the bootlegging business presented continuing dangers. While they had to cultivate on-going relationships with manufacturers and importers, as well as with the local politicians who might protect their warehouses and delivery routes within the city, the very success of their operations often brought them into conflict with other wholesalers in a competition for territories. Often these conflicts were mediated by police and politicians; but sometimes they erupted into organized gang warfare that has remained part of the American vision of the Prohibition decade.

Many successful bootleggers, then, were men who could work within a system of regional, national, and even international cooperation while, at the same time, carrying out brutal murders of rivals.

This had an impact on the urban underworld after Prohibition. Successful bootleggers were young men—often only in their thirties when Prohibition ended in 1933. They still had most of their adult years ahead of them. Some of them became legal liquor dealers and moved directly from the illegal liquor business to the legal liquor business. Some of them, however, sought opportunities within underworld enterprises, especially in various forms of gambling but also in the importation of heroin, in labor union racketeering, and in loansharking.

Ex-bootleggers who remained important underworld figures carried over the lessons learned in their bootlegging days. One of those lessons was the value of regional and national cooperation. This was seen, for instance, in the cooperative development of gambling in such resort areas as Florida and Havana. It culminated in the development of Las Vegas as a gambling and entertainment center after World II—perhaps the most important achievement of the men who first rose to prominence as bootleggers in the 1920s.[21] But there was a second lesson that they carried into their later careers: that violence and the threat of violence could sometimes be a useful economic tool. In those cities in which ex-bootleggers retained significant roles within the underworld, the American underworld became more violent than in the days before World War I. The dual lessons of cooperation and violence lived on after Prohibition as part of the ethos of American underworld activities.

Epilogue

A study of the economics and politics of violence within bootlegging of the 1920s raises the obvious question: Are there parallels with the violence that often accompanies illegal drug markets in American cities in recent years? Since 1960, Americans, in addition to the traditional and legal consumption of nicotine and alcohol, have expanded their use of a variety of illegal drugs. The result has been the emergence of a diversity of networks to supply illegal drugs. With the growth of drug networks has sometimes come violence. Indeed, Miami of the 1970s and 1980s has even begun to rival Chicago of the 1920s as the American city in which to stage movies and television dramas of gang wars and violence. As in the 1920s, young men from ethnic ghettos have assumed the risks of violence and of jail in pursuit of their version of the American dream.

At least three economic systems characterize the illegal drug markets.[22] Drugs such as barbiturates are legally produced by legitimate drug companies and then diverted to illegal drug networks. Other drugs, such as LSD and PCP, originate in illegal laboratories in the United States. Finally cocaine (including "crack"), heroin, and marijuana begin as agricultural products abroad and enter the United States as illegal imports (although somewhat more than 10 percent of the marijuana results from domestic production). Violence has been associated especially with the distribution of heroin and cocaine.

Although the violence of bootleg liquor and illegal drugs are similar in that each occurs in the processing and sale of illegal goods, the economic and political basis for the violence is generally different. Because of its bulk, illegal liquor was often difficult to conceal during shipment and warehousing. The result was that, from the beginning, hijacking attempts were a major source of violence. By contrast, the small bulk and high value of cocaine and heroin increase the ease of concealment, making the drugs more difficult for either law enforcement or hijackers to intercept. Hijacking, then, has not been a major source of violence within drug markets. Unlike bootlegging, in addition, cocaine and heroin are not distributed by wholesalers to retailers over regular routes. In fact, retailers often come to a place designated by the wholesaler to purchase drugs. Wholesalers, as a result, have no special economic need to establish a monopoly of distribution in particular neighborhoods. Because of these differences, the chief causes of violence within drug distribution are not the same as for bootlegging.

Government policies, along with the fact that heroin and cocaine are relatively easy to conceal, combine to create the major sources of violence in drug dealing. As compared with bootlegging (or with most other economic crimes), there are harsh penalties for dealing in heroin and cocaine. Bootleggers might sometimes suffer significant economic losses to law enforcement because of the seizure of a shipment of booze or because a distillery or brewery was closed, but, except for those few bootleggers convicted of subsidiary crimes like tax evasion or murder, bootleggers, even if convicted, generally received modest fines or an occasional short jail term. By contrast, heroin and cocaine dealers, especially importers and wholesalers, risk substantial prison terms as well as seizure of assets.

Bootlegging, as a result, was generally a more open criminal activity. Speakeasy owners who purchased alcohol from the Capone group might even brag about this to customers. Among drug dealers, on the other hand, the fear of law enforcement creates a high level of anxiety and mistrust. Dealers work with a handful of associates and deal regularly with sellers and buyers; yet they do so with a continuing fear that someone will mess up or sell out to the police. In a world in which dealers fear law enforcement and mistrust those with whom they deal, there is often the threat to use violence to enforce silence and discretion. One of the results of high penalties, then, is to create a world of drug dealers within which violence and the threat of violence is part of the way that dealers attempt to protect themselves from the criminal penalties of their business.

Not only have the high penalties worked directly to create a world of violence but, more important, the penalties have indirectly increased violence through their impact on the economics of drug dealing. The marketing of heroin and cocaine differ from other drugs (and from bootlegging of the 1920s) in the high mark-up at each transaction and in the number of wholesalers who handle the drug before it is sold to the consumer. The high mark-up, at least in part, reflects the insistence by dealers that they be compensated for the risks they shoulder in handling drugs. (One estimate is that the price of heroin and cocaine to the consumer is ten times the cost at import.) The large number of dealers between import and final sale to the consumer likewise represents an adjustment to risk. Importers and wholesalers prefer to sell to a small number of reliable wholesalers (each of whom takes a substantial markup), so that drugs pass through several wholesalers before a wholesaler is finally willing to face the risk of sale to a retailer.

As a result, each stage in the sale of heroin or cocaine is potentially an unstable and dangerous transaction. The buyer fears that the seller will take the money but fail to deliver the drug or else deliver inferior drugs; the seller fears that the buyer will attempt to seize the drugs without making payment. While the distribution of illegal drugs could not take place unless dealers were generally able to buy and sell successfully, nevertheless the temptation to cheat remains so strong that suspicion is a realistic and continuing characteristic of drug transactions. The danger that buyer or seller, or both, may be tempted to rip off the other during a deal is the major economic factor leading to drug violence—violence designed to cheat or to protect from being cheated.

The danger of violence continues even after the deal has been consummated. Only later, the buyer may discover that the drugs are of inferior quality and seek out the seller for punishment or restitution. If a sale was made on credit, on the other hand, the seller may later find that the buyer who defaults on payment must be dealt with by threats or violence. The danger of violence—unlike bootlegging of the 1920s—extends even to the final transaction between retailer and consumer. In some neighborhoods, heroin is sold publicly on the streets because the seller, as well as buyer, fear being inside with each other where violence might more easily be carried out. By contrast, some "crack" retailers set up "crack houses" where the seller remains behind a fortified door. The buyer pushes money through a slot in the door and the seller then drops the drugs back through the slot. The seller protects himself through a physical separation from the buyer.

While the dangers inherent in drug transactions are the chief source of drug violence, there is another important economic basis for violence. Although drug distribution differs from bootlegging in that wholesalers lack a strong economic motivation to establish a territorial monopoly of distribution, drug retailers may sometimes have such a motivation. In some cities there are areas well known as drug markets, where consumers can arrive by car or other means of transportation knowing that there is a high likelihood of finding one or more sellers eager to do business. Often sellers collectively profit from this open marketing because of the ready availability of customers in a single location. Nevertheless, if supplies outrun local customers or if new retailers upset the market, violence may break out as some retailers attempt to drive others off the street and thereby become exclusive distributors in the area. From time to time, then, wars break out between heroin or cocaine retailers, especially in poor and ghetto neighborhoods.

Because there are economic and political roots to violence within cocaine and heroin markets, as there were earlier within bootlegging, those unwilling to use violence have often shunned the business. Ironically enough, one effect of policies by local governments and federal authorities to deal harshly with drug dealers may have been to increase violence within heroin and cocaine markets and thus to increase the degree to which drug dealing has been controlled by men willing to kill for profit.

Notes

AUTHOR'S NOTE: I wish to thank Ted Robert Gurr, Nancy Haller, Terry Parssinen, and Peter Reuter for comments and suggestions that have improved the chapter.

1. David E. Kyvig, *Repealing National Prohibition* (Chicago: University of Chicago Press, 1979), 23–9; John C. Burnham, "New Perspectives on the Prohibition 'Experiment' of

the 1920s," *Journal of Social History* 2 (Fall, 1968): 51–68; and Herman Feldman, *Prohibition: Its Economic and Industrial Aspects* (New York: D. Appleton, 1927).

2. Quotation from *Chicago Daily News*, Aug. 23, 1920; discussion of Gennas in *Chicago American*, Oct. 9, 1926, and other newspaper clippings in Chicago Crime Commission, file no. 3485–3; for Philadelphia, see Haller, "Philadelphia Bootlegging and the Report of the Special August Grand Jury,"*Pennsylvania Magazine of History and Biography* 109 (April 1985): 231–2.

3. The notion of economic cooperation is developed in greater detail in Haller, "Philadelphia Bootlegging," 217–23; for economics of bootlegging, see also Herbert Asbury, *The Great Illusion: An Informal History of Prohibition* (New York: Greenwood Press, 1968), esp. chaps. 11 & 13.

4. Concerning rural violence, see Paul M. Angle, *Bloody Williamson: A Chapter in American Lawlessness* (New York: Alfred A. Knopf, 1952); also Donald Bain, *War in Illinois* (Englewood Cliffs, NJ: Prentice-Hall, 1978).

5. Leo Katcher, *The Big Bankroll: The Life and Times of Arnold Rothstein* (New York: Harper & Brothers, 1958), esp. chaps. 17–18; Haller, "Philadelphia Bootlegging," 218–9.

6. Haller, "Bootleggers and American Gambling, 1920–1950," in Commission on Review of National Policy toward Gambling, *Gambling in America*, app. 1 (Washington, D.C.: U.S. Government Printing Office, 1976), esp. 109–115.

7. Harold Waters, *Smugglers of Spirits: Prohibition and the Coast Guard Patrol* (New York; Hastings House, 1971); also extensive materials in Coast Guard Intelligence Files, National Archives, Washington, D.C.

8. From circular in Box 61, Coast Guard Intelligence Files.

9. Based chiefly on materials from Coast Guard Intelligence Files.

10. George Wolf and Joseph DiMona, *Frank Costello: Prime Minister of the Underworld* (New York: William Morrow, 1974), Book II; Waters, *Smugglers of Spirits*, 32; Coast Guard Intelligence files, including "Memo from Charles S. Root on Smuggling Situation as of 30 June 1927," box 80.

11. *Chicago Tribune*, Sep. 25, 1921; Roger Tuohy with Ray Brennan, *The Stolen Years* (Cleveland: The Pennington Press, 1959), 66; *Philadelphia Inquirer*, Sept. 2, 1928, sec. A-5.

12. Dennis Eisenberg, Uri Dan, and Eli Landau, *Meyer Lansky, Mogul of the Mob* (New York: Paddington Press, 1979), 87–8; Hank Messick, *Lansky* (New York: G. P. Putnam's, 1971), 25–7; Joseph Bonanno with Sergio Lalli, *A Man of Honor: The Autobiography of Joseph Bonanno* (New York: Simon and Schuster, 1983), 75–6.

13. Based chiefly on files of Chicago Crime Commission.

14. Lee Kennett and James LaVerne Anderson, *The Gun in America: The Origins of a National Dilemma* (Westport, CT.: Greenwood Press, 1975), chap. 8.

15. See, for instance, Kobler, *Capone*, chap. 17.

16. For ward ties of Chicago politicians and racketeers, mostly for a later period, see Ovid Demaris, *Captive City* (New York: Lyle Stuart, 1969); a brilliant analysis of ward politics is Harold F. Gosnell, *Machine Politics: Chicago Model* (Chicago: University of Chicago Press, 1937). For Dever's enforcement policies, see Dever papers, Chicago Historical Society.

17. This argument was first offered by John Landesco, who claimed in 1929: "Then Dever's administration came, with a genuine attack upon bootlegging as well as upon gambling and vice, and the consequent break-up of the feudal city-wide organization of crime and vice and politics. The system of the orderly allotment of territories and protection that had grown up under the Thompson administrations was suddenly destroyed. It was followed by 'The war of each against all.'" See Landesco, *Organized Crime in Chicago* (Chicago: University of Chicago Press, 1968), 97.

18. Kobler,*Capone*, 191–4; Landesco,*Organized Crime*, 102–3.

19. The discussion of Milwaukee is based on records of federal prosecutions for violation of the Volstead Act and income tax evasion in Central Files of the Department of Justice,

National Archives, Washington, D.C.; also newspaper clippings in Crime Clipping File, Milwaukee County Historical Society; some background can also be found in Jeffrey Lucker, "The Politics of Prohibition in Wisconsin, 1917–1933," (M.A. thesis in History, University of Wisconsin, 1968).

20. Statement of Frank Buckley, after a survey of Wisconsin, in U. S. Senate Document no. 307, vol. 14, p. 1097, 71st Congress, 3rd Session (U.S. Government Printing Office, 1930).

21. For a further development of this theme, see Haller, "Bootleggers as Businessmen: From City Slums to City Builders," in David E. Kyvig, ed., *Law, Alcohol, and Order: Perspectives on National Prohibition* (Westport, CT: Greenwood Press, 1985), chap. 9.

22. The analysis of drug markets is based, in large part, on several excellent articles by Peter Reuter, including Reuter and Mark A. R. Kleiman, "Risks and Prices: An Economic Analysis of Drug Enforcement," in Michael Tonry and Norval Morris, eds., *Crime and Justice: An Annual Review of Research* (Chicago: University of Chicago Press, 1986), 7:289–340; see also Mark Moore, *Buy and Bust* (Lexington, MA: D. C. Heath, 1977).

Chapter 7

Economic Change and Homicide in Detroit, 1926–1979

COLIN LOFTIN, DAVID McDOWALL, and JAMES
BOUDOURIS

The assumption that economic hardship is associated with increases in violent crime is widely shared by both the general public and academic researchers. Economic theorists argue that decreases in legitimate income make the possible gains from crime more attractive and thus raise the probability of criminal violence. Social theorists claim that violent criminal activity is in part a consequence of cultural patterns associated with low incomes. Similarly the frustration-aggression formulation, with its origins in psychology, is used by researchers in a variety of disciplines.[1] Theoretical expectations notwithstanding, empirical research has generally failed to find a strong relationship between economic distress and violent crime rates.

This chapter examines the relationship between economic conditions and two types of homicide rates in Detroit, Michigan, during the period 1926–1979. Like other studies we find that unemployment had no effect on domestic homicides between family members. However, in contrast to other studies, we find that homicides committed in the course of criminal transactions were modestly associated with increases in unemployment rates, and, more important, that both domestic and criminal transaction homicides were strongly influenced by changes in poverty.

Previous Research

The relationship between the economy and crime has been investigated from the earliest days of criminological research.[2] For studies done in Western democracies in the second half of the twentieth century, the overwhelming finding is that there is little association between crime and economic hardship.[3] The lack of relationship between the economy and crime is most apparent in the case of unemployment. Long and Witte,[4] after reviewing almost one hundred studies, done in Western democracies mostly in the post World War II period, conclude that there is essentially no convincing evidence that aggregate unemployment affects crime rates, and only weak evidence of a relationship at the individual level. More recently, Cantor and Land[5] and Cook and Zarkin,[6] looking at U.S. data in the post-World War II period, have pointed out that the effect of cyclical unemployment is likely to be obscured by the long-term trends in other causes of crime. After removing these trends, both sets of researchers find a small relationship between unemployment and property offenses, but neither study finds more than a trivial association between unemployment and violent crime.

The effect of poverty on violent crime is somewhat more clearly established. A number of cross-sectional studies find that members of the lower class are over-represented among violent offenders, and that poorer areas have higher violent crime rates than do relatively more affluent ones.[7] However, the size of the effects of poverty are often small relative to the effects of other variables. Freeman,[8] for example, points out that poverty is usually found to have much less influence on crime than do the deterrent effects of criminal sanctions. In addition, an effect of poverty on crime is not found consistently in all studies, and some researchers dispute the existence of any consistent relationship between crime and economic conditions, including poverty.[9]

Although poverty and unemployment are correlated, the two concepts are analytically distinct. Unemployment rates follow the short-term fluctuations of the business cycle and tend to show little consistent trend over time. Variations in poverty, however, are more strongly determined by long-term changes in the economy and the demographic composition of the population. Low unemployment rates are thus not incompatible with a large and growing underclass.

There are three reasons to believe that, in spite of the inconsistent findings of previous research, it is premature to reject the idea that economic conditions and violent crimes are strongly related. First, economic conditions have not been the primarily focus of most studies. Instead, they have included a somewhat arbitrary collection of economic indicators as controls in analyses directed toward other issues. The relationship between economic hardship and crime may appear to be tenuous and inconsistent because the relationship has been studied in a relatively unsystematic way.

A second reason for the largely negative findings of past research is that they implicitly assume that the full effects of change in the economy on crime are realized immediately. Studies using annual data, for example, typically assume that economic conditions in a given year influence crime rates in that year (or perhaps an adjacent year), but then they presumably disappear. A more reasonable strategy would be to allow for the possibility that the effects are distributed over a relatively long period of time. There are many mechanisms that would distribute the effects of economic conditions over more than one time period. For example, the initial shock of an economic loss is often cushioned by accumulated resources and benefits, so that the total impact is apparent only over the course of several years.

Finally, past research has concentrated on diverse crimes such as violent crime, property crime, or, in the extreme, all crime.[10] If economic conditions result in increases in some types of crime and decreases (or no change) in others, grouping offenses into gross categories would obscure the effect. Although many studies have examined the effects of the economy on specific types of crime, such as homicide or robbery, even these relatively specific categories include acts that are diverse in their motivations and opportunity structures.[11] Therefore it is desirable to investigate the effects of the economy on crime categories that are as homogeneous as possible.

These considerations suggest that a model that provides more detailed attention to measures of economic conditions, that allows for distributed effects across time, and that relies on narrow crime categories may produce clearer evidence of a connection between the economy and violent crime. This type of model is developed below.

Model

This study is based on the annual homicide rate per 100,000 residents of the city of Detroit, between the years 1926 and 1979.[12] Two types of homicides are analyzed separately: domestic homicides and criminal transaction homicides. Domestic homicides are defined as those occurring between family members (husbands, wives, children), while criminal transaction homicides are defined as those committed during the course of another crime (for example, a robbery, or a drug sale).[13] Each type of homicide should be reasonably homogeneous in its causes, and together these categories provide a more refined set of crime categories than in any previous study of this type.

Annual observations on poverty are not available for U.S. cities and even national-level data were not consistently collected until the 1960s. Therefore we estimate trends in poverty with the ratio of infant mortality rates in Detroit to the United States infant mortality rate. There is an extensive literature based on data from both Western and Third World nations in this century that consistently shows a strong relationship between poverty and infant mortality.[14] Taking the ratio of Detroit to U.S. infant mortality removes the effects of technological factors, leaving a residual that will largely reflect variation in the proportion of the population that is extremely poor.

In addition to availability, the infant mortality rate has several other advantages as an indicator of economic distress. It does not depend on an arbitrary poverty threshold, as do income measures of poverty. Also, questions such as how to allow for the value of transfer payments and noncash benefits do not arise. Not only can the inclusion of such benefits have a large influence on estimates of the percentage of the population below the poverty threshold,[15] but also they can create serious distortions in time-series as policies are changed over time.

A second advantage of the infant mortality rate is that in the United States it is measured with a great deal of accuracy, while estimates of income poverty are known to be relatively unreliable. Infant mortality data are derived from the national vital statistics registration system, which is estimated to be more than 98 percent complete in its coverage.[16] In contrast, income poverty estimates are based on surveys, which suffer from substantial under-coverage and response errors.[17]

In addition to the infant mortality ratio, the unemployment rate in the state of Michigan is used as a second indicator of economic conditions. As noted earlier, there is little empirical evidence linking unemployment and homicide rates. However, the inclusion of unemployment allows further investigation of its impact on specific types of homicide, and permits a comparison with the effects of poverty. Although city-level statistics are generally not available for unemployment until the 1960s, Detroit is something of a fortunate exception due to the pioneering work of University of Michigan labor economist William Haber, who developed unemployment estimates as early as the 1930s.[18] Unemployment is measured at the state level because a complete series for the city of Detroit was unavailable. Unemployment in Michigan is very highly correlated with unemployment in Detroit, so the use of state data should provide valid estimates for trends in Detroit.[19]

A dummy variable for the Great Depression (1930–1940 = 1; otherwise = 0) is included as final measure of economic conditions. This variable allows for the possibility that the extremely high levels of unemployment during the Depression had further effects on homicide beyond those attributable to more typical levels of unemployment.

Besides economic indicators, the model includes three additional variables: (1) the proportion of Detroit's nonwhite population, (2) the proportion of all homicide cases cleared by arrest, and (3) a dummy variable for World War II. There is consensus among researchers that nonwhites are over-represented among both homicide victims and homicide offenders, and the proportion nonwhite variable thus allows for variations in racial composition.[20] Similarly, the World War II dummy variable (1942–1945 = 1; otherwise = 0) is included to represent the demographic changes associated with the war years. As a center of industrial production, these wartime changes were especially large in Detroit.[21] Finally, the homicide clearance ratio is intended to measure the deterrent effects of crime control activity on homicide rates. According to deterrence theory, as clearance rates rise, homicide rates should fall.[22]

To complete the specification of the model, the previous year's homicide rate (that is, the homicide rate lagged by one year) is included among the explanatory variables. This is equivalent to a model in which the effects of independent variables are distributed over time in a geometrically declining pattern. Specifically the effect of each independent variable follows a pattern like

$$Y_t = \alpha + \beta(X_t + \omega X_{t-1} + \omega^2 X_{t-2} + \omega^3 X_{t-3} + \ldots) + \varepsilon_t$$

Here β is the slope for independent variable X, and ω is a weight which is multiplied by β in order to distribute the effects over time. The value of ω, however, is estimated by the coefficient of the lagged value of the homicide rate in the equation.[23]

If ω is less than 1 in absolute value, the effects of an independent variable will spread in a declining geometric pattern over succeeding years. The weights (ω^1, ω^2, ω^3, etc.), which are multiplied by the immediate effect of the independent variable β, become progressively smaller, eventually approaching zero. Other types of lag patterns are possible, but the geometric lag is plausible in this context.[24]

A Note on Detroit

Detroit is a particularly good setting for the analysis because of the extensive and rapid transformations in the city during these fifty-four years. In many ways the recent history of Detroit is a paradigm of the rise and fall of the American industrial city. This makes it an ideal location for studying the relationships between economic stress and violent crime as they exist in twentieth century industrial America.

The twenties in Detroit were a period of economic boom and rapid growth in the auto industry. Because of its location across the river from Canada, a thriving bootlegging industry also developed during Prohibition. In 1928 liquor was said to be Detroit's second largest industry, employing as many as 50,000 persons.[25] Violent crime thrived along with speakeasies. There were 326 homicides in 1926—up from 232 in 1925—and many of them were a result of rival gangs fighting for control over vice and liquor business.[26]

The Depression hit Detroit early and hard. In January 1931 as many as one out of every three families in the city was without means of support.[27]

The city was forced to cut relief and eventually went into default when several large banks failed. World War II saw the return of rapid growth to the city as the auto industry adapted to war production. In the eighteen months after the Japanese Attack on Pearl Harbor, Detroit's population increased by 350,000.[28] In many respects Detroit never completely recovered from the Depression. After the war the residential population of the city declined rapidly and a demographic reorganization, which eventually produced a largely black and poor inner city surrounded by affluent and largely white suburbs, began to take shape. Between 1950 and 1970, the population of Detroit fell from 1,850,000 to 1,511,000, but the number of black males under twenty-one tripled from 49,000 to 149,000.[29]

The sixties and seventies were a period of chronic economic and racial strife for the Motor City. Factory employment in the auto industry fluctuated around a pattern of general decline and economic resources of the resident population fell substantially. The continuing reputation as "Murder City" was earned during this period as the number of murders increased explosively, surpassing the bloody twenties. Although the relationships between economic conditions and violent crime are bounded by cultural and historical conditions, the experience of Detroit should weigh heavily in assessing the nature of those patterns for Western industrial societies.

Estimation

Based on a preliminary analysis, all of the variables except for the dummies representing the Depression and World War II were transformed to their natural logarithms.[30] The equations for both types of homicide were then estimated together using the seemingly unrelated regressions (SUR) model. The SUR model allows two or more equations to be estimated jointly, controlling for any contemporaneous correlation between their error terms. A major advantage of this approach is that it provides more precise estimates than would be obtained by estimating each of the equations separately.[31]

In distinguishing the types of homicide, we are assuming that domestic and criminal-transaction homicides are distinct in their cause. Specifically, we assume that some of the independent variables have larger effects on one type of homicide than on the other. Criminal-transaction homicides, for example, may involve a larger component of rational calculation than do domestic ones, and thus may be influenced more strongly by the homicide clearance ratio.[32] If both types of homicide are in fact influenced in an identical way by each of the independent variables, there is nothing to be gained by estimating more than one equation.

To examine whether the effects of the independent variables differed depending on the type of homicide, the coefficients for each variable were tested for equality across the two equations.[33] This analysis indicated that the coefficients for the unemployment rate, the clearance ratio, the Depression, and World War II did differ substantially depending on the type of homicide involved. However, the differences in the effects of the infant mortality ratio, the proportion nonwhite, and the lagged value of the homicide rate were small enough to be due to chance. We concluded that these three variables had identical effects on both types of homicide, and the final model was estimated to constrain the coefficients for these variables to be equal in both equations. Diagnostic tests indicated that the errors for the final equations were not autocorrelated, so the SUR estimates should be statistically consistent.[34]

Findings

Final estimates are presented in Table 7.1. Since the variables have been log-transformed, the regression coefficients in Table 7.1 may be interpreted approximately in terms of percentages. The coefficient for each continuous independent variable represents the expected effect of a one percent change in this variable on the percentage change in the annual homicide rate per 100,000 population. The coefficients for the Depression and World War II represent the expected percentage change in the homicide rate each year these events continued.

As noted above, the inclusion of the lagged value of the homicide rates in the equations implies that changes in the independent variables will continue to influence homicides over a period of several years. That is, in addition to their immediate impacts, each independent variable will also have long-term effects as the homicide rate adjusts gradually to the new conditions. Therefore Table 7.1 provides both the short-term and long-term coefficients for each independent variable.[35]

The most important conclusion to be derived from the analysis is that poverty has a large influence on Detroit homicide rates. As noted earlier, the infant mortality ratio has been constrained to have equal effects on both domestic and criminal transaction homicides. A one percent increase in the infant mortality ratio produced an average increase of slightly more than one percent in the rates of both types of homicide within one year. The total long-term impact of a one percent increase in the infant mortality ratio increase approached two percent in each type of homicide. Poverty was therefore a major risk-factor in determining both domestic and criminal transaction homicide rates.

In contrast to poverty, the effects of unemployment and the Depression differ depending on the type of homicide, and are much larger for criminal transaction homicides than for domestic ones. The immediate effect of each year of the Depression was an increase of about one-half of one

Table 7.1 SUR Estimates for the Detroit Homicide Rate, 1926–1979

Independent Variable	Short-Term Effect	Standard Error	β̂/SE[d]	Long-Term Effect
Domestic Homicides				
Lagged domestic homicide rate	.4399[a]	.0798	5.51	—
Proportion nonwhite	.2228[b]	.0990	2.25	.3978
Unemployment rate	-.1267	.0770	-1.65	-.2262
Infant mortality ratio	1.0399[c]	.3955	2.63	1.8566
Homicide clearance ratio	-.5563	.2627	-2.12	-.9932
Depression (1/0)	.0587	.1447	.41	.1048
World War II (1/0)	-.1398	.1786	-.78	.2496
Constant	.7005	.2177	3.22	1.2507
Criminal-Transaction Homicides				
Lagged criminal-transaction homicide rate	.4399[a]	.0798	5.10	—
Proportion nonwhite	.2228[b]	.0990	2.25	.3978
Unemployment rate	-.3539	.1086	-3.26	-.6319
Infanty mortality ratio	1.0399[c]	.3955	2.63	1.8566
Homicide clearance ratio	-1.7349	.3762	-4.61	-3.0975
Depression (1/0)	.4810	.1841	2.61	.8588
World War II (1/0)	-.9524	.2331	-4.09	-1.7004
Constant	.2049	.2920	.70	.3658

[a,b,c]Pairs of coefficients are constrained to be equal for both domestic and criminal-transaction homicides.
[d]The ratio of the short-term effect (β̂) to the standard error (SE). Ratios greater than 1.96 are statistically significant at the five percent level.

percent in the criminal transaction homicide rate, and each Depression year ultimately increased this rate by somewhat less than one percent. Controlling for other factors, the eleven years of the Depression thus resulted in an increase of more than nine percent in the rate of criminal transaction homicides per 100,000 population.

The impact of the Depression, however, is counterbalanced by the effects of unemployment. Each increase of one percent in the unemployment rate reduced criminal transaction homicides by about one-third of one percent immediately, and by more than one-half of one percent in the long-run. The Depression years had extremely high unemployment rates, of course, and this helped mute the overall effect of the Depression on homicides.

One possible explanation of the pattern of effects for unemployment and the Depression on criminal transaction homicides is that brief and prolonged increases in the unemployment rate influence crime in different ways. Cantor and Land[36] suggest that higher levels of unemployment increase motivations to engage in crime but, at the same time, reduce criminal opportunities. Increases in the unemployment rate result in fewer attractive targets for property crime, for example, and less demand for criminal commodities. They argue that the effect of unemployment on criminal opportunities is immediate, but that motivations are affected only after unemployment continues for some length of time. Therefore, short-term increases in unemployment rates should decrease crime (the opportunity effect), while longer periods of high unemployment should increase it (the motivational effect).

The pattern of results for the criminal transaction homicide rate may therefore reflect the opposing forces of the opportunity and motivational components of unemployment on criminal behavior. Short-term variations in unemployment may reduce opportunities to engage in the crimes of which criminal transaction homicides are the by-product. The prolonged unemployment of the Depression, in contrast, may have resulted in higher homicide rates through its effect on criminal motivations. This explanation is somewhat speculative of course, and replication of the findings in other settings would be necessary before a great deal of faith could be placed in it.

Whatever the explanation of the effects of unemployment and the Depression on criminal transaction homicide rates, it is clear that these variables have much less influence on domestic homicides. Each increase of one percent in the unemployment rate is expected to reduce the rate of domestic homicides by only about one-tenth of a percent immediately, and by a quarter of a percent in the long-run. Although domestic homicides increased by a small amount during the Depression, this effect is not large enough to be statistically significant.

Among the other independent variables, increases in the homicide clearance ratio produce substantial decreases in the annual rates of both types of homicide. Measurable deterrence effects have not been a uniform finding in all past research.[37] However, the results here indicate that a one percent increase in the clearance ratio is accompanied by a long-term decrease of more than three percent in criminal transaction homicides, and of almost one percent in domestic homicides. The fact that the effects are larger for criminal transaction homicides than for domestic ones is in accord with the expectation that domestic homicides involve less rational calculation and therefore are less responsive to criminal sanctions.

The World War II years were associated with lower homicide rates in Detroit, although only the effect on criminal transaction homicides is statistically significant. Each year of the war decreased the criminal-transaction homicide rate by about one percent immediately. The total long-term effect of the four years of war was a decrease in criminal transaction homicides of almost eleven percent. Archer and Gartner[38] suggest a number of reasons why crime might decrease during periods of war. Perhaps the most obvious explanation for the effect in Detroit is that the young males recruited for the war (and hence absent from the city) might otherwise have been disproportionately involved in the activities which are precursors to criminal transaction homicides.

Finally, the proportion of Detroit's population which is nonwhite has a large influence on the annual rates of both domestic and criminal transaction homicides. As discussed earlier, this effect is identical for each type of homicide. An increase of one percent in the proportion nonwhite is thus expected to increase the rates of both types of homicides by a quarter of a percent immediately, and by more than a third of a percent in the long-run.

The coefficients for the lagged values of the homicide rates govern how rapidly homicides adjust to changes in the independent variables. Since the lagged coefficients for each type of homicide have been constrained to be equal, both types of homicide respond to changing conditions with equal speed. About 56 percent of the effect of a change in an independent variable is felt within one year, with the remaining 44 percent spread over the course of several more years.

Discussion and Conclusions

The analysis in this chapter indicates that economic conditions had an important influence on homicide rates in Detroit. In particular, the effects of poverty were larger than those of any variable in the model, and the findings clearly indicate that poverty was a major factor in increasing both domestic and criminal transaction homicides. Our analysis was based on the argument that infant mortality rates provide a more sensitive indicator of poverty than do monetary measures, and our results suggest that many researchers have found little relationship between poverty and violent crime because of the measures they used.

In contrast to poverty, the effects of unemployment were relatively small, and were confined only to criminal transaction homicides. Here the findings suggest that long and short periods of high unemployment affect crime in different ways. Much of the influence of unemployment on crime may therefore be missed if only periods of relative prosperity are examined. Further, the results indicate that aggregations which include several types of offenses may obscure the relationship between unemployment and specific categories of crime. Unemployment may affect only some types of crime, and these effects may not be visible when several dissimilar crimes are combined.

Finally, the results show that the effects of changes in economic conditions (and in the other independent variables) were distributed over time. Homicide rates were to some degree temporally stable, and did not respond instantaneously to changes in the environment. The full influence of the economy on homicide was thus apparent only over a period of several years.

The variability of findings in the existing literature on homicide demonstrates that the results of any single study should be interpreted with a great deal of caution. Our empirical analysis applies to the experience of one American city over a relatively brief period of time. What appears to be a simple linear relationship between economic hardship and homicide may, in fact, be conditional on historical and cultural context.[39] However, our analysis does suggest that the effects of economic hardship on violent crime are more subtle than has often been assumed, and it is thus not surprising that they could have been missed in past research. Careful attention to the conceptualization and measurement of economic effects will clearly be necessary to more fully explicate the links between the economy and violent crime.

Appendix A Variable Definitions

Domestic Homicide Rate Per 100,000 Residents	(Domestic Homicides / Total Residential Population) X 100,000
Criminal-Transaction Homicide Rate Per 100,000 Residents	(Criminal-Transaction Homicides / Total Residential Population) x 100,000
Infant Mortality Ratio	(Detroit Infant Mortality Rate / U.S. Infant Mortality Rate) X 100,000
Unemployment Rate	Percent of persons in the civilian labor force unemployed
Homicide Clearance Ratio	(Number of Homicides Cleared by Arrest / Total Number of Homicides)
Proportion Nonwhite	(Nonwhite Residential Population / Total Residential Population)
Depression	Dummy variable: 1 = 1930–1940; 0 = 1926–1929, 1941–1979
World War II	Dummy variable: 1 = 1942–1945; 0 = 1926–1941, 1946–1979

Appendix B Data Sources

1. Number of Domestic Homicides, Number of Criminal-Transaction Homicides, Total Number of Homicides, Number of Homicides Cleared by Arrest

1926–1968: James Boudouris, *Trends in Homicide, Detroit, 1926–1968*. Unpublished Ph.D. dissertation, Department of Sociology, Wayne State University, 1970.
1969–1979: Collected by Loftin in 1980 from files of the Detroit Police Department Homicide Bureau.

2. Detroit Infant Mortality Rate

1926–1979: *Vital Statistics of the United States*, Volumes I and II. (Washington, D.C.: U.S. Government Printing Office, various years).

3. U.S. Infant Mortality Rate

1926–1970: U.S. Bureau of the Census, *Historical Statistics of the United States, Colonial Times to 1970* (Washington, D.C.: U.S. Government Printing Office, 1975).
1971–1979: U.S. Department of Health, Education, and Welfare, *Monthly Vital Statistics Report* Annual Summary for the United States. (Washington, D.C.: U.S. Government Printing Office, various years).

4. Unemployment Rate

1926–1929, 1934, 1936, 1938, 1939, 1941: regression estimates.
1930–1933: adjusted estimates derived from William Haber and Paul Stanchfield, *Unemployment, Relief and Economic Security*. Second Report of the Michigan State Emergency Welfare Relief Commission, Lansing, Michigan, 1936.
1935, 1937, 1940, 1942–1949: William Haber, *How much does It Cost?* A Report to the Michigan Unemployment Security Commission on Long-Range Unemployment Insurance Benefit Financing and Fund Solvency in Michigan, Lansing, Michigan, 1951.
1950–1955: William Haber, Eugene C. McKean and Harold Taylor, *The Michigan Economy: Its Potentials and Its Problems* (Kalamazoo, Michigan: W.E. Upjohn Institute for Employment Research, 1959).
1956–1979: *Manpower Report of the President* (Washington, D.C.: U.S. Government Printing Office, various years).

5. Total Residential Population, Nonwhite Residential Population

1930–1980: U.S. Bureau of the Census. *Census of Population* (Washington, D.C.: U.S. Government Printing Office, various years). Data for inter-census years were estimated with a modified version of the component method. Population was aged using life-tables, deaths were subtracted and births added. Migration was estimated by redistributing an age category's yearly percentage change relative to the yearly percentage change in the Detroit School Census.

Notes

1. Classic statements include: (for economic theory) Gary Becker, "Crime and Punishment: An Economic Approach," *Journal of Political Economy* 76 (1968): 169–217; Isaac

Ehrlich, "Participation in Illegitimate Activities: A Theoretical and Empirical Investigation," *Journal of Political Economy* 81:3 (May/June 1973): 521–65. A revised and supplemented version appears in *Essays in the Economics of Crime and Punishment*, Gary S. Becker and William Landes, eds. (New York: National Bureau of Economic Research, 1974), 68–134; (for cultural theory) Marvin E. Wolfgang and Franco Ferracuti, *The Subculture of Violence: Towards an Integrated Theory in Criminology* (London: Tavistock, 1967); (for frustration-aggression theory) Carl Hovland and Robert Sears, "Minor Studies in Aggression: VI. Correlation of Lynchings with Economic Indices," *Journal of Psychology* 9 (Apr. 1940): 301–10; Andrew F. Henry and James F. Short, Jr. *Suicide and Homicide: Some Economic, Sociological, and Psychological Aspects of Aggression* (New York: Free Press, 1954); Ted Robert Gurr, *Why Men Rebel* (Princeton: Princeton University Press, 1970).

2. For a summary, see George B. Vold, *Theoretical Criminology*, 3rd ed. by Thomas J. Bernard (New York: Oxford University Press, 1986), 131–32.

3. Since the research literature is vast and several excellent reviews of the research based on contemporary western countries are available, we do not attempt to survey the literature. Readers may wish to consult John Braithwaite, *Inequality, Crime, and Public Policy* (Boston: Routledge and Kegan Paul, 1979); Richard B. Freeman, "Crime and Unemployment," in James Q. Wilson, ed., *Crime and Public Policy* (San Francisco: Institute of Contemporary Studies, 1983), 89–106; Sharon K. Long and Ann D. Witte, "Current Economic Trends: Implications for Crime and Criminal Justice," in Kevin N. Wright, ed., *Crime and Criminal Justice in a Declining Economy* (Cambridge, MA: Oelgeschlager, Gunn, and Hain, 1981), 69–143; Thomas Orsagh and Ann Witte, "Economic Status and Crime: Implications for Offender Rehabilitation," *Journal of Criminal Law and Criminology* 72:3 (Fall 1981): 1055–71.

4. Long and Witte, *Current Economic Trends*, 126–31.

5. David Cantor and Kenneth C. Land, "Unemployment and Crime Rates in the Post-World War II United States: A Theoretical and Empirical Analysis," *American Sociological Review* 50:3 (June 1985): 317–32.

6. Philip J. Cook and Gary A. Zarkin, "Crime and the Business Cycle," *Journal of Legal Studies* 14 (Jan. 1985): 115–28.

7. Many of these studies are reviewed in Allen V. Horwitz, "The Economy and Social Pathology," *Annual Review of Sociology* (Palo Alto, CA: Annual Review Press, 1984), 10:99–100.

8. Freeman, "Crime and Unemployment," 89–119.

9. For example, see Steven F. Messner "Poverty, Inequality and the Urban Homicide Rate: Some Unexpected Findings," *Criminology* 20:1 (May 1982): 103–14; see also Charles R. Tittle, Wayne J. Villemez, and Douglas A. Smith, "The Myth of Social Class and Criminality: An Empirical Assessment of the Empirical Evidence," *American Sociological Review* 43:5 (Oct. 1976): 643–56.

10. See Long and Witte, *Current Economic Trends*, table 5–1, 73–9.

11. Robert Nash Parker and M. Dwayne Smith, "Deterrence, Poverty and Type of Homicide," *American Journal of Sociology* 85:3 (Nov. 1979): 614–24.

12. Appendix A provides a definition of all variables used in the analysis and Appendix B describes the data sources.

13. James Boudouris, "A Classification of Homicide," *Criminology* 11:4 (Feb. 1974): 525–40.

14. An early and influential study was Richard Morris Titmuss, *Birth, Poverty and Wealth: A Study of Infant Mortality* (London: Hamish Hamilton Medical Books, 1943). On the Third World, see Magdi M. El-Kammash, "Stockwell's Infant Mortality Index for Measuring Economic Development," *Millbank Memorial Fund Quarterly* 40:1 (Jan. 1962): 112–9. For other research on the consistency of the relationship, see Aaron Antonovsky and Judith Bernstein, "Social Class and Infant Mortality," *Social Science and Medicine* 11:8/9 (May 1977): 453–70; B. MacMahon, M. G. Kovar, and J. J. Feldman, "Infant Mortality Rates:

Socioeconomic Factors," *Vital and Health Statistics* series 22, no. 14 (Rockville, MD: U.S. Department of Health, Education and Welfare. 1972); Edward G. Stockwell, Jerry W. Wicks, and Donald J. Adamchak, "Research Needed on Socioeconomic Differentials in U.S. Mortality," *Public Health Reports* 93:6 (Dec. 1978): 666–72.

    15. See, for example, U.S. Bureau of the Census, Estimates of Poverty Including the Value of Noncash Benefits: 1979 to 1982, technical paper 51 (Washington, DC: U.S. Government Printing Office, 1984).

    16. Henry S. Shryock and Jacob S. Siegal, *The Methods and Materials of Demography* (Washington, D.C.: U.S. Government Printing Office, 1975).

    17. U.S. Bureau of the Census, Evaluation and Research Program of the U.S. Census of Population and Housing, 1960: Accuracy of Data on Population Characteristics as Measured by Reinterviews, series ER 60, no. 28 (Washington, DC: U.S. Government Printing Office, 1964); U.S. Bureau of the Census, Coverage of Population in the 1970 Census and Some Implications for Public Programs, *Current Population Reports* series P-23, no. 56 (Washington, DC: U.S. Government Printing Office, 1975).

    18. For example, see William Haber, "Fluctuations in Employment in Detroit Factories, 1921–1931," *Journal of the American Statistical Association* 27 (June 1932): 141–52.

    19. Consistent unemployment estimates are available for the six-county Detroit SMSA beginning in 1956, and for the city of Detroit beginning in 1967. The correlations between Michigan state unemployment and both unemployment in the city of Detroit and the Detroit SMSA over these periods are .98.

    20. There is also virtually unanimous agreement that homicide victims and offenders are disproportionately young, and initial specifications of the model included a variable for the proportion of Detroit's population between 15 and 34 years of age. However, the condition numbers for this model were over 60 for each type of homicide, indicating a high degree of multicollinearity between the independent variables. Dropping the proportion 15 to 34 variable produced more acceptable condition numbers of less than 30. Nevertheless, the inferences drawn from the model are not substantially altered if the percent 15 to 34 variable is included. For a description of condition numbers, see David A. Belsley, Edwin Kuh, and Roy E. Welsch, *Regression Diagnostics* (New York: Wiley, 1980).

    21. Alan Cline, *State of War: Michigan in World War II* (Ann Arbor, MI: University of Michigan Press, 1979).

    22. Isaac Ehrlich, "The Deterrent Effect of Capital Punishment: A Question of Life and Death," *American Economic Review* 65:3 (June 1975): 397–417. Ehrlich specifies a simultaneous equation model in which homicide rates and clearance rates have immediate effects on each other. His model assumes that increases in clearance rates immediately reduce crime, and also that increases in crime immediately reduce clearance rates. The latter has been called a "strain effect" because the level of crime strains the resources of law enforcement to respond efficiently. Other researchers—e.g., Llad Phillips and Subhash Ray, "Evidence on the Identification and Causality Dispute About the Death Penalty," in O.D. Anderson and M. Perryman, eds., *Applied Time Series Analysis*, (New York: North Holland, 1982) and Thomas F Pogue, "Offender Expectations and Identification of Crime Supply Functions," *Evaluation Review* 10:4 (Aug. 1986): 455–82—accept the basic notion that crime rates and clearance rates influence each other. However, they argue that, while crime should affect clearance rates immediately, the effects of increases in clearances on crime should occur with some lag. Our model is based on these alternative models, and thus is not estimated as a simultaneous equation system.

    23. It is easy to show that a model with a lagged value of the dependent variable on the right-hand side of the equation implies that the other independent variables follow a geometric distributed lag. For a demonstration and further discussion, see Robert S. Pindyck and Daniel L. Rubinfeld, *Econometric Models and Economic Forecasts*, 2nd ed. (New York: McGraw-Hill, 1981), 232–3.

24. For similar applications, see Lawrence E. Cohen, Marcus Felson, and Kenneth C. Land, "Property Crime Rates in the United States: A Macrodynamic Analysis, 1947–1977; With Ex Ante Forecasts for the Mid-1980s," *American Journal of Sociology* 86:1 (July 1980): 90–118; and James Alan Fox, "The Geometric Distributed Lag and Its Application to Police Expenditures," in James Alan Fox, ed., *Models in Quantitative Criminology* (New York: Academic, 1981), 103–20.

25. Larry D. Engelmann, "A Separate Peace: The Politics of Prohibition Enforcement in Detroit, 1920–1930," *Detroit in Perspective* 1 (Autumn 1972): 71.

26. See Detroit Police Department, *Annual Report* 1925 and 1926.

27. Robert Conot, *American Odyssey* (New York: William Morrow, 1974), 269.

28. Ibid., 376.

29. Ibid., 626.

30. This analysis was performed separately for each type of homicide using Box-Cox methods. See, for example, Jan Kmenta, *Elements of Econometrics*, 2nd ed. (New York: Macmillan, 1986), 518–21.

31. The SUR model increases the precision (efficiency) of estimates by allowing for the contemporaneous correlation between the error terms. Although a contemporaneous correlation between the errors for domestic and criminal transaction homicides could be produced in several ways, one possible mechanism is omitted explanatory variables. If omitted variables influence both types of homicide in the same way each year, the errors for the two types of homicide will be correlated. When this correlation is taken into account, the size of the error term for each equation will be reduced. For further discussion of the SUR model see, for example, A. C. Harvey, *The Econometric Analysis of Time Series* (New York: Wiley, 1981), 67–73, 293–300; or Kmenta, *Elements of Econometrics*, 635–48. All SUR results presented here are maximum likelihood estimates.

32. See, for example, Parker and Smith, "Deterrence, Poverty," 615–6.

33. The analysis was based on a set of F tests, separately comparing each variable across the two equations.

34. To assess the possibility of autocorrelated errors we applied Durbin's *h* test for a first-order autoregressive process to each equation separately. We also applied a Lagrange multiplier test to the equations jointly in order to examine the possibility of vector autoregressive errors. See Harvey, *Econometric Analysis*, 174–6, 298–9 for a discussion of these tests.

35. The long-term effects of an independent variable are calculated as $\beta/(1-\omega)$, where β is the slope for the independent variable and ω is the slope for the lagged value of the homicide rate.

36. Cantor and Land, "Unemployment and Crime Rates," 318–23.

37. Daniel Nagin, "General Deterrence: A Review of the Empirical Literature," in Alfred Blumstein, Jacqueline Cohen and Daniel Nagin, eds., *Deterrence and Incapacitation: Estimating the Effects of Criminal Sanctions on Crime Rates* (Washington, D.C.: National Academy of Sciences, 1978), 95–139.

38. Dane Archer and Rosemary Gartner, *Violence and Crime in Cross-National Perspective* (New Haven: Yale University Press, 1984), 69–70.

39. Ted Robert Gurr, "Historical Trends in Violent Crime: A Critical Review of the Evidence," in Norval Morris and Michael Tonry, eds., *Crime and Justice: An Annual Review of Research* (Chicago: University of Chicago Press, 1981), 3:295–353; Thor Norström, "Theft Criminality and Economic Growth," *Social Science Research* 17:1 (March 1988): 48–65.

Chapter 8

Identifying Potential Assassins: Some Situational Correlates of Dangerousness[1]

JAMES W. CLARKE

In the 200 years since 1789 when George Washington became the first President of the United States, through the term of Ronald Reagan which expires in 1989, forty men have held the nation's highest office. Four of them were killed by assassins,[2] and serious attempts were made on the lives of six others.[3] Thus one out four presidents have been the targets of violent attempts to remove them from office. Furthermore, the political careers of four presidential candidates were interrupted, or ended, by violence.[4] Add to that list of casualties the names of Black Muslim leader, Malcolm X, who was murdered in 1965, and civil rights leader, Martin Luther King, Jr., shot to death three years later, and it would be reasonable to conclude that political prominence in the United States often entails very grave risks.

Especially since 1963. Although three of the four presidential assassinations occurred in the last century, the number of attacks has doubled since 1963. There have been eight assassination attempts on the lives of nationally prominent political leaders in the twenty-five years between 1963 and 1988, as many as there had been in the previous 174 years of the nation's presidential history.[5] Because of that, there is growing interest in developing more accurate methods of identifying the dangerous persons who are likely to commit these acts. Actuarial and clinical approaches have dominated this pursuit to date. My purpose in this chapter is to suggest how *situational* variables may provide more useful clues in *short-term* assessments of dangerousness.

In my previous work on American assassins, I studied the sixteen persons responsible for these earlier attacks.[6] Since then, another, John Hinckley, Jr. has been added to the list. I suggested a typology of assassins and would-be assassins that was derived from an assessment of dispositional and contextual factors. The typology is summarized in Figure 8.1. The

CHARACTERISTICS	TYPE I	TYPE II	TYPE III	TYPE IV
Emotional distortion	Mild	Moderate	Severe	Severe
Cognitive distortion	Absent	Absent	Absent	Severe
Hallucinations	Absent	Absent	Absent	Present
Delusions	Absent	Absent	Absent	Present
Reality contact	Clear	Clear	Clear	Poor
Social relations	Varied	Disturbed	Isolated	Isolated
Primary motive	Political	Personal/Compensatory	Personal/Provocation	Irrational

Figure 8.1: Types of American Assassins

subjects ranged from rational political extremists (Type I) through two shades of mental and emotional disturbance (Types II and III) to the truly insane (Type IV). The distribution of subjects is presented in Figure 8.2.[7]

This relatively small number of only seventeen actual subjects contrasts sharply with the over 26,000 persons who have been investigated by the Secret Service as being potential threats to the president (or other persons in their charge), and the 250 to 400 suspects, drawn from that total, who, at any one time, are considered dangerous and placed on the Service's "watch list" for continued surveillance.[8] Tough decisions. The president's life depends on them—not to mention the Constitutional and legal implications of improper arrests—and they are still based largely on the intuition of Secret Service agents. No one knows how actual assassins differ from the thousands of non-dangerous subjects who are brought to the attention of the Secret Service, or the hundreds of those considered dangerous and placed on the watch list. How does one distinguish between the real threats and the bluffs? Between a Lee Harvey Oswald, for example, who only twelve days before he killed President Kennedy threatened to bomb the FBI's Dallas office, and a harmless drunk who says somebody ought to shot the so-and-so, referring to the president? The FBI apparently assumed Oswald fit the latter category.

There are no formulas to gauge the seriousness of the threat posed; there is no check-list of symptoms, or valid profile of characteristics, to go by; and there are no mental health professionals to call upon who are any better prepared to evaluate dangerousness of this kind than an experienced agent.[9] For reasons that I will explain, there is probably little to distinguish between suspects and actual assassins in actuarial and clinical terms.[10] Yet we know that real assassins are, in some very important way, *different*.

Although I emphasized the importance of *context* in my earlier work on assassins and would-be assassins, I did not define with any operational rigor what elements within those contexts were of critical importance. But despite these operational and predictive limitations, the typology de-

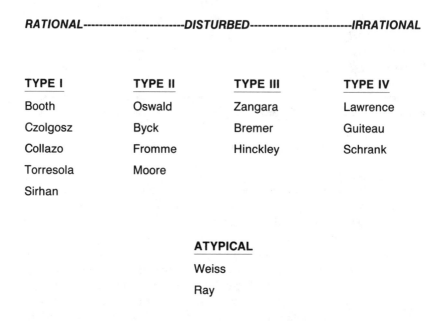

Figure 8.2: Classification of American Assassins and Would-Be Assassins, 1835–1981

scribed in *American Assassins* represents a significant departure from the view of American assassins described in the earlier literature. That work missed important motivational distinctions among assassins because it failed to take into account the varying political contexts of their acts. Considered in this contextual vacuum, it is hardly surprising that assassins as different as John Wilkes Booth and Charles Guiteau were depicted as paranoid schizophrenics.[11]

Perhaps, it is for that reason that law enforcement agencies (including the FBI and the Secret Service, as well as local police) that drew upon such flawed research for guidance have questioned and released as insufficient threats five of the last eight persons who have attacked American presidents. Lee Harvey Oswald, for example, was well-known to the FBI before he killed President Kennedy in 1963; Samuel Byck had been interviewed three times by the Secret Service before his attempt on President Nixon's life in 1974; Lynette Fromme's threats were known to both the FBI and local police before her 1975 attack on President Ford; Sara Jane Moore had hinted at her intentions to local law enforcement officials and was interviewed by the Secret Service the night before she fired a shot at President

Ford, also in 1975; and an armed John Hinckley was arrested and released by local authorities at the Nashville airport during his 1980 stalk of President Carter—the same day Carter was scheduled to arrive in Nashville. One might also include Arthur Bremer whose conspicuous attire and behavior were observed by authorities at a number of presidential candidate George Wallace's rallies in 1972—days, and hundreds of miles, apart— before he finally got close enough to cripple the Governor in the parking lot of a Maryland shopping center.[12]

But concerns about the threat of violence in American society extend well beyond those responsible for the safety of American presidents and presidential candidates. As the incidence of violent crime, in general, increased dramatically in the last two decades, scholarly attention has slowly focused on the violent offender and how such persons can be identified and controlled. But progress has been slow. As with assassins, there is still no valid and reliable method of identifying dangerous persons who pose a threat to the general public, or themselves.[13]

Our knowledge of dangerousness can be characterized as conceptually and theoretically deficient for several reasons: Until recently, there has been much commentary but little actual research on the problem.[14] And, within the relatively small body of research that has appeared, there are significant limitations associated with both the actuarial and clinical approaches that have guided that research. Closely related to these difficulties in approach is the relative lack of systematic attention given to the effect of *situational* variables in violent behavior.

Dangerousness: The Actuarial Approach

Despite the dramatic increase in assassination attempts since 1963, these remain rare events in a statistical sense. Unlike the alarmingly high levels of street violence, eight serious assassination attempts since 1963 are not very many in a population of over 230 million people. Obviously, this reveals something about the effectiveness of the job the Secret Service and other security agencies are doing. But this "low base-rate" of incidents precludes empirically based probability studies of the kind necessary to identify those persons most likely to attempt an assassination.

Actuarial models have achieved some success in identifying, in a statistical sense, the type of person most likely to become involved in ordinary violent crime—assault, murder, and armed robbery. The problem is that actuarial models of street violence do not seem to be applicable to political assassinations.[15] Consider the left column of Table 8.1, the best sociological predictors of individual violence: In a statistical sense, who is the most dangerous person in America? Does such a person also represent the most serious threat to the President?

Table 8.1. A Ranking of Actuarial Predictors of Violent Crime and Their Applicability to Assassins and Would-Be Assassins[1]

Best Predictors	Applicability (n = 17)
1. Previous record of criminal violence	1 (Ray)
2. Age (18–25)	5 (Torresola, Oswald, Sirhan, Bremer and Hinckley)
3. Sex (male)	15 (all except Fromme and Moore)
4. Race (black)	0
5. Social class (lower)	3 (Oswald, Ray, and Bremer)
6. Drug abuse	0
7. IQ (low)	0
8. Education/skills (poor)	4 (Lawrence, Torresola, Oswald, and Ray)
9. Unemployment	14 (all except Booth, Weiss and Collazo)
10. Peer influence	2 (Fromme and Moore)

[1]Adapted from FBI annual crime statistics.

Consistent with Bernard Goetz's enraged assessment, actuarial statistics indicate that the most dangerous person in America is a young black male with a previous record of violent offenses. Would the police chief of Newark, Detroit, or any other large city in America disagree? Unlikely. Those demographic characteristics describe the person most likely to rape, murder, and rob, but such a person has yet to attack a president or a presidential candidate. And if the data were available (and they are not), my guess is few such persons would be found on the Secret Service's watch list of its most dangerous suspects. Why? No one knows. Given the long history of black oppression, and presidential indifference to it, in the United States, it remains one of the mysteries of American political behavior.

To underscore the point, consider the applicability of actuarial indicators to the universe of seventeen assassins and would-be assassins in the righthand column of Table 8.1. With the exception of sex (male) and unemployment, there is scant demographic similarity between the ordinary violent criminal and persons who attack presidents. The best predictor of ordinary violent crime—a previous history of violence—applies to only one of the seventeen subjects, James Earl Ray. Even youth has only limited applicability: most presidential attackers were beyond the crime-prone later teens of their street counterparts.

Dangerousness: The Clinical Approach

Most observers agree with John Monahan's well-known conclusion that "A fair summary of the existing literature on the prediction of violent behavior would be that mental health professionals are accurate at best in one out of three predictions of violent behavior that they make."[16] The conclusion is consistent with other earlier assessments[17] and is empirically grounded in a handful of significant follow-up studies of mental patients who had been institutionalized as dangerous and then released by the courts.[18] There are a number of reasons cited for this gloomy record: First, there is the dubious validity and reliability of a good number of psychological tests regularly employed as diagnostic tools. The relationship between psychometric measures and violent behavior is minimal.[19] Second, in the absence of any empirically verifiable criteria for dangerousness, there has been a well-documented tendency of psychiatrists to overdiagnose mental illness as well as the potential dangerousness of their patients.[20] This was reflected in the subjectivity, and embarrassing diagnostic inconsistencies, that characterized the psychiatric testimony in the trials of assassins and would-be assassins Guiteau, Czolgosz, Sirhan, Bremer and, most recently, John Hinckley.[21] When clinical interviews are successful, it is usually because of some indefinable—and, as yet, unteachable—talent possessed by the interviewer.[22] Third, there is the accompanying clinical inclination to focus on dispositional characteristics while ignoring critical situational factors that contribute to one's potential for violence.[23]

A more general problem that must also be considered is the dominant approach and paradigm of too much behavioral science. Most research is still based on attitudinal studies of what people *say* as opposed to what they actually *do*. Obviously, it is much easier to study attitudes and opinions than it is to study actual behavior, and that fact undoubtedly has something to do with the dominance of the mode of research. But this easier, more convenient approach has contributed much to the barren theoretical landscape that characterizes the study of dangerousness, not to mention other vast areas of the social sciences. Unfortunately, even most honest people cannot accurately report what they will do in the usually stressful, unstructured situations that signal danger; they can only say what they *intend* to do. Heroism and cowardice are difficult to predict. Most of us like to think that we would help another person in distress and would probably state such intentions to an interviewer. Yet one need only recall, for example, when a jetliner hit a Washington bridge in 1982 and plunged into the icy Potomac, that only a handful of persons—out of the thousands of rush-hour onlookers—made any attempt to help the survivors. If ordinary people are so inherently limited in insight and ability to anticipate their future behavior in stressful situations, can we expect any more from those persons whose lives are, shall we say, somewhat more disordered?

Situational variables are not only important determinants of behavior, they also have a bearing on the way persons answer questions and the way those answers are evaluated. Clinical examinations are usually conducted within institutional settings where the setting itself becomes a key factor in the subject's responses *and* the examiner's evaluation of those responses. If we include the possibility of calculated and deliberate deception (common among persons in institutional settings be they mental hospitals, jails, and even, if we can believe the sworn testimony of Oliver North, the staff of the National Security Council), self-reported information regarding criminal behavior, especially serious violence, or one's willingness to commit a violent act in the future, is probably unreliable. Also, it is not clear that what is known about dangerousness within institutionalized populations necessarily applies to those dangerous persons roaming the streets. Self-reported information—or "attitudinal measures"—are especially uncertain guides in assessing dangerousness, whether the attitudes are expressed in clinical interviews or registered in agree/disagree fashion on pencil and paper tests. It is a mistake to assume that rhetoric in any form is a valid and reliable gauge of sentiment—and, especially, action—in unstructured situations.

In summary, the clinical approach, for all these reasons, has yet to produce a reliable empirically-based method of assessing dangerousness. In terms of *clinical* criteria, most American assassins and would-be assassins did not appear to be dangerous prior to their criminal acts. For example, both Samuel Byck and John Hinckley were seeing psychiatrists before their attacks. Neither was considered dangerous. In most cases in which assassins and would-be assassins were brought to trial, mental health experts could not agree on either the *existence*, or *seriousness*, of mental or emotional impairment.

If these difficulties in the clinical approach are so apparent in the courtroom, is there any reason to believe that the same approach would produce more valid and reliable information in the field? How helpful is the clinical approach to an agent in the field when he or she is required to make that important *short-term* prediction of whether an individual is dangerous to the president? Should the suspect be detained for further investigation, or released? How well does that approach supplement the important but intangible skills of insight and intuition upon which such decisions are presently based? Unfortunately, the clinical approach remains almost totally dependent on self-reports that assume the suspect's willingness to answer questions truthfully.

For different reasons, the typology of assassins (described earlier in Figures 8.1 and 8.2) that emerged out of my earlier research is also, as it stands, of little use in assessing dangerousness. But that typology, because it associates types of assassins and would-be assassins with particular incidents and eras, provides a useful starting point for a *situationally* defined strategy for assessing this kind of dangerousness.

A Situational Approach to Predicting Political Dangerousness

Two recent studies have attempted to synthesize what is known about dangerousness, from both the clinical and actuarial literature, and to formulate diagnostic and predictive strategies. Both recognized, but neither was able to define nor to incorporate successfully, situational variables which the authors of one of the studies described as "the socially constructed nature of the dangerousness phenomenon."[24] That is the problem I want to address.

Before I do, let me emphasize once again that my research and the observations here are limited to only seventeen assassins or would-be assassins who have been involved in serious attacks on nationally prominent political figures. I have suggested that they constitute a small, and perhaps unique, subset of dangerous persons. I do not have access to Secret Service information about people who make threats, those who have been placed on watch lists, or the persons who have been arrested before they got within striking range of their intended victims. This restriction, and the "low base-rate" problem mentioned earlier, define the limits of my approach.

How can potential assassins be identified? Obviously, the psychological characteristics identified in Figure 8.1 do not set them apart from millions of other completely harmless persons who are grappling with similar concerns, problems and afflictions. But most assassins are drawn into identifiable behavior patterns before they strike. Those patterns are suggestive of two dominant emotional states common to many of these subjects—anger and depression.

In order to consider this point, I have listed certain behavioral indicators that reflect these two emotional states. In Table 8.2 the seventeen subjects are listed chronologically from left to right. The totals for each indicator are presented in the column on the extreme right. For purposes of brevity, I will emphasize the modern cases, although my observations, except for those about contemporary media influences, apply to the subjects in both eras.

Notice that Table 8.2 is divided, left to right, separating the nine early subjects (1835–1950) from the more recent (1963–1981). This chronological distinction recognizes the advent of television in the 1950s as a new, and profoundly important, influence in American culture. And, as I will suggest, it has become a factor that figures prominently in the motives of most recent assassins. The table is divided from top to bottom into three sets of indicators comprised of twelve items that can be assessed and verified *empirically*. Note that none are solely dependent on self-reported information or the usual clinical assessment techniques.

The detection indicators refer simply to those factors that bring a suspect to the attention of a security officer: suspicious behavior in proximity to the political figure, weapons possession, or an overt threat of some type. Suspicious behavior in proximity to the intended victim is a recent phenomenon. Six of the eight post-1963 subjects exhibited such behavior with only Sirhan and Ray being exceptions. Only two of the nine earlier subjects, the grossly disturbed Lawrence and Guiteau, were conspicuous in this sense. What is

Table 8.2. Situational Indicators of Dangerousness

INDICATORS	Early Subjects:[1] 1935–1950									Recent Subjects[2] 1963–1981								
	LAW '35	BTH '65	GUT '81	CZL '01	SNK '12	ZGA '33	WIS '35	CZO '50	TSA '50	OSW '63	SRN '68	RAY '68	BRM '72	BYK '74	FRM '75	MOR '75	HNK '81	TOTALS (n–17)
Detection:																		
1. Suspicious behavior	X	—	X	—	—	—	—	—	—	X	—	—	X	X	X	X	X	8
2. Weapons possession	X	X	X	X	X	X	X	—	X	X	X	—	X	—	—	X	X	14
3. Threats	—	—	—	—	—	—	—	—	—	X	—	—	—	X	—	X	—	4
Engagement:																		
1. Ideological intensity	X	X	X	X	X	—	—	X	X	X	X	—	—	X	X	—	—	11
2. Stalking	—	X	X	X	X	—	—	—	—	—	X	X	X	—	—	X	X	7
3. Interest/victim	X	X	—	X	X	—	—	—	—	X	X	—	X	X	—	X	X	9
4. Interest/assassins	—	—	—	—	—	—	—	—	—	X	X	—	X	X	X	—	X	6
Disengagement:																		
1. Occupational instability	X	—	X	X	X	X	—	—	X	X	X	X	X	X	X	X	X	14
2. Transience	X	—	X	X	X	X	—	—	—	X	—	X	X	X	X	X	X	12
3. Family estrangement	X	—	X	X	X	X	—	—	—	X	—	X	X	X	X	X	X	11
4. Attention seeking	X	—	X	—	—	—	—	—	—	X	—	—	X	X	X	X	X	4
5. Suicidal	—	—	—	—	—	—	—	—	—	X	—	—	X	X	—	—	X	4
Subject score	8	4	8	7	7	4	1	1	3	11	6	5	10	10	7	7	10	
	Average score = 4.7 (n = 9)									Average score = 8.3 (n = 8)								

1. From left to right the subjects and their targets are: Richard Lawrence (Andrew Jackson), John Wilkes Booth (Abraham Lincoln), Charles Guiteau (James A. Garfield), Leon Czolgosz (William McKinley), Schrank (Theodore Roosevelt), Giuseppe Zangara (Franklin Roosevelt), Carl Weiss (Huey Long), Oscar Collazo (Harry Truman), and Griselio Torresola (Harry Truman).

2. From left to right the subjects and their targets are: Lee Harvey Oswald (John Kennedy), Sirhan Sirhan (Robert Kennedy), James Earl Ray (Martin Luther King), Arthur Bremer (George Wallace), Samuel Byck (Richard Nixon), Lynette Fromme (Gerald Ford), Sara Jane Moore (Gerald Ford), and John Hinckley (Ronald Reagan).

suspicious behavior in proximity to a political figure? A wide variety of behavior qualifies as suspicious. It may be a person in a crowd awaiting the president who is acting oddly, or dressed inappropriately, or it might be something as obvious as someone carrying a weapon. For example, Arthur Bremer was an armed regular at Wallace rallies many days and many miles apart. He was also very conspicuous—usually near the front of the crowd, shouting to the candidate and waving, dressed in a bizarre red, white, and blue outfit with Wallace campaign buttons. Samuel Byck's picketing in front of the White House—*after* he had threatened President Nixon's life and the Israeli Embassy—was clearly suspicious, but officials did not put the threats and the picketing together. Or, if they did, they apparently believed they were legally powerless do anything about Byck. Lynette Fromme's reputation, and well-known attempts to publicize the alleged injustice of Charles Manson's trial, combined with the bizarre red robes she wore as she waited for President Ford to pass by, could be considered suspicious behavior. Or it might be something less obvious such as John Hinckley's arrival at the Nashville airport with three handguns in his suitcase on the day President Carter was scheduled to speak there.

All somehow were ignored or discounted as threats. No one paid any attention to Bremer until after he shot the governor; then many who traveled with Wallace, including his personal security guards, remembered seeing him many times before. And at least a few people in Washington must have cringed when they learned that Sam Byck was serious, that he had killed himself following a failed attempt to crashdive a jetliner into the Nixon White House. Lynette Fromme summed it up for herself when she said after her arrest that *no* one ever took her seriously. And no one made anything out of the coincidence of the Hinckley/Carter Nashville arrivals despite Hinckley's weapons. Hinckley was not even questioned thoroughly when his guns were confiscated and he was fined and released.

Prior weapons possession means little by itself among a people as well-armed as Americans. But in combination with other information, it may be important. Only three of the seventeen subjects—Oscar Collazo, Samuel Byck and Lynette Fromme—did not own weapons prior to their attacks.

Despite the fact that a very large proportion of suspects come to the attention of authorities as a result of threats they have made, only four of the seventeen subjects actually made threats prior to their attacks. On the surface, this finding alone would seem to cast doubt upon the practice of using persons who have made threats as proxies for actual assassins in statistical probability studies. Most threateners are probably very different from actual assassins, but half the recent subjects made threats before they struck. As Oswald, Byck, Fromme, and Moore have taught us, threats still cannot be ignored. Even though three of these subjects owned weapons, and all had behaved suspiciously enough to come to the attention of authorities, their actual threats were not considered serious enough for them to warrant surveillance during presidential visits. Consider, for example, Sara Jane Moore's threat—made seeking arrest, to both the San Francisco police and the Secret Service—that she planned to "test" President Ford's security the next day. And it wasn't until after Lee Harvey Oswald killed President Kennedy that an FBI agent in Dallas remembered that Oswald had threatened to bomb the Bureau's offices only ten days before.

It is after a suspect comes to the attention of authorities that the other indicators—*engagement* and *disengagement*—become important in assessing whether this person constitutes a real threat, or is like so many of the persons who make threats, merely an emotionally-disturbed person seeking attention. The engagement indicators refer to those behavioral attributes that suggest *anger* and *aggression* toward a political figure: they include ideological intensity, stalking behavior, an unusual interest in the intended victim, and an unusual interest in the lives of past assassins.

Disengagement indicators suggest something about the *isolation* and *withdrawal* from ordinary social constraints that often precede violent acts. These indicators—occupational instability, transience, family estrangement, and attention-seeking behavior—are reflective of the interpersonal difficulties, stress and depression that characterize, especially, the Type II and Type III subjects. Consider the empirical and operational basis of each set of indicators.

Engagement Indicators

Ideological intensity. Eleven of the seventeen subjects can be described as having had a strong ideological perspective, especially subjects in the pre-1950 era where seven of nine can be described this way. What may seem odd is that only four of the eight more recent subjects had a strong ideological perspective; for the other half of this group, ideology was unimportant. The rational basis of those perspectives varied greatly from the delusions of the Type IV's, such as Guiteau and Schrank, through the compensatory beliefs of the Type II's, to the rational extremism of the Type I's like Collazo and Sirhan. But rationality *per se* doesn't matter. What does matter is that such persons, for whatever reasons, often have in their possession an unusual amount of political material—books, newspaper articles, campaign literature and the like. This material is often carried with them; it was found in trunks of cars some had used, or in quarters they had recently occupied. Such evidence is probably a much more significant indicator of ideological intensity than assessments based on interviews.

Stalking behavior. Seven of the seventeen subjects stalked their victims; half of those involved in post-1963 attacks were stalkers. Bus and airline ticket stubs, motel and credit card receipts, newspaper clippings from different newspapers and, most obviously, copies of presidential or campaign schedules probably provide the best clues to this type of behavior. *Interest in the intended victim.* Victim interest can be distinguished from ideological intensity although the two may be related since the sources are often the same—newspaper and magazine articles and campaign materials. Arthur Bremer and John Hinckley, for example, had no discernible political perspective, but both had an abiding interest in the *men* they shot. In this sense, interest refers to an unusual and enduring curiosity in the intended victim as a personality. Possession of books and articles, for example, about a president's, or a candidate's, personal life are one important bit of information, as are clipped newspaper, magazine, and postcard photographs. Materials of this kind were found in the possession of nine of the seventeen total subjects and five of the eight since 1963.

Interest in prior assassinations. As time goes on, and assassination attempts continue, it has become common for those contemplating such attacks to read about their predecessors, or persons who have committed comparable violent crimes. Leon Czolgosz was the only assassin in the early period who was so inclined, but since then a definite pattern has emerged among five of the last eight subjects: Oswald read about Huey Long's assassination; Sirhan read about Oswald and European assassins; Bremer read about Oswald and, especially, Sirhan, and described in his diary the profound effect the film *Clockwork Orange* had on him; Byck read about Oswald and Sirhan, as well as other Palestinian terrorists, and followed with great interest the story of rooftop sniper Jimmy Essex; and Hinckley read about them all, plus a book about a skyjacker, and fictional accounts of psychopathic killers (not to mention his well-publicized fascination with the film *Taxi Driver*, nor his post-arrest correspondence with serial killer Ted Bundy). Again, such materials are usually found in the subject's possession—or, in some cases, such as Oswald's and Sirhan's—on well-used library cards. It would be unrealistic to expect to elicit such important information in an interview with a suspect.

Disengagement Indicators

Occupational instability. Unemployment or marginal employment is something assassins and would-be assassins share with common street criminals. Fourteen of the subjects fit this characterization. All but Weiss and Collazo were at least "under" employed, while Booth's unemployment during the year preceding his assassination of President Lincoln can be considered a qualified exception in that it was not due to any decline in demand for his widely acknowledged theatrical talents. Rather, Booth chose not to work so he could devote all his time to the Confederate cause.

All eight of the recent subjects had employment problems. Employment status is one of the easiest things to ascertain and verify; it is an integral part of any criminal investigation.

Transience. Restlessness, moving about, changing addresses and traveling are closely linked to both occupational difficulties and emotional instability. Seven out of the eight most recent subjects and over half of their earlier counterparts lived relatively transient lives. With the exceptions of Booth, Weiss, Collazo, Torresola, and Sirhan, the remaining twelve assassins and would-be assassins frequently moved about before they struck. Transience is a little more difficult to determine than employment, but not much. It is often associated with stalking behavior and the same evidence applies. The salient difference is that the travels of a transient do not usually coincide with the appearances of a political figure. John Hinckley, for example, traveled constantly, even before his stalks of Presidents Carter and Reagan. In these instances, airline and bus ticket stubs, credit card receipts, and motel and rent receipts are usually found somewhere among the suspect's possessions.

Family estrangement. This important indicator that characterizes eleven of the seventeen subjects, and six of the eight most recent, is a bit more difficult to assess, but not much. An attempt to locate next of kin is a standard and innocuous part of most routine investigations. If the suspect identifies no one, that in itself is information; if someone is identified, a phone call or two may be revealing, as it would have when John Hinckley was arrested in Nashville. Given the circumstances of his arrest, a call and interview with his parents might have revealed significant information about what he had been doing, or *not* doing, for the past few months. To an informed and perceptive investigator, that could have shed additional light on whether John Hinckley had something other than a visit to Opryland on his mind that day. The fact that Lee Oswald's and Samuel Byck's family difficulties were not linked by authorities to their threats and other aggressive activities suggests another aspect of the problem. Not only should such information be sought, it must also be carefully weighed for what it might suggest about potential future actions.

Attention-seeking behavior. This attribute is particularly striking among the most recent subjects and relates, often directly, to the importance of publicity,—especially televised publicity—in the motives of most recent assassins. Of the earlier nine subjects, only the bizarre and insane antics of Lawrence and Guiteau qualify, but a different pattern emerges since 1963 when every subject except Ray and Sirhan were involved in some form of attention-seeking activities. What were these? Lee Oswald's picketing and media activities in behalf of his bogus Fair Play for Cuba organization, and the threat made to the FBI; Arthur Bremer's bizarre dress and behavior at Wallace rallies; Samuel Byck's threats and picketing in front of the White House, letters to newspapers, as well as the tapes he made for distribution after his death; Lynette Fromme's repeated, and varied, efforts to attract media attention to Charles Manson's plight; and Sara Moore's not so subtle plea to have herself arrested by making an explicit threat. These all were well-documented and relatively public activities that reflect the concerns and sensitivities of these particular subjects, but attention-seeking may also occur on a more *private* level as it did with Oswald and Byck, with their wives (and Byck's children), and Hinckley, with his parents and actress Jodie Foster.

The behavior is significant because it is linked so closely, especially with the motives of Type II and Type III subjects who, in their rejection and frustration, are eventually drawn to commit acts that can no longer be ignored. This kind of highly neurotic behavior should not be confused with the motives of Type I subjects—namely Czolgosz, Collazo and Torresola, and Sirhan—who sought through their attacks to focus public attention on specific political issues. In an operational sense, the public side of this behavior is self-evident; the private side is more difficult to determine. Certain hints of these activities and frustrations may be observed when a suspect is questioned; but, more likely, the information will come from contacts with estranged wives, parents or significant third parties, such as mental health counselors.

Suicidal tendencies. Suicide or suicidal gestures may be a form of attention-seeking behavior. Suicidal tendencies are a characteristic of more recent subjects. Half of the post-1963 subjects of this study—Oswald, Bremer, Byck and Hinckley—displayed moderate to strong suicidal tendencies. Indeed, the assassination attempts of Bremer, Byck and Hinckley can themselves be considered suicide attempts because each expected to die. Information of this kind is usually the most difficult to get. The only sources are police or medical records (Oswald and Byck), or the reports of family members or friends (Hinckley). In all four cases, the suicidal considerations were also recorded by the subjects in diaries; in Bremer's case, his diary represents the only source of evidence.

It should be apparent that none of these indicators taken *alone* is very revealing of anything, let alone a suspect's dangerousness. It is the total score that is (or may be) significant. In Table 8.3, the seventeen subjects are ranked according to their total scores on these combined indicators. Lest there be some misunderstanding as to purpose, let me emphasize that obviously, by definition, *all* these subjects were dangerous. It is not the purpose of Table 8.3 to restate the obvious. Its purpose is merely a heuristic one, to suggest the possible utility of a situational approach for *short-term* predictions of dangerousness. Note, for example, that with the possible exception of Zangara, the *least* likely assassins and would-be assassins (for example, those who in some sense had the *most to lose*) score below the average of 6.4. Again, with the exception of Zangara, all are either Type I, or Atypical, subjects. Put differently, Type I and Atypical subjects

Table 8.3. A Rank Ordering of Dangerousness Scores: All Cases, 1835–1981

SUBJECTS		
Recent *(n=8)*	Early *(n=9)*	Score
1.Oswald*		11
2.Hinckley*		10
3.Bremer**		10
4.Byck*		10
	5.Lawrence	8
	6.Guiteau	8
	7.Czolgosz	7
	8.Schrank	7
9.Fromme*		7
10.Moore*		7
11.Sirhan		6
12.Ray		5
	13.Booth	4
	14.Zangara	4
	15.Torresola	3
	16.Weiss	1
	17.Collazo	1
Average Score = 6.4		

*Subjects who were known to authorities prior to their attacks.
**Bremer was noticed by authorities, but he was never questioned.

are least afflicted with either mental or emotional problems and their motives are, to that extent, more direct and, therefore, easier to understand.
Obviously, this reflects a bias within the approach toward identifying the
mentally or emotionally disturbed Type II and III, and the psychotic Type
IV suspect.

But there is a reason for this bias: Information on political activities and
affiliations is easy to get. The FBI spends a good bit of its time investigating, infiltrating and monitoring the activities of members of political extremist groups. And the Bureau is very effective, if the present difficulties of the
Communist Party USA and the Ku Klux Klan are any indication. But apart
from international terrorist organizations (which pose a different kind of
threat), it is precisely the disturbed Type II and Type III person who, since
1963, now represents the most serious security threat to political figures.
Why?

In Figure 8.3, notice that six of the eight recent assassins and would-be
assassins fall into the two middle "disturbed" (Types II, III) categories.
The difference between Type II's and Type III's is one only of degree:
Type III subjects are much like Type II's except they have slipped a little
bit further over the edge in terms of their inability to deal with their

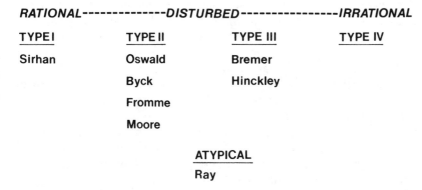

RATIONAL-------------DISTURBED----------------IRRATIONAL

TYPE I	TYPE II	TYPE III	TYPE IV
Sirhan	Oswald	Bremer	
	Byck	Hinckley	
	Fromme		
	Moore		

ATYPICAL

Ray

Figure 8.3: Classification of American Assassins and Would-Be Assassins since 1963

personal problems. They are angry and extremely alienated from society, and dissatisfied with themselves (and not merely with persons with whom they have personal grievances). They see no way out of their difficulties. Both Types II and III displace their aggression on symbols of society as a way of getting even. Those symbols might be a president or a rock star, as John Lennon was for Mark Chapman; it could be even twenty-one ordinary folks having lunch one day in 1984 at that symbol of American life, the "golden arches" of McDonald's—then James Huberty arrived; or people unlucky enough to be strolling across the University of Texas campus in 1966 when Charles Whitman decided to end it all and tried to take forty-five of them with him. It is important to note that both recent Type III subjects considered mass murder before one, Arthur Bremer, decided instead to shoot a presidential candidate, and the other, John Hinckley, Jr., chose a president.

The only difference between the two types is that Type II's attempt to rationalize or justify their personal grievances in terms of some larger political issues or ideals. Type III's do not. They offer no rationales, or if they do, they are vague and idiosyncratic. Instead, they appear to derive some perverse satisfaction from offering no serious explanation for the pain and anguish they have caused. Consider, for example, Arthur Bremer's laconic explanation for shooting Governor Wallace: "Why not, nothing else to do;" or John Hinckley's smiling, "I did it for Jodie."

Both Type II and III are sensitive to the media and use television, especially, as a means of communicating their anger either to significant others in their personal lives (Type II's), or to society at large (Type III's). This is the probable reason for the greater involvement of these two types in the recent era of immediate televised communication that began with the Kennedy assassination in 1963.[25]

The Secret Service spends a disproportionate amount of its time investigating people with psychological problems. Are they really dangerous? No one can be sure. Most mentally disturbed persons are not dangerous. And that, of course, is the problem. But if the false-negative assessments of Oswald, Byck, Fromme, Moore, and Hinckley are considered (not to mention the apparent lapse involving the failure to investigate the very suspicious behavior of Arthur Bremer over the weeks he was observed), Type II and Type III assassins seem to be the most difficult to identify.

How would this situational approach work in identifying dangerous suspects? One possibility might be that a suspect whose score exceeds a certain number, perhaps the 6.4 average, would qualify for immediate preventive detention and further investigation; or, if released, such a person might be marked for future surveillance in the manner of those placed on the Secret Service's watch list. Whatever the method or cutting points used, suspects with scores as high as those of Oswald, Hinckley, Bremer and Byck should certainly create more concern than they apparently have in the past.

Conclusions

The situational approach proposed here is obviously limited by the small data base from which it is derived. And, without a control group to make comparisons, its validity is clearly open to question. It would be interesting to know, for example, how the actual assassins and would-be assassins considered in this chapter compare to the ordinary suspects who come to the attention of the Secret Service, or those considered dangerous enough to be placed on the "watch list," or even the seemingly harmless "White House visitors" who regularly appear at the compound gates with "messages" for the president.

Despite these limitations, the approach seems to offer some advantages over the present data base used for guiding these assessments—for example, highly questionable "proxy" studies.[26] It is important to emphasize that the detection, engagement, and disengagement indicators are reasonably grounded in empirically verifiable evidence. To that degree, the approach is much less dependent on self-reported information. Nonetheless, the situationally-defined engagement and disengagement indicators are suggestive of the critical mental and emotional states of the most common Type II and Type III suspects, namely, *frustration* and *anger*, and their probable *intensity*, as well as their *social isolation*, which may reveal the tenuousness of customary social constraints on the suspect's behavior. Moreover, the operational simplicity of this approach could mean that assessments of dangerousness could be made more expeditiously and confidently in the field. Note that the approach would apply only to decisions on short-term detention, and does not address the more complex clinical/legal issues involved in diagnostic questions that must be answered in cases involving long-term institutionalization.

Obviously, there are many variables that enter into a person's decision to kill a prominent political figure. The task in the short-term is to separate the important from the unimportant. The factors I have identified appear to be important, especially in identifying the danger posed by the most common, but seemingly elusive, Type II and Type III suspects. Clearly, the approach is no substitute for experience and sound intuitive judgments, but it does offer an empirical, if rudimentary, basis to be used in conjunction with such judgments. At present, such a basis does not exist.

Notes

1. This chapter was originally prepared for presentation at Protective Research Briefing No. 18, United States Secret Service, Washington, D.C. (July 29, 1985).

2. They were: Abraham Lincoln in 1865, James A. Garfield in 1881, William McKinley in 1901, and John F. Kennedy in 1963.

3. They were: Andrew Jackson in 1835, Franklin Roosevelt in 1933, Harry Truman in 1950, Richard Nixon in 1974, Gerald Ford (twice) in 1975, and Ronald Reagan in 1981.

4. They were: Theodore Roosevelt in 1912, Huey Long in 1935, Robert Kennedy in 1968, and George Wallace in 1972. Although Long was not a formally declared presidential candidate at the time of his death, there can be little doubt that he was campaigning for the office.

5. Between 1963 and 1988 there have been almost as many assassination attempts (seven) as there have been presidential elections (eight)—not including the two black protest leaders who were slain.

6. J. W. Clarke, *American Assassins: The Darker Side of Politics* (Princeton, NJ: Princeton University Press, 1982).

7. The three convicted killers of Malcolm X, vaguely defined as members of a rival Black Muslim organization, are not included in this study because his death was the result of a gang attack rather than the act of a single assassin, as all the others.

8. J. Takeuchi, F. Solomon, and W. W. Menninger, eds., *Behavioral Science and the Secret Service: Toward the Prevention of Assassination* (Washington, DC: National Academy Press, 1981), 25.

9. See, for example, S. H. Frazier, "On Interviewing Potentially Dangerous Persons," and K. R. Hammond, "On Assessment," in *Behavioral Science and the Secret Service*, 137, 175.

10. This statement cannot be made with complete certainty since the investigative files of the Secret Service are closed.

11. For an extensive review of this literature, see Clarke, *American Assassins*, chap. 1.

12. It is the unfortunate fate of those men and women who are responsible for presidential security that the public rarely learns of their many successes. The fact that there are so few successful assassination attempts in a free and open society of over 230 million well-armed people is worth noting.

13. S. A. Shaw, "Dangerousness and Mental Illness: Some Conceptual, Prediction, and Policy Dilemmas," in C. J. Frederick, ed. *Dangerous Behavior: A Problem in Law and Mental Health* (Washington, DC: National Institute for Mental Health, 1978), 153–191.

14. H. J. Steadman, "Predicting Dangerousness Among the Mentally Ill: Art, Magic and Science," *International Journal of Law and Psychiatry* 6 (1983): 389.

15. See, for example, J. Monahan, "Predicting Violent Behavior: A Review and Critique of Clinical Prediction Studies," in *Behavioral Science and the Secret Service*, 131.

16. Ibid., 129; for a more complete discussion of the problem see Monahan's monograph *The Clinical Prediction of Violent Behavior* (Washington, DC: National Institute of Mental Health, 1981).

17. B. J. Ennis and T. R. Litwack, "Psychiatry and the Presumption of Expertise: Flipping Coins in the Courtroom," *California Law Review* 62:3 (1974): 695–752; B. L. Diamond, "The Psychiatric Prediction of Dangerousness," *University of Pennsylvania Law Review* 123 (1974): 439–452; and A. Dershowitz, "The Law of Dangerousness: Some Fictions About Predictions," *Journal of Legal Education* 23 (1970): 24–46.

18. H. J. Steadman and J. Cocozza, *Careers of the Criminally Insane* (Lexington, MA: Lexington Books, 1974); H. J. Steadman, "A New Look at Recidivism Among Patuxent Inmates," *The Bulletin of the American Academy of Psychiatry and Law* 5 (1977): 200–9; J. Cocozza and H. J. Steadman, "Prediction in Psychiatry: An Example of Misplaced Confidence in Experts," *Social Problems* 25 (1978): 265–76; and T. Thornberry and J. Jacoby, *The Criminally Insane: A Community Follow-up of Mentally Ill Offenders* (Chicago: University of Chicago Press, 1979).

19. E. Megargee, "The Prediction of Violence with Psychological Tests," in C. Spielberger, ed., *Current Topics in Clinical and Community Psychology* (New York: Academic Press, 1970); Monahan, *Clinical Prediction*, 50; and T. Holland, G. Beckett and M. Levi, "Intelligence, Personality, and Criminal Violence: A Multivariate Analysis, "*Journal of Consulting and Clinical Psychology*," 49 (February, 1981): 106–11.

20. A classic experiment in such institutional effects on the examiners is, D. L. Rosenhan, "On Being Sane in Insane Places," *Science* 179 (1973): 250–58; see also J. Rappeport and G. Lassen, "Dangerousness: Arrest Rate Comparisons of Discharged Patients and the General Population," *American Journal of Psychiatry* 212 (1965): 776–83; also, *Baxstrom v. Herold* 383, U.S. 107 (1966) and a discussion of the results in Steadman and Cocozza, *Careers of the Criminally Insane*; Cocozza and Steadman, "Prediction in Psychiatry," 265–76; and Monahan, *Clinical Prediction*, 77–82.

21. Clarke, *American Assassins*, 39–62, 76–104, 174–193, and 198–213.

22. See, for example, C. Montandon and T. Harding, "The Reliability of Dangerousness Assessments: A Decision Making Exercise," 144 *British Journal of Psychiatry* (1984): 149–155; Monahan, *Clinical Prediction*, 21–38; and J. Cocozza and H. Steadman, "The Failure of Psychiatric Predictions of Dangerousness: Clear and Convincing Evidence," 29 *Rutgers Law Review* (1976): 1074–1101.

23. H. J. Steadman, "A Situational Approach to Violence," *International Journal of Law and Psychiatry* 5 (1982): 171–86; Monahan, *Clinical Prediction*; and M. Cohen, A. Groth, and R. Siegel, "The Clinical Prediction of Dangerousness," *Crime and Delinquency* 24 (1978): 28–39. For examples of such myopic, dispositionally focused explanations in the literature of assassins, see L. Z. Freedman, "Assassination: Psychopathology and Social Pathology," *Postgraduate Medicine* 37 (June, 1965): 650–58; and D. W. Hastings, "The Psychiatry of Presidential Assassination," parts 1–4, *The Journal Lancet* 85 (March, April, May, July, 1965).

24. R. J. Menzies, C. D. Webster, and D. S. Sepejak, "The Dimensions of Dangerousness," *Law and Human Behavior* 9 (1985): 49–70; see also H. V. Hall, "Predicting Dangerousness for the Courts," *American Journal of Forensic Psychiatry* 5 (1984): 77–96.

25. Clarke, *American Assassins*, 267–8.

26. Proxy studies seek insights into the behavior of potential assassins by studying substitutes, such as dangerous mental patients, ordinary violent offenders and persons who have attempted suicide.

Chapter 9

Firearms and Violence: Old Premises and Current Evidence

DON B. KATES, Jr.

The *Washington Post* was over-optimistic when it proclaimed in 1965 that "The gun control debate is over; the gun owners lost." Not that the gun lobby itself has wrought any intellectual revolution. In fact it so completely abandoned efforts at academic discourse that its opponents virtually monopolized that arena until neutral scholars began studying gun issues in the last decade. But their more neutral assessments have had the effect of reviving the debate, if only by casting doubt on the shibboleths of both sides. Unable to marshal scholarly resources of its own, the gun lobby could nevertheless cite a series of assessments beginning with Bruce-Briggs' scathing comment that

> [despite the enormous volume of academic writing] it is startling to note that no policy research worthy of the name has been done on the issue of gun control. The few attempts at serious work are of marginal competence and tainted by obvious bias.[1]

In 1978 the Carter Administration's National Institute of Justice funded a complete review of extant social scientific literature on guns, to be done by the University of Massachusetts's Social and Demographic Research Center. This encyclopedic work set the benchmark and point of departure for all later research in the field. Begun with the expectation of ratifying the anti-gun views its senior authors admittedly shared, it ended instead with an almost unrelentingly negative evaluation of the entire corpus of gun control literature. Though not as yet reflected in the *Post* and other popular literature, current scholarly appraisals are epitomized by the sorrowful comment of Duke University's Philip J. Cook, co-author of a Ford Foundation study of gun control, in an unpublished 1976 paper:

While the consistent failure of gun control proposals to pass Congress has often been blamed on lobbying efforts of the NRA, part of the problem may be that the case for more stringent gun control regulation has not been made in any scientific fashion.

By the 1980s study of gun issues was pursued with unparalleled vigor and scholarship. In large part this has further discredited much anti-gun vituperation. But this should not be thought to refute the case for rational control over deadly weapons since vituperation was never necessary to making that case. By analogy, the case for controls over cars does not rest upon vituperation against the sanity, morality or good intentions of those who desire to own and drive cars.

Indeed it is arguable that, in discrediting such extreme anti-gun vituperation, modern research does not refute, but rather advances, the cause of rational gun control. This is because this vituperation fuels fanatic gun owner opposition to the very concept of control. Would not drivers fanatically oppose regulation if it were debated in the vituperative and extremist terms anti-gun proponents insist on injecting into every debate over even modest gun controls: that the ultimate goal is a complete ban (except to the military and police) because "Gun Lunatics Silence [the] Sounds of Civilization," "Handgun Nuts Are Just That, Really Nuts," "Sex Education Belongs in the Gun Store," and "Wretchedness Is a Warm Gun"? These article titles[2] are, unfortunately, all too typical of the counter-productive terms in which some gun control advocates insist on couching the debate. Of course gun owners are often no less vituperative. But there is a crucial difference in the effect of each side's vituperation; anti-gun vituperation assures fanatical defiance from the very people (the gun owners) whose cooperation is necessary if any kind of new controls are to be enacted and, more important, enforced.

In each section that follows I apply modern research findings to thirteen gun control arguments, each of which is indicated by a slogan or stereotype from one or both sides which heads the section. It bears emphasis that even when the findings tend to refute extreme anti-gun claims this may be seen not as vindicating the gun lobby so much as clearing the way for more moderate and rational arguments for more moderate and rational gun regulation.

Gun Control Arguments

(1) GUN CONTROL VIOLATES THE SECOND AMENDMENT VS. THE AMENDMENT ONLY APPLIES TO THE STATE MILITIA, NOT INDIVIDUALS

Both statements are essentially false. On the one hand, the gun lobby is clearly right that what is protected is an individual right to own guns. For instance, Madison was not denoting a right of the states when he phrased the Second Amendment as a "right of the people"—a term he used to describe individual rights just sixteen words earlier in the First Amendment, and again twenty-six words later in the Fourth. The private letters, speeches, and so on, of members of the First Congress and their contemporaries show them including the right to arms in their lists of what they called "human rights" or "personal rights," and discussing it in the same breath as freedom of religion, the press, and so on. Federalist and Anti-Federalist commentaries agreed in explaining the future Second Amendment as guaranteeing the people the right to keep "their own arms," "their private arms." Finally, to recognize an individual right to arms does not militate against a purpose of also protecting the militia: for the "militia" was not some military unit but a system which required that each household have a gun (to deter and defend against both crime and foreign invasion) and that men of military age appear regularly for militia drill bearing their own guns. Thus by guaranteeing the arms of the individual householder, the Amendment guaranteed the arms of a militia composed of those householders.[3]

But recognizing all this does not imply accepting the extravagant claim that what is precluded is not just outright banning of guns but any control the gun lobby happens to oppose. So long as the right of responsible law abiding adults to own handguns and other common defensive weapons is not unduly impeded, the Second Amendment allows not only the prohibition (which the gun lobby itself supports) of arms to felons and the irresponsible, but enforcement of that prohibition by non-discriminatory permit and registration requirements. By analogy, the First Amendment guarantee of freedom of speech does not preclude non-discriminatory permit and registration requirements as to marches and demonstrations, or making it a crime to solicit murder or prostitution.[4]

(2) "THE PROLIFERATION OF HANDGUNS. . . . "

Because exaggerated guesses have been so often offered, it bears emphasis that partisans on both sides of the gun debate have reasons to exaggerate the extent of gun ownership: Anti-gun arguments thrive on the hateful vision of "neighbor arming against neighbor" while the gun lobby happily invokes the grim view of Australian and British experts that U.S. gun ownership long ago passed the point of no return, the point at which guns became too numerous for any realistic hope of reducing their number back to the theoretical "tipping point" that might reduce violence.

It has been easy for both sides to exaggerate the total gunstock since even the relatively hard data are beset with gaping lacunae. We know that surveys find admitted gun possession in about 50 percent of American households, that in about 25 percent it is a handgun and that many households boast several guns. But we can not know how many additional gun owners are not counted because they fail to reveal their gun ownership to the surveyors. We know that Americans purchased more than 200 million guns at retail during this century. But we do not know how many other guns were privately imported (for example, as war souvenirs by returning soldiers) or how many remain from the nineteenth century. Nor, on the minus side, do we know how many have been destroyed by use, poor maintenance or after confiscation by police.[5]

My "guestimate" would put the current civilian gunstock at 60–65 million handguns and 100–110 million long guns (approximately 52–56 million rifles and approximately 48–54 million shotguns). This is deliberately pegged on the low side and takes some account of speculative assumptions about the rate at which guns wear out.[5]

(3) "GUN OWNERSHIP CAUSES VIOLENCE"

Analysis of this extremely complex topic requires keeping in mind a tangential point that is not (because it cannot be) disputed: The gun lobby cannot deny the effectiveness of guns as weapons while it extols their value for self-defense. So it cannot deny that guns augment a criminal's violent capacities (to what extent is discussed below). But what will be addressed in the next three sections is the very different claim that gun ownership causes ordinary citizens to kill—wherefrom it follows that banning guns would necessarily have to reduce homicide.

(4) "IRREFUTABLE STATISTICAL EVIDENCE"

The "proof" most often invoked for the guns-cause-murder theory is the far lower violence rates prevailing in some countries whose laws discourage gun ownership. But these countries' low crime rates seem to have preceded the gun laws that supposedly caused them. Violence was low (and falling) in Western Europe from at least the mid-nineteenth century, but anti-gun policies only came in after World War I aimed not at crime but at the political unrest of that tumultuous era. Also, low violence rates appear in Switzerland and Israel which encourage (even require) gun possession by their entire citizenry; if anti-gun laws explain low Japanese homicide why is the murder rate in Taiwan (where gun possession is a capital offense) higher than in the United States; and why is South Africa's rate twice that of the United States' despite some of the world's strictest anti-gun laws?[6]

Simplistic single-cause explanations of cross-cultural variations are inherently suspect. As discussed below, it is often pointed out that the crime wave of the 1960s coincided with a massive increase in gun sales. But it also coincided with the Supreme Court decisions that so massively expanded the rights of the criminally accused. Does it prove the yahoo claim that those decisions caused that crime wave when we find crime rates so much lower in England, Western Europe, and Japan—where far fewer rights are accorded to criminal defendants and fewer restrictions placed on police and prosecutors? Deriding the fatuousness of such single cause explanations for cross-cultural variation, England's foremost gun control analyst, Colin Greenwood, jocularly asks: Since America so greatly exceeds England not just in the rate of gun crime but in that with knives, should we assume that butcher knives are illegal in England? And if more guns explain the much higher U.S. gun crime rates, what explains the much higher rates of un-armed Americans robbing or beating each other to death: Do Americans "have more hands and feet than" Britons?[7]

Claiming that in any society the number of guns always suffices to arm the few who want to obtain and use them illegally, Greenwood feels the issue is simply one of the relative size of that group: Why is it that perhaps 1 in 300 Americans is inclined toward violent crime while the comparable figure for Japanese and Europeans (including the well-armed Swiss) may be 1 in 30,000? He attributes American crime "not to the availability of any particular class of weapon" but to socio-economic and cultural factors which dictate that American criminals are more willing to use extreme violence. As a report of the British Office of Health Economics put it,

> One reason often given for the high numbers of murders and manslaughters in the United States is the easy availability of firearms. . . . But the strong correla-tion with racial and linked socio-economic factors suggests that the underlying determinants of the homicide rate relate to particular cultural factors.[7]

The other commonly encountered statistical proof that guns cause crime involves the simultaneous major increases in gun ownership and crime after 1965. A difficulty here is that this coincidence fails to hold over any long period: After 1974 crime levels stabilized, even decreased, yet gun (and particularly handgun) ownership continued to increase; and a major in-crease in handgun ownership after World War II actually coincided with a substantial decline from pre-war homicide levels. The leading study is by Kleck who applied modern, computer-assisted statistical techniques in de-termining whether the massive post-1965 increase in American violence was attributable either to increased gun ownership or to that era's virtual cessation of capital punishment. He concludes the latter had no ascertain-able effect but that gun ownership had an ambivalent effect: Increased gun use by criminals contributes to the increasing post-1965 violence, including murders, but increased gun ownership among ordinary citizens was only a reaction to the crime increase, not its cause.[8]

A further difficulty applies both to the overall statistical claim that gun ownership causes ordinary citizens to murder and to a theory commonly advanced to explain this causation. That theory (which is further discussed in the next section) is that owning a gun stimulates hostile impulses or is evidence of a violent nature, or perhaps both. As the encyclopedic evaluation done for the National Institute of Justice (hereinafter NIJ Evaluation) notes, some gun control advocates portray gun owners as little better than "demented and blood-thirsty psychopaths whose concept of fun is to rain death on innocent creatures, both human and otherwise." But sociological studies establish that approximately 50 percent of those who own guns for defense rather than sport are women; and that "while violent crime is much more prevalent in big cities than in rural areas," surveys show that as to gun "ownership just the opposite is true; . . . that private weapons owners of all types are disproportionately [Protestant,] affluent, and middle class" and that "weapons ownership tends to increase with income, occupational prestige, or both."[9] These findings undercut both the specific theory that gun ownership indicates/stimulates violent impulses and the overall claim that gun ownership causes law abiding people to kill. For if either were true it would follow that women, residents of rural areas, Protestants, and the more affluent, prestigiously employed and/or educated all should have higher murder rates than do other, less gun owning, parts of the population, *ceteris paribus*. Needless to say, they do not.

(6) "THE TRIGGER PULLS THE FINGER"

To prove that guns enhance their owners' aggressive inclinations Berkowitz tested for differential hostility levels when laboratory subjects were deliberately annoyed by persons who were associated with guns in some way and when they were annoyed by others who were not. The evidence that there was more hostility when a weapon was present is limited and erratic. Other social psychologists have not been able to replicate Berkowitz's results; indeed, some found their subjects less willing to express hostility against persons whom they associated with weapons.[10] More important, no matter what the results, the very design of these experiments precluded Berkowitz's conclusion that a weapon increases its owner's aggressiveness. For none of his experiments involved a weapon being possessed by the subjects, such as those whose hostility was being tested. Rather, the weapon was always associated only with those against whom the hostility would run. When Buss, Brooker and Buss tested actual gun owners (and hostility levels of non-owners after actually firing a weapon) they found "no evidence that the presence, firing, or long-term use of guns enhances subsequent aggression."[11]

Other empirical efforts to brand gun owners "violence prone" rely on survey evidence showing that they approve of "violence" defined not in terms of illegal violence but of using force when necessary to stop crime or aid its victims.[12] Likewise a *Psychology Today* study of "Good Samaritans" who rescued crime victims or arrested criminals suggests that they are not "good" at all; for 81 percent of them "own guns and some carry them in their cars. They are familiar with violence, feel competent to handle it, and don't believe they will be hurt if they get involved."[13] Assessing these and the few other pre-1981 studies of gun owner psyches/attitudes, the NIJ Evaluation concluded that the evidence "suggests no sharp or distinctive differences between gun owners and non-owners" except that gun owners appear to be less frightened of crime than similarly situated non-gun owners.[14]

Previous research is at once confirmed and largely eclipsed by a much more exhaustive study from 1976, 1980 and 1984 national surveys that inquired into "defensive" as well as "violent" attitudes. Gun owners differed from non-owners only in exhibiting the former, such as approving force directed against violent attackers. In contrast, those who exhibited "violent attitudes" (defined by their approval of violence against social deviants or dissenters) were not more likely to be gun owners than non-owners. Nor did they necessarily approve of defensive force, perhaps because it would be directed against people like themselves.[15]

(7) "MOST MURDERS OCCUR AMONG RELATIVES OR ACQUAINTANCES"

This variant of the guns-cause-homicide theory characterizes murder as being a crime primarily committed not by "real criminals" but by good citizens because they happened to have a loaded gun available in a moment of anger. But the evidence claimed to suggest that ordinary citizens murder—that those killed are relatives and acquaintances—is irrelevant: violent criminals have relatives and acquaintances too. In fact, homicide studies uniformly refute the "myth that the typical homicide offender is just an ordinary person who slipped once . . . "[16] "A more accurate description would be to say that, with comparatively few exceptions, homicide reflects a long-standing pattern [of the perpetrator's prior violent] behavior." Domestic homicide particularly is "just one episode in a long-standing syndrome of violence;"[17] " . . . not an isolated occurrence or outbreak, but rather is the culminating event in a pattern of interpersonal abuse, hatred and violence that stretches back well into the histories of the parties involved."[18]

Homicide studies show that murderers (like most gun accident perpetrators) are "real criminals" in the sense of having life histories of often irrational violence frequently combined with serious felony, alcohol or drug dependence, auto accident and other pathologies indicative of marked indifference to human life. As noted below, the fact that such people are indifferent even to their own welfare undercuts the naive gun owner faith that widespread gun possession will deter them. But it is equally negative to the faith

that much criminal violence, especially homicide, occurs simply because the means of lethal violence (firearms) are readily at hand, and thus that much homicide would not occur were firearms generally less available. There is no persuasive evidence that supports this view.[18]

(8) "GUNS DON'T KILL PEOPLE; PEOPLE KILL PEOPLE"

True, but a gun greatly facilitates both killing (whether legal or illegal) and other violence. Consider the atypical situation of a woman who kills a man: Such killers do not exhibit long histories of prior violence; instead the pattern when a woman kills a man is prior violence by him against her; and usually his death results from her "defensive" use of force (in the sense that she is trying to escape a beating or to leave despite his attempt to stop her— which does not necessarily make her use of deadly force lawful [19]).

Thus the most important value of a gun over other weapons is in allowing a weaker party to overcome a stronger one. So when women kill men it is mostly with guns (usually handguns), but a woman murder victim is, in general, twice as likely to be beaten to death as a male victim.[20] Likewise, because their victims tend to be weaker than they, few rapists, and only a minority of robbers, use guns. Guns are primarily used by more professional criminals to rob stores and other targets that are both more lucrative and less vulnerable than individuals. The total amount lost in gun robberies each year actually exceeds that in non-gun robberies although the latter are much more numerous. Surprisingly, in light of the greater prospect of monetary gain from gun robbery, different levels of gun availability do not affect rates or the raw numbers of robberies in different areas: that is to say, where robbers have less access to guns they commit the same amount of robbery without them; what changes with fewer guns is that robbery is directed more against individuals and less against stores. [21]

This leads Kleck to speculate that it might actually be counter-productive to reduce gun availability to robbers as that would only shift "the burden of robbery from those best able to bear it [stores] to those least able to do so," such as individuals. [22] But this shift is not clearly undesirable, since repeated robberies may literally ruin minority and other businesses in high crime areas where robbery insurance is unaffordable or unavailable. Individuals may be better able to minimize the costs of robbery (by changing their routes, by not carrying large amounts of cash) than are stores; and the overall social cost of losing the remaining shops to which those in high crime areas have access may exceed that of more robberies being directed against individuals.

Also victim death is higher in gun robberies even though serious injury is much higher in non-gun robberies. This reflects the fact that gun robbers rarely have to shoot because the victim is likely to comply with them, whereas he might resist non-gun robbery. Moreover, to preclude this greater prospect of resistance, non-gun robbers may begin by bludgeoning or stabbing their victims in order to maximize compliance. Yet the death rate is higher in gun robbery both because guns are intrinsically more deadly and because robbers who intend to execute victims/witnesses tend to choose a gun as the most effective means.

(9) "THE PROBLEM IS HANDGUNS NOT ALL GUNS"

Here, as with the size of the gunstock, the adverse interests of each side lead, ironically, to their mutual failure to raise important issues. Anti-gun organizations, combining political savvy with woeful technical ignorance of weapons, have long opted to seek a ban on handguns only, believing it too visionary to advocate banning all guns.[23] But, as discussed below, if a ban actually did curb handgun misuse, the tragic result would be to greatly increase homicide unless long guns also were effectively banned: The major criminological work on this point is fittingly titled "Handgun-only Control—A Policy Disaster in the Making."[24] But before discussing that point it is appropriate to ask why the gun lobby ignores what is perhaps the strongest argument against the program of its *bete noir,* the National Coalition to Ban Handguns. The answer is that, though the National Rifle Association is fully conversant with the technical issues, it has ample reason not to make a point which, however negative to banning handguns, shows the need for equally restricting long guns.

To understand that point, remember that the primary argument for banning handguns is to save lives by forcing attackers to rely on large knives, which only kill about 2.4 percent of those they wound, rather than handguns, which are 1.31 to 3 times deadlier.[25] But what if banning handguns led some attackers to rely on rifles, weapons that are 15 times more lethal than knives and, therefore, 5 to 11.4 times deadlier than handguns?[26] Or shotguns, weapons so much deadlier that in medical studies they are not to be "compared with other bullet wounds. . . . At close range they are as deadly as a cannon."?[27] Of course long guns could not be used in all the circumstances in which handgun woundings now occur since long guns are much less concealable (unless sawed off). But, based on a combination of medical studies and gross ballistic comparisons, I have estimated that if a handgun ban caused only 50 percent of the wounds now inflicted with handguns to be inflicted with long guns instead, the number of dead would double—even if not one victim died in the other 50 percent of the cases in which (hypothetically) knives would be substituted![28]

That long guns could be substituted in 50 percent of homicidal attacks is evident from Kleck's finding that "anywhere from 54 percent to about 80 percent of homicides occur in circumstances that would easily permit the use of a long gun".[29] Indeed if a handgun ban actually did disarm criminals long guns might be substituted in far more than 50 percent of gun crimes. In a recent National Institute of Justice survey of about 2,000 felons in ten prisons across the country 82 percent answered that "If a criminal wants a handgun but can't get one he can always saw off a long gun." That would be "easy" according to 87 percent of those felons who had often used handguns in crime and 89 percent of those who had often used shotguns.[30] Based on these responses Lizotte calculates that, far from saving lives, the current handgun death toll could more than triple if a handgun ban led to long gun substitution at the rates indicated.[31] The NIJ Evaluation suggests somewhat facetiously that

> If someone intends to open fire on the authors of this study, our *strong* preference is that they open fire with a handgun. . . . The possibility that even a fraction of the predators who now walk the streets armed with handguns would, in the face of a handgun ban, prowl with sawed-off shotguns instead causes one to tremble.[32]

In sum, the gun lobby is quite right that the basic cause of gun violence (indeed, of all violence) is violent people. But that does not refute the value of controls to keep those people from ultradeadly weapons. By the same token, those controls must be broad enough to force such people to use less deadly weapons rather than more lethal ones. Thus a cardinal rule is to apply any restriction against handguns at least equally rigorously against the ultra-lethal long gun. For instance, states like California, which prohibit felons from buying handguns, and as to retail sales impose a two week "cooling off" period during which police check for criminal record, should move to the broader, more rational Illinois pattern which conditions ownership of any kind of gun on a permit for which only those with a clean record can qualify. But the same considerations dictate a more moderate approach by those whose ultimate goal is moving from control of guns to banning guns. They should recognize the imperative to be content with the strongest controls that are politically feasible for all guns alike rather than pressing for a ban on handguns alone which can only increase the death toll for the foreseeable future.

(10) "FIGHT CRIME—SHOOT BACK"[33]

The defensive use of guns involves two distinct topics (covered in the next two sections): gun use by victims in actual self-defense; and the effect of gun ownership in deterring criminals from even attempting a crime. It is necessary to sharply differentiate these issues because, while the evidence for the value of guns in actual self-defense is stronger than has generally been realized, the evidence on deterrence is much weaker than contended by the gun lobby.[33]

(11) "GUNS PURCHASED FOR PROTECTION ARE RARELY USED FOR THAT PURPOSE"

This standard anti-gun claim is based on statistics showing that burglars are rarely actually killed by householders. But that is doubly misleading: (1) Since burglars avoid confrontation by striking when no one is home, the rarity of burglars being killed has no bearing on the value of a gun to a victim—for example, a shopkeeper or a householder—who is confronted by a robber, or a woman attacked by a rapist or a murderous ex-boyfriend. (2) It is misleading to judge the protective value of guns only by the number of criminals killed, since a gun protects in the (far more common) event that the attacker is wounded, captured, or just scared off no less than if he is killed.

The importance of these objections is that when they are taken into account, a far different picture of the gun as a protective tool emerges. In the past decade four national surveys have included questions about respondents' use of firearms against attackers. All the surveys were sponsored by pro- or anti-gun groups but each was conducted by a reputable independent polling firm. Since the two surveys that were sponsored by the gun lobby might nevertheless be deemed suspect they need not be considered (beyond noting that their results are mutually consistent with those of the other two surveys as well as with public surveys in Ohio and California respectively).[34] Relying therefore only on data from anti-gun groups, it turns out that handguns are used as or more frequently (and with equal success) in repelling crime as in attempting it, about 645,000 handgun defensive uses annually versus about 580,000 handgun criminal attempts.

This survey evidence from victims is further confirmed by recent survey evidence from felons. Some 34 percent of the about 2,000 felons in the NIJ felon survey said they had been "scared off, shot at, wounded, or captured by an armed victim," [quoting the actual question asked] and about two-thirds (69 percent) had at least one acquaintance who had had this experience.[35] In response to two other questions, 34 percent of the felons said that in contemplating a crime they either "often" or "regularly" worried that they "might get shot at by the victim;" and 57 percent agreed that "most criminals are more worried about meeting an armed victim than they are about running into the police."

Also of interest are national victim survey data which show that a gun-armed victim who resists criminal attack is about 50 percent less likely to be injured than a victim who does not resist at all. (In contrast, victims who resisted with a knife were about twice as likely to be injured as non-resisters and much more likely to be injured than gun-armed resisters.) I emphasize that this does not mean that having a gun makes it safe for victims to resist regardless of circumstances. In fact, what is suggested differs startlingly from both pro- and anti-gun stereotypes: keeping a gun for defense may induce sober pre-consideration of the dangers of reckless resistance; their low injury rate suggests that gun owners are not only more able to resist when they decide to do so, but also to decide when it is imprudent to do so. Perhaps gun owners are more likely to have thought seriously about resisting attack than non-owners and are therefore less likely to do it in circumstances when submission is the better course.

(12) "CRIMINALS PREFER UNARMED VICTIMS"

To reiterate, the preceding discussion concerns the actual use of guns to thwart crimes in progress. At first glance the evidence also supports the gun lobby's claim that widespread gun ownership deters the criminal from even attempting confrontation crimes. In 1982 the redneck Atlanta suburb, Kennesaw, became a laughingstock by requiring that a gun be kept in every household. But the joke redounded as the resulting publicity seemed to produce a virtual end to residential burglary which continues to this day.[36] Similar results appeared from a highly publicized 1966 program in which 3,000 civilian women received defensive handgun training from Orlando, Florida, police. As of 1967, rape had dropped 88.2 percent in Orlando and aggravated assault and burglary 25 percent. While rape gradually increased again after the year-long program ended, five years later the rate was still 13 percent below the pre-program level; during that same period rape had increased 64 percent nationally, 96.1 percent in Florida and over 300 percent in the immediate area around Orlando.[37]

If every city adopted such programs to dramatize civilian gun ownership confrontation crime would drop (though not as much as in the examples described which probably involved some displacement of crime to the communities around Kennesaw and Orlando). In fact the experience in Orlando and Kennesaw is by no means unique; similar programs have produced similar results in Detroit, New Orleans and other cities.[37] But, as a practical matter, the controversy of private gun ownership precludes such programs in most cities. That is apparently why the Orlando program lasted only one year.

Moreover one must ask why crime is not equally deterred now since criminals must surely know that gun ownership is widespread. Maybe the massive publicity that accompanied the Orlando and other programs had the effect of dramatizing gun ownership to criminals; maybe such an effect could not be sustained over a period of years even if the publicity continued. Remember also that deterrence is not an absolute bar but only a disincentive to confrontation crime, varying according to the individual felon's personality and opportunities for non-confrontation crime. As the *NIJ Felon Survey* summarizes its data: "Beyond all doubt, criminals clearly worry about confronting an armed victim"—but to "worry" is not necessarily to be deterred. While fear of the armed victim probably causes less hardy and dangerous felons to specialize in non-confrontation crime, it is much less effective with the distinctive subset of felons who are the major perpetrators of violent crime. Although sometimes dubbed "violent predators" for their tendency to extreme violence, they do not specialize in any particular crime, but rather are "omnibus felons" whose daily routines are characterized by "more or less any crime they had the opportunity to commit."[38] Moreover, this omnivorous criminality is matched by omnivorous substance abuse. In his desperation to finance his drug habits, and with his spirits fortified by (singly or in combination) alcohol, cocaine, PCP, and so on, the predator may be indifferent to the danger of confronting an armed victim. Clearly worry about being shot had not deterred many in the NIJ felon survey from a life of confrontation crime. After all, if it had they would not have been in prison to answer the survey.

(13) THE GUN AS WEAPON AGAINST THE POLITICAL ORDER

In July 1984 an unemployed, apparently deranged security guard killed 21 people in a California MacDonald's restaurant. Naturally such incidents, and/or terrorist attacks and assassinations (whether or not politically motivated), generate sentiment for gun policies like those of Japan and those European countries in which political violence is traditionally a major problem. But, realistically, even authorities who are optimistic of anti-gun policies claim only that they reduce domestic murder by the (few) otherwise law abiding citizens who kill in a moment of rage. Serious gun control advocates concede it cannot avail against professional or political criminals or, indeed, anyone who really wants a gun.

A contrasting policy alternative is exemplified by what occurred at a Jerusalem cafe some weeks before the California MacDonald's massacre: Three terrorists who attempted to machine-gun the throng managed to kill only one victim before being shot down by handgun-carrying Israelis. Presented to the press the next day, the surviving terrorist complained that his group had not realized that Israeli civilians were armed. The terrorists had planned to machine-gun a succession of crowd spots, thinking that they would be able to escape before the police or army could arrive to deal with them.[39]

Thus anti-gun policies not only offer no solution to terrorism but may be detrimental by reducing any chance the victims might have to protect themselves before police can arrive. This is not to suggest that Israel provides an appropriate model for American policy. Because terrorism is its most pressing criminal justice problem, Israel maximizes the presence of armed citizens by firearms training and encouraging gun ownership-carrying by almost the entire populace (such as Jews of both sexes and the Druze and other pro-Israeli Arabs). The value of such policy for the U.S., which does not require universal military training even for males, is a far more dubious question, especially since homicide here rarely involves terrorism. A handful of American states freely dispense permits to carry concealed weapons, but even there the number of permittees is comparatively small; there is no clear evidence that such states enjoy less violent crime that other demographically similar states that dispense concealed carry permits less liberally.[40]

Gun Control Options

BANNING ALL GUNS, HANDGUNS, OR SATURDAY NIGHT SPECIALS (SNS)

A basic limitation on gun control policy, however sound, is that continu-ing and substantial majority support is required for initial adoption and for allocation of the long term resources necessary to enforcement. What this means in a country which, by the 1970s, had guns in 50 percent of its households (handguns in 25 percent), is that proposals to generally ban all guns, or even just handguns, are doomed; nor will control proposals of any kind be politically viable when presented in extremist terms that vilify guns and gun owners.

Though the concept of controlling guns enjoys very wide support, ban-ning even handguns has not enjoyed such support since the 1960s, if then. A September 4, 1959, Gallup poll showed a narrow majority favored "out-law[ing] handguns." But handgun sales quadrupled in the 1960s and total ownership doubled by 1980. Not surprisingly, the February 3, 1980, Gallup poll found only 31 percent supporting a handgun ban. Referenda even in states selected as particularly anti-gun saw proposals to ban new handgun sale (California, 1982) or handgun ownership altogether (Massachusetts, 1976) rejected by 66–70 percent of voters. Ironically these intensive refer-enda campaigns seem to have actually and substantially decreased anti-gun sentiment in those states.[41]

Polls do show majority support for banning the small cheap SNS-type handgun. But this is unsupportable as public policy unless one accepts the racist rationales upon which SNS laws have traditionally been based.[42] SNS are disproportionately uninvolved in crime since only the law abiding mi-nority and poor people have to rely on them. The criminals want and can afford high caliber guns.[43] But even if criminals were using SNS, banning SNS would only have the counter-productive effect of encouraging crimi-nals to rely on higher caliber (and thus deadlier) handguns. This would work a "policy disaster" cognate to the banning of all handguns which would greatly increase homicide unless the enormously more deadly long guns were banned.[44]

DISARMING CRIMINALS AND THE IRRESPONSIBLE

The difficulties here are epitomized by the fact that federal (and most states') laws already ban gun ownership by juveniles and those who have been convicted of felony. Unfortunately, these laws are little enforced. In a criminal justice system that is already overburdened with offenders charged with savagely violent crimes, felons charged with nothing more serious than having or carrying a gun need not expect serious penalization. The gun lobby proposes that legislatures remedy the non-enforcement of gun laws by enacting a mandatory two-year (or longer) sentence for anyone convicted of a gun crime. States enacting such laws seem to experience sharp declines in gun crime—until it becomes clear that the courts undermine the law by imposing the gun mandatory sentence concurrently with, rather than in addition to, the two years that an armed robber (for instance) would already receive. The premier study of gun control enforcement concludes:

> It is very possible that, if gun laws do potentially reduce gun-related crime, the present laws are all that is needed if they are enforced. What good would stronger laws do when the courts have demonstrated that they will not enforce them?[45]

But the fault lies equally with prosecutors for cooperating with the judges in subverting the law—and far more with the legislatures for following the gun lobby's advice and adding burdens to an already overburdened system without adding concommitant resources. If a long sentence is mandated for guns crimes, and no plea bargain is possible, felons charged with a gun crime have no reason to plead guilty rather than insisting on trial. So to avoid the addition of innumerable more protracted jury trials to those already inundating them, prosecutors and courts collude in finding inventive ways of dropping the gun charge or otherwise subverting its mandatory penalty requirement. Nor, when they engage in such subversion, are judges and prosecutors just concerned with their crowded calendars. Rather they know how counter-productive a long sentence for every offender who robs at gunpoint is when prisons are already overflowing. To honor the legislative command that mere gun robbers be imprisoned inevitably means early release for far more dangerous offenders, for example, the rapist who mutilated victims with a knife rather than merely threatening with a gun. When reason and institutional pressures unite against sentencing offenders severely just because they used a gun, it is unlikely to occur by legislative fiat, unless accompanied by vastly expanded prosecutorial, judicial and prison resources.

Continuation and Conclusion

Gun control is a matter of supply and demand. In a nation with at least 185 million guns, it is an illusory hope that supply can be so far reduced as to disarm criminals, or even to seriously inconvenience them. But criminal demand for guns (and hence gun crime) might be reduced sharply if criminals knew they would be seriously punished for having or using a gun.[46] But that would require a social commitment to massive new criminal justice expenditure. This is not likely in a society that is both gravely burdened with such expenditures and fragmented between inconsistent views of crime and of the appropriate responses thereto—and when localities clamorously resist becoming sites for even those few new prisons that are funded. It is far easier for the warring opinion groups to continue their antagonistic fragmentation—ritualistically blaming crime on "soft" judges or on gun owners, on the decline of traditional morality or on social inequities, and so on—than to unite in support of a coherent, workable strategy involving serious financial and other costs.

Notes

AUTHOR'S NOTE: I wish to thank the following for their assistance: Professors David Bordua (Sociology, University of Illinois), Philip J. Cook (Public Policy Studies and Economics, Duke University), F. Smith Fussner (History, Emeritus, Reed College), Ted Robert Gurr (Political Science, University of Colorado), Gary Kleck (Criminology, Florida State University), Barbara Stenross (Sociology, University of North Carolina), William Tonso (Sociology, University of Evansville), James D. Wright (Social and Demographic Research Institute, University of Massachusetts, Amherst); Ms. P. Kates, San Francisco, and Ms. S. Byrd and Mr. C. Klein, Berkeley. Of course, for errors either of fact or interpretation the responsibility is mine alone.

1. B. Bruce-Briggs, "The Great American Gun War," *The Public Interest* (Fall 1976).

2. See respectively: editorial columns by G. Braucher in the *Miami Herald,* July 19, 1982 and Oct. 29, 1981; editorial in *U.S. Catholic* magazine (Oct. 1979); and an article by M. Luedens in the *Progressive* (March 1984).

3. See generally: L. Levy and K. Karst, eds., *Encyclopedia of the American Constitution* 1639 (New York: Macmillan, 1986); S. Halbrook, *"That Every Man Be Armed": The Evolution of a Constitutional Right* (Albuquerque: University of New Mexico Press, 1985), chap. 3; D. Kates, "Handgun Prohibition and the Original Understanding of the Second Amendment," *Michigan Law Review* 82 (Nov. 1983), 214–25. See also J. Malcolm, "The Right of the People to Keep and Bear Arms: The Common Law Tradition," *Hastings Constitutional Law Quarterly* 10 (no. 2, 1983) and R. Shalhope, "The Ideological Origins of the Second Amendment," *Journal of American History* 69 (no. 3, 1982).

4. D. Kates, "The Second Amendment," *Law and Contemporary Problems* 49 (no. 1, 1986). For counter-argument from the gun lobby point of view see S. Halbrook, "What the Founders Intended: A Linguistic Analysis of the Right to 'Bear Arms,' " *Law and Contemporary Problems* 49 (no. 1, 1986).

5. Partial figures of arms importation and domestic production for 1899–1968 are collated in G. Newton and F. Zimring, *Firearms and Violence in American Life* (Washington, DC: U.S. Government Printing Office, 1970), app. C. By averaging the partial figures available for importation and domestic production for 1969–88, I estimate that the American gunstock grew during those twenty years by about 100.7 million (34.2 million rifles, 26.4 million shotguns, 40.1 million handguns). For detailed analysis of the available data to 1978, with reasonable, but admittedly unverifiable, assumptions about the "half life" of guns, see the commercially published version of the *NIJ Evaluation,* J. Wright, P. Rossi and K. Daly, *Under the Gun* (New York: Aldine, 1983), chap. 2; originally published as J. Wright, P. Rossi

and K. Daly, *Weapons, Crime and Violence in America* (Washington, DC: U.S. Government Printing Office, 1981).

6. See generally T. Gurr, "Historical Trends in Violent Crime: A Critical Review of the Evidence," in *Annual Review of Crime and Justice* vol. 3 (Chicago: University of Chicago Press, 1981); C. Greenwood, *Firearms Control: A Study of Armed Crime and Firearms Control in England and Wales* 1–3 and chaps. 1–3 (London: Routledge and Kegan Paul, 1971); L. Kennett and J. L. Anderson, *The Gun in America* (Westport, CT: Greenwood Press, 1976), 213; *NIJ Evaluation*, note 5 above, at 125; and D. Kates, ed., *Firearms and Violence: Issues of Public Policy* (Cambridge, MA: Ballinger, 1984), 5–6.

7. C. Greenwood "Comparative Cross-Cultural Statistics" in D. Kates, ed., *Restricting Handguns* (Croton-on Hudson, NY: North River Press, 1979), 37.

8. Gary Kleck's initial conclusions appear in "Capital Punishment, Gun Ownership and Homicide," *American Journal of Sociology* 84 (no. 4, 1979). His data are expanded, and his conclusions modified, in G. Kleck, "The Relationship Between Gun Ownership Levels and Rates of Violence in the United States," in *Firearms and Violence*, note 6 above.

9. *NIJ Evaluation*, note 5 above; see generally chap. 6. For discussion of women's gun ownership see R. Young, "Gender, Region of Socialization and Ownership of Protective Firearms," *Rural Sociology* 51 (no. 4, 1986) and Bordua, "Firearms Ownership and Violent Crime: A Comparison of Illinois Counties," in J. Byrne and R. Sampson, eds., *The Social Ecology of Crime* (New York: Springer-Verlag, 1986) and references there cited.

10. Compare L. Berkowitz, "How Guns Control Us," *Psychology Today*, June 1981, and "Impulse, Aggression and the Gun," *Psychology Today*, September 1968, to G. Kleck and D. Bordua, "The Factual Foundations for Certain Key Assumptions of Gun Control" *Law and Policy Quarterly* 5 (no. 3, 1983): 284–8; and A. Buss, A. Brooker and E. Buss, "Firing a Weapon and Aggression," *Journal of Personality and Social Psychology* 22 (June 1972) and references there cited.

11. Ibid.

12. J. Williams and J. McGrath, "Why People Own Guns," *Journal of Communication* 26 (Autumn 1976).

13. B. Huston, G. Geis and L. Wright, "The Angry Samaritans," *Psychology Today* (June 1976).

14. Note 5 above, 120–2.

15. A. Lizotte and J. Dixon, "Gun Ownership and the 'Southern Subculture of Violence,'" *American Journal of Sociology* 93 (no. 2, 1987).

16. *American Journal of Sociology* as cited at note 8 above, at 893 and studies there cited.

17. M. Straus, "Domestic Violence and Homicide Antecedents," *Bulletin of the New York Academy of Medicine* 62 (no. 5, 1986).

18. *NIJ Evaluation*, note 5 above at 193. See generally M. Howard, "Husband-Wife Homicide: An Essay from a Family Law Perspective," *Law and Contemporary Problems* 49 (no. 1, 1986). As to commonality of characteristics between homicide and fatal gun accident perpetrators see generally P. Cook, "The Role of Firearms in Violent Crime: An Interpretative Review of the Literature" in M. Wolfgang and N. Weiner, eds., *Criminal Violence*, 270–1 (Beverly Hills, CA: Sage, 1982) and G. Kleck, "Firearms Accidents" (draft ms., Florida State University School of Criminology, 1986).

19. See generally Howard, note 18 above at 74 ff., and A. Browne and R. Flewelling, "Women as Victims or Perpetrators of Homicide," paper presented to the 1986 Annual Meeting of the American Society of Criminology (available from the Family Research Laboratory, University of New Hampshire). As to the legality of a battered wife's use of deadly force, note that even where statute-law classifies wife beating as a felony, her only legal remedy is to seek prosecution. A woman must submit to a beating and cannot resist with deadly force unless she reasonably believes she is in imminent danger of death or great bodily harm. *People v Jones*, 191 C.A. 2d 478 (Cal. Ct. of Apr., 1961); see generally D. Kates and N.

Engberg, "Deadly Force Self Defense Against Rape" *U.C.-Davis Law Review* 15 (no. 4, 1982): 876–7. Although the pattern of men who eventually kill their wives is one of progressively more severe beatings until the final one, a wife who only kills after surviving numerous prior beatings may find it difficult to convince police or jury that she reasonably believed this time was different.

20. Browne and Flewelling, "Women as Victims."

21. P. Cook, note 18 above, and "The Effect of Gun Availability on Robbery and Robbery Murder," *Policy Studies Review Annual*, vol. 3 (Beverly Hills, CA: Sage, 1979).

22. G. Kleck, "Policy Lessons from Recent Gun Control Research," *Law and Contemporary Problems* 49 (no. 1, 1986).

23. For example, R. Clark, *Crime in America* (New York: Pocket Books, 1971), 93; and Fields, "Handgun Prohibition and Social Necessity," *St. Louis University Law Journal* 23 (no. 1, 1979).

24. Gary Kleck's paper of that title appears in *Firearms and Violence*, note 6 above.

25. F. Zimring, "Is Gun Control Likely to Reduce Violent Killings," *University of Chicago Law Review* 35 (no. 2, 1968) puts the gun/knife lethality ratio in assaults at 5–1. That is not a true handgun/knife comparison for reasons detailed at length in the *NIJ Evaluation*, note 5 above at 199, and note 9; see also p. 208 where it is suggested that a more accurate assessment is Zimring's later 1.31 to 1 lethality ratio from robbery data and Cook's 3–1 figure from a different robbery sample. But see the same sources at p. 209 for caveats suggesting that even these lower ratios may be too high.

26. S. Baker, "Without Guns Do People Kill People?" *American Journal of Public Health* 75 (no. 6, 1985), and, more generally, M. Fackler, "Physics of Missile Injuries" in N. McSwain, Jr., and M. Kerstein, eds., *Evaluation and Management of Trauma* (Norwalk, CT: Appleton-Century-Crofts, 1987).

27. R. Taylor, "Gunshot Wounds of the Abdomen," *Annals of Surgery* 177 (no. 1, 1973); see also Fackler, "Physics of Missile Injuries."

28. D. Kates, *Restricting Handguns*, note 7 above, 108–11.

29. Kleck, note 24 above, at 186–94.

30. J. Wright and P. Rossi, *Armed and Dangerous: A Survey of Felons and Their Firearms*, 221, table 11.3 (New York: Aldine, 1986) (hereinafter denominated *NIJ Felon Survey*).

31. A. J. Lizotte, "The Costs of Using Gun Control to Reduce Homicide," *Bulletin of The New York Academy of Medicine* 62 (no. 5, 1986) (using Kleck's figures for long gun vs. handgun lethality, which differ from mine in being based on a range of more exhaustive and sophisticated ballistic comparisons that do not, however, include medical study data).

32. *NIJ Evaluation*, note 5 above, at 322–3 (emphasis in original).

33. Except as specifically noted, the assertions in this and the following two sections are based on two works in progress, Gary Kleck's "Guns and Self Defense: Crime Control Through the Use of Force in the Private Sector" *Social Problems*, 35 (Feb. 1988) and D. Kates, "The Value of Civilian Arms Possession as a Deterrent to Crime or Defense Against Crime," in *American Criminal Law Review*, 25 (1988).

34. The polls in question, including the Ohio and California state polls, were: "Gun Control" (DMI poll for NRA—"Attitudes of the American Public Toward Gun Control, 1975") *Congressional Record* 121 (Dec. 19, 1975); Field Institute, *Tabulations of the Findings of A Survey of Handgun Ownership and Access Among a Cross Section of the California Adult Public* (1976); Cambridge Reports, Inc., "An Analysis of Public Attitudes Toward Gun Control: Report for the Center for the Study and Prevention of Handgun Violence" (Cambridge, MA: 1978); Decision Making Information, "Attitudes of the American Public Toward Gun Control, 1978" (Santa Ana, CA: 1979); Peter Hart, "Gun Control" 1981 (Hart Research Associates); State of Ohio Statistical Analysis Center, "Citizen Attitudes Concerning Crime and Criminal Justice" (Columbus, 1982).

35. *NIJ Felon Survey*, note 30 above, 145, 154, table 7.2

36. Kleck and Bordua, note 10 above; "Town Celebrates Mandatory Arms [Policy],' *New York Times*, Apr. 11, 1987.

37. Kleck, *Policy Lessons*, note 22 above, 47. Note that the computations given in the text are my own, based on FBI *Uniform Crime Reports* 1966 (pp. 85, 172), 1967 (pp. 11, 64) and 1971 (pp. 13, 64–8, 88, 199).

38. *NIJ Felon Survey*, note 30 above, 50–4, 71, 76–7, and 150.

39. *The Economist*, Apr. 7, 1984, 34.

40. For a discussion of this by NRA's Research Director see P. Blackman, "Carrying Handguns for Personal Protection," paper presented at the 1985 Annual Meeting of the American Society of Criminology.

41. D. Bordua, "Adversary Polling and the Construction of Social Meaning," *Law and Policy Quarterly* 5 (no. 3, 1983).

42. D. Kates, "Toward a History of Handgun Prohibition in the United States," in *Restricting Handguns*, note 7 above; Halbrook, note 3 above, 196.

43. G. Kleck, "Evidence that 'Saturday Night Specials' Not Very Important for Crime," *Sociology and Social Research* 70 (no. 4, 1986).

44. *Policy Lessons,* note 22 above, at 50; see note 24 above.

45. Bendis and Balkin, "A Look At Gun Control Enforcement," *Journal of Police Science and Administration* 7 (no. 2, 1979): 448.

46. Kleck, *Policy Lessons*, note 22 above, 57–8; Kleck and Bordua, note 10 above, 293–4.

Chapter 10

Homicide in the Twentieth Century: Trends, Types, and Causes

MARGARET A. ZAHN

This chapter reviews what we know about homicide in the United States from 1900 to 1988.[1] It presents an analysis of changing trends; a portrait of the dominant types of homicide in different periods of American history; some analysis of the populations who are differentially affected through time by this type of violent death; and a brief examination of its causes. Since no fully national data bases include these variables for the entire century, the portrait of American homicide is a composite derived from a review of all major studies. These will be presented in chronological sequence. Trend data, as available, are also included.

Homicide Data Sources

Establishing a national portrait of homicide through an entire century, using existing studies, poses a variety of problems. First, studies on homicide lack comparability in a number of ways. One is in how homicide is defined. In some studies, homicides include killings by officers of the law or those occurring in self-defense, in other studies they do not. Studies in the 1920s, for example, seem more likely to include justifiable homicides than do those in the 1960s.[2] Further, in some periods abortion and/or infanticide are included as separate types of homicide, while at other times they are not included or defined as homicide. Further, while many studies discuss the type of relationship between a homicide victim and his or her aggressor, there is no consistent definition across studies of the various types of victim-offender relationship, for example, what constitutes an acquaintance or a stranger. In fact, in many studies of this issue, no definition is offered at all. Even those categories that may seem clear, such as family homicide, are ambiguous. Former spouses may be included as family members but former lovers may not. Further, in some studies only causes in which the offender is known are included while in others those with both known and unknown offenders are included. Additionally, some homicide studies use offenders as their research base, while others use victims and sometimes the two are confused with each other. In all, there are many ways in which the available studies are not comparable and thus difficult to use comparatively. Given these methodological considerations, findings about patterns in homicide at various points in time must be viewed as suggestive, not definitive.

Additional problems revolve around data sources, their availability at different time periods, and biases and difficulties specific to each source. A brief review of some of the kinds of problems with two of the most widely used data sets follows.

CORONER'S AND POLICE DATA SOURCES

There are two sources of data on homicide rates. They are the Vital Statistics, collected by the National Center for Health Statistics, and the Uniform Crime Reports (UCR) compiled by the Federal Bureau of Investigation. Neither of these data sets are fully national prior to the early 1930s.

Mortality data are produced by coroners' and/or medical examiners' offices that forward their results, via death certificates, to the Division of Vital Statistics of the National Center for Health Statistics. As with police departments, patterns and practices of the coroners' offices will affect data collected by them. For example, the coroner, an appointed or elected official, is responsible for determining cause and/or manner of death. Coroners, in contrast to medical examiners, are not required to have medical training. In some places the only requirement for holding office is that they be alive and of legal age to hold office. Early in the century, following late nineteenth century practice, a fee-for-service system among coroners directly affected their reporting of homicides. Coroners received a set fee for each death that they investigated and for which they established cause of death. The fee paid was the same no matter how much difficulty the case involved and the fee was, in cases of murder, often to be collected from the convicted offender. If, then, it was likely that the offender could not be found, as when a victim was found with a slit throat on the highway, or if the victim was an infant, these deaths were not likely to be reported as homicides but rather as a ruptured aorta, in the case of the slit throat, and suffocation for the infant.[3]

Further, the thoroughness of the investigation and detailed determination of cause of death is directly affected by the size, training, and funding of coroners' and medical examiners' staffs. Doing autopsies—and establishing and maintaining toxicology units—is expensive. Some offices, such as large medical examiner offices, have such equipment and thus can tell if the cause of death is drugs in the blood stream, and the like. Many smaller units cannot.

The factors noted above affect data collection at the local level; others affect reporting at the national level; that is, in the Vital Statistics reports. Changes in definition and coding have occurred. For example, if the medical examiner cannot determine whether a suspicious death is an accident or a homicide, he or she may report it as undetermined. Prior to 1968, however, the Vital Statistics did not allow for such a possibility. If a medical examiner was unsure, the case was assigned, through a series of complex procedures, to either the accident or homicide categories.[4] The impact of such shifts in coding schemes on homicide rates is unclear but it is certainly plausible that such changing classification procedures add error to the data produced.

A greater problem is the fact that states entered the national reporting system at different times. While Vital Statistics were available for some states from around 1900, they did not become fully national until the 1930s. Prior to the 1930s, the data available depended on which states and cities were included. Boston was the first entrant and, in general, there were data from East Coast cities very early. Boston had death data in 1880, Pennsylvania in 1906, and Washington, D.C., in 1880. Other states, however, for example Georgia and Texas, entered the registry much later, in 1922 and 1933, respectively. In establishing the homicide trend, then, we have difficulty with obtaining national data prior to 1930 and, throughout the century, there are the aforementioned data-reporting difficulties that affect the quality and the nature of the data.

Police data, too, have numerous problems. Review of the literature on police statistics indicates that these statistics may reflect as much about the activity, size of the police force, ability to do detective work,[5] and tolerance level of the community[6] as they do the actual criminal phenomenon itself. For example, lack of systematic investigation may result from a judgment that the community does not want the investigation done or from low morale because police feel that their work will not result in prosecution. It seems credible that official police data may be fairly accurate on the actual occurrence of a homicide event. Our understanding of the types of homicide or of motives, however, may by influenced by the size of the force, the connections its investigative units have to the community, the priorities of the department, and other organizational variables. Such local problems may be exacerbated when the data are gathered into the national registry, the UCR, compiled by the FBI.

These national level data began to be compiled in 1933. Those early years, however, were not inclusive of all jurisdictions so represented only portions of the United States[7] Furthermore, the sampling and extrapolation procedures were very problematic and underwent a number of revi-

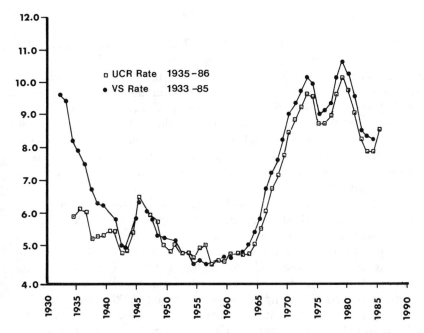

Figure 10.1: U.S. Homicide Rates from the Uniform Crime Reports and from Vital Statistics, 1933–1986

sions, thus time series comparisons through the 1950s are not entirely reliable. Cantor and Cohen provide a detailed analysis of these problems.[8]

While there are numerous problems with the data at both the local and national levels, it is somewhat reassuring to note, when comparing Uniform Crime Reports (UCR) and Vital Statistics rates of homicide through time, that they are very similar and move consistently in the same direction. It also is evident in Figure 10.1 that, in general, Vital Statistics rates are usually somewhat higher than the UCR for the same year. This is due largely to the fact that Vital Statistics use a medical definition of homicide, that is, the intentional taking of another's life, while UCR uses a legal definition, that is, the willful killing of another. Thus, justifiable homicides, for example police officers killing felons, are included in Vital Statistics while they are not in the UCR.

Cantor and Cohen, who compared the two measures on homicide for 1933–1975, conclude that the two time series are highly correlated (.97) from 1936 to 1973.[9] A major discontinuity occurs in 1933–1935 because of problems with the UCR. For this reason this chapter presents data from the UCR only from 1935 to 1986. Data from Vital Statistics are considered highly reliable from 1933 to the present and are thus presented in Figure 10.1.

Homicide Trends

Data on homicide rates from 1900–1933 are mainly local in character. The only data base beyond individual cities, the Vital Statistics, do show a relatively steep increase from a low of 1.2 per 100,000 to 9.7 in 1933. The rate was low and stable from 1900–1905 and then showed steady increases, with 1921–1935 registering rates consistently between 8.0 and 9.7. Data from the Vital Statistics for 1900–1933 should be viewed with extreme caution, since the upward trend is due in large measure to the entry of western and southern states, with high rates of violence, into the registration system. (The 9.7 registered in 1933, for example, occurred when Texas began reporting.)

Local studies of Eastern and Midwestern cities during this time period, however, also generally show increases. Homicide trends in Philadelphia, analyzed in chapter 4 of this volume, showed a modest increase when manslaughter (mainly vehicular) is excluded from the tabulations (see fig. 4.4 in this volume). Sutherland and Gehlke (1933), using arrest data from Baltimore, Buffalo, Chicago, Cleveland, St. Louis, and the state of Massachusetts, also find increasing homicide rates from 1900 to the late 1920s with the peak for the five cities occurring in 1928. For Massachusetts the peak was in 1925.[10] The precise magnitude of increase remains an unresolvable question without more comparability in data sets for these years.

After the mid-1930s the national data sources (police and coroner) are increasingly reliable. Together they show an overall decline in homicide rates through 1964, interrupted by a short spurt of increase in the three years immediately after World War II.

After 1964 the rate began to move up, from 5.9 per 100,000 in 1966 (Vital Statistics) to 10.2 in 1974 and an all-time high of 10.7 in 1980. The national homicide rate in fact was ten times higher in 1980 than it was in the registration area at the beginning of the twentieth century. Since 1980 the rate has declined from 10.3 in 1981 to 8.3 in 1985. Despite this decline the last twenty years remain the most homicidally violent decades in this century in the United States.

The Uniform Crime Reports for the same period show a slightly lower rate each year, since killings by police officers are not included in their definition of homicide. The patterns of increase and decrease and the years at which peaks occurred, however, correspond precisely with those reported by Vital Statistics.

When the rates are disaggregated by race and sex, we find that the changes of most recent years have not affected all population groups equally. While black males continue to have much higher rates than other groups—as they have had throughout this century—the victimization rate for black males (and females) has actually decreased since the 1970s and into the 1980s, while the rates for white males and females have been increasing.[11]

Homicide Types

While the description of changing rates is important, knowledge of the relationships that spawn homicide in different eras and the circumstances that trigger them tell us more about the social organization of homicide than rates can. Data on relationships and "motive" are difficult to obtain and to interpret. They are so not only because of lack of definitional consistency between studies but also because the "motive" for an event and the interpretation of the circumstances are often attributions made by officials, usually police, rather than actual descriptions by participants. Nonetheless, studies that provide description of the participants, their relationship to each other, and some attributed reasons for the lethal violence will tell us something about the nature of homicides and how they change through time.

Homicide: 1900 to the 1930s

Two major studies of early twentieth-century homicide, by H. C. Brearly and by Frederick Hoffman, found a steady increase in homicide rates from 5.0 in 1906 to 8.5 in 1929. Higher victimization rates existed among blacks, among the young, and among men. The South and its northern neighbors (Ohio and West Virginia) had the highest rates while the New England states and the northern part of the Midwest had the lowest. The majority (71.5 percent) of homicides were committed with a gun, with the general tendency being toward an increase in the use of guns throughout the early 1900s.[12]

As to types of motives, only Boudouris's study of Detroit (1926–1968) and Lashley's of Chicago deal with this issue for this period. Boudouris found that Detroit in the late 1920s had a higher homicide rate than any of the other periods he studied. He classified victim-offender relationships into (1) domestic and love affairs; (2) friends and acquaintances; (3) business relationship, for example, landlord-tenant and prostitute-pimp; (4) criminal transaction, that is, homicide resulting from violation of the law, for example, bootlegging; (5) noncriminal, that is, killing of a felon by police or private citizen; (6) cultural-recreational-casual; (7) subcultural-recreational-casual; (8) other; and (9) unknown. He found that for the years 1926–1933, the largest percentage of homicides were noncriminal or justifiable, that is, killing of a felon by a police officer or a private citizen.

Aside from these, there were almost equal proportions of homicide involving domestic relations (18.2 percent), friends and acquaintances (18.2 percent), and criminal transactions (16.6 percent).[13] Thirty percent (71 out of 236) of the criminal transaction homicides during 1926–1934 (prohibition was repealed in 1933) were related to gang wars to control bootlegging. An additional eighteen homicides were police killed in the line of duty, often in the process of enforcing prohibition law.

An analysis of 883 homicides in Chicago for the years 1926–1927 showed a similar pattern. Like Detroit, a large percentage of homicides during this period were justifiable. While the Chicago data do not separate out criminal transactions as a type of homicide, the data do suggest that when "justifiables" are removed from the analysis, the two major categories of homicide were gang and criminal related (approximately 33.3 percent) and altercations and brawls (30.4 percent). Domestic homicides were infrequent, only 8.3 percent of the total.[14]

These two sources, then, suggest that there was not one modal type of urban homicide during the first third of the century. Friends or acquaintances often killed each other in arguments, but homicides resulting from criminal transactions and those considered justifiable were of equal if not greater importance. These latter two types, furthermore, were both closely linked to bootlegging and to the attempted enforcement of prohibition laws.[15] The importance of family-related homicides varied with the city studied. This type was almost as common as criminal and friend homicides in Detroit but was of lesser importance in Chicago.

Homicide: The Mid-1930s to the Mid-1960s

Beginning in the mid-1930s the first fully national data on homicide, both in the Vital Statistics and the UCR, reveal a steady decline of homicide rates from the high of the late 1920s and early 1930s (Vital Statistics data) to a low and fairly steady rate of 5.6 in the 1940s and 4.8 in the 1950s (see Figure 10.1). The low rate of the 1950s persisted until the mid-1960s.[16]

A number of studies of this period examined the relationships in which people were killed, in both southern and northern cities: Houston (Bullock, 1955), Birmingham (Harlan, 1950), Cleveland (Bensing and Schroeder, 1970), Detroit, (Boudouris, 1970), and Wolfgang's (1958) classic study of Philadelphia. All these studies show that domestic and love-related homicides became a more important category than in the preceding years, while males killing males in quarrelsome situations continued to be an important form of homicide. Homicides related to criminal transactions decreased to a small percentage.

Bullock, using police records for the 489 cases of criminal homicide in Houston 1945–1949, found the highest rates of homicide clustered among low-income, black, and Hispanic people, 67 percent of whom were laborers and domestic servants. The homicides occurred most frequently between people who knew each other (in 87 percent of the cases the victim and offender were acquainted with each other) and arguments were the prime precipitating factors. Bullock does not indicate the number killed in domestic quarrels but reports marital discord was the third most important reason for death. The three most frequent patterns precipitating homicide were: (1) arguments originating out of a variety of situations; (2) love triangles and jealousy between friends; and (3) marital discord. The most frequent place of death was a rooming house (42.1 percent of the victims were killed there) followed by a tavern (28.6 percent) and the street (21.1 percent).[17]

Birmingham, Alabama, was studied by Harlan during the same period. In an analysis of 500 cases of criminal homicide from 1937 to 1944, he found that the majority of the victims were black males (67.8 percent) and the modal type of homicide was a black man killing another black man while arguing in a private residence. Murders stemming from such arguments (for example, over dice or money) were the prime circumstance surrounding homicides in Birmingham; marital discord, jealousy, and quarrels over lovers ranked next in frequency as the basis for murder.[18]

In northern cities of that time, Cleveland and Detroit, a similar pattern prevailed. Bensing and Schroeder, using 662 cases of homicide from 1947 to 1953 in Cleveland, found that the majority of homicides involved black males who knew each other. In only 4.5 percent of the cases were the victim and offender unknown to each other. While Bensing and Schroeder's study does not specify the predominant motive for homicide, they do list these three circumstances as important: (1) quarrels of a petty nature; (2) marital discord; and (3) love or sex disputes in which the deceased was slain by someone other than a spouse or common law mate.[19]

The importance of marital and love disputes is further documented in Boudouris's study of Detroit. Analysis of his data shows the 1940s and especially the 1950s to be a time when domestic relations and love affairs claimed most of the homicide deaths. Recomputing his data to combine domestic relations and love affairs into one category, we find that in the 1920s, 21.9 percent of the homicides were domestically related—a figure that rose to 29.3 percent in the 1930s, to 32.6 percent in the 1940s and to a high of 38.4 percent in the 1950s.[20] Friends and acquaintances homicides were consistently second to domestic and love homicides during the 1940s and 1950s.

Wolfgang's classic study further demonstrates the importance of close relationships in homicide during this era. He examined all 588 criminal homicides that occurred in Philadelphia in 1948–1952. He relied primarily on police records that included the investigation reports of the Police Homicide Unit, witnesses' statements, and the like. The data for this period indicated an overall criminal homicide rate of 5.7 per 100,000. The homicide rates for blacks and males were many times greater than for whites and females: black males had a rate of 36.9 per 100,000; black females 9.6; white males 2.9; and white females 1.0. Those in the age group 25–34 were most likely to be victims, and offenders were likely to be in the 20–24 age group. In terms of homicide setting, Wolfgang found that the single most dangerous place in Philadelphia in 1950 was inside a home (50.5 percent of the victims were slain there).

Wolfgang classified the cases both in terms of the victim-offender relationships and in terms of motive recorded by the police for the slaying. In terms of victim-offender relationships, 25 percent of the homicides occurred within the family, with an additional 10 percent involving sexual intimates who were not family members; 42 percent occurred between acquaintances and/or close friends; only 12 percent involved people who were strangers to each other. The most common motives recorded by police included altercations of a "relatively trivial origin" (35.0 percent); domestic quarrels (14.1 percent); jealousy (11.6 percent); and altercations over money (10.5 percent). Robbery accounted for only 6.8 percent of homicides, revenge for 5.3 percent.[21]

In sum, the 1940s and especially the 1950s were a time with a relatively low and stable homicide rate. It was a time, further, when two types of murder seemed most prevalent, that between family members—usually husband and wife or lovers—and that between two males known to each other who were arguing at the time. In some cities, for example, Detroit, the family and love relationship murder was predominant, while in other places deadly arguments between males were more frequent. But in all instances these two types were the dominant ones and, unlike an earlier period, the family and love relationship murder became a more dominant form. In general, family homicides vary least over time; the larger ebbs and surges in homicide rates are due to big changes in other types of murder.

Homicide: The 1960s to 1978

The homicide rate began to increase in 1965 and continued steadily upward throughout the latter half of the 1960s and into the 1970s, peaking in 1980. The most comprehensive study during this time was a 1969 report by the National Commission on Violence, with subsequent analyses by Lynn A. Curtis.[22] A series of local studies was also done in this period.[23]

The Violence Commission Report and Curtis' analyses used a 10 percent random sample of 1967 arrest reports in seventeen large U.S. cities. The Commission found criminal homicide to be intrasexual in nature (63 percent of the cases where the victim-offender relationship was known involved a male killing another male) and intraracial (when race of both the victim and the offender is known, only 10 percent of the murders are interracial). An increase in interracial stranger killings, especially black on white, was suspected. In terms of victim-offender relationships, the seventeen cities in 1967 showed husband and wife killings to account for 15.8 percent of all criminal homicides; 8.9 percent involved other family members; 9.0 percent involved other primary relations, that is, close friends and lovers; 29.8 percent were nonprimary but known to each other. In another 15.6 percent they were reportedly strangers and in 20.9 percent of the cases the offender was unknown, and thus likely to be a stranger.

Regarding motive, the survey revealed that minor altercations were the most frequent reasons for the death (35.7 percent); followed by unknown reasons (21.0 percent); other reasons (10.6 percent); and robbery (8.8 percent). Family quarrels accounted for only 7.7 percent of the homicide deaths.

Other studies of local areas during that time reveal similar homicide patterns although with some variation based, apparently, on differences between northern and southern cities. Studies of northern cities for the 1960s and 1970s include: Chicago (Block, 1974, 1977); Washington D.C. (Reidel and Katzenelson, 1977); Philadelphia (Zahn and Bencivengo, and Zahn and Nielsen, 1973, 1976); and Cleveland (Hirsch, 1973). Studies of southern or southwestern cities include: Atlanta (Mumford, Kazer, and Feldman, 1976); Houston (Lundsgaarde, 1977); and Dallas (Zahn and Snodgrass, 1978).

Block (1974, 1977), using police records, studied 7,045 criminal homicides occurring in Chicago from 1965 to 1974. The homicide rate doubled in that period of time from 11.4 per 100,000 in 1965 to 29.2 in 1974. There are, according to Block, two general patterns of homicide, one of altercation homicide based on domestic feuds or arguments with friends, and the second based on robbery. The second increased much more rapidly than the first in this decade. The annual number of homicides in which the victim and offender did not know each other increased dramatically from 95 to 410 and, in fact, the most common offender became one whose identity remained unknown to the police. Further, there was an increase in homicides using guns.

Riedel and Katzenelson (1977), using arrest data for 3,411 homicides in Washington, D.C., found an increasing rate from 12.2 in 1957 to 31.3 in 1974. The age of offenders decreased but homicide remained an intraracial event, primarily between nonwhite offenders and victims. While they did not analyze victim-offender relationship, they did note a decrease in the percentage of homicides occurring in homes from 58.0 percent in 1957 to 32.7 percent in 1972. One of the largest changes was in method used to kill: In 1957, 35.9 percent of the homicides were committed by firearms, by 1974 this had increased to 82.8 percent.

The findings for Chicago and for Washington, D.C., are similar to those in Cleveland (Hirsch, 1973) and in Philadelphia (Zahn, 1975; Zahn and

Nielsen, 1976). Hirsch, using coroners' records, found that the homicide rate in Cleveland rose gradually in the early 1960s and then dramatically in the latter half of the 1960s. The rate of increase was great for both non-white and white males, although the increase for white male victims was much greater, 600 percent compared to 200 percent for nonwhites. They did not study victim-offender relationships.

Zahn, using medical examiners' records, studied 1,935 homicide victims in Philadelphia from 1969 to 1973. When comparing her results with those of Wolfgang for the 1940s and 1950s, she found a much higher rate of homicide in 1970. There also were more offenders in the youngest age groups. The most frequent reason for homicide was arguments (34.9 percent), followed by those which occurred for reasons unknown (fully 24.3 percent of the homicides occurred for unknown reasons, usually by unknown offenders). Only 15.4 percent of the homicides occurred for domestic reasons. In general while the dominant form was an acquaintance killing another acquaintance in an argument, it was closely followed by a stranger killing someone, with the circumstances immediately surrounding the event remaining unknown.[24]

Findings from studies of northern cities, then, show a consistent picture of an increasing homicide rate in the late 1960s and into the 1970s; an increase in homicides by gun; and an increase in homicides by unknown assailants who may be murdering for money or for reasons other than direct argument. The stranger is, indeed, a more fearful figure in northern American cities in the 1970s than earlier.

Studies of southern and southwestern cities for the same time period show a different pattern. Mumford, Kazer, and Feldman, using police and medical examiners' records for 591 Atlanta victims in 1961–62 and 1971–72, found that there was an increasing homicide rate for both black and white males. The pattern of homicide varied somewhat, however, for each group. While the majority of both blacks and whites were killed at home by relatives or acquaintances, more blacks were killed in such situations than whites. Whites were more likely than blacks to be killed in a public place and this tendency increased from the 1960s to the 1970s. In all situations firearms were the main mode of attack and there was an increase in the use of firearms from the 1960s to the 1970s.[25]

Lundsgaarde studied 300 murders in Houston in 1969. The categories of relationship and kinds of situation had not, he claimed, changed significantly over the past 40 years, with the exception of a slight increase in the number of killings involving strangers (in 17.5 percent of the cases the killer was a total stranger to the victim). In this sample the vast bulk of victims knew their killers—in 31 percent of the cases they were in the family group.[26] Zahn and Snodgrass (1978), studying 202 homicide victims in Dallas, found, as in Houston, that most victims were males; that 33.6 percent of the killings were family related; and 24.5 percent involved acquaintances, 17.3 percent strangers, and 13.4 percent unknown assailants. About equal numbers were killed inside as outside the home, and the most common motive was domestic quarrels, which were the occasion for 38 percent of homicides. As in all other cities, the gun was the main instrument of death.[27]

All studies from the 1960s and the 1970s show a higher rate of homicide than in the time period immediately preceding it. As in other time periods, homicide was intraracial and intrasexual, although there was a slight increase in interracial (black on white) homicide. There was also an increase in stranger murders and in cases where the offender remained unknown, although this increase was much more pronounced in northern cities. In southern and southwestern cities, domestic violence remained a significant category while in the North the stranger and the unknown assailant homicide became a dominant (if not the dominant) murder relationship.

Homicide: 1978–1988

Riedel and Zahn examined types of homicide both for the nation, using UCR Supplemental Homicide Reports, and for eight cities, using local police and detectives' reports. They found that, in 1978, at the national level 18.7 percent of the homicides occurred between family members; 37.7 percent between acquaintances; 13.5 percent between strangers; and 30.1 percent were types without a known offender. Since stranger homicides are the most difficult for police to solve, it is quite likely that the unknown category contains a large percentage of stranger relations. City data bear this out. In the eight cities the percentage of family homicides were consistently lower than the 18 percent nationwide figure and the stranger percentage was consistently higher (averaging 22.6 percent in cities).[28] Straus and Williams compared male and female victims in 1980–84. Seventeen percent of male victims were killed in the family; 54.5 percent in acquaintance relationships; and 28.5 percent by strangers. Stranger homicides, further, were felony linked, usually with robbery. For females, 42 percent were killed by a family member, 41 percent by an acquaintance and 17 percent by a stranger.[29]

Studies in the 1970s and 1980s have specified more clearly the process characteristic of homicide types than studies in earlier periods. Domestic and robbery related homicides have been studied more frequently than homicides between male acquaintances, even though this latter homicide type is the most numerous. Spouse homicides most frequently take place within the home, and, according to analyses by both Luckenbill and Gelles, take place through a series of stages, and after many other assaultive incidents. The process generally involves an escalating set of events where the victim criticizes the offender or refuses to obey a command; the offender interprets this as an affront and demands that some amends be made, with violence being the proposed penalty for lack of concurrence. The victim accepts violence as a way to resolve the situation and does not apologize or flee; the situation escalates and a homicide results.[30]

Recent studies have also focused on women who kill their husbands. While more men kill wives than the reverse, when a woman kills a spouse she generally does so after repeated violent attacks, when she is isolated, and when she seriously fears for her life or for those of her children.[31]

Stranger homicides have also recently been studied.[32] Stranger homicides, however, are quite a diverse phenomenon including, as examples, robbery related killings as well as random slayings in public places. Zahn and Sagi suggest that, at a minimum, stranger felony and stranger nonfelony homicides should be considered separately since they are distinct phenomena.[33] Despite the need, most studies on stranger homicide have dealt with robbery related murders.[34] Even here, the type varies. Some robbery murders result as a mistake, an escalation of violence induced by victim resistance.[35] Others are an after-thought, "You may as well steal from them, since you've killed them." Studies indicate a rise in robbery murders in the 1970s, and while the chance of being killed in a robbery is small, it is greater if the robber has a gun (9.0 per 1,000 with a gun, and 1.4 per 1000 without).[36] Victim resistance and the presence of a gun appear significant determinants of lethal attack during a robbery.[37] According to Cook, robbery murders are much more similar to robberies than to other homicides. Typical robbery murders have younger offenders and older victims; robbers and robbery killers are more likely to be male under 21 years of age and nonwhite.[38] The motives vary yet the fact remains that robbery murder is more common in the 1970s and 1980s than in earlier parts of this century.

In sum, the late 1970s and 1980s continue to have a high percentage, as have the other decades, of acquaintances homicide. The difference in types in the 1970s and 1980s is the increased proportion of homicides associated with robberies and flowing from other stranger relationships.

Types of Homicide Through Time

In summary, comparing homicide studies on victim-offender relationship is difficult to accomplish. There is no consistent definition of what constitutes an acquaintance or a stranger relationship and, further, many studies use motives as the basis of classification—for example, criminal transaction—but do not indicate whether the criminal transaction involved an acquaintance or a stranger relationship.

Nonetheless, these generalizations seem to hold. Throughout the century a young man killing another man of similar age and race with whom he is acquainted is a regular and persistent form of homicide. When homicide rates surge upward, the stranger or economic relationship murder predominates. In the late 1920s murders related to prohibition were common, and from the late 1960s to the present, murder by unknown persons for unknown reasons, or for profit (robbery), increased sharply. In contrast, when homicide rates are low, as in the 1950s, family and acquaintance homicides are most common, with family murders especially so.

In general it seems that the percentage of family-related murders does not fluctuate dramatically through time. The main sources of higher rates are the stranger relationships and so-called economically motivated homicides. While some types of relationships remain associated with homicide throughout time, the prominence of types varies in different periods. The search for causes and for effective intervention strategies needs to take these differences in types into account.

Social Causes of Homicide

Attempts at understanding the social causes of homicide have generally focused on explaining the changes in the overall homicide rate rather than explaining the components of that rate. The variables that have been most frequently examined (not always with consistent results) have been demographic variables such as the size of the youthful male cohort;[39] economic variables, including especially absolute poverty and relative deprivation[40]; and large scale processes such as urbanization, industrialization; and changing sensitivities to violent behavior.[41] The ways in which these factors generate trends in the aggregate homicide rate have been amply discussed elsewhere in this volume and will not be repeated here.

What remains to be done is to deal with the causal processes associated with the various types of homicide. Such analyses are in their infancy. The few studies that have been done along these lines suggest that a very fruitful line of inquiry is to establish how and why variables such as poverty or urban density affect different types of homicide. How and why do the effects of such causes vary for whites, blacks, Hispanics; for males and females; for young and old?

Since a definitive typology of homicide is not yet available, two types of homicide, those between spouses and those between robber and victim, will be used as illustrations. The earliest study comparing rates of primary (family) and non-primary felony homicide, by Smith and Parker, found that poverty was related to primary but not to felony murder. Felony murder was most associated with the percentage of state population that was urban.[42] A recent study similarly found that urbanization was closely associated with stranger homicide but not with family homicide. A 1988 study, however, contradicts Parker and Smith's findings: Poverty was not

Table 10.1 Factors That May Predispose a Person to Kill His/Her Spouse

Structural Factors	Cultural Factors	Interactionist Factors
Poverty Male dominance over females Isolation of nuclear family	Male belief in physical prowess, toughness, that he is "head of house" and has control over females "Hands-off" view of domestic disputes by criminal justice system Lack of safe places for battered women to go	Alcohol and drug consumption Male use of force to compensate for verbal disadvantage

Factors That May Predispose a Person to Commit a Robbery-Motivated Killing

Structural Factors	Cultural Factors	Interactionist Factors	Psychosocial Factors
Income equality Racial segregation and discrimination Urban (population) density Lack of legitimate opportunities for adolescent minority males	Materialism Young male belief in thrills and action Belief that perpetrator will not be caught or severely punished Criminal way of life condoned, and opportunities provided to engage in it Televised violence and media support for "bad guy"	Lack of criminal justice and legal prosecution Alcohol and drug consumption Gun possession	From disorganized home Developmental lack of empathy

associated with family homicide but was with stranger homicide.[43] The contradiction in findings from the two studies has many possible sources, including differences in poverty measures, differences in homicide type categorization, and failure by both researchers to disaggregate homicide type by race. Poverty and income inequality may have very different impacts on whites and blacks, and subsequently on the type of violence each experiences. Sampson's study most forcefully illustrates this. He found that white poverty has a strong positive effect on white juvenile violence, while overall income inequality has no independent influence. For black juveniles, absolute poverty has no effect on violence offenses, whereas income inequality has a very strong positive influence.[44] These studies illustrate the importance of disaggregating the homicide rate by type and by demographic characteristics of participants.

A condensation of suggested causal factors as they relate to killing of spouses and robbery-motivated killing appear in Table 10.1.[45] These diagrams are not definitive but suggestive of an approach to causation that should yield a more informative and policy relevant approach to homicide.

As Table 10.1 shows, most factors have a strong bearing on one type of homicide (for example, the impact of available shelters for battered women on family homicide)[46] but bear no relationship to other types. A few factors affect both types of homicide, including poverty and alcohol and drug consumption. These kinds of associations are grist for studies that are needed if we are to understand and minimize types of violence that take more than 20,000 lives each year.

In sum, reducing this deadly from of violence in the twenty-first century will require clearer understanding of factors associated with specific types of homicide. It also requires knowledge of how events and social forces impact differently on men and women; blacks, Hispanics, and whites; and young and old. For the act of homicide is often a desperate last stand. To understand the routes by which different people reach such desperation may ultimately help us halt its deadly outcomes.

Notes

1. This chapter is a substantial revision and update of an earlier article, "Homicide in the Twentieth Century United States," that appeared in *History and Crime: Implications for Criminal Justice Policy*, James A. Inciardi and Charles E. Faupel, eds. (Beverly Hills, CA: Sage, 1980), 111–31.

2. This difference is at least partially attributable to differences in data sources. In the 1920s National Vital Statistics on causes of death were used as a base of homicide studies and they include justifiable homicides within the overall homicide statistic. Police data (Uniform Crime Reports) that are used more frequently in later studies, do not so classify it.

3. See Roger Lane, *Violent Death in the City: Suicide, Accident, and Murder in Nineteenth Century Philadelphia* (Cambridge, MA: Harvard University Press, 1979).

4. Information regarding this classification change was obtained from a telephone conversation with the former head of the Mortality Unit of Vital Statistics.

5. See Leonard D. Savitz, "Official Police Statistics and Their Limitations," in Leonard D. Savitz and Norman Johnston, eds., *Crime in Society* (New York: Wiley, 1978) and M. Hindelang, "The Uniform Crime Reports Revisited," *Journal of Criminal Justice* 2 (no. 1, 1974): 1–17.

6. See Roger Lane, *Violent Death in the City* and L. J. Center and T. G. Smith, "Criminal Statistics—Can They Be Trusted?" *American Criminal Law Review* 11 (1973): 1046–86.

7. Savitz, "Official Police Statistics." This article and other sources indicate that the number of police agencies cooperating in the voluntary UCR reporting system has changed over time from 400 in 1930 to 8,500 in 1968, the latter representing 92 percent of the national population. National data, then, are not available from police sources until well

after the 1930s, which makes establishing the homicide trend for the early part of the century difficult.

8. David Cantor and Lawrence E. Cohen, "Comparing Measures of Homicide Trends: Methodological and Substantive Differences in the Vital Statistics and Uniform Crime Report Time Series (1933–1975)," *Social Sciences Research* 9 (1980): 121–45.

9. Ibid.

10. Edwin H. Sutherland and C. E. Gehlke, "Crime and Punishment," in *Recent Social Trends in the United States* (New York: McGraw-Hill, 1933), 1114–67.

11. These differences are analyzed by Reynolds Farley, "Homicide Trends in the United States," *Demography* 17 (no. 2, 1980): 179–88; A. Joan Klebba, "Homicide Trends in the United States, 1900–1974," *Public Health Reports* 90 (no. 3, 1975): 195–204; and Patrick W. O'Carroll and James A. Mercy, "Patterns and Recent Trends in Black Homicide," in Darrell F. Hawkins, ed., *Homicide Among Black Americans* (University Press of America, 1986).

12. H. C. Brearly, *Homicide in the United States* (Chapel Hill: University of North Carolina Press, 1932); and Frederick Hoffman, *The Homicide Problem* (San Francisco: Prudential Press, 1925); gun homicide data from Brearly, *Homicide*, 68.

13. James Boudouris, "Trends in Homicide, Detroit 1926–1968," unpublished Ph.D. diss., Wayne State University, 1970; and James Boudouris, "A Classification of Homicides," *Criminology* 11 (1974): 525–40.

14. For detailed analysis of the Chicago data see Arthur V. Lashly, "Homicide (In Cook County)," chap. 13, in *The Illinois Crime Survey* (Chicago: Illinois Association for Criminal Justice, 1929). Also see a reanalysis of this in Carolyn R. Block and Richard L. Block, *Patterns of Change in Chicago Homicide: The Twenties, The Sixties, and The Seventies*, (Statistical Analysis Center of the Illinois Law Enforcement Commission, 1980).

15. For discussion of how violence became associated with bootlegging see chap. 6 by Mark H. Haller, in this volume.

16. The rate for the decades were computed by averaging the UCR Homicide rate figures for the 1940–1949 and 1950–1959 periods, respectively.

17. Henry Allen Bullock, "Urban Homicide in Theory and Fact," *Journal of Criminal Law and Criminology* 45 (1955): 563–75.

18. Howard Harlan, "Five Hundred Homicides," *Journal of Criminal Law and Criminology* 6 (1950): 736–52.

19. Robert C. Bensing and Oliver Schroeder, Jr., *Homicide in an Urban Community* (Springfield, IL: Charles C Thomas, 1970).

20. Boudouris, *Trends in Homicide*. Data for the 1920s do not encompass a whole decade but only the years 1926 to 1929. All figures represent an average of the percentages.

21. See Marvin E. Wolfgang, *Patterns in Criminal Homicide* (Oxford: Oxford University Press, 1958).

22. The Violence Commission Reports are found in Donald J. Mulvihill and Melvin H. Tumin, *Crimes of Violence: Staff Reports to the National Commission on the Causes and Prevention of Violence*, vols. 1, 11- 13 (Washington, DC: Government Printing Office, 1969). See also Lynn A. Curtis, *Criminal Violence* (Lexington, MA: Lexington Books, 1974).

23. The following is a fairly comprehensive list of local studies done on homicide in the 1960s and 1970s. Margaret A. Zahn, "The Female Homicide Victim," *Criminology* 13 (1975): 400–15; Margaret A. Zahn and Mark Bencivengo, "Violent Death: A Comparison between Drug Users and Non-Drug Users," *Addictive Diseases: An International Journal* 1 (1973): 183–296; Margaret A Zahn and Kathleen E. Neilson, "Changing Patterns of Criminal Homicide: A Twenty Year Follow-Up" (paper presented at the American Society of Criminology meetings, Tucson, Arizona, November 1976); Margaret A. Zahn and Glenn Snodgrass, "Drug Use and the Structure of Homicide in Two U.S. Cities," in Edith Flynn and John Conrad, eds., *The New and Old Criminology* (New York: Praeger Press, 1978), 134–50; Marc Riedel and Susan Katzenelson, "Homicide Trends in the District of Columbia 1957–1974"

(paper presented at the American Society of Criminology meetings, Atlanta, 1977); Richard Block, "Homicide in Chicago: A Ten Year Study, 1965–1974" (paper presented at American Society of Criminology meetings, Chicago, 1974); Richard Block, *Violent Crime* (Lexington, MA: Lexington Books, 1977); Charles S. Hirsch, "Homicide and Suicide in a Metropolitan County: Long Term Trends," *Journal of the American Medical Association* 223 (1973): 900–5; Robert S. Mumford, Ross S. Kazer, Roger A. Feldman, and Robert R. Stivers, "Homicide Trends in Atlanta," *Criminology* 14 (1976): 213–323. Henry P. Lundsgaarde, *Murder in Space City* (New York: Oxford University Press, 1977).

24. Additional studies by Zahn and by Zahn and Bencivengo (1975, 1973) above also show a connection between illegal drug use and homicide in the 1960s and 1970s. In a high percentage of Philadelphia cases (appr. one-third in 1972), homicide victims have drugs, usually heroin, in their systems at time of death. Further, 14 percent of these users died in drug-related arguments. How many of the "unknown assailant" homicides involve drug-related arguments remains, of course, a mystery. The connection between illegal substance use and homicide victimization in the 1960s and 1970s, however, warrants closer attention.

25. Mumford, "Homicide Trends.

26. Lundsgaarde, *Murder in Space City.*

27. Zahn and Snodgrass, "Drug Use."

28. Marc Riedel and Margaret A. Zahn, *The Nature and Patterns of American Homicide* (Washington, DC: U.S. Department of Justice, 1985).

29. Murray A. Straus and Kirk R. Williams, "Homicide Victimization and Offense Rates By Age, Gender, Race, Relation of Victim to Offender, Weapon Used, and Circumstances, for the U.S., 1976–79, and 1980–84" (unpublished ms., Durham, NH: Family Research Lab, Feb. 1988).

30. Richard J. Gelles, *The Violent Home: A Study of Physical Aggression Between Husbands and Wives* (Beverly Hills, CA: Sage, 1972); and David F. Luckenbill, "Criminal Homicide as a Situated Transaction," *Social Problems* 25 (1977): 176–86.

31. Angela Browne, *When Battered Women Kill* (New York: The Free Press, 1987). Spouse homicide may not be evenly distributed across ethnic groups. A recent UCLA conference suggested that spouse homicides may be rarer among Hispanic than black or white couples. Papers from that conference will be distributed from the Dept. of Public Health, UCLA, 1989.

32. An entire issue of *Journal of Criminal Law and Criminology* (78, no. 2, Summer 1987) is devoted to stranger violence, especially stranger homicides.

33. Margaret A. Zahn and Philip C. Sagi, "Stranger Homicide in Nine American Cities," *Journal of Criminal Law and Criminology* 78 (no. 2 1987).

34. For examples of studies dealing with robbery murders see Block, *Violent Crime* above, and *Robbery in the United States: An Analysis of Recent Trends and Patterns* (Washington, DC: National Institute of Justice, Sept. 1983); and Franklin Zimring, "Determinants of the Death Rate from Robbery: A Detroit Time Study," in Harold M. Rose, ed., *Lethal Aspects of Urban Violence* (Lexington, MA: Lexington Books, 1979), 31–50.

35. Philip C. Cook, "Robbery Violence," *Journal of Criminal Law and Criminology* 78 (no. 2, 1987): 357–76.

36. Philip J. Cook, ed., "The Effect of Gun Availability on Violent Crime Patterns," *Gun Control. Annals of the American Academy of Political and Social Science* 455 (May 1981).

37. Block, *Violent Crime.*

38. Cook, "Robbery Violence."

39. Travis Hirschi and Michael Gottfredson, "Age and the Explanation of Crime," *American Journal of Sociology* 89 (November 1983): 552–84; Lawrence E. Cohen and Kenneth C. Land, "Age Structure and Crime: Symmetry Versus Asymmetry and the Projection of Crime Rates Through the 1990's," *American Sociological Review* 52 (Apr. 1987): 170–83.

40. Judith R. Blau and Peter M. Blau, "The Cost of Inequality: Metropolitan Structure

and Violent Crime," *American Sociological Review* 47 (Feb. 1982): 114–28; and Scott J. South and Lawrence E. Cohen, "Unemployment and the Homicide Rate: A Paradox Resolved," *Social Indicators Research* 17 (1985): 325–43.

41. See in this volume chap. 1 by Ted Robert Gurr, and chap. 2 by Roger Lane.

42. Dwayne M. Smith and Robert Nash Parker, "Type of Homicide and Variation in Regional Rates," *Social Forces* (1980): 136–47.

43. Ronet Backman-Prehn, Linksy and Murray Straus, "Homicide of Family Members, Acquaintances and Strangers, and State-to-State Differences in Social Stress, Social Control, and Social Norms" (unpublished ms., Durham, NH: Family Research Lab, 1988).

44. Robert J. Sampson, "Structural Sources of Variation in Race-Age-Specific Rates of Offending Across Major U.S. Cities," *Criminology,* 23 (no. 4, 1985): 647–73.

45. These diagrams originally appeared in "Violence: Homicide, Assault, and Suicide," Mark Rosenberg, et al., *Closing the Gap: The Burden of Unnecessary Illness* (New York: Oxford University Press, 1987) 164–78. References that support these causal factors may be found in that article.

46. Support for the notion that the availability of shelters affects the domestic homicide rate can be found in Angela Browne and Kirk R. Williams, "Resource Availability for Women as Risk and Partner Homicide," paper presented at American Society of Criminology meetings, Montreal, Canada, 1987.

Chapter *11*

Social Change and the Future of Violent Crime

WESLEY G. SKOGAN

This chapter examines some of the forces which account for increasing levels of violent crime in the United States over the past 25 years. Prior to the turbulent 1960s, levels of violent crime had been relatively stable for more than a decade; murder rates even declined by about one-third during the two decades following World War II. Then, beginning in about 1963, violent (and property) crime rates began to spiral upward. Between 1963 and 1967 the violent crime rate doubled.

This explosive growth in crime did not go unnoticed. President Lyndon Johnson named a special national commission to investigate the causes and prevention of crime, and presidential contenders like Barry Goldwater and George Wallace attempted to capitalize on the issue. By a number of measures, crime rose to the top of the public's agenda, and opinion surveys pointed to increasing levels of fear of crime all during the 1960s and early 1970s. Researchers have addressed the growth of violent crime as well. Their explanations for events in the post-war era reflect all of the great traditions of research on violence. This chapter focuses on three of them: *demography, economic hardship,* and *family and community social disorganization.* Like most fundamental features of American life, discussion of these factors inevitably involves another one—race. Most of the factors which seem to lead to crime are disproportionately concentrated among black Americans; and, as a result, the condition and experiences of this relatively small group (perhaps 12 percent of the U.S. population) disproportionately affect the crime problem facing the nation as a whole.

Trends in Violent Crime

For the United States as a whole there are perhaps 40 years of data on the national rate of violent crime, depending on the information needed and how far into the past one is willing to trust the figures (see chap. 10 by Margaret A. Zahn).

Those data portray steadily increasing rates of violence in the United States since the mid-1950s. The rate of violent crime rose slowly between then and near the middle of the 1960s, but it rose without interruption every year. Between 1955 and 1975, levels of violent crime increased by a factor of more than four; the property crime rate followed almost exactly the same pattern. Then, there was a three-year respite in this trend, a brief period during which both violent and property crime rates leveled off at nearly their 1975 high; this was followed by a climb to a new high in 1982, and again in 1986. Between 1955 to 1986, the violent crime rate rose almost exactly 600 percent and the property crime rate 400 percent.[2]

The components of this increase might appear somewhat less alarming. In general, the more serious the type of crime the less common it is: Less life-threatening violent crimes are more frequent than deadly ones, and most kinds of property crime are more common than any violent one. In 1986, homicide constituted 1.4 percent of all violent crimes; rape followed at 5.5 percent; robbery (theft using threats or force) and aggravated assault (personal attacks involving either injury or the display of a weapon) were the largest components, at 38 and 54 percent. There were more than twice as many burglaries (thefts from inside homes or businesses) as there were violent crimes of all kinds. The homicide rate also grew the least over this period—between 1955 and 1986, it was up by "only" 150 percent.

There has been a great deal of research on how to explain these trends. This research has linked fluctuations in crime to some of the most central aspects of American life—its population, the economy, and how people live. These factors also provide a basis for predicting the future. To the extent crime is related to features of society which are themselves predictable, their future course can help us forecast the future of crime.

However, there is some question whether the measures of crime upon which all of this research is based can be trusted. Until recently, almost all we knew about the frequency of crime came from official statistics which local police agencies collected and filed with the FBI. Across the country, they voluntarily forward to Washington the number of incidents that citizens have reported to them, and that they in turn have investigated and determined to be crimes. It is clear, however, that both decisions by victims to complain to the police and decisions by the police to make proper records of those incidents are subject to a number of influences which disguise the "true" level of crime lying behind them. Victims often fail to report incidents to the police because their losses were slight or they were not insured, because they see no chance that the offender will be caught or that the police can do anything to help them, and sometimes because they fear retaliation by criminals or their friends. Surveys show that about one-half of all personal crimes are not reported to the police.[3] On the police side, it appears that professional police departments and those with more resources tend to investigate and record more thoroughly all of the complaints brought to them by citizens.[4] The frequent need for top administrators of police departments to point to decreasing rates of crime undoubtedly plays a role in shaping crime statistics as well. Field studies of how official crime data are collected reveal that to an important extent they reflect the organizational arrangements and politics of the collecting agencies.[5] One study found that the Chicago police understated robbery by about 35 percent and rape by 25 percent in 1982, and that this under count had varied widely in prior years.[6] After this practice was revealed on television by an investigative reporter, Chicago's violent crime rate more than doubled.[7]

The tremendous concentration of violent crime in large cities means that only a few instances of serious misreporting (or correcting for such practices when they come to light) can shift the national rate of crime as reported by the FBI by several percentage points, which is its typical yearly level of change. For example, the post-1982 shift in the robbery count for Chicago described above increased the U.S. *national* robbery rate by 2.1 percent. Events in other cities can have similar consequences: New York City, which reports notoriously suspect crime figures and occasionally is chastised for this by the FBI, alone accounts for 15 percent of the national total for robbery, and together the eight largest U.S. cities account for 36 percent. What happens in these cities can account for more than most other sources of yearly variation in national crime rates.

This does not mean that official statistics are useless for any purpose, but it does give us reason for skepticism about apparent fluctuations in crime. It is not clear that the trends depicted by official statistics are even pointing in the right direction. While it would be convenient to conclude that these local perturbations cancel themselves out, and that in the aggregate the official national crime rate is fairly accurate, there is irritating evidence to the contrary. Since 1973, the U.S. Department of Justice has been monitoring crime trends using monthly national surveys which independently measure the incidence of victimization. In the surveys, people are questioned about their recent experiences with crime, whether they reported them to the police, and who they saw committing the crime. As measured by the surveys, crime rates have tracked a somewhat different course than that taken by official figures.

For example, official rates of aggravated assault rose during the 1970s, declined a bit during the early 1980s, and then jumped to new highs in 1985 and 1986; however, national survey measures of the same offense have declined almost every year since 1974. The dramatic differences between trends in the two sets of figures are illustrated in Figure 11.1. Like serious assaults, robberies measured in the surveys have dropped steadily since 1981, while the official robbery rate took off upward again after 1984.[8] In

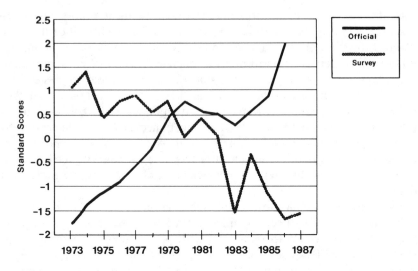

Figure 11.1: Official and Survey Rates of Assault, 1973–1987

1986, violent crime in the surveys stood below its 1973 level, and was off 20 percent from its high.[9] But, as we have seen above, the official total was at its post-war peak in 1986. Attempts to explain fluctuations in survey-based crime rates would point to much different factors than those based on official figures, and presumably would produce more optimistic forecasts for the future.

Age and Crime

Any consideration of the distribution of crime must begin with age, for crime is largely the domain of the young. The strong affinity of young males for getting into trouble with the law has remained fundamentally unchanged over the 150 years or so for which there is data of some sort on the issue. The age-crime nexus is virtually identical for different times and places, under various social and cultural conditions, and for different subgroups. Youth almost seems "pathogenic."[10] Cohen and Land calculate that "indices of the prevalence of teenagers and young adults in the population alone account for about 58 percent of the year-to-year change in the murder series."[11] The typical age of arrest varies by type of crime, but lies between 15 and 21. The median age of arrest for property crime is 16, while the arrest distribution for violent crimes is "two humped," peaking concurrently at ages 18 and 21. What happens after about age 24 is a subject of great interest to criminologists. Sharp declines in offending after age 24 appear to be due to a combination of factors, including imprisonment (generally reserved for older, multiple offenders sporting long records), death ("life in the fast lane" is decidedly dangerous), reintegration into the community through employment and marriage, and "spontaneous burnout" (a concept which bundles together a substantial number of "unknown causes").[12]

The affect of age is so strong that by itself the total number of youths (actually young males, but the numbers go together) in the population is an important determinant of the crime count. The age structure of the U.S. population has taken a roller-coaster ride during the past three decades, and this often is used to explain the 1960s-to-1970s explosion in crime of all kinds. The first wave of the post-World War II baby boom hit age 15 in 1963, the year before the explosion in crime was evident. Baby Boomers made their largest contribution to the pool of high-risk youths in 1973, when the largest number aged into the risky 15-year-old category. Between about 1963 and 1973, each year saw more youths age into the 15-to-21 group than grew out of it. The importance of age was apparent to the President's Crime Commission as early as 1966. They estimated that between 40 and 50 percent of the 1960–65 increase in crime was attributable to changes in the age composition of the population.[13] Recent data for homicide (extending through 1984) set that figure at 58 percent.[14]

Thus, other things being equal, shifts in the age distribution should affect the U.S. crime rate even if the rate at which youths commit crimes (youth crimes per thousand youths) are stable. However, there is evidence that rates of youthful offenders also rose during the 1965–70 period. Not only were there more of them, but they were getting into trouble more frequently.[15] In addition, a study of two groups of Philadelphia youths—all those born there who were 15 years of age in 1960 and those who entered that high-risk category in 1973—uncovered "qualitative" differences in their criminal behavior as well. When they got into trouble, males in the 1970s cohort committed more serious violent offenses, the general seriousness of everything they did went up, their use of weapons in violent crimes went up, and they were more likely to harm or kill their victims.[16] Between how much more they did and how viciously they did it, the more recent cohort of youthful offenders provided a "double dose" of trouble.

There is also evidence that offending members of the Baby Boom cohort are not following patterns of the past. They are not "dropping out" as rapidly as expected.[17] Violent offenders are getting older. For example, between 1975 and 1986 the proportion of those arrested for violent offenses who were under 18 dropped from 32 to 15 percent, and for property crimes from 50 to 33 percent.[18] The emergence of this graying group of unexpectedly high-rate offenders should make forecasts of the future of crime more gloomy than past demographic patterns would predict.

Age effects also interact with economic conditions. We shall consider below the effect of fluctuations in the economy which affect labor force participation and unemployment; here it should be noted that the highest levels of unemployment are concentrated among younger job seekers, and that when recessions hit they often are the first to be laid off. Any criminogenic effects of macroeconomic changes thus could be amplified by both the relative size and the underlying (higher) propensity of youths to get into trouble.

The rising rate of youth crime during the coming of age of the Baby Boom in the late 1960s (which multiplied their cohort's effect on the over-all crime rate) raises tantalizing questions about the impact of historical events on crime. Demographers speculate that the unique size of the Baby Boom generation will shape its development. They argue that the lives of members of that cohort will always be more competitive—for housing, jobs, and advancement—and that their large numbers will multiply the effect of peer-group pressures upon them throughout their lives.[19] James Q. Wilson contends that their numbers have spoken in the marketplace, leading Americans in the 1960s to celebrate dysfunctional aspects of youth culture, including unfettered self-expression and spontaneous behavior.[20] In addition, many Baby Boomers entered their political consciousness dur-ing the divisive period of the Vietnam War, and (just as significant for many black Americans) came of age during the large-scale urban riots of 1964–1969 and the galvanizing appearance (in the summer of 1966) of "Black Power" rhetoric in American politics. At the same time, the Viet-nam War did not appear to have had any short-term crime-control effects. The sharp declines in arrest rates experienced during World War I and World War II were probably due to the sheer number of young males conscripted for service during those periods. The Korean and Vietnam Wars, however, did not mobilize enough youths to have a similar effect on crime. In fact, indicators of the extent of mobilization for these conflicts are associated with *higher* national rates of homicide, a finding some re-searchers attribute to the dislocation of careers, family formation, and family stability caused by those wars.[21]

Race and Crime

Race is another important element in the dynamics of crime in the United States. Racial differences in offending are well known. Blacks are arrested for violent crimes in numbers that are vastly disproportionate to their share of the population. In 1986, they constituted 48 percent of those arrested for murder, 46 percent for rape, and 62 percent for robbery. Since the mid-1970s, black-white differences in youthful arrest rates for violent crimes have averaged about 6.5 to 1. Those arrest statistics closely parallel other ways of detecting offenders. They closely resemble profiles of offend-ers as described by their victims in victimization surveys, and similar black-white differences appear in self-report studies in which people recount their own past offenses in anonymous questionnaires.[22] Only in a few arrest categories—principally those involving alcohol abuse—do whites and blacks appear in numbers proportionate to their share of the population.

Race is also clearly linked to crime at the neighborhood level, where residential segregation and the tendency for victims and offenders to get into trouble near home produces crime rates for neighborhoods which are very highly correlated with their racial composition, and places black Americans at the highest degree of danger.[23] As a result, blacks are much more likely to be victimized by violent crime. In the most recent national victimization survey, blacks were two-and-one-half times as likely as whites to be robbed, and three times as likely to be raped.[24] Black victims also are more likely than whites to be seriously injured, and they are much more commonly threatened, robbed, and raped by criminals carrying guns.[25] Fortunately, blacks have shared with whites the declining rates of violent crime revealed by those surveys. Since 1975, violent victimization (and burglary) rates have been slowly declining for both blacks and whites.[26]

However, the distribution of the population along racial lines cannot do much to explain fluctuations in crime nationally, for the complexion of the nation as a whole changes only at a glacial pace. Statistical studies reveal that at this level the most important feature of the black population is age. In the aggregate, blacks are younger than whites, and since 1960 there has been a steady increase in the non-white proportion of each new high-risk age cohort. Untangled from other factors, blacks' over-representation in the 15-to-24 age category has contributed to increases in the national crime rate over time.[27]

Explanations for this confluence of race and crime abound. In addition to their relative youthfulness, blacks are disproportionately concentrated in the hearts of big cities, where violent crime rates are higher than in rural areas with similar populations. In addition, they disproportionately suffer from several factors to be considered below—poverty, economic inequality, and family and neighborhood disorganization. These problems also are concentrated in big cities, where conditions and events have a substantial impact on national rates of violent crime. Other explanations for high levels of offending among blacks point to cultural factors emerging from those objective conditions of life. For example, the "subculture of violence" explanation for black criminality highlights how values supporting personal toughness and exploitation of others are adaptive to life in oppressed urban ghettos.[28]

Hardship and Crime

The role of economic hardship as a cause of crime has been the object of close scrutiny for at least 150 years. Population wisdom, everyday observation, and official and survey measures of crime all agree that crime problems are much greater in poorer areas of town. The causal linkage between hardship (reflected in high unemployment or low wages) and crime is intuitively obvious in the case of theft, while it takes an indirect, multi-step set of assumptions to link violence to economic conditions.

Most explanations of changing rates of property crime follow Becker's classic application of rational choice theory to crime.[29] An economist, he emphasized the comparative costs and benefits of participating in legitimate and illegitimate enterprises. Becker posited that for each individual the balance of those costs and benefits of crime (for example, what mix of activity "maximizes their expected returns") determines their propensity to rob and steal. This is a powerful rational-economic model of human behavior. It takes into account the threat of sanctions and the opportunities lost while sitting in prison, as well as a comparison between anticipated earnings on the street and those from a lawful job. Research on the effects of hardship use measures of employment and wage rates to index how easy it is to find jobs in the legitimate sector and how lucrative they can be. These studies support common wisdom about the distribution of the inclination to steal, for local levels of employment and real income have been strong predictors of property crime rates.[30]

The theoretical linkage between hardship and violent crime is provided by the "structural strain" approach to understanding violence. In this view, violence is rooted in structurally induced frustration. This frustration stems from the inability of individuals to achieve the lifestyles to which they aspire; the structure is supplied by social forces which shape both their aspiration levels and the likelihood that people will attain them. Violence should therefore be endemic, for the operation of capitalist (and, in practice, probably most other) economies ensures that some-to-most will never achieve their goals.[31]

However, a large body of research indicates that at the national level there is no clear connection whatsoever between changes in the level of criminal violence and measures of the level of hardship.[32] This may be due in part to the fact that the link between hardship and violence is contingent upon mediating factors. For example, in a study of individual and neighborhood factors leading to victimization, Sampson found that area poverty was linked to the incidence of violence only in cities.[33] This finding is in line with the general view that rural poverty is different in character than that concentrated in metropolitan areas. There is also evidence that strain may be better indexed by year-to-year *changes* in unemployment and wages, rather than in their level. In bad times, these measures are lower than last year, signaling that people are not doing as well as before. Changes in homicide levels are related to yearly fluctuations in unemployment, perhaps due to economically-induced stress.[34]

Measures of *inequality* in the distribution of hardship also are linked to levels of crime. Most notably this includes factors like the ratio of black-to-white income and black-to-white unemployment. In 1986, the percentage of black Americans living below the poverty line (31 percent) was almost three times the poverty rate for whites; that year, the median income for adult black males was only 60 percent of that for whites.[35] In 1985, black unemployment (15 percent of those in the labor force) was two-and-one-half times the rate for whites.[36] Race-linked inequality is particularly exacerbated by economic recessions, when blacks lose more than others, are the last to regain their old status, and profit most slowly from "trickle-down" spending by government. Between 1978 and 1986, real wages for white families declined by only 0.2 percent, but for black families the figure was 4 percent, and for Hispanic families it was 5 percent.[37] Across cities, inequality in the distribution of income is related to arrests for violent crimes among blacks, but not among whites. This may be because income inequality reflects concrete conflicts of interest between the poor and the better-off; this generates a sense of discrimination, deprivation, injustice, and hostility among the losers (disproportionately black), which in turn leads to violence.[38]

There is also inequality in the distribution of hardship across generations, a fact which confounds the impact of economic conditions and the age distribution on crime. The youth unemployment rate is one of the factors linked to changing national levels of homicide.[39] The highest levels of unemployment are concentrated among younger job seekers, and when recessions hit they are the first to be laid off. Any criminogenic effects of macroeconomic changes thus may be amplified by both the relative size and the tendency of younger segments of the population to get into trouble. Further, patterns of labor force participation are changing; structural changes in the U.S. economy are channeling youths into low-skill, low-wage, unstable non-union jobs.[40] Being trapped in this kind of work has been characteristic of high-risk populations.

The analysis of hardship effects is further complicated by the fact that they may be mediated indirectly through social and family factors considered in the next section. Declining real wages, unemployment, and business instability are related to indicators of a number of social pathologies, including suicide, illegitimacy, divorce, mental illness, and alcohol and drug use.[41] To the extent to which they then contribute to crime, these pathologies provide an indirect causal connection between hardship and crime. These indirect effects doubtless take some period of time to appear. Even strain-related crime appears only later, for the downward mobility, financial stress, discontent, frustrating social comparisons, and political alienation induced by economic decline also must have time to show its effects.

What does research on the effects of hardship forecast for the future? Forecasting crime based on economic factors is difficult, because forecasting economic trends is itself an elusive art. There is evidence that business recessions set in motion social processes which stimulate national homicide rates over the next few years.[42] However, what business failures and unemployment will be like even a few years from now is difficult to predict. It may even be that in the long run, short-term fluctuations in economic factors like unemployment cancel themselves out, and that we should look for predictions from more stable social and economic factors. In this regard, it may be significant that the real wages of American workers (indexed for inflation) have been stagnant or declining for the last decade, and the position of the United States in the international economy does not suggest that they will rebound significantly. Shifting regional economies have made unskilled jobs increasingly inaccessible to the inner-city poor in Northern cities, and this too does not seem likely to change. The percentage of Americans living below the poverty line has been growing, and now stands at about 14 percent of all persons. We have seen that this percentage varies predictably by race, but between 1978 and 1986 it has grown for whites, blacks, and Hispanics alike.[43] All of these trends portend badly for the future of crime.

Social Disorganization and Crime

The extent of social disorganization is another important determinant of rates of crime. Social disorganization is not the same thing as poverty, although the two often co-exist. In the not-so-distant past, many Americans were ill-housed and illiterate, wages were almost universally low, and levels of cyclical unemployment were often extreme. However, crime rates remained low where the traditional agents of social control were strong: families, churches, schools, traditional values, and ethnic solidarity. Crime problems became worse when those agents lost their hold on the young. Many urban neighborhoods now are disorganized because the informal control once exerted by families and local institutions has largely disappeared.

It is easy to point to figures that signal alarming decreases in the capacity of families and communities to provide opportunities for their young or to exercise control over them. Levels of family abandonment, illegitimacy, divorce, single-adult (usually female-headed) families, teen-age mothers, young mothers in the labor force, school dropouts, and the proportion of children living in households below the poverty line, all rose steadily during the 1960 and 1970s. Currently they stand at their highest point in modern U.S. history. For example, about 25 percent of U.S. children now are living in families headed by single adults, and 22 percent of young children live below the poverty line.[44] These indicators point to a decreasing quantity of "parenting", growing family discord and disruption, and decreased adult supervision of youths.[45] These indicators of the extent of family disorganization are strongly related to neighborhood levels of crime,[46] and national trends in violent crime are linked to such factors as the changing proportion of families with only one adult at home and the divorce rate.[47] Decades of research indicate that a crucial factor in the development of delinquent careers is the early replacement of parents by peers as the figures who set the standards for youthful behavior. This facilitates the development of autonomous neighborhood delinquent subcultures which persist for generations. They can influence the behavior of local youths whose personal family situations are quite stable.

Not surprisingly, family factors which are linked to crime also differ widely by race; the most recent figures paint a stark portrait of the different worlds of black and white families. In 1986, 80 percent of white children were living in two-adult families, but only 41 percent of black children;[48] in 1982, 12 percent of births by white mothers were recorded as illegitimate, while for black mothers the comparable figure was 57 percent;[49] and in 1984, 16 percent of white children and 46 percent of black children were living in poverty.[50] These percentages are changing for all groups, however. Illegitimacy, broken families, and child poverty have grown for blacks, whites, and Hispanics during the past decade.

What does research on family and community factors suggest for the future? There have been few serious attempts to forecast most of them, and without knowing their future course one cannot be precise about their effects on crime trends. The Urban Institute tracked the size of the "underclass" in American cities, and found that it quadrupled between the 1970 and 1980 censuses. It continues to grow. The underclass is made up of persistently poor families, chronically on welfare, who live in neighborhoods with high concentrations of unemployment, high rates of school drop-out, and many families headed by lone women. They account for a vastly disproportionate share of teen-age pregnancies, drug addicts, and homicide victims.[51] It seems unlikely that the strength of families and urban communities indexed by this trend will rebound significantly. They reflect a complex of problems that have come to be known as "social poverty," to distinguish them from the more tractable financial problems linked to aging, widowhood, physical disability, chronic illness, or factory layoffs.[52] Families caught up in this web of pathologies do not seem to respond to traditional social service or income-maintenance strategies. The United States faces a deep intellectual crisis about how to deal with social poverty. In addition, the lagged effects of this cluster of variables probably are strong. As Cook and Laub point out, family factors play important roles in the socialization of the very young;[53] this implies that we will see the effects of the current state of American families perhaps 15 years from today, at just the time when the age structure forecasts reviewed below indicate that the proportion of teenagers in the population will be growing again. In this light, the fact that indicators of so many family pathologies now stand at historical highs does not bode well for levels of crime in the early twenty-first century.

Crime in the Twenty-First Century

We have seen that crime is firmly rooted in many fundamental aspects of American life. Some of those factors have been changing rapidly and some more slowly, but they all have implications for the future. Those implications are easiest to draw out for the most predictable aspects of life in coming decades, those which involve demography. Almost all of those who will be filling the high-risk age categories during the first decade of the twenty first century have already been born; we know their numbers, and who they are. *What* they will do is less predictable, but some research suggests they will engage in more and more serious acts of criminal violence than generations in the immediate past.[54] The influence of poverty, racial and generational inequality, and family and community disorganization also seem clear, and while it is less certain that those forces will worsen, there seem to be few reasons to be particularly sanguine about their near-term trends.

What do changes in the age structure of the U.S. population forecast for the future? They seem to portend well for the remainder of this century. This can be seen in Figure 11.2, which displays on the same scale both the reported rate of violent crime between 1950 and 1986 and U.S. Census Bureau estimates of the proportion of the U.S. population aged 18 to 21 (the high-risk years for violent offending) from 1950 to 2010.[55] The early, pre-1957 dip in the relative size of the 18-to-21 group displayed in figure 11.2 was due to the very large number of births taking place during that period; later, as the birth rate subsided and early Baby Boomers aged into their late teens, their population share soared. The violent crime rate also rose noticeably every year following 1960, lagging behind the rate of population change by just a few years.

Just as dramatic as the size of the Baby Boom cohort is the tremendous decline in the relative size of the youth population forecast by the Census Bureau for the following decades. The proportion of the U.S. population in the highest risk category for violent crime peaked in 1977, and through 1995 will drop as rapidly as it rose. Thereafter it should rebound a bit, while 18-to-21'ers born in the peak year of 1977 are having *their* children. However, no reasonable assumptions about the fertility rate in the near future reproduce the post-World War II Baby Boom, which should serve to reduce levels of violent crime. In nations where the collapse of the post-boom birthrate has been even more extreme than in the U.S., those declines will be even more dramatic. For example, age-structure changes forecast a decline in German robbery rates of 28 percent by the year 2000, reflecting that nation's extremely low fertility rate.[56]

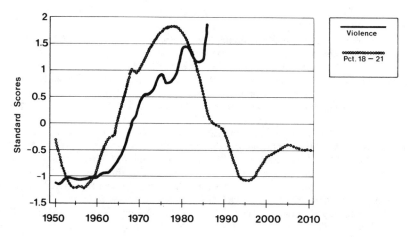

Figure 11.2: Violent Crime and the Age Structure of the U.S. Population, 1950–2010

These projections may be tempered by other factors. One is the apparently tenacious criminality of Baby Boomers, who we saw may not drop out of crime as rapidly as anticipated. Also as long as race continues to track the distribution of other hardship and family problems, the relative size of the youthful black population will add significantly to our expectations concerning future rates of crime. In 1963, when rates of violent crime began to climb sharply, blacks made up 12 percent of the 14–21 year old age group. The same Census Bureau projections cited above forecast a steady increase in that percentage every year through 2010. In 2010, when the youth share of the population will again have risen, blacks are projected to make up 21 percent of that then-larger group. This should boost the youthful offending rate, canceling some of the gains otherwise attributable to their smaller numbers.[57] Also, none of these projections take into account the growth of the Hispanic population. Hispanics evidence many of the problems facing American blacks. However, because they are not a "race," they are not accounted for separately by most local police departments (either as victims or offenders), nor have their numbers in the population been projected separately by the Census Bureau.

On the other hand, we also saw evidence above of worsening economic conditions and family disorganization among whites as well as blacks and Hispanics. They all face declining real wages, increasingly fall below the poverty line, and show evidence of family disruption. The diffusion of hardship and disorganization throughout the population will multiply its effects on crime by a much larger "at risk" group, also to the detriment of future social order.

Notes

1. For an exception, see Eric Monkkonen, *Police in Urban America, 1860–1920* (Cambridge, UK: Cambridge University Press, 1981).

2. In this discussion, "violent crime" refers to the sum of murders, rapes, robberies, and aggravated assaults. The figures from which these trends were calculated can be found in yearly editions of the FBI's *Uniform Crime Report*.

3. Wesley G. Skogan, "Citizen Reporting of Crime," *Criminology* 13 (Feb. 1976): 535–49.

4. Wesley G. Skogan, "Crime and Crime Rates," in W. Skogan, ed., *Sample Surveys of the Victims of Crime* (Cambridge, MA: Ballinger, 1976), 105–19.

5. Richard McCleary, Barbara C. Nienstedt, and James M. Erven, "Uniform Crime Reports as Organizational Outcomes: Three Time Series Experiments," *Social Problems* 29 (Apr. 1982): 361–72; David Seidman and Michael Couzens, "Getting the Crime Rate Down: Political Pressure and Crime Reporting," *Law and Society Review* 8 (Spring 1974): 457–93.

6. Wesley G. Skogan and Andrew C. Gordon, "Detective Division Reporting Practices," *Crime in Illinois 1982* (Springfield, IL: Illinois Department of Law Enforcement, 1983), 167–82.

7. Wesley G. Skogan, "Crime and Public Safety," *Chicago: The State of the Region* (New York: Associated Faculty Press, 1988).

8. Michael Rand, *Violent Crime Trends* (Washington, DC: Bureau of Justice Statistics, U.S. Department of Justice, 1987).

9. Bureau of Justice Statistics, *Households Touched by Crime, 1986* (Washington, DC: Bureau of Justice Statistics, U.S. Department of Justice, 1987).

10. Travis Hirschi and Michael Gottfredson, "Age and the Explanation of Crime," *American Journal of Sociology* 89 (Nov. 1983): 552–84.

11. Lawrence E. Cohen and Kenneth C. Land, "Age Structure and Crime: Symmetry Versus Asymmetry and the Projection of Crime Rates Through the 1990s," *American Sociological Review* 52 (Apr. 1987), 170–83.

12. Alfred Blumstein, Jacqueline Cohen, and Daniel Nagin, eds., *Deterrence and Incapacitation: Estimating the Effects of Criminal Sanctions on Crime Rates* (Washington, DC: National Research Council, 1978).

13. President's Commission on Law Enforcement and Administration of Justice, *Task Force Report: Crime and Its Impact* (Washington, DC: U.S. Government Printing Office, 1967), 25.

14. Lawrence Cohen and Kenneth Land, personal communications, 1987.

15. Philip J. Cook and John H. Laub, "The (Surprising) Stability of Youth Crime Rates," *Journal of Quantitative Criminology* 2 (Sept. 1986): 265–78.

16. Paul E. Tracey, Marvin E. Wolfgang, and Robert M. Figlio, *Delinquency in Two Birth Cohorts* (Washington, DC: U.S. Department of Justice, National Institute of Justice, 1985).

17. David Klepinger and Joseph G. Weis, "Projecting Crime Rates: An Age, Period, and Cohort Model Using ARIMA Techniques," *Journal of Quantitative Criminology* 1 (Dec. 1985): 387–416; David F. Greenberg, "Age, Crime and Social Explanation," *American Journal of Sociology* 91 (no. 1, 1985): 1–21.

18. Federal Bureau of Investigation, *Uniform Crime Report, 1987* (Washington, DC: U.S. Government Printing Office); Cook and Laub, "Stability of Youth Crime Rates,"(1986).

19. Robert A. Easterlin, "What Will 1984 Be Like?: Socioeconomic Implications of Recent Twists in Age Structure," *Demography* 15 (1978), 397–421.

20. "Crime and American Culture," *The Public Interest* 70 (1983): 22–48.

21. M. Harvey Brenner and Robert T. Swank, "Homicide and Economic Change: Recent Analyses of the Joint Economic Committee Report of 1984," *Journal of Quantitative*

Criminology 2 (March 1986): 81–104; see also M. Harvey Brenner, *Estimating the Effects of Economic Change on National Health and Social Well Being* (Washington, DC: Joint Economic Committee of the U.S. Congress, U.S. Government Printing Office, 1984); for a comprehensive analysis of the effect of wars on domestic crime, see Dane Archer and Rosemary Gartner, *Violence and Crime in Cross-National Perspective* (New Haven: Yale University Press, 1984).

22. Michael J. Hindelang, "Race and Involvement in Crimes," *American Sociological Review* 43 (Feb. 1978), 93–109; Michael J. Hindelang, "Sex-Race-Age Specific Incidence Rates of Offending," *American Sociological Review* 46 (Aug. 1981): 461–74; Michael J. Hindelang, Travis Hirschi, and Joseph G. Weis, *Measuring Delinquency* (Beverly Hills, CA: Sage, 1981).

23. Ronald Beasley and George E. Antunes, "The Etiology of Urban Crime," *Criminology* 11 (Feb. 1974): 439–61; James M. Byrne and Robert J. Sampson, "Key Issues in the Social Ecology of Crime," 1–22 in J. Byrne and R. Sampson, eds., *The Social Ecology of Crime* (New York: Springer-Verlag Publishers, 1986).

24. U.S. Department of Justice, *Criminal Victimization in the United States, 1985* (Washington, DC: U.S. Government Printing Office, 1987), table 6.

25. Richard Block and Wesley G. Skogan, *The Dynamics of Violence Between Strangers* (Evanston, IL: Center for Urban Affairs and Policy Research, Northwestern University, 1984).

26. U.S. Department of Justice, *Households Touched by Crime, 1986* (Washington, DC: U.S. Government Printing Office, 1987), 2.

27. Klepinger and Weis, "Projecting Crime Rates."

28. Marvin E. Wolfgang and Franco Ferracuti, *The Subculture of Violence: Toward an Integrated Theory in Criminology* (London: Tavistock, 1967); Lynn Curtis, *Violence, Race and Culture* (Lexington, MA: Lexington Books, 1975).

29. Gary S. Becker, "Crime and Punishment: An Economic Approach," *Journal of Political Economy* 76 (March/Apr. 1968): 169–217.

30. Theodore G. Chiricos and Edmond J. True, "Unemployment and Property Crime: Aggregate Effects in the 1970s," unpublished paper presented at the annual meeting of the Society for the Study of Social Problems, 1987; David Cantor and Kenneth C. Land, "Unemployment and Crime Rates in the Post-World War II United States: A Theoretical and Empirical Analysis," *American Sociological Review* 50 (June 1985): 317–32.

31. Judith R. Blau and Peter M. Blau, "The Cost of Inequality: Metropolitan Structure and Violent Crime," *American Sociological Review* 47 (Feb. 1982), 114–28; Richard A. Cloward and Lloyd E. Ohlin, *Delinquency and Opportunity: A Theory of Delinquent Gangs* (New York: Free Press, 1960).

32. For reviews, see Cantor and Land, 1985; Scott J. South and Lawrence E. Cohen, "Unemployment and the Homicide Rate: A Paradox Resolved," *Social Indicators Research* 17 (1985): 325–43; Sharon K. Long and Anne D. Witte, "Current Economic Trends and Implications for Crime and Criminal Justice," 69–146 in K. Wright, ed., *Crime and Criminal Justice in a Declining Economy* (Cambridge, MA: Oelgeschlager, Gunn and Hain, 1981); Thomas Orsagh, "Empirical Criminology: Interpreting Results Derived from Aggregate Data," *Journal of Research in Crime and Delinquency* 16 (July 1979): 294–306.

33. Robert J. Sampson, "The Effects of Urbanization and Neighborhood Characteristics on Criminal Victimization," in R. Figlio, S. Hakim and G. Rengert, eds., *Metropolitan Crime Patterns* (Monsey, NY: Criminal Justice Press, 1986), 3–25.

34. South and Cohen, "Unemployment and the Homicide Rate"; Brenner and Swank, "Homicide and Economic Change."

35. U.S. Department of Commerce, "Money Income and Poverty Status of Families and Persons in the United States, 1986," *Current Populations Reports: Consumer Income*, series P-60, no. 157, table B and table 7

36. U.S. Department of Commerce, *Statistical Abstract of the United States, 1987* (Washington, DC: U.S. Government Printing Office, 1988), table 638.

37. U.S. Department of Commerce, "Money Income and Poverty Status of Families and Persons in the United States, 1986," table A.

38. Robert J. Sampson, "Neighborhood Family Structure and the Risk of Personal Victimization," 25–46 in J. Byrne and R. Sampson, eds., *The Social Ecology of Crime* (New York: Springer-Verlag Publishers, 1986); Robert J. Sampson, "Structural Sources of Variation in Race-Age-Specific Rates of Offending Across Major U.S. Cities," *Criminology* 23 (Nov. 1985): 647–75; Blau and Blau; Colin Loftin and Robert H. Hill, "Regional Subculture and Homicide," *American Sociological Review* 39 (Oct. 1974), 714–25.

39. Brenner, *Estimating the Effects of Economic Change.*

40. Barry Bluestone and Bennett Harrison, *The Deindustrialization of America* (New York: Basic Books, 1982).

41. Brenner, *Estimating the Effects of Economic Change.*

42. Brenner and Swank, "Homicide and Economic Change." For a contrary finding, see Philip J. Cook and Gary A. Zarkin, "Crime and the Business Cycle," *Journal of Legal Studies* 14 (Jan. 1985): 1–17.

43. U.S. Department of Commerce, "Money Income and Poverty Status of Families and Persons in the United States, 1986," table B.

44. U.S. Department of Commerce, *Statistical Abstract of the United States, 1987.*

45. Cook and Laub, "Stability of Youth Crime Rates," (1986); Philip J. Cook and John H. Laub, "Trends in Child Abuse and Juvenile Delinquency," 109–127 in F. Hartmann, ed., *From Children to Citizens, Vol. II: The Role of the Juvenile Court* (New York: Springer-Verlag Publishers, 1987).

46. Byrne and Sampson, "Social Ecology of Crime.

47. Brenner and Swank, "Homicide and Economic Change"; Kenneth Land, personal communication.

48. U.S. Department of Commerce, "Marital Status and Living Arrangements," *Current Population Reports* (series P-20, no. 418, 1987), table 7.7.

49. National Center for Health Statistics, *Vital Statistics of the U.S., Vol. 1* (Washington, DC: U.S. Government Printing Office, 1986).

50. U.S. Department of Commerce, "Characteristics of the Population Below the Poverty Level," *Current Population Reports* (series P-60, no. 152, 1986), table 22.

51. *New York Times*, Dec. 20, 1987.

52. Edward Marciniak, *Reclaiming the Inner City* (Washington, DC: National Center for Urban Ethnic Affairs, 1986).

53. Cook and Laub, "Stability of Youth Crime Rates," (1986).

54. Tracey, Wolfgang, and Figlio, *Delinquency in Two Birth Cohorts.*

55. The yearly population estimates and projected figures can be found in two reports by the U.S. Department of Commerce: "Estimates of the Population of the U.S. by Age, Sex, and Race," *Current Population Reports* (series P-25, for various years); and "Projections of the Population of the U.S. by Age, Sex, and Race: 1983 to 2080," *Current Population Reports* (series P-25, no. 952, 1984).

56. Ulrich C. H. Blum and Thomas Feltes, "The Long Term Development of Criminal Offenses in the Federal Republic of Germany, 1985–2030," *Journal of Contemporary Criminal Justice* 3 (May 1987): 70–82.

57. Klepinger and Weis, "Projecting Crime Rates."

Chapter 12

Crime, Law, and Society: From the Industrial to the Information Society

RICHARD MAXWELL BROWN

On December 22, 1984, on a Manhattan subway train a slight electronics specialist bearing some resemblance to Woody Allen fired shots at four young blacks, wounding all, in what he claimed was an act of self-defense. The event was front-page news in the next day's Sunday *New York Times* and soon became not just a New York but a national media sensation. The massive show of support for Bernhard H. Goetz, the young white man who fired the shots and whom the media soon labeled the "subway vigilante," was the most significant aspect of the episode, which attracted strong public interest for three months, a relatively long period in a media-sated nation. The case generated heavy newspaper reporting, national newsmagazine cover stories, featured attention by the major TV networks, a Congressional hearing, and statements by the President, the Governor of New York State, and the Mayor of New York City.[1] More than ten months later, the occasional stories about the aftermath of the Goetz episode were relegated to the inside pages, and the public had largely forgotten the whole thing. Yet, the case was one of those news events that had great symbolic significance and the leverage to focus our attention on long-term trends and implications.

The premise of this essay is that "great social and demographic changes seem to work profound changes on patterns of crime," and that "the criminal law, police courts, and prisons together can only restrain common crime if they reinforce underlying social forces that are moving in the same direction."[2] Trends in American crime and law, some of them exemplified by the Goetz episode, will be examined in relation to the long-term evolutions of Industrial Society, Postindustrial Society, and the current Information Society.[3]

The common wisdom used to be that the destabilizing impact of industrialization and urbanization resulted in social chaos and high levels of crime, but careful studies in the last twenty years have shown that just the opposite occurred—that the great forces of industrialization and urbanization were, rather, stabilizing forces that drove down crime. This trend has been charted in England, the protagonist of the Industrial Revolution, and in our own country. Roger Lane's studies of nineteenth-century Boston and Philadelphia reveal a decline of crime in conjunction with triumph of the Industrial Revolution. As in the case of Boston, Lane found that in Philadelphia the city was " 'working' better as its population grew. The apparent increase of problem behavior of all sorts . . . was not 'real' but 'official,' the product of stricter standards more strictly enforced "by the agents of society."[4] In Boston and other American cities a surge of crime "began in the 1850s and crested in the 1870s."[5] All of this was a result "of the discipline demanded by the industrial revolution and taught in the classrooms, on the railroads, and in factories and offices of nineteenth-century America."[6] Crucial to this process of socialization, which was "broad and continuous" and affected virtually everyone in society—not just those "directly exposed to industrial or bureaucratic discipline"—was "the growing system of public schools" which "inculcated" the "kinds of behavior demanded by the changing economy" of industrialism.[7] Moreover, the downward trend in homicide that began in the 1870s continued (with, perhaps, an upward surge from 1900 to about 1930) until the 1950s.[8]

The process of industrialization produced a broad national campaign against the misfits—the "marginal men, those left behind or new to the demands for order and discipline" of the new age.[9] These demands were not restricted to the growing industrial cities of the Northeast but were to be found, also, on the frontier and in the West. In the West of the middle and late nineteenth century, classic American vigilantism reached a peak as the economic elite and its middle-class compatriots converged in hundreds of local vigilante movements to purge the new country of outlaws so that fields, ranges, and mines could be worked in peace to produce raw materials for the factories of the East and profits for the middle and upper classes of the West.[10] Regular peace officers—exemplified by the Earp brothers of Kansas and Tombstone—joined in this process. Wyatt Earp, leader of the clan, was an ambitious petty capitalist and speculator in Tombstone real estate whose strong membership in the Republican Party helped make him the chosen instrument of the mining aristocracy of Tombstone against the aggressive bandit element of surrounding Cochise County.[11] Neovigilante campaigns headed by the coalition of corporate leaders and local members of the middle class continued in the early twentieth-century West as field hands, loggers, sawmill workers, and miners—many of them members of the radical IWW—felt the force of the "conservative mob."[12]

The capitalistic backlash of neovigilantism was also found in the North and East, but in these regions the spearhead of reform in behalf of a more orderly industrializing, urbanizing society, was the growing police establish-ment. Increasingly stringent and widely approved urban policing was brought heavily to bear upon the drunken and disorderly individuals whose rhythms were out of tune with Industrial Society, and upon the "class of transients, drifters, and newcomers to the city" whom Lane found to be the most prone to homicide in Philadelphia.[13] The upward trend of industrial-ization and the downward trend of crime that characterized America from 1870s on dissolved in the 1950s and 1960s. The evidence of the crime surge from the 1950s to the 1980s has been well summarized by Weiner and Wolfgang (1985) and, most recently, by Ted Robert Gurr in this volume. Between the late 1950s and 1973, for example, the urban murder rate increased by 250 percent.[14] As a result of their 1985 reconciliation of the technical indices of crime, Weiner and Wolfgang concluded that the level of violent crime in the United States increased during the 1970s but that, even if it had not, it was "unacceptably high."[15] The figures provided by these two scholars show increases in the years from 1969 to 1982 of 34 percent in criminal homicide, 92 percent in forcible rape, 69 percent in robbery, and 82 percent in aggravated assault.[16]

Lane's statement that since 1952 "the patterns of homicide in the post-industrial city of 1960s and 1970s have reverted in many respects to those of the preindustrial city of the 1840s and 1850s"[17] introduces what some, including myself, see as the most general explanation for the crime surge of the late 1950s to the early 1980s: namely, the destabilizing context of Postin-dustrial Society. Gurr's comparative cross-national data show that the asso-ciation of increased crime and Postindustrial Society is a general affliction among the advanced industrial democracies of the world except for Japan. Thus, the United States is far from being alone in this pattern, but crime has increased to its highest levels in our own country. Asserting that "the most devastating episodes of public disorder . . . seem to occur" when major "social crises coincide with a change in values," Gurr wrote in 1979 that the institutions of the criminal justice system and their policies were effective in bygone industrial societies "dominated by a self-confident mid-dle class convinced that prosperity in this life and salvation in the next could be achieved through piety, honesty, and hard work. All authorities spoke with the same voice. The institutions of public order were effective because they reinforced the dominant view. They did not merely punish those who transgressed. They were missionaries to the under class, inform-ing them of the moral order through arrest, trial, and imprisonment."[18] Holding that "it is not entirely convincing to attribute crime increases of 300 or 500 percent [in America] to 50 percent increases in the size of the youthful population," Gurr put his main emphasis on "value change"—on a crucial shift in Postindustrial Society toward an ethic of "aggressive hedo-nism": that is, "a mutation of Western materialism, stripped of its work ethic and generalized from material satisfactions to social and sexual ones" in coexistence "with a sense of resentment against large, impersonal organizations or indeed any external source of authority that might restrain people from 'doing their own thing.' "[19]

Elliott Currie has reminded us that the Violence Commission's 1969 specter of an American society split between the protected (the "upper-middle and high-income populations" sequestered from street crime by elaborate private security systems) and the unprotected (the remainder of the population moving through high-risk streets and vehicles of public transportation, or isolated in the terror-ridden ghetto slums) has become the reality of the 1980s.[20] Back in the 1960s the emergent gap between the protected and the unprotected inspired such high-visibility quasi-vigilante movements as the Deacons for Defense and Justice in the South, the Maccabbees of Brooklyn, and the North Ward Citizens' Committee of Newark. These examples of militant urban self-protection were seen in terms of the American vigilante tradition. Yet, as neighborhood patrol groups they ordinarily stopped short of taking the law into their own hands.[21] In retrospect they may be seen as the rough nucleus of the by-now well-established, well-respected community crime-prevention movement (of which more later). But the gap between the protected and the unprotected grew during the 1970s and 1980s. It was not merely ghetto blacks (the most victimized of all) but also members of the solid white middle class who were increasingly the prey of murderers, muggers, and rapists on the streets, in their own homes, and on the buses and in the subway and elevated trains of the great cities. A growing but largely silent public resentment seethed below the surface until it broke out in the massive approval for the shots fired by Bernhard Goetz on December 22, 1984. A nationwide poll taken as late as two months after the event showed that 57 percent (including 39 percent of nonwhites) approved of Goetz's action and that 78 percent, following Goetz's presumed example, would use deadly force in self-defense.[22]

The Goetz episode was rife with social symbolism for crime and law in America as it moved into the new era of the Information Society. Goetz himself was virtually a personal prototype for the emergent Information Society: an upwardly mobile entrepreneur with a college education in his chosen field of electronics. On the boundary between the protected and the unprotected, Goetz was safe in his elegant and highly secured Manhattan apartment but, like so many others, he put himself at risk when he took to the city's subways. Thus, he was prototypical as both a victim of crime and an active participant in his own neighborhood version of the community crime-prevention movement—that is, he was a leader in FAB 14 (the association For a Better 14th Street). Goetz's first moment of victimization came on a day in early 1981 when, in a Canal Street subway station, he was mugged by three youths who beat him and robbed him of a thousand dollars' worth of equipment used in his electronics business. Goetz was prototypical, too, in his frustration with the criminal-justice system that allotted only four months of jail time to one of his assailants. Disgusted, Goetz became part of a growing national trend when he obtained a gun and carried it for the personal protection of which, so he claimed, he availed himself on December 22, 1984.[23]

In June, 1987, a New York jury found that Goetz was a victim rather than a victimizer[24] but, in retrospect, the four targets of his .38 caliber pistol shots may also be seen as personal prototypes of the current situation of crime and law in America. All four were almost classic examples of the ghetto black underclass of the 1980s: high-school dropouts, products of shattered homes, drug prone, and crime prone. One of them, Darryl Cabey, was typical of the black-ghetto residents whose lives are permanently ruined by the crime of others: The Cabey family was thriving in a small-business endeavor until the husband and father was killed in a street accident as he defended his truck against theft in Harlem. The bereaved family lost its home and fell into a hapless existence in a dangerous public-housing project in the South Bronx from which the young Darryl lapsed into a pattern of petty theft that brought him, along with the three others, face to face with Bernhard Goetz on the subway train three days before Christmas, 1984.[25] These four—Troy Canty, Barry Allen, James Ramseur, and Darryl Cabey—are prime examples of those excluded from today's Information Society: "those left behind" and "more and more out of step" with today's high-tech, computerized life. But even here there is irony and more social symbolism, for Canty, Allen, Ramseur, and Cabey had their own prototypically underclass relationship with our increasingly pervasive Information Society: Their occupation, so to speak, was a criminal one—robbing video machines, an errand on which they were bound when their destinies intersected Goetz's on the subway train.[26]

The Goetz episode—the event itself and the public reaction to it—was a flash of lightning revealing the problems and possibilities of the social scene of the 1980s. It encourages reflection on where we are today and where we are going. However, to be noted first is another irony: namely, that the massive public outcry in favor of Goetz, widely and correctly interpreted as an index of public frustration over intolerably high levels of crime, occurred at a time when crime in America was going down and was significantly below its all-time peak in 1980–1981. Yet, public concern over crime in the 1984–1985 winter of the Goetz episode was well taken, since the decline in crime from the level of 1980–1981 was not steep.[27]

The remainder of this essay will discuss the possibility that "underlying social forces . . . are moving in the same direction" as current and future efforts of "the criminal law, police, courts, and prisons" to "restrain common crime."[28] In this case, the underlying social forces are those embodied in our new Information Society. I will return to the concept of the Information Society in due course, but first I will identify elements in the current situation that both exemplify and have helped to produce the 1980s' decline in crime:

—A strong 1980s trend in favor of a de facto nationwide rationalization and regularization of "the laws under which people are sent to prison and in the mechanisms that control how long they stay there," with the result that more hardened, dangerous criminals get to prison and stay there longer. For example, discretionary early-release programs by parole boards are on the wane.[29]

—A 1980s sentencing-reform movement aimed at increasing the odds of repeat offenders going to jail and staying there longer. This movement includes the replacement of indeterminate sentencing with the stricter system of determinate sentencing in state after state and, overall, a more rationalized, structured system of sentencing which, with the exception of the popular panacea of mandatory sentencing, has worked well.[30] As early as 1983 one result of this movement was that the odds of a robbery leading to an arrest and imprisonment increased to 3-to-1 from 4-to-1 in 1978.[31] At the federal level, the sentencing-reform movement is exemplified by a major piece of legislation, the U.S. Sentencing Reform Act of 1984. As this is written in August 1988 the constitutionality of the legislation is yet to be upheld by the U.S. Supreme Court, but it is estimated that if it is upheld, the result will be harsher sentences, especially for drug offenses, which will increase the federal prison population by 15 percent in the first year of full implementation of the law.[32] Related to the sentencing-reform movement is an effective federal law of 1984 for the pretrial detention of dangerous defendants, major drug offenders, and hardened criminals.[33]

—Prison space has significantly increased since 1970 and so has the prison population. From 1970 to 1986 the prison population nearly tripled and, in line with that increase, the national incarceration rate per 100,000 Americans doubled as it rose from 110 in 1970 to 227 in 1986.[34] This increase in overall prison space and population was heightened by a 1979–1984 increase of state prison space by 29 percent and of the state inmate population by an even greater 45 percent.[35] These increases, both for the longer term of 1970–1986 and the shorter term of 1979–1984, are a major reason for the decline of the murder and crime rates in the early 1980s and their leveling off thereafter.

—Private security expenditures have hugely increased since 1979, and by the early 1980s more money was being spent on private security (over $20 billion) than on public police forces ($15 billion).[36]

—Community self-help and computerization against crime are very significant. (They are discussed below.)

—With President Ronald Reagan having appointed nearly one-half of its members,[37] a more conservative federal judiciary, in conjunction with a somewhat more conservative U. S. Supreme Court since the recent appointment of Anthony M. Kennedy, has been rolling back the 1960s-1970s emphasis on due process of law for those accused of crime in favor of the older focus on the repression of crime.[38]

—Symptomatic are the following movements which cut across the ideological lines of liberal and conservative and have been notable for their vitality and zeal:

> —the victim-rights movement.[39]
> —the drives against child abuse and wife abuse.[40]
> —movements against rape and incest.[41]
> —the anti-pornography movement.[42]
> —the campaign against drunken driving.[43]
> —new techniques to detect and forestall serial killers.[44]

These developments reflect a trend to tighten the bonds of society that *Washington Post* columnist Michael Barone refers to as a new "Age of Restraint."[45] In addition to the waning of sexually-permissive behavior (partly in reaction to the threat of genital herpes and, even more, of Acquired Immune Deficiency Syndrome), the use of alcohol and tobacco is off,[46] and among the mainstream population drug use is in significant decline.[47]

The new tightening up of society against crime and what Gurr referred to as the ethic of "aggressive hedonism"[48] is all, I am convinced, a part of the increasingly inclusive Information Society whose impact will be, as was that of Industrial Society, "broad and continuous" in terms of "changes in the socialization process" that will affect "virtually every aspect" of our life, and not just those who are directly engaged in high-tech, computer-oriented occupations.[49] Just as Industrial Society, a decline in crime, and repression of crime were all linked, it is my view that the Information Society will converge with and reinforce a new decline and a new repression of crime.

The two aspects of the Information Society that I wish, now, to emphasize in regard to the future of crime in this country are the linked entities of high technology and computerization and, second, the trend of decentralization in America.

In regard to high tech and computerization, the "war on crime" is increasingly being computerized, and longer and longer strides will be made in that direction. For example, computerized analysis of information, now underway, holds high hopes for increasing significantly the ability of the criminal-justice system to deal effectively with the elusive serial killers who as recently as 1984 were believed to be responsible for an annual toll of over 3,000 unsolved murders.[50] Even more broadly, there is the remarkable expansion in the scope of such criminal-justice data bases as those of the FBI's National Criminal Justice Information Center and the U.S. Treasury Department's Treasury Enforcement Communication System.[51]

Not all of this is pretty. One of the growth areas of American law enforcement that seems destined to become bigger and bigger is in the realm of undercover work and the high-tech domain of what sociologist Gary T. Marx terms the "new surveillance."[52] The new surveillance is spearheaded by burgeoning, ever-more sophisticated electronic means that include—among a staggering array of devices—potent lasers, parabolic microphones and other "bugs" with more powerful transmitters, subminiature tape recorders, improved remote camera and videotape systems, advanced ways of seeing in the dark, voice-stress analyzers, and powerful new tracking devices.[53] In the course of his searching study of the new surveillance, Marx came to be more reconciled to the need for undercover tactics as an aid to law enforcement, but he remains deeply troubled by the frightening potential for the abuse of undercover work in the interest of an oppressive extension of governmental power. Yet, in a time when a "choice between anarchy and repression" may too often be forced on society, the new surveillance, concluded Marx, "may be a necessary evil. The challenge," he writes, is to prevent it "from becoming an intolerable one."[54] His forebodings are appropriate, for the trend, noted earlier, away from emphasis on the due process of law toward the bald repression of crime, are likely to reinforce the fixation on the new surveillance made possible by the technology of the Information Society.

Much more benign is the Information Society's converging trends of decentralization and of community self-help for neighborhood revitalization and the prevention of crime. Here is an area in which the popular prophet of the Information Society, John Naisbitt, and scholarly criminologists and urbanologists seem to be in agreement. In his 1982 best-selling book, *Megatrends*, Naisbitt presented neighborhood crime prevention as a prime example of decentralization in the Information Society. He wrote that "citizens are responding to the 1980s crime wave with fear, anger and activism. No longer willing to delegate the responsibility for their safety to the government or the police, citizens are taking matters into their own hands. Once an innovation, crime-watch groups and crime-stopper programs are fast becoming commonplace across the country and are compiling an impressive track record."[55] By the same token, a significant recent book, edited by Lynn A. Curtis, *American Violence and Public Policy* (1985), emanating from the prestigious Eisenhower Foundation, reveals that community self-help against crime is the avant garde of scholarly thought on the subject. As contributions by Elliott Currie, James P. Comer, Paul J. Lavrakas, and Curtis, himself, show, the emphasis in the book is to play down the criminal-justice system (or what might be called "government help") in favor of community self-help. Currie holds "that informal sanctions applied by family, peers, and community have more effect" in deterring crime than " 'tough' criminal justice policies" and advocates "the search for ways of strengthening the infrastructure of local communities and enhancing their capacity to deal with problems of crime and disorder" in preference to the traditional approach of a massive criminal-justice bureaucracy with what he sees as its an overemphasis on incarceration.[56] In his contribution, Lavrakas—a leading authority—presents what is virtually a success-manual for "citizen self-help and neighborhood crime prevention,"[57] and Curtis in his epilogue for the volume commends such model community programs as Umoja in West Philadelphia, El Centro in Puerto Rico, and Argus in the South Bronx, and calls for "neighborhood or community-based crime prevention" as the best hope, one which, he informs us, is being funded and fostered by the Eisenhower Foundation.[58]

The technique of community self-help to prevent crime is being tested as never before in the black-ghetto neighborhoods whose residents are both the most crime-prone and the most victimized by crime of all Americans. A triple crisis of epidemic drug use, youthful gang activity, and black-on-black crime in America's inner-city neighborhoods is colliding with the emergent Information Society and its imperatives for a new structure and order in American life. Potent and pervasive youth gangs in the ghettos and barrios of Los Angeles, New York, Miami, Washington, and Chicago have become, in reality, drug-dealing crime confederations specializing in the highly addictive, smokable cocaine known as "crack." The most famous of these gangs are the ubiquitous Crips and Bloods—competing gangs of young blacks based in south-central Los Angeles (and environs) that are rapidly expanding their operations into Denver, Portland, and other Western cities. Also prominent are similar gangs of young Hispanos, Asians, and Jamaicans. In 1987, 55 percent of the more than 800 homicides in Los Angeles were believed to have been drug related, mostly in connection with the gangs. The drive-by shootings of warring gangs have become a dauntingly familiar feature of life in the afflicted urban zones. In some ways resembling the Mafia of the 1920s-1940s, these new inner-city gangs are, however, much more violent than their earlier counterparts. The cost, personnel, and time involved in fighting the Crips, Bloods, Jamaican "posses," and other gangs is overwhelming the police. As *Newsweek* reported in early 1988, the "war on drugs" is being lost in the inner-city battle grounds. To many—perhaps the majority—of Americans, the drug-danger was the Number-One concern in the presidential-election year of 1988.[60]

In related fashion the carnage inflicted by young black males upon each other is jeopardizing neighborhood after neighborhood of inner-city black people. Statistics show that young black males are by far the most violence-prone and violence-vulnerable of all Americans and have been for some time.[61] At the root of the crime crisis in inner-city black life is the shockingly high rate of unemployment among young black males, which has hovered around 40–50 percent for a number of years.[62] Currie has long since made the common-sense point that America will get its problem of crime under control only by a massive publicly-funded program of work for black youth—and not just lowly-paid make-work jobs but jobs in which pride may be taken and families supported above the poverty line.[63] Aside from the problem, acknowledged by Currie, of gaining political support for such an endeavor, the whole notion of such a massive employment program seems increasingly irrelevant. Once the conventional but arbitrary distinction between legal and illegal employment is put aside, it becomes evident that black-male youth employment in inner-city areas is not low but quite heavy in a combination of legal work and drug-dealing illegal gang work. The estimated 70,000 gang members in Los Angeles are, to greater or lesser degree, employed in illicit but highly remunerative jobs in a drug-dealing hierarchy that brings millions of dollars, annually, into the city's ghettos and barrios. The illegal employment of drug dealing produces, in effect, wages that are far above the level afforded by the legal private sector or contemplated, even, in Currie's proposed employment program.[64] Many law-abiding black-ghetto residents have, out of economic desperation and without approving illegality, become dependent upon income brought in by those in their families who are affluent drug-dealing gang members.

The picture is indeed bleak, and there is in this volume[65] ample basis for pessimism in regard to a significant decline in the black-youth offending that is at the center of the late-twentieth century onslaught of crime. Yet, neither scholars nor the public should underrate the resiliency of black Americans in this time of crisis. There is, in fact, a mood among them that, at all costs, the challenge of inner-city crime and disorder must be met and repelled. In recent years, black leaders and urban residents have come strongly to the view that community self-help more than government aid is the key to the reduction of the size of the under class of the black ghettos.[66]

In this new mood of resolve, education is seen as the key both to the alleviation of the plight of the demoralized and violence-prone underclass and to black survival in the era of the Information Society. The black media magnate, John H. Johnson, has warned that "we are losing a whole generation" of black youth "in a new high-tech environment in which the disadvantages of one generation multiply in the next" and "create no-win scenarios" that could last until the twenty-first and twenty-second centuries unless the trend is reversed.[67]

With John E. Jacob, president of the National Urban League, also warning that "black survival" is at stake in the present crisis,[68] many are rallying around the revitalization of black community educational institutions. A strategy has come to the fore that focuses on creative new model schools. With such great black high schools of an earlier generation as Dunbar in Washington, D.C.; Frederick Douglass in Baltimore; St. Augustine and Xavier Prep in New Orleans; and Booker T. Washington in Atlanta now in decline, there has arisen a new array of model schools where academic achievement and pride are thriving. Among them are Wheatley Elementary in Dallas; Audubon Junior High and George Washington Preparatory High in Los Angeles; Renaissance High in Detroit; Eastside High in Paterson;[69] Orangeburg-Wilkinson High in South Carolina;[70] Murry Bergstrum High in Manhattan;[71] Kelly Miller Junior High in Washington, D.C.;[70] and Simeon Baldwin and Martin Luther King, Jr., elementary schools in New Haven.[73] In these and other schools energetic and innovative principals (Joe Clark of Eastside High, George J. McKenna III of George Washington Preparatory High, Gene McCallum of Audubon Junior High, Claude Moten of Kelly Miller Junior High, and Melvin Smoak of Orangeburg-Wilkinson High are only five among many),[74] talented teachers,[75] eager and impressive students,[76] and involved parents are leading the black-community educational comeback. In once-chaotic classrooms and crime-ridden hallways, discipline has been restored, and prideful students have responded to the keynote motif that unites the ferment and diversity of these vibrant schools: high expectations of student achievement. A black business-magazine publisher, Earl Graves of New York City, rightly characterized all of this as a new battle for education in the post-slavery, post-segregation era.[77] There is widespread recognition that black students must be trained for "tomorrow's highly technical, super-competitive job market."[78]

Thus, local black neighborhoods and schools are responding to the crisis of violent, drug-dealing gangs along with the high rate of homicidal deaths among young black males and to the challenge of the Information Society. "Education is the fundamental ingredient in the prescription for saving our children," asserts Los Angeles black principal George J. McKenna III.[79] Blacks will be no less immune than whites, Hispanics, and Asians to the transformation of "the feelings, sensibilities, perceptions, expectations, assumptions, and, above all, the possibilities that define a community" stemming from the creation of the Information Society.[80]

Blacks and all Americans will share, therefore, in the new order and structure to be provided, after decades of Postindustrial chaos, by the Information Society. Japanese scholar and planner Yoneji Masuda has written that the Information Society will "bring about fundamental changes in human values, in trends of thought, and in the political and economic structures" of the times.[81] These changes are well underway in America and are making a revolutionary impact as Shoshana Shuboff, the most thorough and perceptive student of the emerging Information Society, has recently shown. Her case studies of computerized workplaces demonstrate that the alteration in employee attitudes is as significant as that which occurred at the dawn of Industrial Society.[82] Shuboff and other authorities are revealing that the "intellective skills" of our computer-dominated era are producing a new age structured by mental discipline rather than the machine discipline of the earlier Industrial Society.[83]

The radically different ethos of the Information Society (in contrast to that of Industrial Society) is emerging not only in the workplaces but in the minds of the young: By 1985–1986 students in 92 percent of the nation's public schools were being exposed to desktop computers.[84] Most adaptable of all to the Information Society are these "microkids"—journalist Frederick Golden's term for the school children who, he declares, "will surely confront the world differently from their parents. The precise orderly state of logic required to use and program the machines [for example, microcomputers] promises to shape—and sharpen—the thought processes of the computer generation."[85] Similarly, Stephen Toulmin, a philosopher of science at the University of Chicago, announces that computers are "re-intellectualizing" the mentally passive members of the TV generation.[86] Mathematician Seymour Papert, developer of the computer language, LOGO, for elementary-school pupils, underscores the potential for educating children according to theorist Jean Piaget's concept of the child as builder of ideas—one who structures reality according to the Piagetian maxim that "to understand is to invent." "*The child programs the computer,*" says Papert, and thus gains a "sense of mastery over a piece of the most modern and powerful technology and establishes an intimate contact with some of the deepest ideas from science, from mathematics, and from the art of intellectual building."[87]

The destiny of crime, law, and society in America on into the 1990s and the next century is likely to be governed by a combination of short-term and long-term developments that will affect all Americans in an increasingly multi-cultural society:

—An increasing emphasis on education and an increasingly effective educational system (a trend already underway in the 1980s)[88] will gradually introduce an important element of structure into society that will counteract crimogenic factors.

—Leavened by a more conservative federal judiciary, the system of criminal justice will reduce its emphasis on due process of law in favor of repression of crime.

—High technology and computerization will increase the effectiveness of the criminal-justice system and efforts to prevent crime.

—Community self-help will strengthen local neighborhoods and help reduce the inroads of crime.

—An expanded prison population will take out of circulation more and more members of the relatively irreducible hard core of those who commit a highly disproportionate amount of violent crime.[89]

Transcending as well as influencing these short-term developments will be the most important factor of all: a revitalization of education and a freely-chosen, self-imposed renewal of social discipline—both resulting from the Information Society [90]—that will shape a new structure and order in American life whose impact will reduce crime in the long run.

Notes

1. The Goetz episode is discussed below.
2. Ted Robert Gurr, "On the History of Violent Crime in Europe and America," in Hugh Davis Graham and Ted Robert Gurr, eds., *Violence in America: Historical and Comparative Perspectives* (Beverly Hills, CA: Sage, 1979), 353, 370.
3. The Information Society is discussed below.
4. Roger Lane, *Violent Death in the City: Suicide, Accident, and Murder in Nineteenth-Century Philadelphia* (Cambridge, MA: Harvard University Press, 1979), 119. See also Lane, *Policing the City: Boston, 1822–1885* (Cambridge, MA: Harvard University Press, 1967).
5. Gurr, "History of Violent Crime," 359.
6. Lane, *Violent Death*, 124.
7. Ibid., 359–61.
8. Ted Robert Gurr, "Historical Trends in Violent Crime: England, Western Europe, and the United States, " chap. 1, this volume. Two authorities in this volume are in disagreement over whether homicide increased significantly in the period from 1900 to about 1930: Margaret A. Zahn, in chap. 10, finds a significant increase; Roger Lane, in chap. 2, finds no such "homicidal crime wave" (his term). Zahn, ibid., found that the American homicide rate was at its lowest in the late 1950s.
9. Lane, *Violent Death*, 131.
10. Richard Maxwell Brown, *Strain of Violence: Historical Studies of American Violence and Vigilantism* (New York: Oxford University Press, 1975), chaps. 4–6.
11. Richard Maxwell Brown, ed., *Helldorado: Bringing the Law to the Mesquite* [1928] by William M. Breakenridge (Chicago: R. R. Donnelley, 1982), xxviii-xxxv.
12. Brown, *Strain of Violence*, 127–8, 134. Two recent studies of the widespread phenomenon of neovigilantism against industrial laborers are James W. Byrkit, *Forging the Copper Collar: Arizona's Labor-Management War of 1901–1921* (Tucson: University of Arizona Press, 1982), and John M. McClelland, Jr., *Wobbly War: The Centralia Story* (Tacoma: Washington State Historical Society, 1987).
13. Lane, *Violent Death*, 131.
14. Gurr, "History of Violent Crime," 361.
15. Neil Alan Weiner and Marvin E. Wolfgang, "The Extent and Character of Violent Crime in America, 1969 to 1982, " in Lynn A. Curtis, ed., *American Violence and Public Policy: An Update of the National Commission on the Causes and Prevention of Violence* (New Haven: Yale University Press, 1985), 34.
16. Ibid., 25.
17. Lane, *Violent Death*, 137.
18. Gurr, "History of Violent Crime," 370.
19. Ibid., 369–70. I find Gurr's 1979 interpretation (quoted here) of the crucial role of value change in Postindustrial Society to be as compelling as ever, but in his contribution to this volume he places less emphasis on this factor; see his Introduction and chap. 1.
20. Elliot Currie, "Crimes of Violence and Public Policy: Changing Directions," in Curtis, ed., *American Violence*, 41–2. See also Currie, *Confronting Crime: An American Challenge* (New York: Pantheon, 1985), 7–9; this elegant piece of scholarship has devastating critiques of the wrong-headed ways in which both the politically conservative and the politically liberal schools of criminology have reacted to 1960s-1980s crime. Currie's own views, which transcend the conservative and liberal schools, are compellingly presented throughout his book.
21. Brown, *Strain of Violence*, 129–30.
22. *Newsweek*, March 11, 1985, 50–3.
23. Robert D. McFadden, "Bernhard Goetz: A Private Man in a Public Debate," *New*

York Times, reg. ed., Jan. 6, 1985, sec. 1, pp. 1, 22. See also the psychological study of Goetz by Lilian B. Rubin, *Quiet Rage: Bernie Goetz in a Time of Madness* (New York: Farrar, Straus & Giroux, 1986).

24. On June 16, 1987, a lower-middle-class and middle-class jury composed of nine whites, two blacks, and two Hispanos acquitted Goetz of the charge of attempted murder. Altogether, the jury of eight men and four women found Goetz not guilty of ten felony and two lesser charges and found him guilty of only one charge: the minor one of illegal weapons possession in regard to the gun he used in the shootings. The State Supreme Court trial in Manhattan lasted seven weeks: *New York Times,* nat. ed., June 17, 1987, 15; *Oregonian* (Portland), June 17, 1987, 1, 3; *Register-Guard* (Eugene), June 17, 1987, 1A, 4A, 5A. On the composition of the jury: *Register-Guard,* 5A, and *USA Today,* June 17, 1987, 3A. A legal study is George P. Fletcher, *A Crime of Self-Defense: Bernhard Goetz and the Law on Trial* (New York: Free Press, 1988). While his jail sentence of six months was under appeal Goetz, who was also sentenced to pay a fine of $5,075 and serve four and a half years of probation (including 280 hours of community service), was free on bail. Fletcher, *Crime of Self-Defense,* 216–7. In acquitting Goetz of all charges but the one of illegal weapons possession, the jury, in effect, accepted his plea of self-defense during the incident on the subway train.

25. Derrick Jackson and Marily Milloy of *Newsday,* "A Victim of a Vigilante,"*Register-Guard* (Eugene), March 24, 1985, 1E, 2E.

26. Ibid., 2E.

27. The "murder rate" (i.e., the number of murders and nonnegligent manslaughters per 100,000 Americans) peaked at 10.2 and 9.8 in 1980 and 1981, respectively, and fell to 9.1 in 1982. From 1983 through 1987 it has held steadily at a lower but still high level in the range of 7.9 (1984, 1985) to 8.6 (1986). The figure for both 1983 and 1987 was 8.3. U.S. Department of Justice, Federal Bureau of Investigation, *Uniform Crime Reports for the United States: Crime in the United States*—annual reports for 1980–1987. The "crime rate" (i.e., the percentage of American households affected by the crimes of rape, robbery, assault, personal theft, and theft or burglary in the residence) was 24.4 percent in 1987 and has been holding steady at about 25 percent since 1985 and, as such, is way down from the 1985 figure of 32 percent. *National Journal,* June 11, 1988, 1576, reporting figures from the U.S. Department of Justice's Bureau of Justice report on the crime rate for 1987.

28. Quoted from Gurr, "History of Violent Crime," 370.

29. *Society,* July/Aug., 1984, 3. On the waning of discretionary early-release programs: Robert J. Sampson, "Crime in Cities: The Effects of Formal and Informal Social Control," in Michael Tonry, and Norval Morris, eds., *Crime and Justice: An Annual Review of Research* vol 8, *Communities and Crime* (Chicago: University of Chicago Press, 1986), 271–311. Sampson, 271, found that the "high risk of jail incarceration" had a significant deterrent effect on robbery.

30. Michael Tonry, "Structuring Sentencing," in Tonry and Morris, *Crime and Justice,* vol. 10 (1986), 267–337. Tonry found that mandatory sentencing was largely a failure, because attorneys and judges frequently managed to evade it and because it often produced injustice in individual cases.

31. *National Journal,* Mar. 30, 1985, 215.

32. *New York Times,* nat. ed., Aug. 25, 1988, 8. The law was found to be unconstitutional by a panel of the U.S. Court of Appeals for the 9th Circuit, but the chairman of the sentencing commission appointed under the act is confident that it will be approved by the Supreme Court.

33. U.S. Department of Justice, Bureau of Justice Statistics, *Special Report: Pretrial Release and Detention: The Bail Reform Act of 1984* (Feb., 1988), 2, 5.

34. Alfred Blumstein, "Prison Populations: A System Out of Control?" in Tonry and Morris, *Crime and Justice* vol. 10 (1986), 232. Despite the very high rate of incarceration in

1986 which found 1 of every 300 Americans in jail, Blumstein found, also, that, contrary to the "conventional wisdom" of scholars, the United States is not one of the most punitive nations in the world. Ibid., 236.

35. U.S. Department of Justice, Bureau of Justice Statistics, *Special Report: Population Density in State Prisons* (Dec. 1986), 1.

36. Joseph Kraft. "Law is in Disorder in America Today," *Register-Guard* (Eugene), Jan. 10, 1985, 11A. See also Currie, "Crimes of Violence," 42–3.

37. *New York Times*, nat. ed., Aug. 9, 1988, 1, 8.

38. For the distinction between an emphasis on due process of law vs. an emphasis on the repression of crime in regard to the criminal-justice system, see Herbert L. Packer, *The Limits of Criminal Sanction* (Stanford: Stanford University Press, 1968), 149–73.

39. Robert Elias, *The Politics of Victimization: Victims, Victimology, and Human Rights* (New York: Oxford University Press, 1986), chaps. 6–7, and Robert Reiff, *The Invisible Victim: The Criminal Justice System's Forgotten Responsibility* (New York: Basic Books, 1979), an advocacy book.

40. Terry Davidson, *Conjugal Crime: Understanding and Changing the Wifebeating Pattern* (New York: Hawthorn, 1978), is an advocacy book while Jean Giles-Sims, *Wife Battering: A Systems Theory Approach* (New York: Guilford, 1983), is a scholarly study.

41. On rape: Susan Brownmiller, *Against Our Will: Men, Women, and Rape* (New York: Simon and Schuster, 1975), which significantly raised the consciousness of people on the subject, and Susan Estrich, *Real Rape* (Cambridge, MA: Harvard University Press, 1987), a legal study. On incest: W. Arens, *The Original Sin: Incest and Its Meaning* (New York: Oxford University Press, 1986), a cultural study.

42. *Newsweek*, Mar. 18, 1985, 58–66, Andrea Dworkin, *Pornography: Men Possessing Women* (New York: Perigee Books, 1981). A quite new thrust has been the movement against child pornography resulting in, among various initiatives, an increase in federal child-pornography prosecutions from 3 to 249, annually, in the last five years. *New York Times*, July 8, 1988, A27.

43. James B. Jacobs, "The Law and Criminology of Drunk Driving," in Tonry and Morris, *Crime and Justice*, vol. 10 (1988), 171–229. A profile of Candy Lightner, founder of Mothers Against Drunk Driving (MADD), appears in Bill Berkowitz, *Local Heroes* (Lexington, MA: Lexington Books, 1987).

44. Ronald M. Holmes and James DeBurger, *Serial Murder* (Beverly Hills: Sage, 1987). *Newsweek*, Nov. 26, 1984, 100, 104–5, discusses the creation of the National Center for the Analysis of Violent Crime (Quantico, Virginia) with its focus on serial killers.

45. Michael Barone, "An Age of Restraint," *Washington Post National Weekly Edition*, Sept. 30, 1985, 27.

46. *National Journal*, Oct. 17, 1987, 2628. *New York Times*, nat. ed., July 10, 1988, sec. 4, 5, on the decline in alcohol use.

47. *New York Times*, nat. ed., sec. 4, p. 5. citing two recent research studies and the opinion of David F. Musto a historian of drug-abuse trends. The mainstream decline in drug use is countered by a powerful surge of inner-city drug activity (discussed below).

48. Gurr, "History of Violent Crime," 369–70.

49. Quoted from Lane, *Violent Death*, 120–1.

50. *Newsweek*, Nov. 26, 1984, 100, 104–5.

51. Gary T. Marx, *Undercover: Police Surveillance in America* (Berkeley: University of California Press, 1988), 208–9.

52. Ibid., 3.

53. Ibid., 54–9, 208–16.

54. Ibid., 206, 233.

55. John Naisbitt, *Megatrends: Ten New Directions Transforming Our Lives* (New York: Warner Books, 1982), 114; see also 154–5.

56. Currie, "Crimes of Violence," 44–5, 48, 57. For Comer's contribution to Curtis, ed., *American Violence*, see note 66, below.

57. Paul J. Lavrakas, "Citizen Self-Help and Neighborhood Crime Prevention Policy," in Curtis, ed., *American Violence*, 87–115.

58. Lynn A. Curtis, "Neighborhood, Family, and Employment: Toward a New Public Policy against Violence," in Curtis, ed., *American Violence*, 206–9, 213, 217–8. A balanced, perceptive study of the movement, as a whole, is Wesley G. Skogan, "Community Organizations and Crime," in Tonry and Morris, *Crime and Justice*, vol. 10, (1986), 39–78.

59. Weiner and Wolfgang, "Violent Crime," 27, 29, 32, 34.

60. *Newsweek*, Mar. 14, 1988, 16–18, and Mar. 28, 1988, 20–7.

61. See Weiner and Wolfgang, "Violent Crime," 34, and contributions to this volume by Gurr, chap. 1; Zahn, chap. 10; and Skogan, chap. 11.

62. Currie, "Crimes of Violence," 58–9. In their study of Detroit, Colin Loftin and David McDowall (chap. 7, this volume) found that homicide was not significantly related to the unemployment rate per se, but they did find a significant connection with the level of poverty—the basic issue addressed by Currie (see below) and other advocates of a crime-alleviating full-employment policy for black youth.

63. Currie, *Confronting Crime*, chap. 7.

64. See Skogan, chap. 11, this volume, on "rational choice theory," which applies to the propensity of young black males to join high-profit drug-dealing gangs.

65. Gurr, chap. 1, this volume; Lane, chap. 2, this volume; Skogan, chap. 12, this volume.

66. A precipitating event in the movement stressing community self-help was a 1984 conference in Nashville attended by representatives of 100 black organizations. Among black leaders who have endorsed the self-reliance approach are John E. Jacob, executive director of the National Urban League; William H. Gray III, chairman of the budget committee, U.S. House of Representatives; Mayor Tom Bradley, Los Angeles; Robert Woodson, chairman of the National Center for Neighborhood Enterprise; Benjamin L. Hooks, executive director of the National Association for the Advancement of Colored People; and presidential candidate Jesse Jackson, leader of People United to Save Humanity. *New York Times*, nat. ed., June 15, 1986, 1, 18. Typical is the view of the late M. Carl Holman who in 1985, as president of the National Urban Coalition, reflected upon the future of black children and saw them in trouble: "slipping academically to the point where a shocking percentage of the next generation will be economically expandable—not because of racism but because they will lack the skills to compete in the labor market" of the computer era. "Much of our help," he continued, "has to come from our own community—churches, clubs, fraternities, sororities, fraternal orders, and professional organizations" whose members Holman urged to enlist in an educational crusade for black children. "Black people," he concluded, "really need to take charge of their own success and not look exclusively to those outside our community." Quoted by William Raspberry in *Oregonian* (Portland), Oct. 29, 195, B7. The same theme has been expressed by leading black scholars, including psychiatrist James P. Comer, who can recall from his own youth youngsters of "chaotic backgrounds" who became neither criminal nor violent. Comer focuses on child rearing and education within the black community as the realm where progress must be made. Comer, "Black Violence and Public Policy," in Curtis, *American Violence*, 63, 80, 84–5, and below for Comer's own effort to revitalize education in the black ghetto of New Haven. Notable, too, during the 1980s have been many nationally-syndicated newspaper columns promoting black community self-help, especially in regard to education and the reduction of crime, by journalist William Raspberry whose home newspaper is the *Washington Post*. See, for example, Raspberry, "Blacks' Ability Must Rest in Attitude," *Oregonian* (Portland), Sept. 27, 1985, D7, and "Blacks Need to Seize Own Educational Reins," Ibid., Oct. 29, 1985, B7.

67. *Ebony*, Aug., 1988, 31—Johnson's keynote editorial for a special issue of *Ebony* devoted entirely to the problem of revitalizing education in the inner-city black areas. Aside from its informative content, this special issue is significant, because *Ebony* is a high-circulation, "slick" magazine catering to the affluent black middle class that has often been accused of indifference to the plight of crime-plagued ghetto blacks.

68. *Ebony*, Aug. 1988, 164.

69. Ibid., 52–63.

70. *Newsweek*, May 2, 1988, 56–65.

71. Allyson Reid-Dove, "Of Minds and Money," *Black Enterprise*, Sept. 1988, 67–70.

72. William Raspberry, "Black Children Succeed at Strong D.C. School," *Oregonian* (Portland), Sept. 24, 1985, B11.

73. James P. Comer, "The Social Factor," *New York Times*, Aug. 7, 1988, sec. 4A, 27–31, in which Comer recounts the success of a "social-skills" approach in the two schools in the course of a five-year project directed by him.

74. On McCallum and McKenna: *Ebony*, Aug., 1988, 58, 124–26, respectively. On Clark: Ibid., pp. 120, 122, and *Newsweek*, Jan. 18, 1988, 80–1. On Moten: Raspberry, "Black Children Succeed." On Smoak: *Newsweek*, May 2, 1988, 56–65.

75. Profiles of ten such teachers appear in *Ebony*, Aug. 1988, 78–87.

76. For example, the ten "top achievers" presented in Ibid., 40–50.

77. *Black Enterprise*, Sept. 1988. Graves edits and publishes this magazine.

78. Reid-Dove, "Of Minds and Money," 67.

79. *Ebony*, Aug. 1988, 124.

80. Quoted from Shoshana Zuboff, *In the Age of the Smart Machine: The Future of Work and Power* (New York: Basic Books, 1988), 388.

81. Yoneji Masuda, *The Information Society as Post-Industrial Society*, trans. Bernard Halliwell (Bethesda: World Future Society, 1981), viii. Masuda was the formulator of a nationwide cooperative public/private plan for an "Information Society" in Japan which, with 2000 as its target year for completion, is being impressively realized.

82. Shuboff, *Age of Smart Machine*, xiii and here and there.

83. Ibid., 70–6 and here and there. See also J. David Bolter, *Turing's Man: Western Culture in the Computer Age* (Chapel Hill: University of North Carolina Press, 1984), 232–3, 236–7; Eugene F. Provenzo, *Beyond the Gutenberg Galaxy: Microcomputers and the Emergence of Post-Typographic Culture* (New York: Teachers College, Columbia University, 1986), 16–17, 73, 75; Tom Forester, ed., *High-Tech Society: The Story of the Information Technology Revolution* (Cambridge: MIT Press, 1987), 167; Tom Forester, ed., *The Information Technology Revolution* (Cambridge: MIT Press, 1985), 227–8; Masuda, *Information Society*, 30–1. "Intellective skills" is Shuboff's appropriate term for a concept that all of these authorities, in their own terminology, emphasize. A significant statement is by Daniel Bell, "The Social Framework of the Information Society" (1979), repr. in Tom Forester, ed., *The Microelectronics Revolution* (Cambridge: MIT Press, 1981), 500–49.

84. *National Journal*, May 7, 1988, 1220.

85. Frederick Golden, "Here Come the Microkids," in Forester, ed., *Information Technology Revolution*, 227.

86. Quoted in ibid., 228.

87. The emphasis in the quotation is by Papert who is cited and quoted in Provenzo, *Beyond the Gutenberg Galaxy*, 15, 76.

88. For example, *Newsweek*, May 2, 1988, 54–5, which among other things mentions the widely noted improvement in Scholastic Aptitude Test scores.

89. On this disproportionately violent element, see Weiner and Wolfgang, "Violent Crime," 32.

90. Shuboff in *Age of the Smart Machine* is far from being a Pollyannna, but she has high

hopes for humanity in the Information Society in which, on the basis of trends discovered in her field research, she envisions a "socially integrated high technology workplace" in which the "hierarchical or other status-based distinctions" of Industrial Society will dissolve or, at least, "hold less power." Shuboff, *Age of Smart Machine,* 206, 404, and here and there. Her view is typical of many authorities on the Information Society.

Index

Abernathy, Lloyd M., 79n
Adamchak, Donald J., 176n
Adams, James Truslow, 145n
African Americans, see race and crime
alcohol and crime, 136, 230-231, 243; see also Prohibition and crime
Anderson, Harry H., 144n
Anderson, James LaVerne, 161n, 213n
Anderson, O. D., 176n
Angel, Myron, 144n
Angle, Paul M., 161n
Antonovsky, Aaron, 175n
Antunes, George E., 249n
Archer, Dane, 43, 48, 53n, 99n, 172, 177n, 249n
Arens, W., 265n
Asbury, Herbert, 161n
assassins of U.S. presidents, 178-195
assault trends, 25, 237-238; in England 30-31, 33-34; in Europe, 42-45; in Philadelphia, 112, 114-115, 117
Atlanta, rape, 132; types of homicide, 226
Aurora, Nevada, auto accidents and crime, 66-67, 117; crime (1861-1865), 123-142 passim
Austria, crime trends, 43-44
Avison, N. Howard, 51n
Ayers, Edward L., 101n

Baby Boom, 239-240, 246; see also youth and crime
Backman-Prehn, Ronet, 234n
Bain, Donald, 161n
Baker, S., 214n
Barone, Michael, 257, 265n
Bayley, David, 53n
Beasley, Ronald, 249n
Beattie, J. M., 30-31, 33, 34, 50n, 51n
Becker, Gary S., 174n, 175n, 242, 249n
Beckett, G., 196n
Belden, Frank A., 145n
Bell, Daniel, 267n
Belsley, David A., 176n
Bencivengo, Mark, 121n, 225, 232n, 233n
Bensing, Robert C., 223, 232n
Berkowitz, B., 265n
Berkowitz, L., 202, 213n
Bernard, Thomas J., 175n
Bernstein, Judith, 175n

Birmingham, Alabama, types of homicide, 223
Black Death and crime, 32, 51n
Blackman, P., 215n
Blau, Judith R., 233n, 249n, 250n
Blau, Peter M., 233n, 249n, 250n
Bloch, Herbert A., 49n
Block, Carolyn R., 225, 232n
Block, Richard L, 225, 232n, 233n, 249n
Bluestone, Barry, 250n
Blum, Ulrich C. H., 250n
Blumstein, Alfred, 177n, 248n, 264n, 265n
Bodie, California, crime (1878-1882), 18, 123-142 passim
Bolter, J. David, 267n
Bonano, Joseph, 161n
Bonger, William A., 95
Booth, John Wilkes, 17, 180, 189, 190
bootleggers, social origins, 148-149; see also Prohibition and crime
Bordua, David J., 53n, 212, 213n, 215n
Boston, 252; crime rates, 13, 35, 126-127, 132-134 passim; crime trends, 37, 105, 118-119
Boudouris, James, 15, 43, 174, 175n, 221, 223, 232n
Bradley, Tom, 266 (n66)
Braithwaite, John, 175n
Breakenridge, William M., 263n
Brearly, H. C., 40, 50n, 52n, 221, 232n
Bremer, Arther, 181-194 passim
Brennan, Ray, 161n
Brenner, M. Harvey, 248n, 249n, 250n
Britain, crime trends, 22, 31; see also England; London
Brooker, A., 202, 213n
Brown, Richard Maxwell, 18, 19, 137, 145n, 263n
Browne, Angela, 213n, 214n, 233n, 234n
Brownmiller, Susan, 265n
Bruce-Briggs, B., 212n
Buckley, Frank, 162n
Buffalo, New York, crime trends, 105
Bullock, Henry Allen, 222, 232n
Bulmash, Kathleen Jones, 144n
Bundy, Ted, 189
Burnham, John C., 160n
Buss, A., 202, 213n
Buss, E., 202, 213n

Byck, Samuel, 180-194 passim
Byrd, S., 212
Byrkit, James W., 263n
Byme, James M., 213n, 249n, 250n

Cantor, David, 164, 171, 175n, 177n, 219n, 232n, 249n
Capone, Al, 146, 153-154, 155
Carter, James Earl, 181, 187, 190
Center, L. J., 231n
Chapman, Mark, 193
Chenquan, Jia, 99
Chicago, and Prohibition crime, 13, 146-147, 151-156 passim; crime rates, 237; types of homicide, 222, 225
Chiricos, Theodore G., 249n
churches and crime, 46
cities and crime, 31-32, 43-44, 83-84, 105, 237, 242, 252-253; see also specific cities
Civil Rights Movement, 9
Civil War, 13-14, 18, 47, 93, 129; and crime rates, 35
Clark, Joe, 261
Clarke, James W., 16-17, 195n, 196n
class and crime, 46-47; see also poverty and crime
Clemens, Samuel L., 145n
Cleveland, Ohio, homicide trends, 226; types of homicide, 223
Clinard, Marshall, 44, 53n
Cline, Adam, 176n
Cloward, Richard A., 249n
Cockburn, J. S., 29, 30, 50n, 51n
Cocozza, J., 196n
Cohen, Jacqueline, 177n, 248n
Cohen, Lawrence E., 53n, 177n, 219, 232n, 233n, 234n, 238, 248n, 249n
Cohen, M., 196n
Collazo, Oscar, 187-191 passim
Comer, James P., 258, 266 (n66), 267n
community self-help and crime, 254, 258-259, 262, 266 (n66); see also vigilantism
Connolly, Patrick, 141, 145n
Conot, Robert, 177n
Conrad, John, 121n, 232n
Cook, Philip J., 164, 175n, 197, 212, 213n, 214n, 233n, 245, 248n, 250n
coroners' offices, as sources of homicide data, 65-66, 83, 96-97, 217-218
Coser, Lewis A., 8, 10n
Costello, Frank, 146, 150

Count-van Manen, Gloria, 52n
courts, see criminal justice
Courtwright, David T., 99n
Couzens, Michael, 248n
Crane, Amanda, 78n
Crawford, Richard, 144n
crime, defined, 60; see also homicide; robbery
crime data, accuracy of, 23-28, 34, 49 (n5), 65-70 passim, 82-83, 94-98, 105-109, 216-219, 236-238
crime trends, causes, 42-49, 56-64, 229-231, 235-247; see also homicide trends, causes
criminal justice, 11, 13-14, 18, 75, 251; contemporary reforms, 255-257, 262; in medieval England, 28; in 19th century U.S., 96; on the frontier, 139-140; see also policing and crime; vigilantism
cultural diversity and crime, 75-76; see also immigrants and crime; race and crime
Currie, Elliott, 254, 258, 260, 263n, 266n
Curtis, Lynn A., 224, 232n, 258, 263n, 266n
Czolgosz, Leon, 183, 189, 191

Dallas, types of homicide, 226-227
Dan, Uri, 161n
Davidson, Terry, 265n
DeBurger, James 265n
Demaris, Ovid, 161n
Depression of the 1930s, effects on crime rates, 14-15, 43; and crime in Detroit, 166-171; see also poverty and crime; unemployment and crime
Dershowitz, A., 196n
Detroit, correlates of homicide, 165-172; crime patterns, 15, 208; crime rates, 12, 67; economic history, 167-168; types of homicide, 221-223
Dever, William E., 147, 155
Diamond, B. L., 196n
DiMona, Joseph, 161n
Dixon, Jo, 20n, 54n, 213n
drugs and crime, 16, 117, 158-160, 230-231, 233 (n24), 243, 245, 259-260; see also Prohibition and crime
Dudden, Arthur, 79n
Durkheim, Émile, 95
Dworkin, Andrea, 265n
Dykstra, Robert R., 134-135, 144n

Earp, Wyatt, 252
Easterlin, Robert A., 248n

Ehrlich, Isaac, 174-175n, 176n
Eisenberg, Dennis, 161n
Eisenhower, Milton S., 7, 10n
Elias, Norbert, 45, 50n, 53n
Elias, Robert, 265n
Elliot, Mabel A., 145n
El-Kammash, Magdi M., 175n
Emerson, Haven, 97
Engberg, N., 214n
Engelmann, Larry D., 177n
England, medieval crime, 11-12, 27-29, 32-33; see also Britain
Ennis B. J., 196n
Espy, M. Watt, 51n
Estrich, Susan, 265n
Europe, Eastern, crime rates, 44
Europe, Western, crime rates, 21; see also specific countries
executions, U.S. trends, 35-36
Exner, Franz, 53n
Eyre Courts, 28

Fackler, M., 214n
families and crime, see homicide within the family; morality and crime; social disorganization and crime; youth and crime
Farley, Reynolds, 232n
Farquhar, Francis P., 144n
Faupel, Charles E., 49n, 77n, 120n, 231
Federal Bureau of Investigation, 34, 106, 217, 236-237; and potential assassins, 179-180, 188, 192; see also *Uniform Crime Reports*
Federal Centers for Disease Control, 40
Feldman, Herman, 161n
Feldman, J. J., 175n
Feldman, Roger A., 225, 226, 233n
Felson, Marcus, 52n, 177n
Feltes, Thomas, 250n
Ferdinand, Theodore N., 37, 51n, 104, 105, 118, 120n, 121n, 126, 143n, 144n
Ferracuti, Franco, 175n, 249n
Figlio, Robert M., 248n, 249n, 250n
firearms, as cause of crime, 200-203; as deterrent to crime, 127, 129-131, 203, 206-209; possession in Europe, 200-201; possession in U.S., 199-200; right to ownership, 198-199; use in crime, 14, 17-18, 29, 70, 81, 93, 101 (n12), 112, 116, 118, 136-137, 144-145 (n59), 153, 203-206, 221, 225, 227-228; see also gun control policies
Fletcher, George P., 264n

Flewelling, R., 213n, 214n
Flynn, Edith, 121n, 232n
Ford, Gerald, 180-181, 186-187
Forester, Tom, 267n
Fox, James Alan, 177n
France, crime trends, 42, 44
Frantz, Joe B., 145n
Frazier, S. H., 195n
Frederick, C. J., 195n
Freedman, L. Z., 196n
Freeman, Richard B., 164, 175n
Freud, Sigmund, 58
Friedman, Lawrence J., 135, 144n
Fromme, Lynette, 180-194 passim
frontier crime 13, 55, 122-142; property crime, compared with Eastern cities, 125-129; violent crime, compared with Eastern cities, 131-134
Fulbrook, Mary, 53n
Fussner, F. Smith, 212

Glavez, José, 99
gangs and crime, 141, 259-260; see also drugs and crime; Prohibition and crime
Garavaglia, Louis A., 145n
Gartner, Rosemary, 43, 48, 53n, 99n, 172, 177n, 249n
Gastil, Raymond D., 53n
Gatrell, V. A. C., 26, 31, 49n, 50n, 51n
Gehlke, C. E., 232n
Geis, Gilbert, 49n, 145n, 213n
Gelles, Richard J., 227, 233
Germany, crime rates, 246; crime trends, 42-44
Giles-Sims, Jean, 265n
Gilje, Paul A., 52n
Gillis, A. R., 54n
Given, James Buchanan, 50n, 53n
Godman, Thomas, 150
Goetz, Bernard, 182, 251, 254-255, 264 (n24)
Gold, Martin, 59, 77n
Golden, Frederick, 262, 267n
Goldwater, Barry, 235
Gordon, Andrew C., 248n
Gorn, Elliot J., 99n
Gosnell, Harold F., 161n
Gottfredson, Michael, 233n, 248n
Grabosky, Peter N., 49n, 50n, 51n, 52n, 53n, 54n, 77n
Graham, Hugh Davis, 7, 9, 10n, 49n, 77n, 120, 145n, 263n
Graves, Earl, 261

Gray, William H., III, 266 (n66)
Greenberg, David F., 248n
Greenwood, C., 213n
Groth, A., 196n
Guiteau, Charles, 180-190 passim
gun control policies, 205-206, 210-212
Gurr, Ted Robert, 7, 10n, 49n, 50n, 51n, 52n,
  53n, 54n, 56-64, 66, 75, 76, 77n, 78n, 79n,
  99n, 103, 104, 105, 106, 119, 120n, 121n,
  145n, 160n, 175n, 177n, 212, 213n, 253,
  257, 263n, 265n
Guzik, Jack, 146, 153-154

Haber, William, 174, 176n
Hacker, Andrew, 52n
Hackney, Sheldon, 53n
Hadden, T. B., 49n
Hair, E. H., 50n, 51n
Hakim, S., 249n
Halbrook, S., 212n
Hall, H. V., 196n
Haller, Mark H., 13, 16, 52n, 161n, 162n, 232n
Haller, Nancy, 160n
Hammer, Carl I., Jr., 28, 50n
Hammond, K. R., 195n
Hanawalt, Barbara A., 28, 32, 50n, 51n, 53n
Harding, T., 196n
Hardy, Charles, III, 79n
Harlan, Howard, 232n
Harrison, Bennett, 250n
Hart, Peter, 214n
Hartmann, F., 250n
Harvey, A. C., 177n
Hastings, D. W., 196n
Haven, Charles T., 145n
Hawkins, Darrell F., 232n
Hay, Douglas, 50n
Henderson, Dwight F., 96
Henry, Andrew F., 175n
Hernnstein, Richard J., 58, 77
Hill, Robert H., 54n, 250n
Hinckley, John, Jr., 178-194 passim
Hindelang, Michael J., 231n, 249n
Hindus, Michael Stephen, 35, 51n
Hirsch, Charles S., 225, 226, 233n
Hirschi, Travis, 233n, 248n, 249n
Hispanics, 247; economic status, 243-244;
  homicides, 40, 223
Hoffman, Frederick Ludwig, 52n, 83, 96-97,
  99n, 101n, 221, 232n
Hofstadter, Richard, 102, 120

Holland, T., 196n
Holman, M. Carl, 266 (n66)
Holmes, Ronald M., 265n
homicide, types of victim-offender relations,
  75, 89, 91-94, 100 (n10), 122-123, 203,
  221-231
homicide rates, in Elizabethan England, 29-
  30, 33-34; in Europe, 42, 53 (n67); in frontier towns, 132-137; and gun ownership,
  199-206 passim; in medieval England, 27-
  29, 32-33; in U.S., 11-16 passim, 21, 35-41
  passim, 133-134, 219-228 passim, 264 (n27)
homicide trends, 21-23, 26; causes, 30, 32-33,
  37; in Europe, 41-44; in Liverpool, 80-94;
  in London, 27-34, 82-89; in New York City,
  65-67, 82-94; in Philadelphia, 64-74, 107-
  109, 112-113, 117-119; U.S. and England
  compared, 80-94
homicide within the family, causes, 168-172,
  229-231; patterns, 91-93, 222-229
Hooks, Benjamin J., 266 (n66)
Horwitz, Allen V., 175n
Houston, homicide rates, 93; types of homicide, 222-223, 226
Hovland, Carl, 175n
Howard, M., 213n
Huberty, James, 193
Hula, Richard C., 49n, 50n, 51n, 52n, 53n,
  54n, 77n
Huston, B., 213n

immigrants and crime, 12-13, 15-16, 34-38,
  41, 60, 73-74, 84, 89-91, 124, 148; Germans,
  37, 84, 91, 99 (n8); Irish, 35, 37, 51-52
  (n36) (in Liverpool, 84; in New York City,
  84, 89, 91, 94; in Philadelphia, 99 (n8); and
  violence, 51-52 (n36)); Italians, 60, 70-73;
  Jews, 73, 148
Inciardi, James A., 49n, 77n, 120n, 231n
industrialization, see modernization and crime
Information Society, 251-262 passim
Israel, firearms and public order, 209

Jackson, Derrick, 264n
Jackson, Jesse, 266 (n66)
Jacob, John E., 260, 266 (n66)
Jacobs, James B., 265n
Jacoby, J., 196n
Japan, crime rates, 44, 63
Johnson, Eric A., 42, 52n, 53n
Johnson, John H., 260, 267n

Johnson, Lyndon B., 7, 235
Johnston, Norman, 231n

Kalish, Carol B., 49n
Kamimura, Naoki, 99
Karst, K., 212n
Katcher, Leo, 161n
Kates, Don B., Jr., 17, 29, 213n, 214n, 215n
Kates, P., 212, 212n
Katzenelson, Susan, 225, 232n
Kaye, J. M., 50n
Kazer, Ross S., 225, 226, 232n
Kennedy, Anthony M., 256
Kennedy, John F., 179, 180, 188, 193
Kennedy, Robert, 7
Kennesaw, Georgia, crime rates, 208
Kennett, Lee, 161n, 213n
Kerstein, M., 214n
Kilar, Jeremy W., 135, 144n
King, Martin Luther, 17, 178
Klebba, A. Joan, 232n
Kleck, Gary, 143n, 201, 204, 205, 212, 213n, 214n, 215n
Kleiman, Mark A. R., 162n
Klein, C., 212
Klepinger, David, 248n, 249n, 250n
Kmenta, Jan, 177n
Kovar, M. G., 175n
Kraft, Joseph, 265n
Kuh, Edwin, 176n
Kyvig, David E., 160n, 162n

Lalli, Sergio, 161n
Land, Kenneth C., 53n, 164, 171, 175n, 177n, 233n, 238, 248n, 249n, 250n
Landau, Eli, 161n
Landes, William, 165n
Landesco, John, 161n
Lane, Roger, 12, 15, 16, 24, 34, 35, 37, 39, 50n, 51n, 52n, 77n, 78n, 79n, 95, 96, 99n, 103, 104, 105, 107, 108, 109, 117, 120n, 121n, 133, 143n, 144n, 231n, 234n, 252, 253, 263n, 266n
Lansky, Meyer, 146, 151
Lashley, Arthur V., 221, 232n
Lassen, G., 196n
Laub, John H., 245, 248n, 250n
Lavrakas, Paul J., 258, 259, 266n
Lawrence, Richard, 185, 190
Lee, Mathew, 99
Leonard, John, 10n

Lenman, Bruce P., 50n
Lennon, John, 193
Levi, M., 196n
Levy, L., 212n
Liepmann, Moritz, 53n
Lincoln, Abraham, 17, 189
Linebaugh, Peter, 50
Litwack, R. T., 196n
Lizotte, Alan J., 20n, 54n, 205, 213n, 214n
Lodhi, Abdul Qaiyum, 52n
Loftin, Colin, 15, 43, 52n, 54n, 174, 250n, 266n
London, England, crime trends, 22, 26; medieval murder rates, 28; murder rates (1820-1974), 31-32; (1850-1931), 82-89
Long, Huey, 189
Long, Sharon K., 164, 175n, 249n
Los Angeles, gangs and crime, 141, 259
Luckenbill, David F., 227, 233n
Lucker, Jeffrey, 162n
Luedens, M., 212n
Lunden, Walter A., 53n
Lundsgaarde, Henry P., 93, 101n, 225, 226, 233n

MacMahon, B., 175n
McCallum, Gene, 261, 267n
McCleary, Ricahrd, 248n
McClelland, John M., Jr., 263n
McClintock, F. H., 51n
McDowall, David, 15, 43, 266n
McFadden, Robert D., 263n
McGrath, J., 213n
McGrath, Rogert D., 13, 17-18, 41, 77n, 91, 142n, 143n, 145n
McHale, Vincent E., 42, 52n, 53n
McKanna, Clare V., Jr., 135, 144n
McKean, Eugene C., 174
McKenna, George J., III, 261, 267n
McSwain, N., Jr., 214n
Madison, James, 199
Malcolm, J., 212n
Malcolm X, 178, 195
manslaughter, *see* homicide
Manson, Charles, 187, 191
Marciniak, Edward, 250n
Marohn, Richard C., 145n
Martin, Lydia, 78n
Marx, Gary T., 258, 265n
Masuda, Yoneji, 261, 267n
Mead, Margaret, 58

Megargee, E., 196n
Menninger, W. W., 195n
Menzies, R. J., 196n
Mercy, James A., 232n
Messick, Hank, 161n
Messner, Steven F., 175n
Michelson, Rob, 99
Milloy, Marily, 264n
Milwaukee, Wisconsin, crime, 13; Prohibition era, 155-156
modernization and crime, 42-43, 57, 59, 61-62, 71-72, 104, 252-253
Monahan, Joh, 182, 196n
Mondy, R. W., 145n
Monkkonen, Eric H., 12-13, 16, 24, 37, 38, 49n, 51n, 52n, 53n, 64-65, 67, 74, 77n, 78n, 79n, 104-105, 120n, 134, 143n, 144n, 248n
Montandon, C., 196n
Moore, Mark, 162n
Moore, Sara Jane, 180-194 passim
Moore, Will, 51n
morality and crime, 57-58, 61, 63, 253-254
Moran, George "Bugs," 153-154
Morris, Norval, 49n, 77n, 99n, 120n, 162n, 264, 265n, 266n
Moten, Claude, 261
Mulvihill, Donald, 49n, 22
Mumford, Robert S., 225, 226, 233n
murder, defined, 24; see also homicide
Musto, David F., 265n
Myers, Samuel L., Jr., 52n

Nagin, Daniel, 177n, 248n
Naisbitt, John, 258, 265n
National Advisory Committee on Civil Disorders (Kerner Commission), 102
National Commission on the Causes and Prevention of Violence (Violence Commission), 7, 9, 102-103, 224
National Rifle Association, 198, 205
National Security Council, 184
Naylor, Timothy J., 103, 120n
Neilson, Kathleen E., 225, 232n
New York City, crime rates, 134; crime trends, 37, 39, 65-68, 82-94; Prohibition era, 152
Newton, G., 212n
Nickoll, Ben, 135, 144n
Nienstedt, Barbara C., 248n
Nitti, Frank, 146
Nixon, Richard M., 180, 187
Norstroem, Thor, 20n, 177n
North, Oliver, 184

Oakland, California, crime rates, 135
O'Carroll, Patrick W., 232n
O'Hare, Sheila, 99
Ohlin, Petre, 249n
opportunity theory, 43
Orlando, Florida, crime rates, 208
Orsagh, Thomas, 175n, 249n
Oswald, Lee Harvey, 179-194 passim
Oxford, England, medieval homicide rates, 28-29

Packer, Herbert L., 265n
Papert, Seymour, 262
Parker, Geoffrey, 50n
Parker, Robert Nash, 175n, 177n, 229, 134n
Parssinen, Terry, 160n
Peirce, David, 51n
Percival, Robert V., 135, 144n
Perryman, M., 176n
Philadelphia, crime rates, 14, 23-24, 133-134, 252; crime trends, 13, 35, 37, 59-60, 64-74; Prohibition era, 147-148, 151; types of homicide, 223-224, 226; violence arrests, 109-112; youth crime, 239
Phillips, Llad, 176n
Piaget, Jean, 262
Pindyck, Robert S., 176n
Pleck, Elizabeth, 101n
policing and crime, 24, 67-69, 141, 218, 237, 253, 258; during Prohibition, 146-157 passim; see also criminal justice
politicians and crime, Prohibition era, 146-156
Pollack, Eric, 78n
post-industrial society and crime, 76-77, 243-244, 253-262 passim
poverty and crime, 12, 15, 17, 20 (n2), 40, 48-49, 163-173, 229-231, 241-244, 259-260; see also unemployment and crime
Powell, Elwin H., 37, 51n, 104, 105, 120n
President's Commission on Law Enforcement and Administration of Justice (Katzenbach Commission), 102
President's Crime Commission (1966), 239
Preyer, Kathryn, 96
prisons, 256; see also criminal justice
Prohibition and crime, 13, 16, 38, 146-160, 167, 222
property crime rates, contemporary U.S., 13-14, 21, 236; Europe, 21, 42-44 passim; 19th century U.S., 125-129; see also robbery trends

Provenzo, Eugene F., 267n

Quetelet, Adolphe, 95-96

race and crime, 15-16, 19, 20 (n1), 38-41, 45, 47, 52 (n44), 59-60, 63, 70-73, 81-82, 84-91, 139-140, 220-221, 223-231 passim, 240-241, 243-247, 259-261
Rand, Michael, 248n
Rappeport, D. L., 196n
Raspberry, William, 266 (n66), 267n
Ray, James Earl, 17, 182, 185
Ray, Subhash, 176n
Reagan, Ronald, 178, 190, 256
Redfield, Horace V., 99n
Redo, Slawomir, 53n
Reid-Dove, Allyson, 267n
Reiff, Robert, 265n
Reiss, Albert J., Jr., 264n
Rengert, G., 249n
Reuter, Peter, 160n, 162n
Ridel, Marc, 225, 227, 232n, 233n
robbery, defined, 25; in medieval England, 28; trends, 25-26, 44-45, 112-119 passim, 237; use of firearms in, 204
Rogers, Kevin, 141, 168n
Rose, G. N. G., 51n
Rosenberg, Mark, 234n
Rosenhan, D. L., 196n
Rossi, P., 212n, 214n
Rubenfeld, Daniel L., 176n
Rubin, Lilian B., 264n
Rule, John G., 50n

St. Valentine's Day Massacre, 153-155
Sagi, Philip C., 228, 233n
Salem, crime rates, 126-128 passim, 133
Samaha, Joel, 29, 30, 50n, 51n
Sampson, Robert J., 213n, 230, 234n, 242, 249n, 250n, 264n
Savitz, Leonard D., 231n
schools and crime control, 260-262
Schrank, 188
Schroeder, Oliver, Jr., 223, 232n
Schryock, Henry S., 176n
Schultz, Dutch, 146
Sears, Robert, 175n
Seidman, David, 248
Sepejak, D. S., 196n
Serven, James E., 145n
sexual assault, in frontier towns, 131-132; trends, 25, 44, 112-119 passim

Shalope, R., 212n
Sharpe, James A., 51n, 82, 94, 99n
Shaw, S. A., 195n
Short, James F., Jr., 7, 175n
Shuboff, Shoshana, 261, 267n, 268n
Shulman, Peter, 78n
Siegal, Benjamin, 151
Siegal, Jacob S., 176n
Siegal, R., 196n
Silver, Alan, 53n
Simms, Margaret C., 52n
Sirhan Sirhan, 183-191 passim
Skogan, Wesley G., 15, 16, 19, 20n, 21, 49n, 50n, 52n, 53n, 248n, 249n, 266n
Smith, Douglas A., 175n
Smith, Dwayne M., 175n, 177n, 229, 234n
Smith, Grant H., 143n
Smith, T. G., 231n
Smoak, Melvin, 261, 267n
Smylka, John Ortiz, 51n
Snodgrass, Glenn, 121n, 225, 226-227, 232n, 233n
social disorganization and crime, 244-245; see also community self-help and crime; morality and crime
Soloman, F., 195n
Soman, Alfred, 24-25, 46, 50n
South, Scott, 234n, 249n
Southern subculture of violence, 47, 53-54 (n74), 67, 93-94
Spielberger, C., 196n
Stanchfield, Paul, 174
Steadman, H. J., 195n, 196n
Stenross, Barbara, 212
Stivers, Robert R., 233n
Stockholm, crime trends, 22, 42, 44
Stockwell, Edward G., 176n
Stone, Lawrence, 49n, 51n, 82, 99n
Straus, Murray A., 213n, 227, 233n, 234n
suicide and crime, 59
Sutherland, Edwin H., 52n, 232n
Sutherland, R. Q., 145n
Swank, Robert T., 248n, 249n, 250n
Sweden, causes of theft, 20n
Switzerland, crime rates, 44
Sydney, Australia, crime trends, 22, 41-42

Takeuchi, J., 195n
Taylor, Harold, 174
Taylor, R., 214n
Teeters, Negley K., 79n
Thompson, E. P., 50n

Thompson, William Hale "Big Bill," 154, 155
Thornberry, T., 196n
Tilly, Charles, 52n
Titmuss, Richard Morris, 175n
Tittle, Charles R., 175n
Tonrey, Michael, 49n, 77n, 99n, 120n, 162, 264n, 265n, 266n
Tonso, William, 202
Toplin, Robert B., 99n
Torresola, Griselio, 190, 191
Touhy, Roger, 151, 161n
Toulmin, Stephen, 262
Tracey, Paul E., 248n, 250n
True, Edmond J., 249n
Tumin, Melven, 49n, 232n

U-curve in crime trends, 21-22, 49 (n4), 56-64, 74, 104, 119
underclass and crime, 245; see also poverty and crime; race and crime; social disorganization and crime
unemployment and crime, 129, 164, 189-190, 242-243, 259-260; see also poverty and crime
Uniform Crime Reports (UCR), as sources of crime data, 38, 64, 111, 143-144 (n39), 217-220, 227, 231 (n7)
U.S. Coast Guard, 150, 151
U.S. Secret Service 17; and potential assassins, 179-185 passim, 188, 194
U.S. Sentencing Reform Act (1984), 256
Urban Institute, 245
urbanization and crime, see cities and crime

victimization surveys, 23, 236-238, 241
Vietnam War, 47, 102, 240
vigilantism, 18, 125, 137-139, 252, 254
Villemez, Wayne J., 175n
violent acts, prediction of, 182-195
Vital Statistics, as sources of homicide data, 217-220
Vold, George B., 174n
Volstead Act, 146

Wallace, George, 181, 193, 235
Wallace, Michael, 102, 120n
Waters, Harold, 161n

war and crime, 47-48; in England, 30, 32; in Europe, 43; in U.S., 35, 38, 41, 93, 129, 172, 240
Washington, DC, crime trends, 39-40; types of homicide, 225
Washington, George, 178
Webster, C. D., 196n
Weigley, Russell, 79n
Weiner, Neil Alan, 12, 23, 35, 37, 51n, 213n, 253, 263n, 266n, 267n
Weis, Joseph G., 248n, 250n
Weiss, Carl, 190
Welsh, Roy E., 176n
white-collar crime, 60
Whitman, Charles, 193
Wicks, Jerry W., 176n
Wilentz, Sean, 99n
Williams, J., 213n
Williams, Kirk R., 227, 233n, 234n
Wilson, James Q., 56-64, 70, 76, 77n, 78n, 79n, 175n, 240
Wilson, R. L., 145n
Winslow, Cal, 50n
Winter, Carole, 99
Witte, Ann D., 164, 175n, 249n
Wolf, George, 161n
Wolfgang, Marvin E., 7, 78n, 175n, 213n, 223-224, 226, 232n, 248n, 249n, 250n, 253, 263n, 266n, 267n
Woodwon, Robert, 266 (n66)
Worman, Charles G., 145n
Wright, James D., 212, 212n, 213n, 214n
Wright, Kevin N., 175n, 249n
Wrigley, E. A., 49n

Young, R., 213n
youth and crime, 44, 48, 57, 117-118, 140-141, 158, 230, 238-240, 244-247

Zahn, Margaret A., 12, 14, 18, 21, 23, 34-35, 37, 38, 51n, 52n, 121n, 225-227 passim, 228, 232n, 233 (n24), 236, 263n, 266n
Zangara, Guiseppe, 191
Zarkin, Gary A., 164, 175, 250n
Zehr, Howard, 42, 50n, 52n, 53n
Zimring, F., 212n, 214n
Zuboff, Shoshona, 267n

About the Contributors

JAMES BOUDOURIS does research and trial consulting for Starr & Associates in West Des Moines and teaches criminology at Grand View College. He formerly was Director of Research and Evaluation for the State of Iowa Department of Corrections and the City of New York Office of Probation. He is the author of *Prisons and Kids* (1985).

RICHARD MAXWELL BROWN is Beekman Professor of Northwest and Pacific History at the University of Oregon. His numerous books include *The South Carolina Regulators* (1963) and *Strain of Violence: Historical Studies of American Violence and Vigilantism* (1975). He is completing a book on violence and American values to be titled *No Duty to Retreat: An American Theme.*

JAMES W. CLARKE is Professor of Political Science at the University of Arizona where, in 1987, he received the Burlington Northern Foundation Award for his teaching. He is the author of *American Assassins: The Darker Side of Politics* (1982) and *Last Rampage: The Escape of Gary Tison* (1988).

TED ROBERT GURR is Professor of Political Science and Director of the Center for Comparative Politics at the University of Colorado, Boulder. His fourteen books and monographs include *Why Men Rebel* (recipient of the Woodrow Wilson Foundation Award as the best book in political science of 1970) and *The Politics of Crime and Conflict: A Comparative History of Four Cities* (1977). In 1988–1989 he was a Fellow of the U.S. Institute of Peace in Washington, D.C.

MARK H. HALLER is Professor of History and Criminal Justice at Temple University. His research is chiefly in the history of crime and criminal justice in American cities since the Civil War. He is author of numerous publications concerning the development of police, gambling, loansharking, and vice in the cities.

DON B. KATES, Jr., a San Francisco criminologist and civil liberties lawyer, attended Reed College and Yale Law School. He is the editor of *Firearms and Violence: Issues of Public Policy* (1984), a special issue of *Law and Contemporary Problems* on firearms regulation (Winter 1986), and a special issue of *Law and Policy Quarterly* on gun control (Summer 1983).

ROGER LANE is Benjamin R. Collins Professor of Social Sciences at Haverford College. He is author of *Policing the City: Boston 1882–1888* (1967), *Violent Death in the City: Suicide, Accident and Murder in 19th Century Philadelphia* (1979), and *Roots of Violence in Black Philadelphia, 1860–1900* (1986) which won the Bancroft Prize for 1986.

COLIN LOFTIN is Professor in the Institute of Criminal Justice and Criminology at the University of Maryland, College Park, where he serves as Director of its Violence Research Group. He has written extensively on violent criminal behavior and collective responses to crime.

DAVID McDOWALL is Associate Professor in the School of Criminal Justice, State University of New York at Albany. His major interests are in quantitative methods and the social distribution of violent crime.

ROGER D. McGRATH is Lecturer in History at the University of California, Los Angeles, where he teaches the History of the American West. He is the author of *Gunfighters, Highwaymen, & Vigilantes: Violence on the Frontier* (1985) as well as numerous articles and reviews that have appeared in scholarly journals, magazines, and newspapers. His principal research interests and writings have focused on the nineteenth-century, trans-Mississippi West.

ERIC H. MONKKONEN is Professor of History at the University of California, Los Angeles. He has published several books and articles on the history of criminal justice in the U.S., historical methods, and urban history, including *Police in Urban America, 1869–1920* (1981). His most recent book is *America Becomes Urban: The Development of U.S. Cities and Towns, 1790–1980* (1988).

WESLEY G. SKOGAN is Professor of Political Science and Urban Affairs at Northwestern University. He is the author of *Coping with Crime; Sample Surveys of the Victims of Crime* (1976), and a new book, *Disorder and Community Decline*. His research focuses on crime, the police, and crime policy.

NEIL ALAN WEINER is Senior Research Associate at the Sellin Center for Studies in Criminology and Criminal Law at the Wharton School of the University of Pennsylvania. He directs the Center's Interdisciplinary Study of Criminal Violence and has co-edited several books and special journal volumes on criminal violence. His major research interests include violent criminal careers, situational aspects of violence escalation, the prediction of violent recidivism, the effectiveness of programs for violent juvenile offenders, and disparities in the imposition of the death penalty.

MARGARET A. ZAHN is currently Professor of Sociology and Chair of the Department of Sociology, Social Work and Criminal Justice at Northern Arizona University. She directed a nationwide study of homicide for the National Institute of Justice from 1980 to 1982. She has extensive publications dealing with homicide and is co-editor of a forthcoming book on the *Sociology of Violence: Patterns, Causes and Public Policy.*